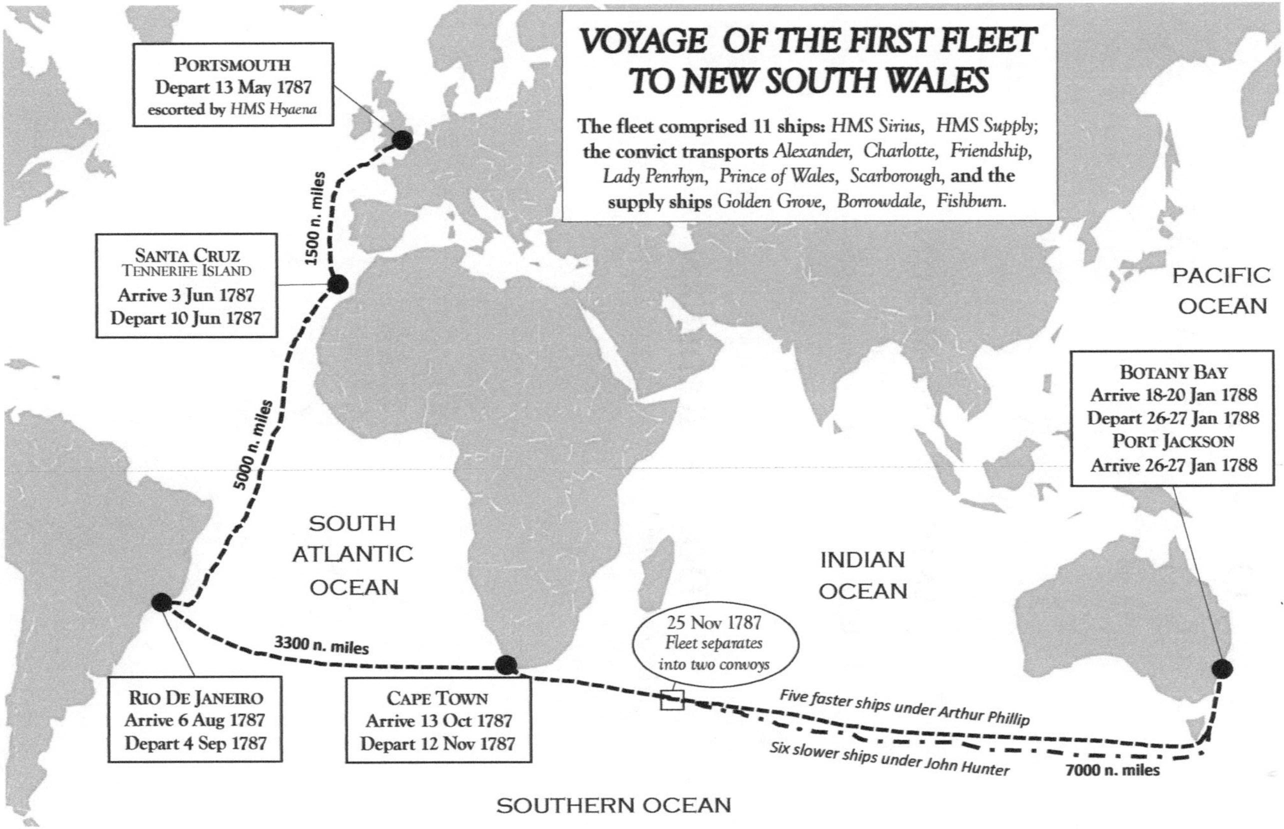
VOYAGE OF THE FIRST FLEET TO NEW SOUTH WALES
The fleet comprised 11 ships: HMS Sirius, HMS Supply; the convict transports Alexander, Charlotte, Friendship, Lady Penrhyn, Prince of Wales, Scarborough, and the supply ships Golden Grove, Borrowdale, Fishburn.
PORTSMOUTH
Depart 13 May 1787
escorted by HMS Hyaena
1500 n. miles
SANTA CRUZ
TENNERIFE ISLAND
Arrive 3 Jun 1787
Depart 10 Jun 1787
5000 n. miles
RIO DE JANEIRO
Arrive 6 Aug 1787
Depart 4 Sep 1787
3300 n. miles
CAPE TOWN
Arrive 13 Oct 1787
Depart 12 Nov 1787
SOUTH ATLANTIC OCEAN
INDIAN OCEAN
PACIFIC OCEAN
SOUTHERN OCEAN
25 Nov 1787
Fleet separates into two convoys
Five faster ships under Arthur Phillip
Six slower ships under John Hunter
7000 n. miles
BOTANY BAY
Arrive 18-20 Jan 1788
Depart 26-27 Jan 1788
PORT JACKSON
Arrive 26-27 Jan 1788

OTHER BOOKS ON COLONIAL AUSTRALIA BY THE AUTHOR

ANDREW THOMPSON
*From Boy Convict to
Wealthiest Settler in Colonial Australia*

DOCTOR REDFERN
Mutineer, Convict, Medical Pioneer, Rights Activist

www.annegrethall.com

In For The Long Haul

First Fleet Voyage & Colonial Australia:
The Convicts' Perspective

ANNEGRET HALL

First published in 2018.
Revised editions published in 2019, 2020 and 2023.

Copyright © Annegret Hall 2018
www.annegrethall.com

ESH Publication, Nedlands 6009, Australia

All reasonable attempts have been made to communicate with copyright holders of the images reproduced in this book. Any corrections to information provided about these images should be communicated to the author.

This book is copyright. Apart from any fair dealing for the purpose of private study, research, criticism or review, as permitted under the *Copyright Act*, no part of this book may be reproduced by any process without written permission from the author.

 A catalogue record for this book is available from the National Library of Australia

ISBN: 978 0 9876292 0 3   (paperback)
ISBN: 978 0 9876292 1 0   (ebook)

Text set in Garamond typeface
Cover design by Robert Hall

Printed in Australia by Ingram Lightning Source

To Syd

and

his twelve convict ancestors

Contents

Prologue	A Truly Epic Adventure		1
Chapter 1	Poverty & Punishment		4
Chapter 2	Poor Rural Youth		12
Chapter 3	Female Servitude		21
Chapter 4	Botany Bay Scheme		35
Chapter 5	Assembling the Fleet		49
Chapter 6	Portsmouth to Rio		60
Chapter 7	Female Convict Behaviour		73
Chapter 8	Long Haul to Botany Bay		83
Chapter 9	A Colony at Sydney Cove		92
Chapter 10	A Hearty Wedding Supper		109
Chapter 11	A Struggling Colony		121
Chapter 12	Second Fleet Arrival		128
Chapter 13	First Settlers		140
Chapter 14	Phillip's Departure		153
Chapter 15	The Rum Corps	1793-1796	163
Chapter 16	Floods & Debts	1797-1801	179
Chapter 17	Governors King & Bligh	1802-1806	200
Chapter 18	The Rum Rebellion	1807-1808	214
Chapter 19	Bligh Defies the Rebels	1808-1810	230
Chapter 20	Macquarie & Equality	1810-1815	241
Chapter 21	Prosperity for Emancipists	1816-1821	257
Chapter 22	Currency Lads & Lasses	1822-1825	272
Chapter 23	Despotism & Dysfunction	1825-1831	288
Chapter 24	End of the Convict Era	1832-1843	302

LIST OF MAPS & ILLUSTRATIONS	viii
CONVERSION CHART & ABBREVIATIONS	x
ROPE-PULLEY DESCENDANT TREE	322
ACKNOWLEDGEMENTS	323
BIBLIOGRAPHY	325
NOTES	330
INDEX	362

MAPS & ILLUSTRATIONS

Page

i   Voyage of the First Fleet to New South Wales.

18   An 1800 engraving showing prison hulks on the Thames River near Woolwich. Printed for Bowles & Carver. (SLNSW: V*/Conv/1).

20   Rope & Pulley Sites in England.

31   Norwich Castle prison in 1809. Printed by W. Stevenson, J. Matchett and S. W. Stevenson. (NWHCM: 1954.138.Todd7.Conisford.74)

48   First Fleet Ports in England.

61   Watercolour painted by William Bradley, 13 May 1787, showing HMS *Sirius*, HMS *Supply* and convict transports leaving Needle Point in England, in the company of HMS *Hyaena*. (SLNSW ML: Safe 1/14)

62   Captain Arthur Phillip with his plan for New South Wales in 1787. Engraving by W. Sherwin in 1789. (NLA: nla.obj-136095976)

84   Miniature portrait of Marine Captain Watkin Tench in 1787. (SLNSW ML: FM5/650)

84   Judge Advocate and diarist Lieutenant David Collins, engraving by A. Cardon in 1804. (NLA: nla.obj-136055593)

90   A 1937 oil painting by John Allcot of the First Fleet arriving in Sydney Cove in 1788. (NLA: nla.obj-135776002)

93   A 1937 painting by Algernon Talmage of the founding of the New South Wales colony by Governor Arthur Phillip on 26 Jan 1788. (SLNSW ML: FL3141725)

104 Sketch and description of the Sydney Cove settlement at Port Jackson made by convict Francis Fowkes on 16 Apr 1788. (NLA: nla.obj-230578175)

108 Survey map of the Sydney Cove settlement in 1792. (UML: 810.879a 1792)

118 Engraving by E. Dayes after a sketch by John Hunter, showing the Settlement on Sydney Cove, 20 Aug 1788. (SLNSW: C689)

120 A 1789 sketch of Sydney Cove viewed from the Rocks at the rear of the General Hospital. (SLNSW ML: DG V1/14)

126 Watercolour painted by William Bradley in 1791, showing Governor Phillip's house at Sydney Cove. (SLNSW ML: FL1113942)

138 View of the Government House in Rose Hill, *An Account of the English Colony in New South Wales*. (NLA: nla.obj-135688446)

147 Extract of the 1900 Parish map of the Field of Mars showing the original land grants at the Ponds. (HLRV: AO MAP 25765)

155 Excerpt of a 1796 map of the New South Wales settlement, *An Account of the English Colony in New South Wales*. (SLNSW ML: D Q79/60-61)

167 Sketch of an old slab hut drawn by Conrad Martens in 1840s. (SLNSW ML: DL Pd 697)

182   Part of St Matthew parish map showing the land allotments on the South and Eastern Creeks. (HLRV: AO MAP 26055)

191   Portrait by W.M. Bennett of John Hunter, the colony's second governor (1795-1800). (NLA: nla.obj-134293340)

191   Miniature portrait of Philip Gidley King, the colony's third governor (1800-1806). (SLNSW ML: MIN 62)

194   A sketch showing the 1816 flood in Windsor. (SLNSW ML: PX*D 264)

195   Illustration of the plight of families in the 1867 Hawkesbury flood. (Illustrated Sydney News, 16 Jul 1867)

203   Irish convict uprising at Castle Hill, 5 Mar 1804. (NLA: nla.obj-135226428)

206   Part of the 1820 Parish map of Castlereagh showing the land grants at Agnes Banks. (HLRV: AO MAP 203)

207   A view of the junction of the Nepean, Hawkesbury and Grose Rivers, painted by George William Evans in 1809. (SLNSW: SV/123)

213   Part of the Londonderry parish map. (HLRV: AO MAP 237)

217   Localities in the colony where Anthony and Elizabeth Rope lived.

225   Watercolour of Government House at Sydney Cove painted in 1807 by John Eyre. (SLNSW ML: SV/31)

237   Portrait by A. Huey of William Bligh, the colony's fourth governor (1806-1808). (NLA: nla.obj-136207002)

237   Miniature portrait of Lachlan Macquarie, the colony's fifth governor (1810-1821). (SLNSW ML: MIN 236)

244   View of the King Estate Dunheved on South Creek painted by Conrad Martens in 1837. (SLNSW ML: ML 1140)

246   Watercolour painted by John William Lewin of the settlement at Green Hills (Windsor) on the Hawkesbury River in 1809. (SLNSW ML: PXD 388 v.3 no. 7)

254   Watercolour painted by Joseph Lycett of the town of Windsor in 1824. (SLVIC: 30328102131561/16)

276   Watercolour painted by Joseph Lycett of Port Macquarie in 1825. (NLA: nla.obj-134636052)

300   Part of a portrait painted by Augustus Earle of Sir Thomas Brisbane, the colony's sixth governor (1821-1825). (SLVIC: H5407)

300   Portrait painted by John Linnell of Ralph Darling, the colony's seventh governor (1825-1831). (NLA: nla.obj-134769948)

316   Portrait of Richard Bourke, the colony's eight's governor (1831-1837). (SLNSW ML: ML 125)

316   Part of a portrait painted by Eden Upton Eddis of Sir George Gipps, the colony's ninth governor (1838-1846). (SLVIC: H1536)

319   The graves of Elizabeth and Anthony Rope in the Castlereagh General Cemetery on Church Street, Cranebrook, New South Wales.

CONVERSION CHART

For historical accuracy, imperial measurements have been retained in the text.

1 inch (in)	2.54 centimetres
1 foot (ft)	30 centimetres
1 yard (yd)	90 centimetres
1 mile	1.6 kilometres
1 nautical mile (nm)	1.85 kilometres
1 rod	5 metres
1 (square) rod	25.3 square metres
1 cup	284 millilitres
1 pint (pt)	570 millilitres
1 quart (qt)	1.14 litres
1 gallon	4.5 litres
1 ounce (oz)	28 grams
1 pound (lb)	450 grams
1 hundred weight	50.8 kilograms
1 ton	1016 kilograms
1 bushel wheat	27.2 kilograms
1 bushel maize	25.4 kilograms
1 pound Sterling (£)	20 shillings
1 shilling (s)	12 pence
1 pence (d)	

ABBREVIATIONS

Col.	Colonel
Lt.	Lieutenant
RN	Royal Navy
Rev.	Reverend

To preserve historical accuracy quotations are given verbatim with original spelling and grammar. Some insertions are made, inside square brackets, to aid understanding.

The land maps were reproduced with the permission of the New South Wales Government Office of the Registrar General, a unit of the Department of Finance, Services and Innovation.

Prologue

A TRULY EPIC ADVENTURE

> .... *it was one of the most ambitious and optimistic voyages of all time. It's like today sending a group of citizens against their will to establish a colony on the moon.*[1]

At daybreak on the morning of 13 May 1787 a flotilla of eleven small ships commanded by Captain Arthur Phillip set sail from the Spithead anchorage off Portsmouth heading through the Needles into the English Channel.[2] It was the start of an 8-month 17,000-mile voyage across often-uncharted seas to New South Wales on the east coast of New Holland. The flotilla, later to be known as the *First Fleet*, carried 1500 people, half of whom were convicts sentenced to transportation *Beyond the Seas*. The primary purpose of the expedition was to create a new colony on an unknown continent on the other side of the world. By any measure, this was a truly epic venture, and few on board these small ships understood the enormity of what lay ahead.

The story of the First Fleet voyage, and the establishment of a New South Wales colony, will be told wherever possible *through the eyes of the transported convicts*. For the most part this uses the life experiences of actual transported convicts, and two people, in particular, Anthony Rope and Elizabeth Pulley. Information about transported convicts has been sourced from many places but these two young transportees will provide the common thread throughout the story. Their experiences in this venture were not special; they mirror those of many other convicts. Anthony and Elizabeth both came from Norfolk but did not know each other before transportation, and as was the case for most single men and women about to be sent to this remote land.

Anthony Rope, aged 30, was placed on the First Fleet ship *Alexander* and Elizabeth Pulley, 25, on the *Friendship*; both were transported because of dangerously overcrowded prisons in England. The First Fleet's departure from Portsmouth in May 1787 initiated the *Botany Bay Scheme* – a scheme only acted upon when the overflowing British prisons had reached a crisis point, and public anger became a political threat to the government. Sending convicts to a remote location on the east coast of New Holland was now seen as the only realistic substitute for the practice of shipping convicts to the American colonies, which had stopped with the American Revolutionary War. Even so, transporting convicts so far away was a risky undertaking, both for ships and the government. Many believed it would fail totally and that the ships and their company would never be seen again. Michael Pembroke the author of *Arthur Phillip – Sailor, Mercenary, Governor, Spy* claims that it was one of the most ambitious projects ever attempted.[3] Indeed, since very little was known of the southern oceans or New South Wales in the 1780s, this expedition was just as challenging as the incredible Man-on-the-Moon attempt almost two hundred years later.

At the time of sailing, Lloyd's of London, contrary to its motto *Fidentia*, would have had little confidence in the Scheme succeeding and, for that matter, nor did most of the British politicians. Arthur Phillip understood better than anyone the risks that this expedition entailed, and he was meticulous in provisioning his fleet for the long journey ahead. In the hope of restricting the endemic diseases present in confined quarters on long passages at sea he had also insisted on the best possible sanitary conditions for the convicts and crew.

Despite the importance of the occasion, there were no special farewells as the flotilla departed Spithead on the morning of 13 May 1787 – no fanfares, no gun salutes from the Portsmouth harbour fort, no special flags fluttering and no government dignitaries waving their hats as the rag-tag little fleet set sail. Commander Phillip did not expect any such ceremony and probably would have discouraged any suggestion of it; he needed to concentrate on the difficult task ahead. He knew that his convoy of mostly prisoners would face many physical and medical obstacles before it would reach the coast of New South Wales.

One can envisage that, as the flagship HMS *Sirius* bore south through a blustery English Channel, Phillip stood confidently on the quarterdeck knowing that he had done everything possible for the success of the voyage and was looking forward to the challenges ahead. Fancifully perhaps, we can imagine him humming the andante of a piano concerto he had recently heard in London; the No. 21 in C major, written by the young musical celebrity of the time, Wolfgang Amadeus Mozart, then only 31 years of age. After all, the Royal Navy was a service that greatly valued music and Arthur Phillip was a veteran mariner fluent in several languages with broad cultural interests.

Critical episodes in the lives of Anthony Rope and Elizabeth Pulley, the two central people in our history told from a convict perspective, occur well before HMS *Sirius* led the First Fleet out into the English Channel. Knowledge of Anthony and Elizabeth's early lives is relevant because it gives insights into why many illiterate rural convicts found themselves on board ships bound for the *ends of the earth*, and, more importantly, why Britain needed to resort to the precarious Botany Bay Scheme at all. Many of the answers to these questions can be found by studying the living and working conditions of common people, especially rural workers, at that time.

The historical narrative opens with an examination of Anthony and Elizabeth's early upbringing and livelihoods prior to being convicted of stealing. Their experiences replicate those of many fellow convicts who were unemployed young labourers. For the young men and women starving in the land of plenty – and 18th century Britain certainly offered much to the upper and middle classes – stealing had become the only way to stay alive. Their daily existences were subject to continual unemployment, social disruption and economic destitution – the prosperous and expanding British economy was mostly inaccessible to them. In this sharply stratified society, it was the incarceration of the underprivileged in great numbers that became the overwhelming motivation for establishing a new penal colony in New South Wales.

This book also delves into the politics, influences and causes that led to the eventual choice of the remote coast of New Holland as the site for the penal colony, and explains the careful preparation and logistics needed to ensure the success of the long voyage and prison settlement. Later chapters describe the dangerous 8-month sea voyage of the flotilla as it traversed largely unexplored seas. Telling the story of this journey is, in itself, a remarkable chronicle of the skill and courage of the seamen, and the resilience of convict transportees who were closely confined below decks in dreadful conditions.

The story will explain the enormous physical, emotional and political challenges that confronted convicts, emancipists and settlers – these were the men and women that would eventually ensure the very survival of the colony. The hardship and suffering sustained by the transported cohort, in an environment of servitude, deprivation and hunger, will be revealed through documented cases. Just staying alive in this isolated harsh environment, let alone flourishing, required much fortitude and sacrifice. That these mostly illiterate people prospered and became the stalwarts of a free and democrat government was the major impetus for Australia developing into a land of opportunity and equality.

Chapter 1

POVERTY & PUNISHMENT

There are prisons, into which whoever looks will, at first sight of the people confined there, be convinced, that there is some great error in the management of them: the sallow meagre countenances declare, without words, that they are very miserable: many who went in healthy, are in a few months changed to emaciated dejected objects.[1]

The 18th century in England was a time of enormous social, economic and political change. There were a multitude of reasons for these upheavals, but the principal ones were the all-embracing industrial and agrarian revolutions. These dramatically altered the lives of both urban and rural working classes by eroding traditional employment opportunities, and, ultimately, decimating the cottage-based industries. These changes took place when Britain's colonial empire, along with its African slave trade, was burgeoning, but they also occurred in a period of major military conflicts with France, Spain and the American colonies. The burgeoning growth in international trade and commodity markets at the time contributed significantly to the overall wealth of the mercantile classes but, in most respects, it reduced the opportunities and living standards of unskilled and illiterate workers.

The advent of new industrial and transportation technologies proved a major factor in Britain's increasing mercantile success. John Kay's invention of the flying shuttle in 1733 and the carding machine in 1754 accelerated cloth weaving and were the forerunners of innovations that ultimately led to the complete automation of textile manufacturing. James Hargreaves invented the spinning jenny in 1765; Matthew Boulton and James Watt began producing steam engines for factories in 1774. By 1780, the combination of Hargreaves' inventions, Richard Arkwright's water frame, and the increased access to canals linking major population centres, made Britain a world leader in the manufacture of high quality textiles.

These industrial advances increased the prosperity, sophistication and leisure pursuits of the British upper and middle classes of society and provided the intellectual environment for the appreciation of progressive social concepts, including the abolition of slavery. The mid 18th century in Britain was a time of far-reaching intellectual advances in scientific knowledge, politics and philosophy and is commonly referred to as the *Age of Enlightenment and Science*. The outspoken views of William Wilberforce, Thomas Paine, Voltaire, Isaac Newton, Victor Hugo, Benjamin Franklin and many others, were discussed within literate and political circles and became catalysts for significant shifts in the social attitudes of the educated. The tolerant views of King George III cultivated a relatively liberal approach to social mobility and political change. George III suffered from bouts of porphyria during his 50-year reign but for most of this time he remained politically astute and active.

The rapid increase in national prosperity and liberal attitudes did not reward everyone in Britain. The upper echelon of society – the landed gentry and mercantile classes – profited but there were far fewer benefits for the rest. The prospects for rural workers were further damaged by legally enforceable changes to land-management practices. At the start of the 18th century, tenant farmers had small leaseholds to grow cereal crops and those with sheep and cattle were allowed to graze on the common land. This provided a basic subsistence living that supported many rural families: freehold and tenant farmers, cottagers, squatters and farm labourers. In effect, the traditional communal sharing of land allowed the 'humblest and poorest labourer to rise in the village'.[2] This basic agrarian lifestyle had existed since feudal times, and it was how most of England's country population survived. The mostly illiterate rural poor were largely unaware of the changes that were soon to disrupt their traditional livelihood.

Agricultural land practices altered dramatically in 1710 when laws permitting major landholders to fence off farming lands were enacted, thus restricting their communal use. Successive changes to the Enclosure Act (*Inclosure Act*) led to the consolidation of small farms into larger estates. This encouraged more efficient farming practices but seriously reduced the earnings of rural villages and small freehold farmers. It also meant that there was much less need for agricultural labour.

The new laws reduced the income and food-producing capacity of farmers who did not own land. Large numbers of rural labourers and their families, most of whom had for many generations scrounged a meagre living as small tenant farmers became destitute. Some moved to towns hoping for work in the industrialised textile factories, but they usually discovered that the machine-based industries offered little opportunity for unskilled labourers. As a consequence, unemployment, poverty and hunger became commonplace in many parts of rural and urban Britain by the mid-18th century.

Although the full impact of the Enclosure Act was not felt until the 19th century, by 1760 up to 40% land in Norfolk County had been enclosed.[3] By the 1780s life for the poor in rural Norfolk, where both Anthony and Elizabeth lived, became a bleak struggle for survival. There was little or no social assistance for the unemployed, and many poor people stole to feed their families. The disparity between the rich and poor at that time was seen in the spending by the wealthy on "fad foods" such as tea and sugar. It was claimed that 'as much superfluous money is expended on tea, sugar, etc as would maintain four millions more of subjects in BREAD'.[4]

It is difficult today to fully appreciate the gulf that existed between the gentry and the working classes in Britain up until the 20th century. The famous author Jane Austen (1775-1817) lived in England at the same time as Elizabeth and Anthony. Jane's father was a country pastor, and this meant that the Austen family was of 'modest means' and were even considered poor by their relatives. But because they were educated and well connected, all of the Austen family members were able to forge successful careers. Nevertheless, for this enlightened Christian family their social separation from the lower classes 'remained absolute and unquestioned; both sides believed that God had arranged the system'.[5] The stark reality of the 18th century was that the upper and lower classes lived in separate worlds – one full of privilege, education, smart clothing, witty theatre, coaches, glamorous balls, parties and opportunity – the other full of deprivation, hard work, poor housing, illiteracy, poverty and frequent hunger. These two worlds rarely intersected, and when they did it was only if advantageous to the gentry; usually when cheap labour or rent income was needed. To the majority of the privileged classes the poor remained nameless beings invisible in their daily lives, even when present in their houses as servants. Consequently, the wealthy had scant concern for their wellbeing. The common belief was that the working classes existed because it was God's Will, and they deserved to be where they were. This was an unrelentingly hard and miserable time to be poor.

The movement of rural workers in search of work to urban centres led to overcrowding and increased unemployment in the major industrial towns. It inevitably fuelled increased property and debtor crimes. Local authorities and communities in Britain were not accustomed to, and ill prepared for, the growing level of lawlessness. The demand for improved 'law and order' grew. But solving the high petty crime rate was not simply a matter of expanding the existing police force. Law-enforcement officers were virtually non-existent in England and very few offenders were ever brought to justice. In fact, prior to the

Metropolitan Police Act of 1829, laws were enforced by volunteer parish constables in villages, or by Justices-of-the-Peace in larger towns.

In the early 18th century, a lawbreaker convicted of minor property or debtor crimes was usually imprisoned for a short time in a local gaol. Because serious crimes, such as murder and treason, usually incurred the death penalty, rural gaols, which were mostly private, were unsuitable for lengthy incarceration. However, the practice of giving light sentences for petty crimes was about to undergo dramatic change.

By mid-century the fear that increasing crime rates would lead to widespread social disruption spawned new penalties intended to discourage property theft. The legal imperatives for these were bolstered by a growing concern about the civil insurrection in France, especially after the French Revolution took place in 1789. The British Parliament passed bills reclassifying many petty crimes as *capital offences* (to which the death sentence applies). Capital crimes now included burglary, highway-robbery, house-breaking in daytime, private stealing or picking pockets above 1 shilling, shoplifting above 5 shillings, stealing above 40 shillings, maiming or stealing a cow, horse or sheep, or breaking into a house or church.[6] The official punishment for these offences was now the same as for murder and treason – *death by hanging*.

Quite unfairly the new laws came into effect rapidly and were little understood by the poor, of whom 90% were illiterate. Consequently, the severity of the changes went largely unappreciated by the working class, which Thomas Paine – author of *The Rights of Man* – claimed was intentional to disadvantage the poor. Other enlightened members of English society, including the judiciary, strongly opposed the imposition of the new capital sentences for minor offences and this became a *cause célèbre* for many social reformers; the same people advocating for the abolition of the slave trade in the 1770s.

Mercifully, there were several *ad hoc* legal options available to those members of the judiciary who were inclined to avoid the imposition of a capital sentence. The legal loopholes were not recognised officially, but they were commonly applied, nonetheless. In particular, juries could be encouraged to apply *pious perjury* in assessing the severity of an offence when a prisoner was charged with a minor property or financial crime. Such actions permitted judges to assign *imprisonment by transportation* rather than the death sentence. For example, a court clerk could routinely understate the value of stolen property on the charge sheet in order that it was below the capital offence threshold.[7]

This practice is especially important to this story since, as will be detailed later, Anthony Rope was sentenced to 7 years transportation although the initial charge sheets clearly show that he stole goods to the value of 55 shillings, well in excess of the listed capital offence threshold of 40 shillings. Across the nation, judges and juries displayed an admirable reluctance to commit criminals to the gallows for minor offences, especially if they were women. Of course, some magistrates strictly applied the new capital sentences and became known as Hanging Judges. Their sessions were to be avoided at all costs. Fortunately, even when a crime was ruled as a capital offence by the court, it could be, and often was, commuted by Royal Pardon. The other person central to our story, Elizabeth Pulley, benefited from such an amnesty. In the last of her five court appearances she was sentenced to death, which was later commuted by a Royal Pardon to transportation for 7 years.

In fact, the widespread application of judicial leniency in the late 1700s meant that *transportation beyond the seas* became the *de facto* sentence imposed by courts for minor crimes. Relaxation of the capital sentencing laws was tolerated because a sentence of *transportation* satisfied the political imperative of removing petty lawbreakers from decent society. Ironically, the lenient judicial practices posed a new problem for the prison system in England; where were all these transported prisoners to go? After 1775, the American Colonies no longer accepted transportees and there was no other offshore prison to send them to.

A brief overview of earlier British convict transportation practices is relevant here. In 1717, the British Parliament passed the *Act for the Further Preventing Robbery, Burglary, and Other Felonies, and for the More Effective Transportation of Felons, etc.* (4 Geo. I cap. XI), which established penal transportation to America with a seven-year convict bond service for minor offenders, and a fourteen-year convict bond service for more serious crimes. Between 1718 and 1775 an estimated 50,000 convicts were transported to the British-American colonies.[8] This represented about a quarter of all British migrants to the North American colonies at a time when they were desperately short of labour. The American colonists saw convict transportation as beneficial socially, politically and economically. It disposed of minor criminals at a cost that was less than gaoling them and a boon to the colonies by providing cheap labour. This was, in effect, and indeed in fact, a *slave trade* under a different guise. From its inception, transportation to the American colonies was a private business enterprise. Shipping contractors managed the movement of the convicts, obtained contracts from the sheriffs and in the colonies recouped their costs by selling the prisoners at auctions. Colonists would buy a convict as an indentured servant for the duration of their sentence. During an indenture the living and working conditions imposed on convicts differed little from those of slaves.[9]

However, by the mid 18th century, convict labour had become less attractive to American colonialists and, moreover, in the 1770s the prospect of antislavery laws in England spelled the end of this practice.

Maryland was the last colony to accept convicts and by 1775 the American Revolutionary War ended the trade of imported British goods and convicts. On 11 Jan 1776, the London *Gazetteer* reported 'there will be no more convicts sent to America whilst the country remains unsettled.'[10] The article suggested that transportation would resume just as soon as peace was restored. This never took place.

With the loss of the American colonies, the systematic disposal of convicts to places *beyond the seas* came to a halt. Nevertheless, most judges consistently refused to apply capital punishment to relatively minor crimes and, where it was applied, capital sentences were often commuted to transportation. Consequently, the land gaols in the 1770s and 1780s overflowed with prisoners awaiting the imposition of a sentence that could not be enacted and, importantly, could not be altered. It was a serious judicial stalemate.

The *Hulks Act* (16 Geo III, c. 43) was passed by parliament in 1776 as a two-year temporary measure to house prisoners committed for transportation in decommissioned naval ships, called 'hulks', moored on the Thames River. These floating prisons were intended as a short-term solution to gaol overcrowding until somewhere could be found to send the transportees. The Hulks Act made an important distinction between prisoners sentenced specifically to transportation or hard labour. Male convicts given the death sentence, but commuted to transportation, were required to do 3 to 10 years hard labour; specifically, to dredge the Thames and improve its navigability.

The government awarded the first contract for overseeing prisoners on the hulks to Duncan Campbell, who had been involved in convict transportation to the American colonies from 1758 to 1775. One of his ships, the *Justitia*, became the first hulk on the Thames. Parliament regularly reviewed the 1776 Hulks Act and, although there was opposition to the practice, the Act remained in effect for 80 years.

Throughout this time the overall control and maintenance of prisoners on hulks was, on the whole, more rigorous than those in gaols. Hulk prisoners were usually better clothed and fed and, with good behaviour, could have their period of confinement reduced. Moreover, in early 1776 the government offered pardons for any transportees who joined the army or navy or could remove themselves from England for the duration of their sentence. The last option was clearly only possible for those with money or influential friends. The wars with the American colonies, France and Spain created a demand for soldiers and sailors, who were increasingly drafted from hulks and gaols. This reduced hulk numbers, but prisoners from the overcrowded land gaols quickly took their place.

The conditions on hulks may have been better than gaols but the work regimes aboard were brutal and harsh, and the mortality rates were high. In 1776, the prison reformer John Howard surveyed British gaols and hulks and determined that the high death rate on the hulks was due mainly to typhus prisoners invariably contracted in land gaols.[11] In 1777, the hulk contractor Campbell reported that convicts were seldom free from illness they contracted in gaols. Between August 1776 and March 1778, of the 632 prisoners sent to hulks, 176 had died (28%). To promote better sanitation, a new *Hulks Act* was passed in 1779 that required all male convicts sent to hulks be washed, given new clothes and isolated for four days at a secure place so that diseases could be detected. An additional hospital ship was provided for this purpose. On a subsequent visit to the hulks in 1779, Howard observed that the conditions and health of the convicts had improved.[12]

The hulk death rate slowly decreased and by 1783 had sunk to 19%. By 1785-86, when Anthony Rope was on a hulk, the mortality rate had fallen significantly. When Campbell's contract was renewed in 1779, he purchased another ship as a replacement for the aging *Justitia* with the same name and fitted her out to accommodate 260 prisoners.[13]

However, land gaols had some advantages for the rich. Prisoners with money could make their life much easier, as gaolers were prepared to provide better food, quarters and clothing to those who could pay. Such practices were prohibited on hulks and the same food, bedding and work conditions applied to all. Moreover, few visitors were allowed on hulks and alcoholic drinks were banned, except for small (low alcohol) beer. Hulk prisoners were confined to bed at 7 pm.[14]

In 1779, out of the total of 4379 prisoners in England and Wales, 526 were held on hulks. Three years on, out of a total of 4439 prisoners, only 204 were on hulks because of expired sentences, deaths and pardons to those enlisted in the military.[15] The end of the American and Continental wars in the 1780s meant that this last way to escape from prison life had disappeared. In 1784, the government passed a new Act making all hulk prisoners, independent of sentence, liable to hard labour pending transportation. At the end of 1785, the overcrowding of gaols saw two more naval hulks fitted out as floating prisons. In 1786 there were 1240 prisoners on five hulks; three moored on the Thames at Woolwich, the *Justitia*, *Censor* and *Ceres*; one in Plymouth, the *Dunkirk* and one in Portsmouth, the *Fortunée*.[16] The convicts who were to be eventually transported on the First Fleet mainly came from these hulks, the rest from metropolitan and county gaols across England.

In the early 18th century, most towns in England used local gaols and bridewells to incarcerate minor felons. The bridewells were primarily for rehabilitating petty criminals; their role in the legal system was based on a 16th-century penitentiary housed in King Henry VIII's old London residence, *Bridewell Court* that had been used to house petty criminals doing hard labour. Later bridewells also imprisoned disorderly women and homeless children.

Most of the gaols and bridewells across England were decrepit old buildings and although Justices of the Peace had been granted powers to rebuild them in 1698, they were not obliged to, and most did not. As a consequence, decades later 30 of the major gaols were housed in decaying medieval castles, while smaller prisons were crammed into city gates or old fortified buildings. This meant that often prisoners had to be permanently chained to prevent escape. These cells were not intended for prisoners with lengthy sentences, and inmates were reliant on the whims of their turnkeys for their food and clothing. John Howard wrote in his 1777 edition of *The State of the Prisons in England and Wales*:

> The fallow meagre countenances declare, without words, that they are very miserable; many who went in healthy, are in a few months changed to emaciated dejected objects. Some are seen pinning under diseases, *"sick and in prison"*; expiring on the floors, in loathsome cells, of pestilential fevers, and the confluent small-pox victims, I must say to the cruelty, but I will say to the inattention, of sheriffs, and gentlemen in the commission of the peace.[17]

It was not uncommon for infectious diseases to decimate prison populations. Howard recorded how poorly fed and clothed prisoners were and he strongly recommended a system of state-controlled, rather than privately owned, gaols. He personally advocated a tough prison regime within a healthy environment of solitary confinement, hard labour and religious instruction in which prisoners were rehabilitated, not just punished. Howard argued that the main cause of gaol overcrowding was the large number of debtors sent to prisons. Insolvents often entered the gaols accompanied by their wives and children. By 1782, debtors comprised 2197 of the total number of 4439 prisoners.[18]

When a prisoner's gaol sentence had expired, they were not released until prison fees had been paid. The amount charged varied according to the gaol, the gaoler, the length and type of sentence and the food and bedding provided. Those without money could linger in gaol months longer than the length of their sentence. During this time food was often not provided, and prisoners were dependent on fellow inmates for food until their fee had been paid. These delays further contributed to overcrowding in prisons. In 1777 John Howard applied, without success, to legal authorities for gaolers to receive a salary instead of depending on income from prison fees.[19]

Chapter 2

POOR RURAL YOUTH

Important incidents in his [life] have entirely vanished beneath the political horizon.... However, just about enough is known to tell a life and describe the times. .... We have very little information about [his] childhood and youth, but are well informed about the events of the day, so at least we can give an account of what he witnessed or heard about when he was a boy[1]

The majority of convicts transported on the First Fleet were poor illiterate males, younger than 30, and a high proportion of these came from the rural areas of England. It was here that poverty and unemployment was rampant, and, in the absence of any form of social or government support, men stole to keep themselves and their families alive. In the countryside, part-time magistrates, who were mostly landed gentry, sentenced the rural youth to death, prison and transportation for trivial offences – even for leaving their workplace without permission wearing servants' clothing. Not all offenders were rural, but many of the crimes committed in London (Middlesex) districts were country youths who had migrated there in search of work and food. The enclosure laws and the industrial manufacture of textiles had destroyed the livelihoods of the small farmers, agricultural labourers and many others in small villages. It was here that the full impact of land aggregation and industrialisation was most severely felt. Without work or social support, these people were destitute. The brutal reality of the mid to late 18th century was that starving workers with no prospect of employment had no other choice but to become a felon.

This story explores the lives of young men and women who were transported to Australia for relatively petty felonies. In particular it will trace the history of two young rural workers, Anthony Rope and Elizabeth Pulley, who lived through these tumultuous times. We shall see that their punishment for stealing was incarceration and, eventually, transportation as convicts on the First Fleet. Both came from small villages in Norfolk, but they did not know each other until they reached New South Wales. The story is not specifically about them however, their lives are typical of the convicts sent to establish a new colony on the continent that would eventually become Australia. Their individual stories replicate, in so many ways, those of mostly illiterate and underprivileged workers who were transported to the Ends of the Earth for stealing to prevent starvation.

There is little information about Anthony Rope's life prior until 1784 when he appeared in court, at the age of 28. We do know whom his parents and siblings are from church documents but, since Anthony and his family were uneducated, no written record of his boyhood and youth has survived. Nevertheless, as historians are wont to claim, and Anthony Everitt aptly demonstrates this in his biography of Emperor Hadrian, even without citable records considerable knowledge of an individual may be deduced from the events and social conditions of the period.[2] Anthony Rope lived through a turbulent and well-recorded era of English history and this biographical strategy will be applied to his story as well. While this approach involves a degree of speculation, Anthony's whereabouts are known at various times, and we can predict with some confidence the sort of early existence he is likely to have led.

Anthony Rope was born in Norton Subcourse, Norfolk in 1756, the tenth child of John and Ann Rope, and was baptised on August 1st in the St Mary's Church.[3] The small rural parish of Norton Subcourse existed prior to the Norman Conquest in 1066 and lies on the edge of the marshes of the River Yare, 24 km southeast of Norwich. In 1760, about 70 people over the age of 16 were living in the parish of St Mary and St Margaret (referred to hereafter as *St Mary*).

Anthony's maternal grandparents Robert and Susanna Curtis also lived in Norton Subcourse, and as freehold farmers they had the right to vote. Voting was the entitlement of people owning property worth at least 40 shillings a year. The Norfolk Voting Register for Norton Subcourse (from the 1734 Poll) lists 24 freeholders and includes the name of Robert Curtis.[4] The polls from the years 1734 and 1768 reveal the cruel effects of the land Enclosure Acts on small landowners. Over the span of those 34 years, the number of freeholders in Norton Subcourse decreased from 24 to 7, indicating how difficult it had become for small farmers to purchase and retain their existing freeholds.

Anthony was only 4 years old when, on 4 Apr 1760, his mother Ann died aged 45. His father John lived a further 25 years, dying on 12 Nov 1785 at the age of 84. The gravestones of Ann and John are still in excellent condition in St Mary's churchyard and located next to the graves of Ann's parents Robert and Susanna Curtis.

The repercussions of Ann's early death would have been calamitous for the family. Anthony had a baby sister less than one year old, three brothers below 12 years and three sisters aged between 17 and 23 years. The older sisters Susannah, Ann and Mary are likely to have taken over the running of the household and the raising of the younger children. Susannah married 4 years later in 1764, Mary 11 years later in 1771 and Sarah in 1781. The eldest son John, as well as Sarah, remained in Norton Subcourse and both are buried in St Mary's churchyard.

Anthony, like most poor commoners, was illiterate. Education in rural Britain was rare, and the few schools that existed were usually private and expensive. A village church might provide some classes, and girls were occasionally schooled at home, but it was a luxury affordable only to the wealthy. Most families needed their children to work.

From an early age, the Rope children would have worked with their father on their leasehold land. In rural families this was a matter of survival. Children were part of a tenant farmer's work force; the boys minded livestock and helped with seeding and harvesting. The girls did the cooking, milking and fed the chickens. On reaching the age of five, a child in a poor rural family was expected to earn his keep either on a farm, at sea, in a mine or in a factory. Even as the youngest child, Anthony would have shared in the heaviest jobs. His efforts nurturing animals, draining ditches and repairing fences was essential in keeping the family afloat, and were skills that would prove invaluable in later life.

Because rural families and villagers traditionally built their own houses, most farm labourers had rudimentary construction skills. Farmers in England were expected to be jacks-of-all-trades and Anthony probably had building experience. Norton Subcourse borders on marshes and the Yare River, and water transport to the nearby North Sea coastal towns of Lowestoft and Great Yarmouth was common, so it is quite likely that Anthony became an experienced boatman and shipper.

In the 1750s, freeholder and tenant farmers in England numbered around 350,000 families – most earning between £40 and £150 a year. It is probable that the Ropes were small leaseholders prior to the land Enclosure Acts. A subsistence livelihood was feasible in the early 18th century provided the farmers worked hard, their rented land was arable, and their animals could graze on the village common.[5] Tenant farmers were often allowed to scavenge for fallen branches, to cut peat for fuel and to dig local clay for making bricks but the enclosure laws prohibited many of these practices. Moreover, the custom of levying rents *in kind* – by barter or labour – had changed by mid-century to the requirement to pay rents in cash. For poor families this proved almost impossible.

In effect, the Enclosure Acts eliminated small freehold farms in many parts of England. Before the land realignments, freehold and tenant farms on quite small plots of an acre or so were labour intensive and required numerous farm workers and domestic servants. These workers were hired on a yearly basis and often resided in the farmer's household where they frequently helped with the spinning and weaving activities. Producing textiles was an important local cottage industry. The textiles, which were usually sold back to the merchants who supplied the raw materials, were a critical source of income for farmers who had to pay cash rents. Typically, females did the spinning and, depending on the season, the farming men helped with the weaving. By the 1750s, however, the availability of cheap textiles from factories had challenged the viability of cottage weavers and reduced the income of many small farmers.

We know from court records that, years later, Anthony ended up in the small Essex town of Rochford over 170 km south of Norton Subcourse, not far from the Thames River estuary. He may have been on his way to London where many rural unemployed went to seek work, or he may have recently been employed on boats at the many ports and docks in the area. Getting to Rochford from Norton Subcourse is a relatively long journey by land, especially on foot at a time when most villagers rarely travelled more than 10 miles from home. However, if Anthony was a crewman aboard a boat trading at the many ports on the southeast coast, then the historic market town of Rochford on the river Roche is close by and only 40 miles from London.

On the 3 Sep 1784, Anthony, aged 28, appeared before magistrate John T. Bull in Rochford on the charge of stealing from Robert Gosling and Robert Bradley. He had been caught in the act and seen by several witnesses making off with the goods. Anthony was convicted of felony, grand larceny and fraud.[6] This was a major crime on which the local magistrate at the Quarter Court had no authority to adjudicate, so the case was transferred to the March 1785 hearings of the Assizes Court in Chelmsford. Until this hearing could be arranged six months' hence, Anthony was held in Chelmsford prison.

Chelmsford had recently built a gaol, which the prison reformer John Howard wrote about: 'There is a new Gaol, which exceeds the old one in strength & almost as much as in splendor. The County, to their honour, have spared no cost'.[7] In October 1783, this gaol housed a total of 46 prisoners, 21 debtors and 25 felons. A prisoner was fed 1½ lb of bread a day and 1 qt of small beer, requiring a weekly fee of 3s 6d for 'garnish'. A sign in the prison taproom warned 'Prisoners to pay garnish or run the gauntlet'. Men and women had separate cells 15¾ x 14½ feet in size, lined with stone and with straw for sleeping. There was also a workroom in which prisoners could weave garters to pay for their keep and for extra food.[8]

The next Assizes Court hearing in Chelmsford began on Monday, 7 Mar 1785 before Justices, Sir Henry Gould and Sir Richard

Perryn. On Thursday morning, 10 Mar 1785, the Judges delivered the verdict on Anthony Rope as follows:

> *Anthony Rope, late of the parish of Rochford in the co. of Essex Labourer: Burglary by breaking and entering the house of Robert Gosling about 7 in the forenoon on 2 September 1784, and stealing:*
> - two printed cotton Gowns – value 20s
> - one Petticoat made of Silk and Worsted – value 5s
> - one Silk Neck Handkerchief – value 18d
> - one pair of Women's Leather Shoes – value 1s
> - one pair of Metal Buckles plated with Silver – value 6d
> - one Man's Hat – value 6s
> - one fustian Frock – value 5s
> - one pair of Men's Leather Shoes – valve 2s
> - one pair of other Metal Shoe Buckles plated with Silver – value 1s
> - one Hempen Sack of Robert Gosling – value 6d
> - one pair of others Men's Leather Shoes – value 5s
> - one pair of other Metal Buckles plated with Silver – value 3s
> - one cotton Waistcoat – value 2s
> - one linen shirt – value 6d
> - two silk Handkerchiefs – value 2s
> - one piece of Silver Coin called an Half Crown – value 2s 6d
> - one piece of proper Silver coin called a Shilling of Robert Bradley
>
> *Verdict: Not guilty of breaking and entering. Guilty of stealing. Goods value 35s. No Chattels.*
>
> *Sentence: Transported for 7 years.*[9]

A seven year transportation sentence for burglary may sound harsh but Anthony was fortunate that the judges had exercised *pious perjury* by undervaluing the stolen goods to 35s. The actual value totalled 58s 6d. The new sentencing laws mandated that if the value of stolen goods exceeded 40s, the sentence had to be *death by hanging*. The petty larceny charge incurred the lesser sentence of transportation *'Beyond the Seas'*.[10] The next day the trial was reported in *The Chelmsford Chronicle*. 'At our assizes, which began on Monday, the following prisoners received sentences … Anthony Rope, for burglary, seven years transportation.'[11] *The Ipswich Journal* published details of the trial a day later, with a similar text. Four months on, *The Chelmsford Chronicle* observed that the Quarter Sessions had reviewed Anthony's sentence and it remained the same.[12] His fate as a *transportee* was now sealed, and, as such, the Chelmsford gaoler would almost certainly have been trying to move him elsewhere to make space for lesser criminals.

Prisoners sentenced to transportation were usually sent to a hulk moored on the Thames River. It is not known exactly when Anthony was moved to the hulk *Ceres*, but it was probably after the Quarter Session review of his sentence. His name appears for the first time on the *Ceres* hulk record of April 1786, which lists his age as 26 (he was 28) and his sentence on 7 Mar 1785 in Chelmsford as 7 years transportation. The record also shows that, with four fellow inmates from Chelmsford gaol, Anthony was transferred from the hulk *Ceres* to the *Justitia* on 1 Jun 1786.[13] The likely reason for the transfer was that the number of convicts on the *Ceres* exceeded the contracted quota.

Prison hulks had been moored on the Thames River since 1776. Even with five hulks in service by 1786 the land gaols were grossly overcrowded, and the prisoner quotas for hulks exceeded those agreed to by hulk contractors.[14]

Hulk (location)	Period for 1786	No. on Board*	
Justitia (Thames)	July – October	292	(250)
Censor (Thames)	July – October	255	(240)
Ceres (Thames)	July – October	311	(250)
Fortunée (Portsmouth)	August – November	336	(300)
Dunkirk (Plymouth)	June – September	214	(200)
		1408	(1240)

* *The maximum number contracted for each ship is in brackets*

Incarceration on hulks differed from that in land gaols. Depending on the severity of the crime, convicts might be chained two-on-two and others were in heavy fetters, and they were required to do hard labour dredging the Thames to improve its navigation. Depending on the weather, the prisoners' worked from 7 am to 6 pm, with a break for lunch, and in winter from 8.30 am to 3 pm. A high brick wall was built on the land facing the hulks to prevent any escapes when irons had to be removed so men could work more freely and effectively. This wall also served to keep curious visitors and anxious family away.[15]

The *Justitia* hulk muster record of July 1786 lists Anthony Rope.[16] A statement at the end of the muster by Duncan Campbell, the contractor for the hulks, describing work performed by convicts in the past months.

> The Convicts names in the above Return, since last Report have been employed when Health & Weather permitted in raising Gravel from Barking or Woolwich Shoals in wheeling the same for the purpose of making considerably higher the surface of all the Ground continuous to the Proof of Practise Butts which they have erected and are now repairing, in filling up large Ditches, scraping & cleaning of Cannon, sawing of Timber for the Laboratory and in other occasional Works in the Warren at Woolwich under the Direction of the Officers of the Board of Ordnances.[17]

Dredging was exhausting work and sufficient diet was needed to keep the convicts fit enough to do it. The hulk food ration was much better than in the Chelmsford gaol, where Anthony received only a bread ration, and this he had to pay for. At meals hulk prisoners were grouped into messes of six men, with each group receiving the following food rations. For breakfast: 1 pt of barley made into 3 qt of soup. For lunch: half a bullock's head with 7 lb bread or 2 lb cheese with 7 lb bread. For Sunday lunch: 7 lb of salt pork or 8lb of beef with 6 lb of biscuit or 7 lb bread. For dinner: ½ pt of pea and ½ pt of barley was to be made into ¾ qt of soup, or 1 qt of oatmeal to be made into porridge. Each mess received 5 qts of beer a day.[18] These were far from starvation rations.

An 1800 engraving showing prison hulks on the Thames River near Woolwich. Convicts can be seen dredging the river and working on adjacent land and docks.

In August 1786, after the recommendations of innumerable parliamentary committees, the Pitt government announced that it would establish a new convict settlement on the remote continent of New Holland. The following announcement was published in *The Public Advertiser* at the end of September 1786.

> A muster is ordered to be made immediately of all convicts which are now confined on board the Prison hulk here, and a return to be made thereon to the Secretary of State's officer. We have it current here, that the ships for Botany Bay will sail the beginning of November next, and that all the convicts now here will be sent aboard.[19]

Government orders were now sent to the turnkeys of each gaol and hulk, instructing them to select prisoners for the voyage. From October onwards individual prisoners are likely to have been told if they were one of the "lucky ones" to be shipped to Botany Bay. It is entirely possible that the chosen prisoners welcomed the chance to escape the hard labour aboard the *Justitia*. For the unmarried, the prospect of a new life in a distant land would have been a lot less unsettling than for those with a wife and children. Family members would have to stay behind.

Not surprisingly, preparing the ships that would transport the convicts on the long voyage to Botany Bay took much longer than expected. Modifying merchant ships to install secure convict bunks was a major undertaking and loading of supplies for the voyage took longer than anticipated. It was not until early January 1787, that the Under Secretary of the British Home Office, Evan Nepean, asked Duncan Campbell to convey 202 transportees from his hulks to the transport ship *Alexander*, at anchor in the Thames. Of the 799 male prisoners on the three Thames hulks at the time, 52 male convicts went from the *Justitia*, 31 from the *Censor* and 102 from the *Ceres*.[20] The final decision on who would be sent to the *Alexander* appears to have been left entirely to Duncan Campbell. However, the Home Office had recommended that men be selected for their fitness and health to make the arduous sea journey and for the skills they would bring to the new settlement. On 3 Jan 1787, Campbell submitted his final list of 185 men who he thought suitable for the journey.[21] Anthony Rope and two other Chelmsford inmates were among the names appended to the Transportation Warrant:

> Whereas a contract has been entered into for transporting to New South Wales or some other of the Islands adjacent the several Convicts now in your custody on board the Hulks in the River Thames whose Names are contained in the list hereunto annexed. Our Will and Pleasure is, that you forthwith do deliver over to the Contractors Mr William Richards, Ship Broker and Mr Duncan Sinclair, Master of the Transport Ship called the Alexander the said Convicts whose Names are specified in the said list, in order that they may be transported to the said Coast of New South Wales, or some one or the other of the Islands adjacent on board the said Ship Alexander for the Terms of Years for which such Convicts are severally sentenced or ordered to be transported. And for doing this shall be your warrant.[22]

On 6 Jan 1787, the selected convicts were transferred to the *Alexander* moored at Woolwich, in readiness for her departure to Portsmouth to rendezvous with the other ships of the First Fleet at Spithead.[23] Anthony Rope was, at 30 years of age, one of the older convicts to be transported, and because he had been in prison since September 1784, he had only five years of his seven-year sentence left to serve.

It is unrecorded whether Anthony's father, John, in Norton Subcourse, knew anything of his son's fate or was even aware of his son being sent to prison. Since all of the Rope clan were probably illiterate communications outside of Norton Subcourse would have been difficult and news of family who left the village was rare. This was an age when years might pass before someone would receive word from a family member residing in a distant place, or news of a major event elsewhere in Britain. News came to rural areas mostly through travellers, or from someone who was asked to carry a report to a family. It is possible that a literate person from Norton Subcourse had read in *The Chelmsford Chronicle* about Anthony being sentenced to transportation, but without spoken communication or a hand-borne letter, it is unlikely that anyone in the Rope family knew of his imprisonment, or that he was destined for Botany Bay. This would have been a common problem for most of the transportees aboard the First Fleet ships.

One hopes that Anthony knew a fellow prisoner who he could dictate a letter to his father John about his Chelmsford conviction in March 1785, because he died at the end of that year.

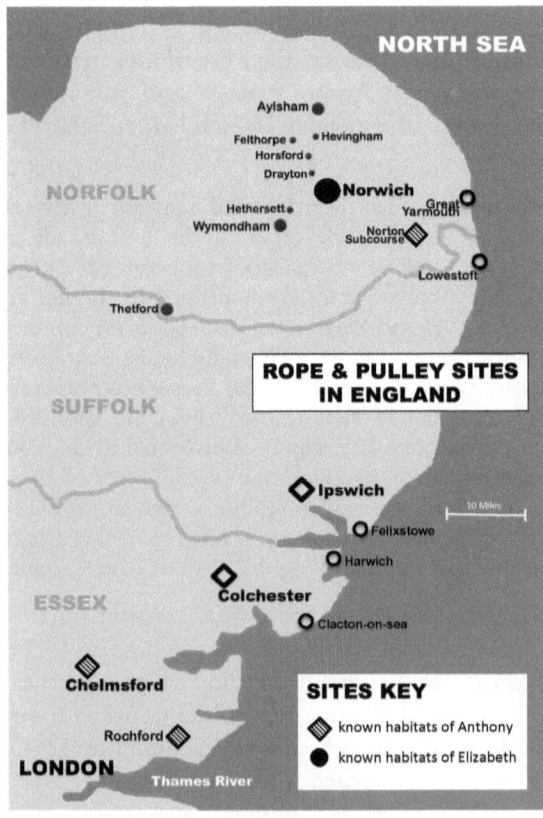

Chapter 3

FEMALE SERVITUDE

In their day-to-day existence, in which total obedience to the demands of their master and mistress was expected, they became morally, economically, financially, and even sexually, dependent on their master and wholly confined in the isolated and tight little world of one household.[1]

The other rural convict central to our story is Elizabeth Pulley. As with Anthony Rope, few written records exist about her childhood and youth. She was orphaned at the age of six, and until she was 17 there are no information on her activities and whereabouts. We do know, however, what her family ties were, and from the social conditions prevailing at the time conclusions can be drawn about her early life. These provide reasonably credible insight into what it was like to be a poor female orphan and a young woman in servitude in rural 18th century England. It was an era when there was little support for orphans, who were considered a burden on local parish authorities and were moved on quickly to a placement in servitude. The deprivations experienced at that time by the destitute and homeless, and especially by female children, would have been horrible and unavoidable.

From the outset, we know that Elizabeth's childhood as an orphan would have been one of insecurity and personal hardship. She was born in 1762 in Felthorpe, Norfolk, and baptised in the 14th century parish church St Margaret on 21 Feb 1762 as Elizabeth *Puly*. Felthorpe is part of the district of Taverham Hundred, 13 km northeast of Norwich.

Elizabeth's family name is recorded with multiple spellings. As she was illiterate, her orally communicated name was often misspelt. Elizabeth's surname in early official papers appears as Pulley, Pully and Puly. In some later books and diaries her name was spelt as Powley, and in Ralph Clark's First Fleet diary, Elizabeth is addressed as Pully.[2] In this narrative her surname will be spelt *Pulley*.

For centuries the Pulleys had lived in Horsford. Her father, Tobias, was born there in 1736. There were also Pulleys in adjacent villages, though their surnames often appear as *Pooley* or *Poley*. None of the Pulleys appears to have owned land, and the 1734 Poll Book shows that there were only four freeholders in the Horsford area. This suggests that the Pulleys were poor, and employed as weavers, farm labourers, servants or maids in the local manor house and larger farms.

On 10 Aug 1752, Tobias, aged 15, was registered as a weaver apprentice in the Norfolk Apprenticeship Records (shown as *Tobiah*). He was indentured to a Thomas Brown in Drayton (misspelled *Drainton*), about 3 km south of Horsford, for a 7-year apprenticeship commencing on 24 Jun 1751 at a premium of £2.[3] At the age of 20, Tobias married Alice Brighton on 18 Dec 1756 at St Peter's church in Haveringland. Their marriage certificate shows the surname *Pully* and both signatures as marks. In 1757 Alice had a son, William, and two years later the family moved to Felthorpe where another son, Tobias, was born. On 21 Feb 1762 a daughter was baptised 'Elizabeth Puly' in St Margaret's Church.

In 1764, shortly after the family moved back to Haveringland, tragedy struck. Both father and son Tobias died within two weeks of each other, presumably from a contagious illness. Elizabeth was just two years of age at the time and would not have understood what a calamitous effect this would have on her life. Her brother, aged 5 years, was buried on 6 Feb 1764 at St Peter's churchyard in Haveringland and her father on 19 Feb 1764, aged 27.

Elizabeth's mother Alice was now a young widow with two small children and a third on the way. Without income or property the young Pulley family faced a bleak future. There were few job opportunities for a female with small children, especially when pregnant. Alice most likely sought out the most menial tasks such as laundry washing, ironing and clothing repairs. These were low paying jobs usually done by the poor. As a destitute young family their survival may have depended on the Haveringland Church Parish or Brighton and Pulley relatives who could afford to feed extra mouths. An even worse possibility is that they were sent to the poorhouse. Late in 1764 Elizabeth's mother gave birth to another brother named Tobias.

Even greater trauma lay ahead. Three years after Tobias' birth, Alice died suddenly, and was buried in Haveringland on 21 Apr 1768. The young Pulley children were now orphaned; William at 11 years of age, Elizabeth at just 6 and Tobias at only 3. Nothing is known of their immediate fate, but it is likely they were adopted by relatives or sent to an orphanage. Often the local parish would pay relatives to care for orphans. There were workhouses for orphans in the area, and it is possible the children were sent there. If so, William and Elizabeth would have been immediately put out to work.

Bridget Hill writes in her book *The Servants: English Domestics in The 18th century*, that it was a common practice for pauper children to be placed in bonded service or signed up as apprentices, in order that parish ratepayers would not have to maintain them. A master responsible for a servant or an apprentice who was a pauper child would receive a small fee from the parish for their support. Little consideration was given to the type of work or trade the child was given, as training was secondary to employing the child and minimising the cost to the parish. A pauper child was usually bound to the master for seven years or until the age of 21. Bridget Hill writes 'in parishes where the only opening for such girls was domestic service they were often several years older before a situation could be found for them... The prospects for such parish apprentices were almost always grim. Some of their masters and mistresses ill-treated them.'[4]

It is not known how Elizabeth, or her brothers, fared in this system, but it is probable that the parish sought to get them off its books as quickly as possible. The rural economy was severely depressed, so the small fee from the parish to take care of a child would have been very attractive for many households. Even so, most orphans were treated no better than farm animals and in the smaller households the life of a servant or labourer would be grindingly hard and miserable.

No trace has been found of Elizabeth's older brother William after his mother's death. Tobias, the younger brother, stayed in the area and later married Martha Lavender and had a son, William. In 1802, one year after the birth, Tobias died in Norwich, aged 37. Young William would appear before the Norfolk Assizes for stealing some 20 years later and was sentenced to 7 years transportation to New South Wales. In 1822 he arrived in Australia on the *Asia* and died in Orange in 1870. It is not known if Elizabeth ever had any contact with her nephew or even knew that he had arrived in the colony.

Documentary evidence of Elizabeth Pulley's whereabouts next appears when she was 17. In 1779, Elizabeth was imprisoned in the Norwich Castle prison, where she appeared on July 14th before the General Quarter Session charged with stealing. Elizabeth defended herself on the charges of 'stealing one Cheese, one Womans Bonnet, one short Gown, Two gowns, two Aprons, one Shift, one Silk Handkerchief and two Caps the property of Stephen Coulson'.[5] The jury found her *not guilty* and she was acquitted. This was reported by *The Norfolk Chronicle*.

> Thursday ended the session for the county of Norfolk, when one prisoner, viz. Elizabeth Pulley, charged with stealing wearing apparel was tried and acquitted.[6]

The circumstances and location of the alleged crime are unknown. Elizabeth may have been employed as a washerwoman or as a domestic servant in laundry work. The loss of clothing from a laundry had serious consequences for a servant because it could lead to a charge of stealing.

To laundry workers, smart clothing and bed linen were expensive items and they could ill afford to replace them if they were lost.

By February 1780, Elizabeth was living in Hethersett, 16 km south of Felthorpe, 10 km southwest of Norwich. In the 18th century, the large estates and farmhouses in Hethersett offered much-needed employment as labourers and servants and it is quite likely that Elizabeth became a maid or servant in one of these. On the 19 Feb 1780, close to her 18th birthday, Elizabeth was committed for disorderly conduct to the Norwich Workhouse, which was the nearest and largest workhouse to Hethersett. This was a gaol intended for the correction of vagrants, minor offenders and the disorderly. No details are known of the charge, other than the fact that Elizabeth *was released the same day*.[7] At that time, anyone unemployed, or with no fixed address, could be prosecuted as a vagrant. So it seems possible that this had happened and that she was released after someone had vouched for her respectability.

A month later, in March 1780, Elizabeth announced by banns her impending marriage to Thomas Howes in the Wymondham Abbey Church.[8] Aged only 18, Elizabeth was a minor and needed permission from a guardian to be married. However, in view of a later court committal giving her an older age, it is doubtful if she would have considered this an obstacle. It is likely that she was then employed as a servant and that her master needed to approve the marriage. If permission were refused, her only option would be to leave the service. This was a discriminatory process. Households often objected to servants marrying because it inconvenienced the lives of the master's family. To prevent such liaisons, servants could be confined to the master's house, thus restricting outside contacts.[9]

Elizabeth may have also been considered too young to marry. In the 18th century the average marriage age of men was 28 and women 27. The typical marriage age of commoners was even higher, as they usually avoided formal unions until they could support a family. In any case, for reasons unknown, the marriage to Thomas never took place, and, soon after, Elizabeth's life took a much worse direction. On June 26th she was again imprisoned in Norwich Castle for stealing. *The Norfolk Chronicle* reported her arrest:

> Monday was committed to the castle by Charles Weston, esq., Elizabeth Pulley, of Hethersett, charged on oath of John Coulsey, of Drayton, with stealing divers [various] goods from the dwelling-house of his father, which she has confessed.[10]

The court committal suggests Elizabeth had left her work in Hethersett and returned to Drayton, the village where her father Tobias had once worked as a weaver apprentice. The reason for the move is uncertain.

Was it to seek family permission to get married, or had her fiancé Thomas jilted her by then? We will probably never know but her arrest adds a serious impediment to Elizabeth's already complicated life. A month later, in August 1780, her fiancé Thomas Howes was sentenced to death in Norwich for horse stealing in Heigham, six km south of Drayton. His death sentence was later commuted.

Two weeks after her arrest, the 18-year-old Elizabeth was arraigned before the Norfolk Quarter Sessions for her stealing offence and sentenced to imprisonment, and to *whipping*. It read; 'To be conveyed to Wymondham Bridewell, there to be confined 3 Weeks, then whipt, afterwards examined. Elizabeth Pulley of Drayton. Felony.'[11] *The Norfolk Chronicle* reported the court findings.

> Thursday ended the sessions for the county of Norfolk, when Elizabeth Pulley was found guilty of stealing wearing apparel, and sentenced to be committed for three Weeks to Wymondham Bridewell, then to be publicly whipped in the market there.[12]

Not only was Elizabeth to be whipped but it was to take place in the public market. Bizarrely, before this punishment could be imposed in Wymondham, a Norwich Castle gaoler's fee of 13s 4d had to be paid, or she would have to stay at the castle prison.[13] One wonders if Elizabeth chose to pay the fee or was it simply overlooked in lieu of the more severe punishment. In any case, when Elizabeth reached the Wymondham bridewell, she was taken bare footed 150 m down the road to the marketplace and publicly whipped. Males were regularly flogged, but it was uncommon for females. It seems that the authorities in the community wanted Elizabeth's punishment to be a conspicuous warning to other miscreant servants. The magistrate, Charles Weston Esq., an estate owner in Drayton, presided over the charges laid by John Coulsey, a landholder in Drayton. The gentry were sending out a strong message.

Today, the Wymondham Bridewell Museum refers to Elizabeth Pulley as a *cause célèbre* prisoner 'who had helped found Australia'. For a small fee, the museum offers a dungeon audio tour in which an effigy of Elizabeth delivers a speech about her punishment and ultimate transportation to Australia. It is an intriguing example of how moral and legal standards change over time – someone can be publicly whipped in one era and recognised as a pioneer settler in another!

However, "celebrity status" was no help to Elizabeth in the 18th century. In the damp bridewell dungeon she would have nursed her flesh wounds – infection was a real threat to life in those times – and was bedridden for days. It remains unclear what aspect of her offence led to this treatment. The 'stolen wearing apparel' cited in the charge sheet was probably her servants' uniform and she may have worn this when leaving. The charge of stealing was often used at that time to deter servants and labourers from protesting about working conditions, or poor treatment, or sexual harassment. [14] Some employers actively supported flogging so as to discourage other servants who might be tempted to do the same. Whipping posts were placed in prominent places and their use was timed for busy occasions such as market days.

In 1779, a year prior to Elizabeth's incarceration, John Howard wrote about conditions in the Wymondham Bridewell.

> A day-room; with three closets on one side of it, for night-rooms; about 6 feet by 4. .... There is another room for women, in which, at my visit in 1779, there were four dirty and sickly objects at work with padlocks on their legs, though they were never out in the court except on Sundays. The very small quantity of straw on the floor was worn almost to dust. There is a dungeon down eight steps with the stocks in it. It is 15½ feet by 8, and 6 feet high; now arched with brick; a dirty floor; has two apertures at the top, of a foot diameter. .... Neither the rooms nor the spacious court secure. Prisoners in this bridewell are not only confined within doors, but generally in irons. ... no fees.[15]

Elizabeth spent three weeks in the dungeon and was released in August 1780. This was her first real taste of judicial punishment and prison, and it had been brutal and humiliating. It would be surprising if it had not permanently prejudiced her views about laws and justice.

All of Elizabeth's appearances in court during this early period of her life were of a similar nature. They seem to have arisen while working as a servant in a laundry where clothing had been lost or if she departed from the household service without permission. A servant who left employment without authorisation, no matter what the reason, was usually severely punished. In the rural areas where Elizabeth lived and worked, landholders administered the law and acted as the local magistrates. The late 18th century may have been the *Age of Enlightenment* in England, but few commoners benefited from the increased liberty and rights, especially in rural areas. It is doubtful whether the harshness of the laws applied by rural magistrates would have been acceptable in the London courts where a permanent professional judiciary presided.

All indications are that Elizabeth, raised as an orphan, had become a strong independent, perhaps vocal, woman. This was dangerous in a female servant and most masters would rail against any signs of it in a household. Grace Karskens observes that men then commonly referred to rebellious working-class females, and especially those who spoke-out, as 'damned whores'. [16] This expression is sometimes used to label women in the First Fleet diaries and probably referred more to their feistiness than sexual misconduct.

Bridget Hill writes that female servitude could be particularly difficult in large households because of the sexual liberties taken with serving staff. On the larger estates, liaisons with junior female servants were often considered the prerogative of males in the household. Servants were on constant call, and many were not given adequate sleeping or living accommodation. The fortunate ones would sleep in the attic, but the younger servants often slept in bedroom closets close to those they served or in a corner of the kitchen. In addition to low annual wages, a servant would usually receive board and lodging, and often servant clothing was included as part of the board. A servant wishing to seek work elsewhere generally required a character reference from her present employer. The threat of dismissal or any other misdemeanour could be used to bind a servant to a household. A sacked person might receive back wages but no character reference. Servants who chose to leave were made to depart empty-handed and, if so inclined, a master could try to have them arrested on a charge of vagrancy.[17]

For the next year, Elizabeth seems to have avoided trouble. But in mid-1781 she was again arrested for stealing; this time from the weaver Samuel Pightling in Hethersett. Because of prior convictions her trial was assigned to the next session of the twice-yearly Assizes Court in Norfolk and was placed on remand in Norwich Castle until her case could be heard. The *Norfolk Court Calender* reported the hearing:

> ELIZ. PULLEY. Committed the 5th May, 1781, by Thomas Starling, Esq.; charged by Samuel Pightling of Hethersett, weaver, on a violent Suspicion of having in the Night between Thursday and Friday, then last past, burglariously and feloniously broke open and entered his Dwelling House in Hethersett, aforesaid, and from thence took, stole and carried away one Hat, one old Cloth Cloak, one silk Handkerchief, one coloured Apron, three loaves of Bread, and Threepence Halfpenny the Copper Coin of his Realm, with various other Things to the Value of Three Shillings, the Property of the said Samuel Pightling.[18]

On the 6 August 1781, Lord Chief Justice Baron Skyner and Justice Arhurst opened the Assizes of Norwich and County with a Grand Jury comprising 23 men: 5 Barons and 18 Esquires. *The Norfolk Chronicle* reported that Elizabeth was found guilty and sentenced to 12 months hard labour.

> Elizabeth PULLEY for stealing out of the house of Samuel Pightling, of Hethersett, weaver, an old cloth cloak, one silk handkerchief, a coloured apron, and three pence halfpenny, with various other articles to the value of three shillings, was

sentenced to be kept to hard labour for twelve months in the house of correction at Aylsham.[19]

The circumstances that led to Elizabeth's return to Hethersett and to the committal of the crime are not known.

This is one of the more puzzling episodes in Elizabeth's life. What were the reasons for this stealing charge? Was she so destitute that she stole just to survive? Or did it result from a domestic situation of the kind discussed above, where she departed without consent? Whatever her reason, if Elizabeth departed wearing clothing given to her by Pightling, such as the old cloak, she was liable to a charge of stealing. These circumstances appear almost identical to those a year earlier and it begs the question: why would Elizabeth steal such a paltry assortment of apparel and items? If it was a premeditated theft, then it must have been an act of desperation. Why else would she repeat such a trivial crime when it had led to so much misery, so recently?

One possibility is that, as an orphaned female without support, Elizabeth had not learnt from the consequences of her previous actions. While such an explanation is credible, it is not supported by her actions much later in life. Perhaps she was a desperate strong-minded woman who had decided to rebel against anything or anyone who deprived her of personal liberty, or an ability to eke out a living. Elizabeth served out her one-year sentence in the Aylsham Bridewell. John Howard, in his book, *The State of the Prisons*, wrote of this bridewell:

> In the floor of the work (or day) room is a trap-door into a dungeon, which is 9½ feet by 6. Above stairs are three rooms, not secure. No fire-place; no straw; court not secure; prisoners in it only on Sundays; no water; no sewer; no implements for work; no allowance, but two pennyworth of bread a day to vagrants.[20]

It is not known if Elizabeth had a food allowance. If not, she would have had to use her handicraft skills to make things to sell outside. Female prisoners engaged in sewing, spinning and making textiles for sale to the public. John Howard was highly critical of the food rations in bridewells. The bridewell turnkeys often pleaded with magistrates for better food allowances but were usually silenced with the instruction 'Let them work or starve'. This meant that many prisoners in bridewells were clothed in dirty rags and permanently sick.[21]

In August 1782, Elizabeth, aged 20, was released. Because of high unemployment at the time, it would have been extremely difficult for her to get work, especially as a female with a criminal record. Her experiences with the rural justice system had left her embittered and angry. The last thing she would have wanted was another encounter with the justice system that she saw as unfair. Despite this, only four months passed before she was in conflict with the law again.

On Christmas Eve 1782, Elizabeth was arrested for burglary and felony in Hethersett and gaoled in Norwich Castle Prison on 6 Jan 1783. The Prison record lists Elizabeth, then aged 21, as being 25.[22] The charge was reported in *The Norfolk Chronicle*:

> Monday last was committed to the Castle by Thomas Beevor, Esq., Elizabeth Pulley, an old offender, charged with breaking into the shop of Mrs Elizabeth Minns, of Hethersett, in the night of the 24th of December last, and stealing from thence two cheese, four pieces of Bacon, several half pints of butter, a quarter of a stone of raisons, half a stone of flour, and two rolls of worstead, the property of the said Mrs Minns, which she has confessed. - The above offender has been in the Castle four times, and convicted of a burglary at the assizes in 1781 in the same town, and sentenced to hard labour one year in Aylsham bridewell.[23]

The burgling of Mrs Minns' house might be viewed as Elizabeth's first serious act of lawlessness. Her previous convictions had been for the removal of clothing, which, in all likelihood, was servant-assigned or related to laundry losses. The sentences levied for the previous two offences were, even by the prevailing standards of the day, harsh. In the few months leading up to the bleak, bitterly cold Christmas of 1782 – a year of record low temperatures – Elizabeth was desperate, cold, hungry and in need of clothes to replace her prison rags. There is no doubt that a young strong female could easily have carried the 11 kg of food and two rolls of cloth she was accused of stealing. Perhaps she wanted to make up for past Christmases, and in this frame of mind, she decided: *I deserve something out of life, and to hell with the law*!

The next Norfolk Court of Quarter Sessions met in Thetford and Elizabeth was transferred from the Norwich Castle to a Thetford dungeon for four days.[24] The Norfolk Lent Assizes met on 17 March 1783, with the judges Baron James Eyre and Fleetwood Bury presiding. A jury of 20 men was in attendance. The court extract reads:

> *Elizabeth Pulley spinster: 24th December last at Hethersett abt. 12 in the Night Burgl. Dwelling House of Elizabeth Mimms [sic] widow and stealg:*
> 10 pounds weight of Cheese value 3s
> 3 pounds weight of Bacon value 18d
> 24 ounces weight of Butter value 12d
> 3 pounds weight of Raisins value 12d
> 7 pounds weight of Flour value 12d
> 2 rolls of Worsted value 12d goods of sd. Elizabeth Mimms [sic].
> *Verdict: Guilty, to be Hanged by the neck until she is dead.*
> *Sentence: Reprieve not recorded; 7 years.*[25]

Elizabeth had been sentenced to death for stealing goods worth 8s 6d. This was consistent with the mandatory sentence for 'house breaking in daytime' and 'removing goods in excess of 5 shillings value'. One can only guess at Elizabeth's feelings when the Judge stood up, put on his black cap and sentenced her to be *hanged by the neck until she was dead.*

Shortly after the trial, the senior judge, Baron Eyre, wrote a letter requesting the King's mercy on behalf of Elizabeth and the others convicted at the Norfolk Lent Assizes. Such applications were standard and usually resulted in a Royal reprieve. On 22 Mar 1783, *The Norfolk Chronicle* reported:

> Elizabeth Pulley for burglariously breaking and entering the shop of Elizabeth Minns of Hethersett, and stealing thereout divers goods; and Henry Cabell, jun. for burglariously entering the dwelling house of Abigail Hambling of Alburgh, received sentence of death, but afterwards reprieved.[26]

The stated reprieve was premature but was later granted.

Between her arrest on 6 Jan 1783 and the Assizes session in March, Elizabeth was imprisoned in the Norwich Castle gaol, a medieval fortification used as a prison since about 1350. This was the fourth time Elizabeth had spent time in the castle gaol and it would have been familiar to her. Prison reformer John Howard had toured its facilities in 1782 and wrote in his report:

> There is a dungeon down a ladder of 8 steps, for men-felons; in which has been sometimes an inch or two of water: here are now barracks and mats. Only a small room for women-felons; and they cannot be separated from the men, when decency would most of all require it. There are three airy rooms for the sick; so distinct from the rest of the prison, that there is no danger of spreading any infection from thence. The gaoler is humane, and respected by his prisoners. These, felons as well as debtors, sell at the grates of their separate day-rooms, laces, garters, purses, nets, etc, of their own making. There is a nurse or matron to attend the sick; and provide for them, when the surgeon orders it, broth, gruel, milk-pottage and extra-firing. It is also her business to see that prisoners be duly served with their allowances of bread, which is remarkably good.[27]

In Elizabeth's time the castle prison housed 25 debtors and 23 felons. A felon received a 20 oz loaf of bread each day and every week shared a 14 lb wheel of cheese. The prisoners sold their goods directly to the public through the barred windows and used the cash to buy extra food, clothing and to pay the gaoler's fee. It is likely that Elizabeth had a cell in the lower gaol of the castle, where the poorer prisoners were kept.

At the same Thetford Assizes Elizabeth had been sentenced,

Henry Kable (*aka* Cabell, Cable) was convicted of burglary with his father. Both were sentenced to death. They had been part of a robbery gang who broke into barns to steal grain and farm animals. Later Henry's sentence was reprieved to 7 years transportation, and he was sent to Norwich Castle prison. His father was promptly hanged. A few months later Susannah Holmes was also sentenced to death for burglary and also imprisoned in Norwich Castle. Her sentence was later commuted to 14 years transportation. In prison, Henry Kable, Susannah Holmes and Elizabeth became good friends and they would later be transported together on the First Fleet to New South Wales.[28]

An 1809 engraving of Norwich Castle prison. Elizabeth was imprisoned here on four occasions. The last time was in 1783 prior to her transfer to the *Dunkirk* in Sep 1786.

On 1 Dec 1783, nine months after Judge Eyre's submission for a Royal Pardon, Lord North announced those receiving mercy:

> Elizabeth Pulley Spinster at the same time and place for a Burglary. ... And You having by Certificate under your Hand humbly recommended them as fit Objects of His Majesty's Mercy on the following Conditions, that is to say, the said ......to be transported to America ..., Elizabeth Pulley, and ...... for and during the Term of Seven Years respectively.[29]

It is interesting to note that Elizabeth's sentence for burglary and felony was commuted to transportation *to America*.[30] The British government was still hopeful in 1783 of renewing its lucrative convict trade to the American colonies. In August 1784, the Norfolk Assizes sat again and one of the matters it considered was the severity of Elizabeth's 1783 sentence; it remained unchanged. One year later, in July 1785, Elizabeth, Susannah and Henry were still in custody of the Norwich Castle prison awaiting transportation. The government had not yet decided where to send the convicts, and gaolers cross England were eager to remove these transportees to make room for new prisoners.[31] In the meantime, Henry Kable and Susannah Holmes had become a couple, and in 1786 Susannah gave birth to a son, Henry.

In August 1786, the government announced that prisoners sentenced to transportation would be sent to Botany Bay in New South Wales in ships commanded by Captain Arthur Phillip. It was a momentous decision that would shape the future lives of many young convicts, including Anthony Rope, Elizabeth Pulley, Susannah Holmes and Henry Kable. In October 1786, the Home Office asked the sheriffs of the counties to submit details of women who were in their gaols. Elizabeth, after almost four years in gaol, was told she was one of the convicts selected for transportation to Botany Bay.

On 21 Oct 1786, Lord Sydney informed the sheriff of Norwich Castle prison 'to remove Elizabeth Pulley, Susannah Holmes and Hannah Turner Convicts under Sentence of Transportation in the Castle at Norwich, on board the *Dunkirk*, by the first Week in the ensuing Month'.[32] The women were to be sent to the hulk *Dunkirk* in Plymouth, where they would await embarkation on the transport ship *Friendship*. It was requested that the transfer be done promptly, as women from London gaols were also being embarked on the *Friendship*, and any latecomers would be returned to their gaols.

The Norwich sheriff acted quickly and sent Elizabeth to Plymouth in the first group. *The Bury and Norwich Post* reported the departure of the prisoners from Norwich Castle.

> A few days since a letter was received by Mr Gynne, Keeper of the Castle, signifying his Majesty's pleasure, that Elizabeth Pulley, Susannah Holmes, and Ann Turner, should be conveyed to Plymouth in the course of the first week in November, and there put on board his Majesty's ship the Dunkirk, which is bound for the New Settlement at Botany Bay. - They were accordingly on Monday last taken from the said gaol, and seemed not in the least dismayed at the length of their voyage, or their future fate.[33]

The *Post* journalist was clearly surprised that prisoners would be looking forward to the prospect of leaving the mouldy old gaol. On 11 Nov 1786, *The Norfolk Chronicle* printed a half page article on the women transportees. Although Elizabeth's name is not mentioned, it is clear, that she was one of the 'Three unhappy women, who had been a long while in the Castle under sentence of transportation, were accordingly sent, and were committed to the care of Mr. John Simpson, the turnkey of the prison'. The other two were Ann Turner and Susannah Holmes. The repeated requests of Henry Kable to marry Susannah, the mother of his child, were refused and he was very distressed when the order came for her to be sent to Plymouth. An application was made to the government for him to go as well but this was turned down. Susannah and the baby had to leave without him.[34]

The Norwich Castle gaoler John Simpson was in charge of taking the females and baby Henry by coach to Plymouth, a journey that took three full days. The prisoners would have travelled, in the winter wind and rain, chained to the exposed seats of the coach. Compared to prison they may not have found this particularly difficult, and in any case, none had probably experienced travelling *inside* a coach. The hulk *Dunkirk* in Plymouth harbour would be the interim prison for females until the transport ship *Friendship* was ready to take them aboard. When the coach arrived in Plymouth the hulk Captain refused to take the infant, saying he had no explicit orders to take children. The refusal to accept Susannah's baby shocked Simpson but he resolved to reunite mother and child. The story attracted wide interest in newspapers across the country. In the meantime gaoler Simpson and little Henry travelled back to London, where he left the child with some responsible women. He immediately petitioned Lord Sydney for the baby and father to join Susannah on the *Dunkirk*. *The Norfolk Chronicle* observed:

> that Capt. Phillips, who is to go out with the convicts to Botany Bay, is a man of a very different disposition to the person alluded to in this narrative, but he, unfortunately, had no power to interfere.[35]

Simpson's petition eventually proved successful, and he returned to Norwich from London to take the two Henrys, father and son, to Plymouth. It was another continuous three day and night coach journey and led to a very emotional reunion. John Simpson described the journey in a letter dated 16 Nov 1786, which was printed in *The Derby Mercury*, and other newspapers.

> It is with the most utmost Pleasure that I inform you of my safe Arrival with my little Charge at Plymouth; but it would take an abler Pen than mine to describe the Joy that the Mother received her Infant and her intended Husband with. Suffice it to say their Transports, and the Tears which flowed from their Eyes, with the innocent Smiles of the Babe on sight of the Mother, who had saved her Milk for it, drew the Tears likewise from my Eyes; and it was with the utmost Regret that I parted with the Child, after having travelled with it on my Lap more than seven hundred Miles backwards and forwards. But the Blessings I received at the different Inns on the Road have amply paid me.[36]

This may have been one of the few positive episodes in Elizabeth's short and difficult life. Despite the brutality of her encounters with the British legal system, she had met people such as John Simpson who tried to provide fair justice to the underprivileged. The prison reformer, John Howard, wrote of John Simpson in a subsequent report 'The gaoler is humane, and respected by his prisoners.'[37]

Elizabeth, Ann and Susannah embarked on the *Dunkirk* hulk on 5 Nov 1786 and the two Henrys on November 16th.[38] The 25-year-old Elizabeth is recorded on the embarkation list as aged only 23. She remained for four months on board the *Dunkirk* hulk before boarding the transport *Friendship* on 11 March 1787. Sadly, 44-year-old Ann (*aka* Hannah) Turner died in early February 1787, just one month before being transferred to the *Friendship*.[39]

The long and dangerous voyage across vast uncharted oceans to an unexplored remote continent was about to begin.

Chapter 4

BOTANY BAY SCHEME

The establishment at Botany Bay, however ridiculed at present, will probably, in future, give birth to a colony highly advantageous to this country.[1]

In August 1786, after years of discussion and indecision, the British government announced that Botany Bay in New South Wales would be the location of a new colony for transported convicts. This decision had been a difficult one and was reached only after the English prison system was in crisis. The land and hulk prisons were overflowing with riotous prisoners and Londoners were concerned for their safety. It became apparent to Prime Minister William Pitt that the hulks moored on the Thames would not solve the prison over-crowding and the Tory government had little choice but to remove prisoners awaiting transportation to an overseas destination as quickly as possible.

As early as 1778, most prison authorities had realised that hulks were, at best, a temporary solution to the rapidly growing convict population. A parliamentary House of Commons committee had been formed by the then Whig government to consider the establishment of convict colonies in remote locations, such as West Africa, the East Indies and New Holland. When Sir Joseph Banks, who accompanied James Cook on his first voyage to New Holland, was interviewed at one of these enquiries, he strongly supported Botany Bay as a settlement location. He praised the area's climate, fertile soil and abundance of water, food and timber. Banks's opinion was considered, but the prison situation was not yet serious enough to justify the cost of creating a prison colony so far away, on the other side of the globe.

The parliamentary committee on transportation continued to meet regularly but no firm recommendations were made. Four years later, in Aug 1783, the American-born James Matra suggested to the committee that a civil colony for Loyalists displaced by the American Rebellion be established in New South Wales. Matra had been a midshipman aboard Cook's ship HMS *Endeavour* in 1770. He pointed out that the climate in New South Wales was favourable and the soil fertile, suitable for growing hemp or flax. The site offered commercial opportunities that would increase Britain's influence in that part of the world. Sir Joseph Banks agreed to endorse Matra's 1783 proposal.[2] However, the plan failed to provide a permanent settlement for transported convicts and was not supported.

The British Whig government was defeated in December 1783 and the Tories, with William Pitt the Younger as the Prime Minister, came to power. Changes to the House of Commons committee and the appointment of Lord Sydney as the new Home Office Secretary, gave a new impetus to finding a prison settlement location. Following an interview with Lord Sydney in March 1784, James Matra amended his proposal to promote the transported convicts as future settlers.

> When I conversed with Lord Sydney on this subject, it was observed that New South Wales would be a very proper region for the reception of criminals condemned to transportation. I believe that it will be found that in this idea good policy and humanity are united. ... Give them a few acres of ground as soon as they arrive in New South Wales, in absolute property, with what assistance they may want to till them. Let it be here remarked that they cannot fly from the country, that they have no temptation to theft, and they must work or starve. I likewise suppose that they are not, by any means, to be reproached for their former conduct. If these premises be granted me, I may reasonably conclude that it is highly probable they will be useful; that it is very possible they will be moral subjects of society.[3]

After considerable debate Matra's proposal was turned down. The Tory government seemed more interested in closer destinations. Between 1783 and 1786, three different sites for convict colonies were under consideration – in Senegal, on the Gold Coast of Africa and in New South Wales on the east coast of New Holland. In December 1784, an exploratory expedition to transport convicts to Lemain Island, 700 km up the river Gambia in Senegal, was put forward. Following strong public and parliamentary criticism, the Lemain project was abandoned because of the region's unsuitable climate. In May 1785, James Matra once again testified before a committee enquiring specifically into the suitability of Botany Bay as a penal colony. Even at this late stage, the committee was not prepared to rule out the *free* colonisation of this site. Despite much testimony in favour of a New Holland location, the majority of the committee believed that an African site would be more practical. In parallel with committee's enquiries, the government was independently exploring various settlement options. The Home Office was increasingly anxious at the burgeoning number of transportees in prisons and Lord Sydney and Evan Nepean, thought that closer sites in Africa could be settled sooner.

The strain on the prison system by the end of 1785 was so great that additional naval ships had to be converted into prison hulks. The hulk *Fortunée* was moored at Portsmouth and the *Dunkirk* at Plymouth. The political and public pressure on the government was intense, and the Home Office commissioned a ship to explore possible locations on the west coast of Africa between Das Voltas (Orange River) and Angola. This expedition returned in July 1786 and reported that the soil in the Das Voltas was not suitable for cultivation. This report effectively ended any further consideration of Africa as a place for a British convict settlement.

In March 1786, riots broke out aboard several prison hulks and 44 prisoners were shot, 8 fatally. This caused a huge public outcry, and the Lord Mayor of London urged the government to take urgent action to reduce convict numbers on the Thames hulks. The Pitt government desperately needed to find a quick solution. After years of deliberation only the east coast of New South Wales appeared suitable as a long-term settlement, and in August 1786 the government announced its intention to establish a convict colony in Botany Bay. This choice was strongly influenced by reports from the explorations of Captain James Cook and Joseph Banks 16 years earlier. The government saw no reason to question the accuracy of their assessments. After all, Cook was the greatest navigator of the time and Banks was England's most famous botanist.

The Home Office immediately started the planning for the prodigious voyage to New Holland. Under Secretary Evan Nepean prepared estimates on the cost of transporting 750 convicts, three marine regiments and a handful of officials to Botany Bay. He had calculated that to transport a single male convict to New South Wales and to support him for the first three years would be about £32 per annum. This compared favourably with the cost of keeping a prisoner on a hulk in Britain of £28 per annum.[4] Based on this, Evan Nepean drafted a report: *Heads of a plan for effectually disposing of convicts, and rendering their transportation reciprocally beneficial both to themselves and to the State, by the establishment of a colony in New South Wales.*[5]

After endorsement by Cabinet, Evan Nepean wrote to Treasury announcing the decision, signed by the Home Office Secretary, Lord Sydney, dated 18 Aug 1786:

> The several gaols and places for the confinement of felons in this kingdom being in so crowded a state that the greatest danger is to be apprehended, not only from their escape, but from infectious distempers, which may hourly be expected to break out amongst them, his Majesty, desirous of preventing by every possible means the ill consequences which might happen from either of

these causes, has been pleased to signify to me his royal commands that measures should immediately be pursued for sending out of this kingdom such of the convicts as are under sentence or order of transportation.[6]

The *Heads of a Plan* document was included. It read in part:

Heads of a plan for effectually disposing of convicts, and rendering their transportation reciprocally beneficial both to themselves and to the State, by the establishment of a colony in New South Wales, a country which, by the fertility and salubrity of the climate, connected with the remoteness of its situation (from whence it is hardly possible for persons to return without permission), seems peculiarly adapted to answer the views of Government with respect to the providing a remedy for the evils likely to result from the late alarming and numerous increase of felons in this country, and more particularly in the metropolis.[7]

At the conclusion of the *Heads of a Plan,* additional advantages were described: the cultivation of hemp or flax for use by the navy, the cultivation of spices and cotton, and the procurement of timber from New Zealand for masts and ship timber. The climate appeared healthy and would not be 'a grave' for European settlers, unlike Gambia. The *Heads of a Plan* expounded the voyage and settlement arrangements for ships, stores, tools, marines, surgeons, clothing, seeds, livestock etc., but it did not mention any strategic or commercial intentions.

The often-cited belief that Botany Bay was planned solely as a dumping ground for convicts is unsupported by available documents. It may have been the main objective, but there is clear evidence the Pitt government saw tangible benefits in establishing commercial bases in the South Pacific. At the time, Britain was embroiled in conflicts with France, Spain and America, so there were also strategic reasons for establishing a territorial claim on the continent. Nevertheless, the endless debates on whether New South Wales was suitable suggests a begrudging recognition by the Tory government that this was a good locality – *it was just a pity one had to go so far to dispose of the convicts, and to achieve these objectives.*

Early assessments of the Botany Bay Scheme logistics by the Home Office appreciated that it would be quite different to sending convicts to America, which had been privately financed and organised. The Botany Bay Scheme would be administered by the government, transported by the Royal Navy and guarded by Royal Marines. This enterprise had no precedent in previous British convict transportations. The government, rather than private merchants, would be involved in convict transportation on a scale that they had never before attempted.

In August 1786, Lord Sydney informed the Admiralty of what he needed to transport 750 convicts to Botany Bay. He requested a naval warship that would escort and protect transport ships carrying the convicts and 160 marines as guards to the new settlement. The marines would be responsible to the Home Office for a term of three years.[8]

The public was first made aware of the Botany Bay decision on September 2nd through a rather obscure notice in the *White Hall Evening Post*.[9] This was in the form of a Navy request to 'be ready to treat for about 1500 Tons of Shipping, by the ton, to carry Persons and Provisions to Botany Bay on the Coast of New South Wales'. Five days later, it was announced in *The London Chronicle* that convicts under the sentence of transportation were to be sent to Botany Bay 'where they are to have some singular privileges in case of good behaviour'.[10] Shortly after this *The British Evening Post* observed, somewhat erroneously, that the government was to settle a new colony in New Holland *in the Indian Seas*. Several London newspapers reported that a settlement was to be in Botany Bay, where Captain Cook had landed in 1770, and that marines would guard the 750 convicts.[11] Later, *The London Chronicle* and *The General Evening Post* informed the public in some detail about the new settlement, with descriptions of the land excerpted from Cook's logs.[12]

By the end of September, further details of the expedition were published. *The London Chronicle* told its readers that Captain Arthur Phillip was appointed as Commodore of the squadron and that he was to be the governor of the colony with a salary of £500 per annum. It added that 700 men and 150 women convicts were to be transported.[13] Most Londoners seemed to welcome the decision to resume transportation, believing that it signalled the end of hulks on the Thames and that all future convicts would be confined to the new hulks in Portsmouth and Plymouth.[14] This was not the case; prison hulks would remain on the Thames until the mid 19th century.

In general, newspaper articles and editorials supported the Botany Bay decision. *The Morning Chronicle and London Advertiser* stated that keeping convicts on the hulks was too expensive and pointed out the impossibility of sending them to Africa or America. They praised the Botany Bay site as the only place where convicts 'may become useful to the empire'.[15] Also, the ever-vigilant *Norfolk Chronicle* was enthusiastic of the scheme.

> Under proper direction they will be able to plough, sow, plant, and provide themselves, by their industry, with the means of a comfortable future subsistence…. If that active and enterprising young man can be brought to conform to the scheme, there is no doubt but he would soon make himself a Squire of renown in the colony.[16]

Approval also came from *The Northampton Mercury* reporter, who observed that transportation was the most rational way to dispose of petty criminals driven by their distress to thieving, who would now 'have an Opportunity to regain, by Industry and good Behaviour, that Character which it is impossible for them to attain in this Country'. This insightful reporter went on to say that there were many more poor people in London with no other means of support than those that had brought these convicts to such a sad end.[17]

Approval of the Botany Bay scheme was, however, by no means universal. Public letters about the future 'Thief Colony' were published in various newspapers that claimed 'transportation was too expensive' and that convicts 'could acquire property and hence become persons of affluence'.[18] Others insisted that convicts work for their food or starve; if this 'would not conform them, and inure them to work, then let them die'.[19] There was also some weird commentary, such as: 'The plan of transporting convicts to Botany Bay is considered as a lunatic scheme, and it is wisely compared to that of Dean Swift, who founded an hospital for insane persons in Dublin, and became the first patient in that hospital'.[20]

In October, *The Morning Post* told its readers 'The establishment at Botany Bay, however ridiculed at present, will probably, in future, give birth to a colony highly advantageous to this country.' And went on to compare it with the American colonies and how they had eventually benefited the British Empire.[21]

Political opinions on the strategic importance of Botany Bay also appeared in the press. *The Derby Mercury* observed that Botany Bay's position on the globe 'cannot fail of giving it a very commanding Influence in the Policy of Europe'. The article concluded with the comment that 'When this Colony from England is established, if we should ever be at War with Holland or Spain, we might very powerfully annoy either State from the new Settlement'.[22] A couple of days later, *The General Evening Post* remarked that the new settlement would be an advantage to the China trade and ships would no longer be obliged to stop in Batavia (East Indies).[23]

But the reporters and their readers were by no means constant in their support. Later, when the departure of the First Fleet from Portsmouth was delayed, several journalists suggested that it would never leave. In November, there was a spurious report that the Botany Bay Scheme had been abandoned altogether on the grounds of cost. On 17 Nov 1786, *The Morning Herald* questioned the legality of the Scheme.

> That so important a design should have been set on foot, without the concurrence of Parliament, is, we believe, the most daring step that has taken place in this country since the Revolution; and as its sanction, in the first instance, was not applied for by the

Minister, it is hoped there is spirit enough remaining in the Commons and Peers, to part a heavy reproof upon the measure.[24]

Two days later, the same newspaper told their readers that New South Wales 'must inevitably become a nest for pirates'.[25]

The Hereford Journal followed this with a report 'that the Botany Bay scheme is not totally abandoned, as has been asserted'.[26] These stories flourished because of the delays in the departure of the fleet. Captain Arthur Phillip was refusing to set sail for Botany Bay until the provisioning and other preparations met his demanding standards. Very few people, including most newspaper Editors, appreciated the scale of planning needed to send eleven ships with 1500 people, and two years' supplies, to the other unknown side of the world. Public speculation and ridicule increased with the inordinate time it took to prepare for this complex expedition – it was much longer than the Admiralty planners had anticipated.

In response to incessant newspaper criticisms on the cost of the expedition, someone close to the government with a detailed knowledge of the preparations wrote to *The Morning Chronicle*. This appeared as a two-column article explaining why a colony at Botany Bay was preferred to Africa and America. It also gave detailed costing of the expedition and the expenses currently paid to Duncan Campbell for keeping prisoners on the hulks.[27]

In November 1786, *The General Evening Post* informed its readers that the Botany Bay scheme was at a standstill because the Dutch had protested against the 'planning of a settlement in those regions of the South, the habitation of cannibals'.[28] It is uncertain if these protests were true, as no diplomatic records to this effect have been found.[29] The likely fate of the convicts sent to Botany Bay was widely speculated on, sometimes very positively. Such optimism is expressed in a letter submitted from Portsmouth to *The Northampton Mercury* newspaper:

> The Convicts having got Information that they are to be sent to Botany seem quite rejoiced at it, declaring there is no Place in the whole World that would be so agreeable for them to be sent. The Reason of this is, that some of the Convicts having been there with Captain Cook, have described it to be a perfect Paradise, abounding with every Necessary of Life, which may be obtained without much Toil or Labour; where they may breathe the free Air, and not be confined under Hatches, which has carried a Number of them off.[30]

The Morning Herald observed that there must be honour among thieves since prisoners in Newgate gaol had shown their approval of the Scheme by toasting 'Pitt and Botany Bay'. Soon after, the claims in some newspapers that the Botany Bay Scheme had been abandoned led 3875 prisoners to present a petition to William Pitt. This was printed in *The Morning Herald* and pleaded with the government to adopt the Botany Bay Scheme again.[31] Other newspapers wrote that prisoners had revolted when hearing from their turnkeys 'that no volunteers could be taken to this desirable settlement'. The convicts then declared 'that they would find a way of being sent thither according to Law'. It was also reported that felons had committed petty crimes and asked judges at court hearings to be sentenced for *transportation to Botany Bay*.[32]

In December 1786, *The Gazetteer* claimed, that the government had abandoned the Botany Bay location and would instead send the convicts to Norfolk Island.[33] This was quickly dismissed by *The General Advertiser* and reported a First Fleet contractor had just signed an agreement with the East India Company 'to proceed from thence to China, to bring back tea'.[34] At the same time *The Morning Chronicle* announced 'The Botany Bay expedition may in the end keep in this island much of the money now sent to Holland for spices.' The newspaper thought the evidence for this came 'from the vast number of persons daily applying for leave to go out to share the fortune of the new colonists'.[35]

But there were also fierce critics. Lord George Gordon opposed the Botany Bay Scheme and in 1786 published a pamphlet entitled *The Prisoners Petition, to preserve their Lives and Liberties, and prevent their banishment to Botany Bay*. He used this pamphlet as a reason to seek access to Newgate Prison to speak to prisoners sentenced to death, but the turnkey denied him entry.[36] Gordon was an inveterate protester, who seven years earlier had caused the notorious *Gordon Riots*. These had set London, including Newgate Prison, ablaze, and caused prisoners to be set free. In February 1787, Gordon was arrested and charged with inflaming mutiny among the Newgate prisoners sentenced to transportation to Botany Bay.[37] Fittingly, Gordon, himself, was later incarcerated in Newgate Prison for three years.

In early September 1786, Captain Arthur Phillip was officially commissioned to become the governor of the colony in New South Wales. This would prove to be an excellent choice; Phillip was a veteran mariner with vision and humility and had enlightened views on equality. Support for Phillip's appointment had not been unanimous. On 3 Sep 1787, Lord Howe wrote to Lord Sydney 'I cannot say the little knowledge I have of Captain Philips [*sic*] would have led me to select him for a service of this complicated nature'.[38] Arthur Phillip is certainly not the focus of this story but his importance to the ultimate success of the First Fleet and the New South Wales settlement cannot be overstated. Because of this, a short overview of his career is warranted.

Excellent biographies of Arthur Phillip's life have been published.[39] Michael Pembroke writes 'He was a man with a good head, a good heart, lots of pluck, and plenty of common sense. To those qualities he brought an uncommon amount of integrity, intelligence and persistence'.[40] As an experienced sea captain, Phillip appreciated the dangers of the voyage ahead and from his time as a farmer he knew that establishing a new settlement would be challenging. He had progressed through the ranks of the Royal Navy from Ordinary Seaman to Post Captain mostly by merit and had held numerous important commands during his long naval career.

Like the great maritime navigator and explorer James Cook, Arthur Phillip had risen to some eminence from quite unprivileged beginnings. Born in London in 1738, he was the son of Jacob Phillip, a language teacher from Germany, and Elizabeth, née Breach, widow of RN Captain Herbert. His father Jacob died young leaving the Phillip family financially bereft. Even so, Arthur was properly educated and at the age of nine joined the Royal Navy and sailed with Captain Michael Everitt, a cousin of his mother. In 1751 Arthur was admitted to the Charity School of the Royal Hospital for Seamen at Greenwich. His acceptance into this school was probably through the naval connections of his mother's family.

The 14-year-old Arthur Phillip left the Charity School two years later to embark on a seven-year apprenticeship aboard the whaling ship *Fortune*.[41] In late 1755, he entered the Royal Navy with the rank of Ordinary Seaman. He saw meritorious naval action against the French and Spanish and was promoted to Lieutenant. In 1763 he married a wealthy widow, Charlotte Denison, 16 years his senior, and in 1766-68 they settled at Lyndhurst in Hampshire where Phillip became a gentleman farmer. However, the marriage was not a success and the childless couple separated in 1769.

From 1770 Phillip spent several years in France and Holland supposedly recovering from an illness but, because of his language skills, it seems likely he was in service gathering intelligence for the Royal Navy, which was in desperate need to know about military expansion in Europe.[42] In 1774 Phillip was seconded to the Portuguese Navy and captained a warship that fought on the South American coast. He had several notable victories against the Spanish in 1779 and was promoted to Commander. In 1781 Phillip returned to England and the Royal Navy as Post Captain and commanded a ship that sailed to India in 1782. In the following year he did more naval reconnaissance in France.[43]

In April 1787, Captain Phillip received details of his commission as Governor of New South Wales.[44] They included the authority to establish a new settlement at Botany Bay. Somewhat controversially Phillip was ordered to govern the colony alone, without a council. Much later, during the establishment of the settlement, some officers questioned the extent of the powers granted to Phillip. Arthur Bowes Smyth, the Fleet Surgeon, observed that Phillip's commission was 'a more unlimited one than was ever before granted to any Governor under the British Crown'.[45] This concern was understandable. Although the governor was subject to the rule of British law, he had been given the power to appoint justices and officers of the law, to raise an army, to erect fortifications and to exercise sovereign naval powers. Phillip also had full authority to pardon and reprieve, either absolutely or conditionally, according to the seriousness of the crimes, and, most importantly, to make land grants to emancipated convicts.[46]

Matters of particular concern for Phillip with his commission were the rights and official status of transportees. He had been appalled by the slavery he had seen in South America and Africa, and he was determined that New South Wales *not* be another *convict slave* colony.

> The laws of this country will, of course, be introduced in [New] South Wales, and there is one that I would wish to take place from the moment his Majesty's forces take possession of the country: That there can be no slavery in a free land, and consequently no slaves.[47]

Somewhat at variance with this view was his belief that the convicts' ultimate status in the settlement, even after the expiration of their sentences, could not be equal to that of the soldiers and free settlers. He explained this at end of February 1787, before his departure from Portsmouth.

> As I would not wish convicts to lay the foundations of an empire, I think they should ever remain separated from the garrison, and other settlers that may come from Europe, and not be allowed to mix with them, even after 7 or 14 years for which they are transported may be expired.[48]

Fortunately, these views would change during the voyage and, by the time the fleet had arrived in New South Wales, his observations of the behaviour of the soldiers and the convicts on the ships caused him to adopt a more conciliatory attitude.

Another major objective of Arthur Phillip was that a fair and harmonious relationship be cultivated between the settlement occupants and the indigenous peoples of New South Wales. In April 1787, he wrote a proclamation that indicated his intentions with respect to Aborigines 'Any man who takes the life of a Native, will be put on his trial as if he had killed one of the Garrison. This appears to me not only just, but good policy.'[49] Despite these intentions, the British government deemed New South Wales to be *terra nullius*, and nothing is mentioned in his commission about negotiations with the Aboriginals regarding land ownership. The British maintained that Captain Cook had 'discovered' this part of the country and this gave them the right to occupy the land. The Dutch certainly claimed the sovereignty of New Holland, but they were clearly not prepared to defend it, and the British knew that.

From October 1786 to when the First Fleet departed in May 1787, Phillip was constantly busy organising the expedition. The successful private tender for maintaining the non-naval ships of the fleet was the London shipbroker, William Richards. With the approval of the Admiralty, Richards chartered five merchant vessels to be used as convict transports – the *Alexander*, the *Charlotte*, the *Friendship*, the *Lady Penrhyn* and the *Scarborough*. He also contracted the *Borrowdale*, the *Fishburn* and the *Golden Grove* to be accompanying store ships. The Navy added two naval warships to the flotilla, HMS *Sirius* and HMS *Supply*. The Navy board appointed Lieutenant John Shortland as the naval agent for the First Fleet. He issued contracts for the supplies loaded onto the fleet ships and was in command of all the masters of the private vessels.

To balance the male-to-female ratio in the colony, the Home Office increased the original complement of 70 female convicts to 150, and later to 190. The extra convicts meant that the space for supplies and personnel on ten ships was insufficient, and in early December 1786, another convict transport ship, the *Prince of Wales*, was added. This ship was fitted out in January 1787.

In early 1787, the first prisoners boarded the convict transports. The diminutive size of the 11 wooden ships comprising the First Fleet is shown below with their carrying capacity, dimensions and function.[50]

Ship	Cargo (tons)	Length ft (m)	Width ft (m)	Purpose
HMS *Sirius*	540	110 (30.5)	32 (10)	Flagship
HMS *Supply*	170	70 (21.3)	26 (8)	Support
Alexander	452	114 (34.7)	31 (9.4)	Convict
Scarborough	430	111 (33.8)	30 (9.1)	Convict
Charlotte	335	105 (32.0)	28 (8.5)	Convict
Prince of Wales	350	103 (31.4)	29 (8.8)	Convict
Lady Penrhyn	338	103 (31.4)	27 (8.2)	Convict
Friendship	278	75 (22.9)	23 (7.0)	Convict
Borrowdale	272	75 (22.9)	22 (6.7)	Supplies
Fishburn	378	103 (31.4)	29 (8.8)	Supplies
Golden Grove	331	103 (31.4)	29 (8.8)	Supplies

The merchant ships used as convict transports required considerable conversion; in particular the prisoners' quarters needed strengthening. Details of these renovations have been lost, but Lt. Philip Gidley King wrote in his journal of the voyage that the transports 'are fitted up for the convicts in the same way as for carrying troops, except for the security'. Thick bulkheads served as the walls to confine convicts. These were constructed from side-to-side between decks, studded with nails, and had loopholes through which marines could fire at the convicts in case of insurrection. King observed that 'The hatches are well secured down by crossbars, bolts and locks and are likewise rail'd round from deck to deck with oak stanchions' in order to prevent access. Above decks an exercise area in front of the main mast was rendered secure and was separated from the quarterdeck by a wooden wall armed with pointed prongs of iron. An armed guard would always be present to prevent misbehaviour by convicts.[51]

The headroom between decks was so low that only a child could stand up. For example, on the *Scarborough* the headroom was only 1.35 m. Portholes and other viewing areas below decks were blocked, which meant that it was permanently dark. The flow of fresh air to the confined convict quarters was virtually non-existent, and windsails had to be fitted to the stairways to try and direct air into the hold. When the weather conditions were calm these areas became stifling, and in a storm, when the hatches were battened down, the atmosphere was putrid.

Legal aspects of the prison sentences still needed to be resolved before convicts could be transferred to the transport ships. In particular, the sentences of convicts varied between *transportation to America*, or *to Africa*, or, more generally, *to Beyond the Seas*. On 6 Dec 1786, the Home Office issued an *Order for Transportation* stating that the place of transportation for all prisoners was to be *to New South Wales*.[52] This order was followed by warrants sent to the relevant gaols authorising the delivery of those convicts selected to the designated ports.[53]

Another commercial issue also had to be resolved. The East India Company had a monopoly on all British trade routes between the Cape of Good Hope and Cape Horn, and the transportation of goods on these routes by the First Fleet contravened this. On 19 Sep 1786, *The London Chronicle* reported that the government had made a contract with the East India Company. The convoy to Botany Bay would carry 1500 tons of goods to Botany Bay for £7 per ton, and the returning ships would bring cargoes of tea from China for which the East India Company would pay £10 per ton.[54]

Provisioning the First Fleet was logistically difficult. Long sea voyages usually rely on ships being able to purchase provisions at ports of call, and at their destination. On the route to Botany Bay, supplies could only be replenished at the ports of Santa Cruz, Rio de Janeiro and Cape Town. There were certainly no supplies at the final destination of New South Wales. This meant that food supplies aboard the fleet had to be sufficient for the long passages between ports, and provisions had to include special equipment needed at the settlement. Since the small ships had limited cargo space, the success of the expedition depended critically on adequate replenishment of supplies at the ports of call.

The contractor, William Richards, was in charge of victualling the ships while in Portsmouth and on the voyage; the government was responsible for supplies once the ships reached New South Wales. These supplies had to be sufficient for the *first two years* of the colony. The Home Office authorities estimated what was needed by assuming that after the first year, the settlement would approach self-sufficiency – that is, food grown in the colony, supplemented by transported provisions, were expected to suffice over the second and third years. This plan was highly optimistic by any measure. The biggest constraint on supplies was the limited cargo space on the small ships and that most food was perishable. The acknowledged, but unwritten, reality in this plan was that the settlement would eventually have to find a way to "make-do"!

The quantities of food needed for the voyage were determined from the standard weekly rations. No distinction was made between the requirements of marines or convicts, except for alcohol, which were not supplied to convicts. The weekly ration for males was set at:[55]

7 lb bread or 7 lb flour	7 lb beef or 4 lb pork	3 pt peas
6 oz butter	1 lb flour or ½ lb rice	

Convict women would receive two-thirds of the men's rations and convict children half of a mother's allowance. Marines would have a daily alcohol ration of ½ pint of rum; the convicts would not receive alcohol unless wine was prescribed as medicine.[56]

A wide variety of tools were required to build the settlement housing and farm the land, and this equipment needed to be brought from England. Additionally, medicine, medical instruments, plants, seeds and grains, animals, bricks, tents, clothing, guns and ammunition, implements to manufacture cloth, and bedding were loaded into the eleven vessels.[57] Replacement clothing and shoes for convicts was essential with the government providing two years' supply. The annual clothing allowance for a male convict was:[58]

2 jackets	4 woollen drawers	1 hat
3 shirts	4 pairs stockings	3 frocks
3 trousers	3 pairs shoes	

The annual allowance for a female convict was set at:[59]

4 pair of drawers	4 white shifts	1 grey cotton jacket
1 white cotton jacket	2 check cotton jackets	3 pairs shoes
4 pair yarn stockings	2 linsey cotton jackets	2 caps
3 handkerchiefs	1 serge petticoat	1 hat
2 canvas petticoats	2 linsey woolsey petticoats	

In late 1786, skeleton crews commenced rigging and modifying the naval, store and transport ships moored on the Thames and loaded supplies from the Deptford docks. The First Fleet was gradually taking shape.

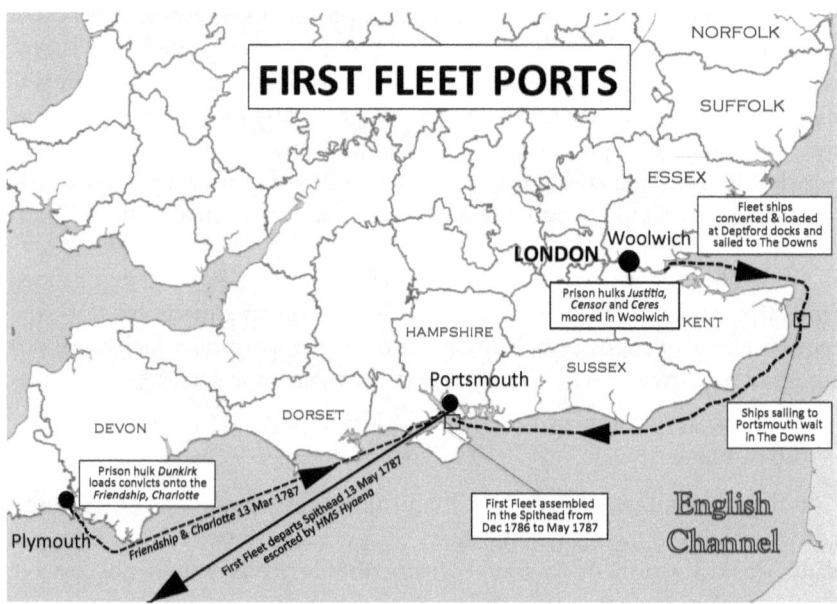

Chapter 5

ASSEMBLING THE FLEET

> *It being the intention of government to remove the inconvenience, which this country suffered, from the gaols being so exceedingly crowded with criminals, who had been by the laws condemned to transportation, the east coast of New Holland was the place determined upon to form a settlement for this salutary purpose.*[1]

From October 1786 onwards, ships of the First Fleet flotilla began to muster at the Deptford dockyards on the Thames River.[2] Two naval warships, HMS *Sirius*, a three-masted fully rigged ship with 20 guns, and HMS *Supply*, a two-masted armed tender with 8 guns, were the first to arrive.[3] The flagship of the First Fleet, HMS *Sirius*, had two captains, Captain Arthur Phillip, the Commander of the Fleet, and Captain John Hunter, responsible for the navigation of the flagship. Hunter was also designated as the alternate commander of the expedition.[4] Lieutenant Philip Gidley King, a naval officer on HMS *Sirius*, had served with Phillip on other naval assignments since 1782. Marine Lieutenant David Collins was appointed as the Judge Advocate in the colony, and he was also to be Phillip's Secretary. Collins would prove in future years to be Phillip's closest ally and confidant.

Major Robert Ross, aboard HMS *Sirius*, was the Commander of the Marines contingent and had been commissioned as Lieutenant Governor, second in command to Arthur Phillip. He was known to be an opinionated soldier, and he would prove to be a difficult and abrasive subordinate to Phillip. John White, the appointed Surgeon General, was in charge of six other ship surgeons: Arthur Bowes Smyth, George Worgan, William Balmain, Thomas Arndell, John Altree and Dennis Considen. Reverend Richard Johnson was appointed as the Fleet Chaplain and Augustus Alt as the Surveyor General.

Among the officers, marines and seamen who would sail on the fleet, thirteen later became well known as the authors of journals and diaries documenting the voyage and the establishment of the colony. The historical details in these journals are crucial to our story. They provide eyewitness accounts of the arduous journey, the ports of call visited and of the eventual formation of a settlement in New South Wales. The assembling of ships on the Thames River aroused much public interest in the Botany Bay Scheme, and London newspapers were soon seeking written reports of the forthcoming voyage and of the convict settlement. It is unlikely that financial gain motivated the diaries, notes, letters, logbooks and drawings recording the First Fleet expedition, though many later were published as books and in newspapers.

The initial fitting out of the convict transport ships at the Deptford docks was almost complete by mid-December 1786. After modification and provisioning, the transports would sail to Portsmouth and Plymouth to embark the marines and convicts. The transport ship *Scarborough* and the three store ships, *Borrowdale*, *Fishburn* and *Golden Grove*, sailed directly to Portsmouth, and the convict transports *Friendship* and *Charlotte* sailed to Plymouth. The transports *Alexander* and *Lady Penrhyn* would remain at the Deptford docks to embark convicts from the London prisons and hulks.

At 452 tons, the three-masted, two-decked barque *Alexander* was the largest of the convict transport ships. Her Master was Duncan Sinclair. On 6 Jan 1787, the *Alexander* received 184 male convicts from the Thames hulks *Justitia*, *Censor* and *Ceres*. The convicts, who included Anthony Rope, were transferred in long boats under strong marine escort and were assigned bunks aboard the *Alexander*.[5] Anthony and his fellow transportees may well have welcomed the transfer. Their quarters on the *Alexander* were cramped and dark, but they had new bedding and fit-outs and were probably an improvement on the damp hulk cells. Being aboard a real ship with sails would be a different experience, and, importantly, they no longer had to do hard labour dredging the river.

The *Lady Penrhyn*, a three-masted barque, the newest of the transports, was designated as an all-female convict ship. It expected to receive the inmates of London gaols, but naval authorities had become concerned about the sanitation and health of the convicts. The females were in a dreadful state, badly clothed and filthy. Phillip was appalled and wrote a blunt missive to Under Secretary Evan Nepean.

> The situation in which the magistrates sent the women on board the Lady Penrhyn, stamps them with infamy – tho' almost naked, and so very filthy, that nothing but clothing them would have prevented them from perishing, and which could not be done in time to prevent a fever, which is still on board that ship.[6]

On January 6th, 54 ragged women convicts from Newgate gaol arrived to board the *Lady Penrhyn*. They were immediately washed and issued new clothing from supplies already stored on the ships. The unexpected use of these clothes was later to have adverse consequences for the settlement. Also, there was a last-minute decision to increase the number of female convicts from 70 to 190 and this further depleted the planned clothing stock. Additional clothing was immediately ordered from the London suppliers, but they failed to arrive before the fleet departed. The navy knew that unsanitary convicts in the confined quarters posed a health risk on such a long voyage and insisted that those boarding meet basic hygiene standards. All convicts were washed and reclothed before being allowed on board.[7]

Surgeon General White was in charge of hygiene on board. As the chief medical officer he set high sanitary standards for the ships. The low death rate on the First Fleet voyage was later attributed to his diligence and to Phillip's insistence on adequate food and medical care for all on board. Despite the vigilance of the surgeons, disease did occur and spread aboard the *Lady Penrhyn*. There was also serious sickness on the *Alexander* moored on the Thames. On 11 Jan 1787, it was reported that four of the sick convicts on the *Alexander* were liable to infect others and deemed unfit to make the voyage.[8]

Phillip complained to the Home Office about overcrowding on the *Alexander* and that 'there are amongst the men several unable to help themselves'. He observed that 184 convicts on board made it difficult to limit the spread of disease. The congestion was compounded because the Thames moorings were close to land and convicts exercising on deck were a security risk. Phillip wanted the *Alexander* and the *Lady Penrhyn* to sail for Portsmouth, where convicts had greater liberty to come on deck. He requested that the remaining convicts be embarked at Portsmouth, observing 'the most fatal consequences may be expected if the full number is kept on board any length of time before we sail'.[9]

However, his request went unheeded. Four days later, another 26 convicts were embarked on the *Alexander*, bringing its complement to 210. On 19 Jan 1787, the Master of the *Alexander* recorded in his log that he 'Found the convicts to be very troublesome, and the convicts could take their hands out of irons'. The close proximity of the transports to the Thames shoreline alarmed him and he wrote 'Boats rowing around the ship to prevent the convicts making their escape'.[10] Lt. William Bradley on HMS *Sirius*, felt that it was impossible for convicts to escape because 'They were handcuff'd two together or had chains on, those that were handcuffed were never separated but obliged to move together upon all occasions'.[11]

On January 28th, the *Alexander* left the Deptford docks to join HMS *Sirius*, HMS *Supply* and the *Lady Penrhyn* anchored at The Downs, south of the Thames River channels.[12] All was seemingly ready for the small convoy to sail around the coast to Portsmouth when another medical crisis arose. An outbreak of the 'fluxes' (dysentery and cholera) occurred among marines and convicts on the *Alexander*. On February 7th Surgeon White told Phillip that medical supplies aboard were inadequate to cope with this outbreak.[13] The Navy Board responded quickly, and the requested medicine was sent from the Thames dockyards to the vessels assembled as a flotilla at The Downs.

On February 10th the *Lady Penrhyn* departed for Portsmouth. Because of heavy seas, HMS *Sirius*, HMS *Supply* and the *Alexander* remained at The Downs, but set sail when the winds abated on February 19th. The flotilla reached Spithead anchorage outside Portsmouth's inner harbour on February 22nd. Waiting there were the three store ships and the convict transports *Scarborough* and *Lady Penrhyn*. The convict transport *Prince of Wales*, a recent addition to the fleet, joined them a day later.[14]

Shipboard illnesses were common in the 18th century; wooden sailing ships were natural incubators for all sorts of contagious diseases, particularly if those aboard were closely confined. The problem was just as acute for ships anchored in ports; visitors and embarked convicts brought diseases from ashore. The prevalence of sickness aboard the anchored fleet was such that in March 1787 the surgeons White and Balmain warned Phillip that a combination of fresh food, warm clothing and better ventilated quarters were desperately needed for the ill.[15] The Navy Board's response was surprisingly swift. It promptly told the victuals contractor in Portsmouth, Lt. John Shortland, to supply more fresh meat and vegetables with the meals. Shortland took this as an order to provide better victualling to *all* convicts, sick and healthy.[16]

The Royal Navy had no such lavish intentions and instructed that extra fresh food be given *only* to the sick convicts. This petty mindedness irritated Phillip, and he wrote to Lord Sydney that 'orders may be given for the supplying both marines and convicts with fresh meat and vegetable while they remain at Spithead, and that a small quantity of wine may be allowed for the sick'.[17] He emphasised that sailing crowded ships for six months to the extremities of the globe was quite different from a six-week passage to America, and that on such an arduous voyage many would die unless there was an adequate supply of flour for bread and anti-scorbutic food. Phillip feared that he would be remembered as the person that had 'lost half of the garrison and convicts'.[18] His plea was listened to, and the quality and quantity of food improved. Within two weeks, Surgeon White reported an overall decline in sickness.[19] Even so, 15 convicts, and an unknown number of marines, had died by the end of April; 13 of these were on the *Alexander*.[20]

During the long period the fleet anchored at Spithead, newspapers regularly reported on shipboard matters, and particularly on the illnesses and fatalities. *The Northampton Mercury*, in keeping with the prevailing gloom and doom concerning the expedition, was pessimistic about the Botany Bay Scheme and predicted calamitous consequences.

> The Transportation to Botany Bay has the Advantage of the former Mode of Transportation to America, in securing the Kingdom from the Dread of being again infested with these pernicious Members of Society. From the Mortality which has already taken Place on board the Transports, it is supposed not more than one in five will survive the Voyage; and should the Remainder live to the Expiration of their Sentence, they can never pay the Expense of a Passage Home.[21]

In an effort to counter this poor publicity, Surgeon General White made assurances to newspaper editors that the fleet's personnel were, overall, in good health. However, after a routine ship inspection in mid-March, White ordered that the *Alexander* be completely disinfected. The convicts aboard were temporarily housed on a barge while the ship was scrubbed and smoked. The *Alexander*'s bunks were also whitewashed with lime to combat dampness caused by the convicts' breath. These precautions significantly improved the sanitation on board.[22]

It is claimed that the health of the male convicts transferred from the Thames hulks was better than that of the marine privates on board. This may well have been true. Male convicts on hulks received regular medical attention and were kept clean and well fed. The hygiene standards for the lower ranks of the military were not always a priority. That was also the case for convicts in land gaols who were often poorly dressed and fed and had little or no medical care. Official medical records show that the health of the convicts, crew and marines on board the First Fleet ships was remarkably good. Some had boarded ill but, because of shipboard hygiene and food, they had recovered quickly.[23]

The early illnesses on the *Alexander* had alerted Phillip to what might occur on a long journey with few ports of call, and he put in place special preventative measures. Phillip wrote to Evan Nepean in the Home Office that a lack of fresh provisions meant 'scurvy must make a great ravage amongst people naturally indolent and not clean'. He asked to have the power if necessary to change the regular salted meat diet for flour rations, otherwise 'scurvy must prove fatal to the greatest part' of crew and convicts.[24] Phillip also requested that anti-scorbutic remedies, such as sauerkraut and wort of malt, an extract from brewing, be part of the provisioning. He insisted that Treasury bills be issued so that fresh meat, fruit and vegetables could be purchased *en route* in the ports of Santa Cruz, Rio de Janeiro and Cape Town.

In early March 1787, the *Friendship* and the *Charlotte* were still moored in Plymouth harbour, awaiting the embarkation of convicts. Surgeon General White travelled from Portsmouth to Plymouth to oversee the transfer of convicts to both ships. The marines had already embarked. One of them, Marine Captain Watkin Tench on the *Charlotte*, would prove to be one of the expedition's most able chroniclers. Another marine, Second Lieutenant Ralph Clark, who boarded the *Friendship* on 9 Mar 1787, also kept a diary, and Elizabeth Pulley would be one of the female convicts to receive considerable attention in his diary entries.

Elizabeth was one of 249 convicts waiting on the hulk *Dunkirk* to be transferred to the *Friendship*.[25] Heavy gales delayed the transfer but on March 11th, 76 men and 26 females were embarked, they included Elizabeth, Susannah Holmes, Henry Kable and baby. On the same day, 89 men and 15 females boarded the *Charlotte*. Surgeon White recorded that the convicts were 'placed in the different apartments allotted for them; all secured in irons; except the women'.[26]

The poor hygiene of the female convicts transferred in Plymouth gave rise to sanitary concerns similar to those raised in London. The women were in a very poor state, and Phillip complained again to Under Secretary Nepean.

> The giving of cloths [clothes] to those convicts who have been embarked at Plymouth is so very necessary that I have ordered it to be done, and presume the Navy Board will replace the clothing, but as there are more convicts to be sent on board the different ships, unless orders are being given for their being washed and clothed on their leaving the prison or the hulks, all that we may do will be to no purpose.[27]

Presumably, Elizabeth Pulley was one those who greatly appreciated getting out of her hulk rags, washing and putting on the new clothes. It would have been a rare and luxurious experience for most convicts, and probably generated much excitement and pleasure among the females in particular. For many it would have seen as their first taste of a new life. When the loading and stowing was completed, the *Friendship* and *Charlotte* weighed anchor on 13 Mar 1787 in Plymouth Sound and sailed for Portsmouth to join the rest of the fleet.[28]

The assembly of the flotilla at Spithead and the transfer of so many convicts to Portsmouth caused fears among some residents. *The British Chronicle* proclaimed 'The villains are supposed to have belonged formerly to the hulks at Woolwich, and to have come down to see their former friends and companions' and that 'Portsmouth was now infested with numerous gangs of thieves'. It claimed that people were being robbed and their houses broken into.[29] During the last week in February 1787, around 210 additional convicts had been disembarked from the Thames hulks and transported, with a cavalry escort, to Portsmouth in open horse-drawn wagons.[30] The arrival of the convict wagons in Portsmouth after a two-day journey was, according to one naval officer, not warmly received.

> All the ship windows and doors of Portsmouth [were] closed on this occasion, and the streets were lined with troops, while the wagons ... passed to Point Beach, where the boats were ready to receive them; as soon as they were embarked, they gave three tremendous cheers.[31]

Strong winds prevented an immediate transfer of convicts by long boat to the *Scarborough,* and the transportees had to be kept in chains on board the HMS *Gorgon* until the winds dropped.[32] By March 16th the entire fleet of 11 ships had anchored at Spithead outside the entrance to Portsmouth harbour.[33] However, various administrative matters needed to be finalised before the ships could depart, and the fleet would remain at anchor for another two months.

In the meantime, the newspapers were having a field day at the Navy's expense. They published multifarious rumours circulating about the fleet, claiming that 8 to 10 people were dying each day, 'a malignant disease raged with great violence on board the transports', and much more.[34] The veracity of these reports was unimportant to the newspapers – such news always had a following, and it sated the readers' appetite for gossip about this *ill-fated voyage to the ends of the earth.* The reality, diarised by Marine Captain Tench aboard the *Charlotte,* tells a quite different story:

> In this period, excepting a slight appearance of contagion in one of the transports, the ships were universally healthy and the prisoners in high spirits. Few complaints or lamentations were to be heard among them and an ardent wish for the hour of departure seemed generally to prevail.[35]

Supplies continued to be loaded onto ships while the fleet waited for the last convicts to be embarked on the *Prince of Wales.* The constant victualling of the 1500 persons aboard was, in itself, a major industry. Not surprisingly, given the confined quarters on the convict transports, some of the seamen and female convicts sought out one another's company, despite explicit orders prohibiting liaisons. Marine Lt. Johnston on the *Lady Penrhyn* reported that he twice had to remove women from the bunks of sailors and had put them in irons and recommended that a Second Mate be dismissed.[36]

While the fleet was at anchor in Portsmouth, Phillip was in London receiving final instructions from the Home Office and Navy Board. He was kept well abreast of fleet preparations and transmitted orders to Portsmouth when needed. On April 2nd he officially received his commission as governor of the new colony, and on April 25th was given instructions for the governance of the voyage and the settlement.[37] In London Phillip also studied Captain James Cook's records and the

Admiralty's charts and finalised his route to Botany Bay. Sea-lanes in the Atlantic Ocean were well established but in 1787 little was known about routes through the Southern and South Indian Oceans. The charts and logs of the voyages of Abel Tasman in 1642, and James Cook in 1772-5 and 1776-80 were used to plan the preferred route of the First Fleet.

On May 7th, Phillip returned to Portsmouth, bringing with him a sextant and an accurate marine chronometer. The chronometer was one of the Navy's most valuable instruments, a 'rare jewel of timekeeping'.[38] The Royal Navy used clocks for navigation following the development of the marine chronometer by John Harrison. The longitude of a ship's position could be calculated from the interval between Greenwich time on the clock and the local noon determined by the navigator's sextant.

How did the convicts cope aboard the transport ships during their long wait in the relatively open seas at Spithead? Most would never have experienced the open sea before and to dark bunks aboard a small ship in often-rough seas would have been distressing and many were seasick. However, all of the convicts would have been used to much greater hardships and they quickly adapted to the shipboard routines of feeding, washing and sleeping in an incessantly moving bunk. Despite promises, little, if any, deck exercise was permitted for the convicts while in Portsmouth. Watkin Tench aboard the *Charlotte* diarises this period:

> the behavior of the convicts being in general humble, submissive, and regular. Indeed, I should feel myself wanting in justice to those unfortunate men were I not to bear this public testimony of the sobriety and decency of their conduct.[39]

At the end of April, Major Ross ordered the marine officers to inspect convicts' letters. Watkin Tench writes that inspecting the letters brought to, or sent from, the ship 'was not one of the least tiresome and disagreeable'.[40] Almost all convicts were illiterate and letters they sent would have been dictated to someone who could write. Tench was surprised at the content of the letters, which 'varied according to the dispositions of the writers' and 'their constant language was an apprehension of the impracticability of returning home, the dread of a sickly passage and the fearful prospect of a distant and barbarous country'. One wonders if Anthony dictated a letter to his family in Norton Subcourse. As for Elizabeth, it is doubtful that she had any family to whom she could communicate, or who could read.

Ten days before the fleet departed Portsmouth, the last cohort of convicts arrived from London's Newgate prison. Records about the fleet's personnel on departure and on arrival in Port Jackson differ widely.[41] However, based on a reasonably accurate name list, the *convict* count on 13 May 1787 was 752 with 13 accompanying children.[42]

ASSEMBLING THE FLEET

Number of Convicts on Departure

Convict transport	Men	Women	Accomp. Child
Alexander	191		
Charlotte	89	15	2
Scarborough	205		
Friendship	76	26	4
Prince of Wales	1	49	2
Lady Penrhyn		100	5
Totals	562	190	13

The total of 752 adult convicts agrees with the estimate of Lt. Philip Gidley King.[43] The numbers recorded for *non-convict* personnel vary widely. Lt. King states that HMS *Sirius* carried 160 officers and crew, and HMS *Supply* 55 men. There were another 240 crew on the transport and store ships.[44] These numbers are unlikely to be reliable, as crew were often not counted – they were expected to return to England after unloading in Botany Bay.

The military compliment is better known. The marine soldier contingent comprised a total of 212 men. This includes the Commandant Major Ross and his staff on board HMS *Sirius*. Additionally, there were 28 marine wives and 17 accompanying marine children.[45] It is estimated that there were about 680 *non-convict* personnel on board. This would give a grand total of 1459 people (ignoring the crew numbers) aboard the First Fleet, but a precise count of the fleet's full complement may never be known. However, based on the recorded names of those on board, the distribution of the *non-convicts* among the fleet is as follows:[46]

Non-convict Personnel on the First Fleet

	Navy	Crew	Marines	Marine wives	Marine children	Civilians
Sirius	15	121	53	7	2	4
Supply	1	44	16			
Alexander	1	36	42	4	1	
Charlotte	1	9	26	4	3	1
Friendship		21	34	3	6	
Lady Penrhyn	1	37	17	2	3	1
Prince of Wales		11	20	13	11	1
Scarborough	1	15	47	1	1	1
Borrowdale		9	1	1		
Fishburn		10				
Golden Grove		5		2		2
Total	20	318	256	37	27	10

ASSEMBLING THE FLEET

The number of *non-convict* personnel known by name is 668. The crew numbers are uncertain, though Lt. King records that each store ship had 22 crew.[47] Taking this into account would indicate that about 1500 people departed Portsmouth on the First Fleet.

Some demographical data on the First Fleet convicts are known. About 38% of the male and 56% of the female convicts had been sentenced in the Old Bailey in London. The rest were tried at various English and Welsh courts. When the First Fleet set sail the majority of convicts were in the age group of 21-30 years (55%).[48]

Age	Male	Female
13-15 years	3	5
16-20 years	70	32
21-30 years	319	96
31-40 years	109	31
41-50 years	28	7
51-60 years	11	2
61-70 years	3	3
Unknown	19	15

Convict numbers according to sentence duration were:[49]

Duration	Male	(Death)*	Female	(Death)*
5 years			2	
7 years	513	(153)	173	(28)
14 years	16	(8)	11	(7)
Life	33	(31)	4	(4)

Number of people whose death sentence was commuted to transportation.

About 91% of the convicts were sentenced to seven years transportation. The crimes committed by First Fleet convicts were:[50]

Crime	Male	Female
Stealing	366	131
Burglary & robbery	91	34
Highway robbery	70	9
Forgery & fraud	10	1
Receiving stolen goods	6	8
Unknown	18	6

Two-thirds (66%) of the convicts were convicted of stealing – if you classify 'robbery' as 'stealing' then 93% involved theft of some kind. All in all, most transported convicts were punished for stealing offences that today would be pardoned under the First Offenders Act.

ASSEMBLING THE FLEET

In early May 1787, the fleet was still awaiting the delivery of important papers from London and the loading of additional stores. The latter included the women's clothing recently ordered to replenish supplies consumed on the *Lady Penrhyn* and *Friendship*. The most critical documents yet to arrive were the details of the convict's sentences. Phillip needed information on the crimes, sentences and skills of the convicts to ensure their proper administration into the foreseeable future.[51] But navigational priorities aboard the ships were more pressing. The ships' captains feared that the favourable sailing conditions currently gracing the fleet would be lost before they could set sail into the English Channel. In addition, HMS *Hyaena*, a 24-gun frigate, who joined the fleet temporarily to secure the convict transports while in English waters, was only available for a limited time. HMS *Hyaena* was considered necessary because of a mutiny in 1784 on the convict ship *Mercury* sailing to America. The limited availability of HMS *Hyaena* put additional pressure on Phillip to depart soon. On May 10th, with provisioning complete, Phillip hoisted his Commodore's flag on HMS *Sirius* signalling the flotilla to prepare for departure.

The prospect of imminent departure brought both exhilaration and remorse to those aboard the fleet. Some seamen regretted leaving their loved ones for such a long voyage, others aboard HMS *Sirius* and HMS *Supply* saw it as an opportunity to recoup wages. The Royal Navy had a dreadful reputation for missed payments to lower ranks, and some seamen demanded two-month's wages in advance. Phillip was furious and threatened to exchange the protesters for seamen on HMS *Hyaena*. This caused even more problems, and eventually Lt. King took over negotiations, and the seamen received their advance payments in cash.[52]

Two days later, on May 12th, the Commodore ordered all ships to weigh anchor and the fleet set sail for Santa Cruz on the Island of Tenerife. But the favourable winds suddenly calmed, and HMS *Sirius* signalled all ships to drop anchor immediately – three of the convict transports had not even had time to set their sails. That afternoon the *Prince of Wales* unexpectedly received four more convicts, one male and three females.[53]

Our story now re-joins the moments of departure described in the opening Prologue. At daybreak on the 13 May 1787, the First Fleet flotilla of twelve ships, including the temporary escort ship HMS *Hyaena*, weighed anchor at Spithead and set sail for the English Channel.[54] Their destination, and first port of call, was to be Santa Cruz, on the Isle of Tenerife.

Chapter 6

Portsmouth to Rio

We may now consider the adventurers in this small fleet as finally detached, for the present, from their native country; looking forward, doubtless with very various emotions, to that unknown region, which, for a time at least, they were destined to inhabit.[1]

Late on 13 May 1787, all ships in the First Fleet flotilla were in full sail bearing southwest in the English Channel towards the Atlantic Ocean. As they passed the Isle of Wight, Marine Captain Watkin Tench, on the *Charlotte*, diarised the mood of the convicts.

> A very few excepted, their countenances indicated a high degree of satisfaction, though in some the pang of being severed, perhaps for ever, from their native land could not be wholly suppressed. In general, marks of distress were more perceptible among the men than the women.[2]

By the close of the first day, it was apparent that the transport ships *Charlotte* and *Lady Penrhyn* were labouring in the choppy seas and were struggling to keep up with the rest of the fleet. Phillip ordered HMS *Hyaena* to put the *Charlotte* in tow until they cleared the Channel. On May 16th, the fleet continued to battle its way west in heavy rain and blustery winds. Just three days into the journey, some seamen aboard the *Friendship* demanded increased food rations and went on strike. Phillip sent Lt. Shortland from HMS *Sirius* to investigate the protest. On the *Friendship* Marine Second Lt. Clark recorded the incident in his diary:

> the Seamen refused to doe there duty on Account of there Provisions -- the agent came on board by the Commd. orders to enquire in to the complaint which was that the[y] would have two pounds of Beef a day in the room of having 1½ pound which is at present a half a pound a day more than we are alloud -- the[y] all agreed to goe to work again Since the other Seamen in the rest of Transports have no more but if any Ship in the fleet gives ther Ships Company more they are to expect the same.[3]

Clark claims that the seamen wanted the additional food to supplement the rations of female convicts. It is not known if this was a humane gesture or seamen expected appropriate favours in return. Sensing an escape opportunity in the open seas, two convicts on the *Scarborough*, both experienced ex-sailors, were plotting to take over the ship. Another convict had informed the captain before the mutiny could be started. The two ringleaders were taken to HMS *Sirius*, flogged, put in double irons and moved to the *Prince of Wales*, where they remained for the voyage. For his own safety, the informant was transferred to another transport.

Watercolour showing HMS *Sirius*, HMS *Supply* and convict transports leaving Needle Point in England, in the company of HMS *Hyaena*, 13 May 1787.

On May 20th the fleet was 270 nautical miles (500 km) west of the Isles of Scilly, an archipelago off the coast of Cornwall, and Phillip ordered HMS *Hyaena* to return back to Portsmouth, carrying letters from various writers.[4] One was printed later in *The London Chronicle*.

> By a letter from an officer on board the Friendship transport (one of the Botany Bay fleet) dated May 20, lat. 47, 51, brought by the Hyaena frigate, there is advice that the convicts were very healthy, and had behaved perfectly well since their departure on board every ship, except the Scarborough transport, which they had formed a scheme to take on the night of the 17th; but luckily just as their design was about to be put in execution, they were discovered, and ten of the most notorious were secured, and wait the sentence the Commodore means to pass on them.[5]

The person who wrote this letter (either Meredith, Clark or Faddy on the *Friendship*) had exaggerated the mutiny and the arrest; only the two ringleaders were secured. Most Captains in the Royal Navy would have immediately hung the mutineers after a cursory trial, and then enforced much stricter security on the ships. Phillip did the opposite; he ordered that the convicts be treated leniently. His rationale was to gain the confidence and cooperation of the 752 convicts who would be in his charge for years ahead. Hanging the two miscreants would achieve little, other than entrench hostility among convicts for the whole expedition.

Captain Arthur Phillip with his plan for New South Wales in 1787, prior to the departure of the First Fleet. Phillip was the colony's first governor (1788-1792) and is considered the *Founder of Modern Australia*.

After clearing the English Channel, Phillip turned the fleet southwards into the Atlantic Ocean. Foremost on his mind must have been the recent mutiny aboard the *Scarborough*. Was this indicative of the lack of discipline he would face ahead? His benevolent handling of the mutineers was characteristic of Phillip, and this was to prove important to the success of the First Fleet and the later settlement. On the same day that HMS *Hyaena* left the fleet, he ordered that all the convicts *be released from their irons*.[6] Captain Tench on the *Charlotte* thought Phillip's actions fair, and he praised the decision. When convicts on the *Charlotte* were released from their fetters, he noted in his diary:

> I had great pleasure in being able to extend this humane order to the whole of those under my charge without a single exception. It is hardly necessary for me to say that the precaution of ironing the convicts at any time reached [applied] to the men only.[7]

Ralph Clark aboard the *Friendship* vehemently disagreed, writing that the Captain of the *Friendship*, Francis Walton, had spoken to Phillip about removing all convicts from their irons 'as Capt Merideth and Self don't think is Save for so great a number to be out of irons at once'.[8]

The records of the convicts' crimes or sentences had not reached Phillip before the fleet sailed, and he ordered that each prisoner be questioned individually on details of their charges, sentence and on their past work experience. The officers performing the survey were sceptical that the responses would be reliable but agreed that even the convicts' version of their past history was better than nothing. Anthony Rope would have provided details of his conviction and sentence (stealing, 7 years). Regrettably none of the survey responses from the *Alexander* have survived. In fact Anthony Rope is not mentioned in any of the diaries or records of the First Fleet, which suggests that he behaved himself.

The absence of Anthony's name in shipboard records is in stark contrast to Elizabeth Pulley, who achieved regular star billing in Lt. Ralph Clark's diaries on the *Friendship*. Her name is first mentioned in the convict interviews ordered by Phillip. Clark conducted these on the *Friendship* and recorded Elizabeth's responses in the *List of female convicts on board the Friendship Transport May 13th 1787* as follows:

Elizt. Pully Age 26 Trade: none Crime: Shope Lifting 7 years[9]

There are some inaccuracies here. Elizabeth's age was in fact 25, and her recorded crime of *Shop Lifting* is also incorrect. She was charged with the more serious offence of *Daylight Burglary* and that had earned her an initial death sentence. The errors were probably unintentional. It is quite possible that Elizabeth did not distinguish, or appreciate, the difference between the two crimes. In any case, she would have been reluctant to reveal too much of her miserable past. Elizabeth was on a voyage to a new future and the less said about the past, the better.

By now, Elizabeth would have become accustomed to ship life and in all likelihood experienced the same 'high degree of satisfaction' felt by convicts on the *Charlotte*.[10] However, discipline aboard the *Friendship* was quite different to that on the *Charlotte*, and the potential for conflict on Elizabeth's ship was much greater. In the first place, it carried convicts who were part of the 1784 mutiny on the *Mercury*. Phillip had already instructed Marine Captain Meredith to put these convicts into irons whenever he thought it necessary. Among the 102 convicts (76 males and 26 females) aboard the *Friendship*, 54 had been on the *Mercury* during that mutiny.[11] Most had been quickly captured and the ringleaders hanged; the rest were imprisoned on the hulk *Dunkirk* in Plymouth to await future transportation. These females were brutally treated by the marines, and this was to have long-term repercussions. The ex-*Mercury* females were mostly from London, and six of them were now aboard the *Friendship*. Four in particular, Elizabeth Barber, Elizabeth Dudgeon,

Margaret Hall and Charlotte Ware are repeatedly cited in Clark's diaries. They had gained a tough reputation among convicts because of the 1784 mutiny, and probably expected to rule below decks. On the other hand, Elizabeth Pulley was an orphaned rural lass who had fended for herself since childhood, and she was not about to be bossed about by any city girls. Unsurprisingly, for much of the voyage she was in regular conflict with these four females, and some First Fleet histories have referred to them as the 'Fighting Five'.[12]

Because of the mistreatment of ex-*Mercury* females on the *Dunkirk*, the convicts on the *Friendship* shared a low opinion of the marine guards and frequently defied them. Lt. Ralph Clark was punctilious in diarising the behaviour of the females, and particularly any dalliances with the crew. On July 18th, he wrote that Elizabeth Barber, while intoxicated, had abused Surgeon Arndell 'in a most terrible manner'. Later, Barber did the same to Marine Captain Meredith when he put her in irons, shouting 'she was no more a Whore than his wife'. As convicts had no alcohol ration, a sailor or marine must have given her the grog. Soon after, Clark records that Margaret Hall was put in irons for foul behaviour and Elizabeth Dudgeon was flogged for being impertinent to Captain Meredith.[13]

These young women rebelled against the marine guards and protested bitterly about insults and punishment. In the pressure cooker confinement of the small, crowded ship, one wonders to what extent the women's bad behaviour may have been provoked. Undisciplined guards may have felt that goading the young, shackled females was an acceptable and entertaining sport, but Phillip was fiercely against such behaviour and strived to maintain strict discipline among the naval and marine officers. After a marine had flogged several seamen for a minor issue, Phillip forbade any corporal punishments without explicit orders from a senior officer.[14] Flogging was common in the British Navy, but Phillip was determined to apply the lash only when necessary. The goodwill and cooperation of everyone on board was his first priority, and his humane approach proved judicious.

The small town of Santa Cruz on the Tenerife Island was to be the first port of call for the fleet. It was about 1500 nautical miles (2778 km) from Portsmouth and directly *en route* to the major staging port of the voyage, Rio de Janeiro in Brazil. Rio had been selected as the main victualing port for the voyage, and where most of the supplies and livestock needed for the settlement would be purchased. The plan to visit Rio was especially attractive to Phillip, who was familiar with the region from his time as a Captain in the Portuguese navy engaged in fighting the Spanish from 1774-78. He spoke Portuguese and would have been looking forward to meeting up with old colleagues in familiar Rio haunts. But the port of Rio de Janeiro was another 5000 nautical miles (9300 km) away, and an earlier port of call was needed to replenish essential victuals. The Spanish port of Santa Cruz on Tenerife Island was to be their first destination.

The fleet sailed south along a well-known route to the Canary Islands taking full advantage of the trade winds and permanent sea currents of the Atlantic Ocean. However, in doing so, they encountered heavy seas and exceedingly high winds that made many of the convicts and marines seasick. Weather conditions eventually improved and on June 3rd the fleet anchored in Santa Cruz harbour on the Island of Tenerife.[15] Within a week they had replenished their fresh food and water. Phillip writes in his diary that for the sake of the convict's health:

> In this, and every port, the crews, soldiers, and convicts, were indulged with fresh meat, fruit, vegetables, and every thing which could conduce to preserve them from the complaints formerly inevitable in long voyages. The allowance was, to the marines, a pound of bread, a pound of beef, and a pint of wine per man, daily: the convicts had three quarters of a pound of beef, and of bread, but no wine. The fruits obtained here were only figs and mulberries, but these were plentiful and excellent.[16]

However, food was not as plentiful in Santa Cruz as Phillip had hoped. The only fruits in season were figs and mulberries, and vegetables were limited to potatoes, onions and pumpkins.[17] With the new provisions quickly loaded, Phillip allowed most of the officers and marines to go ashore. With three weeks of the journey complete Phillip proudly reported in his letters to Lord Sydney and Evan Nepean that 'the convicts are not so sickly as than when we sailed'. Moreover, the convicts were on the whole well behaved and 'are quiet and content, tho there are amongst them some complete villains'. Eight convicts had died so far, and five were on Anthony's ship the *Alexander*.[18] The fleet remained in Santa Cruz for one week. During this time the convicts were released from irons to exercise, but with strict orders to lock them up on the smallest offence.[19]

Phillip was eager to resume the passage to Rio de Janeiro, and at first light on June 10th the fleet weighed anchor and set sail. The winds stayed in their favour and despite tropical storms the ships maintained a close convoy. A week later they approached the Cape Verde Islands where Phillip considered purchasing additional fruit and vegetables because of the shortfall in Tenerife. But when they sighted the Cape Verde Islands Phillip realised the current and high winds were too dangerous and decided that the additional victualling was not worth the risk. The fleet continued sailing towards Rio.[20]

For most convicts the heat, humidity and heavy rain of the tropical latitudes was a new and oppressive experience. The temperature below decks was so high that female convicts frequently fainted, and this often resulted in fits. The convicts suffered most in calm conditions when the air was still. It was then necessary to remove the hatches and erect a small windsail to try and direct more air down into the convict bunks. Below decks on still nights it was stifling, almost suffocating.[21]

The unrelenting heat and humidity led to fierce competition among convicts to find the coolest places in the bunk areas. On June 9th, Ralph Clark diarised, in his inimitable style, that Captain Meredith had placed four females in irons for 10 days because of fighting.

> Capt Meridith put the four Convict women Elizh. Dudgeon, Marget Hall, Elizh. Pully, Charlott Ware out of Irons whome I had put in Irons on the 9 of this month for fighting ther was never three great whores living than they are, the four of them that Went throu the Bulk head while we lay at the Mother Bank.[22]

Clark's harsh condemnation of both the convicts and the crew on the *Friendship* continued for most of the voyage. Surgeon White wrote of similar concerns about the behaviour of the convicts on board the *Charlotte* but in more measured tones.[23] A month later he recorded that three seamen on the *Charlotte* had made their way into the women's area through a hole cut in the windsail.[24] The men were detained and put on trial. No record exists of what happened after that but because Marine Captain Watkin Tench was in charge of guards on the *Charlotte*, it is likely that the convicts and crew were appropriately and fairly treated.

Heavy tropical squalls, rain, thunder and lightning continued to batter the ships. When the weather allowed, the crew were encouraged to catch fish to supplement the ship's diet, and during rain showers to use sails to funnel water into barrels. The hot tropical conditions greatly increased the consumption of drinking water.

Thus far on the passage, the discipline and hygiene standards on board the ships were better than anticipated. When Surgeon White inspected the convict transports in late June he recorded that he 'found the troops and convicts from the very great attention paid to cleanliness, and airing the ships, in much better health than could be expected in such low latitudes and unfavourable weather'.[25] Watkin Tench aboard the *Charlotte* attributed the general good health to 'frequent explosions of gunpowder, lighting fires between decks, and a liberal use of that admirable antiseptic, oil of tar were the preventives we made use of against impure air; and above all things we were careful to keep the men's bedding and wearing apparel dry'.[26]

On July 3rd four women on the *Friendship* were caught on the seamen's side of the bulkhead. Ralph Clark diarised the episode:

> was cald up by the Capt of the Ship last night informing use that his men had brock throu the Womens Convicts Bulk head again and that he had caught four of the women in the mens place -- four of the Number that had gone throu while we lay at the Mother Bank & two of them that I had put in Irons while we lay at Teneriff for fighten -- I thought as I have Said before that these D....d troubelsem Whores it would not be long before the[y] gott ther again.[27]

The matter was brought before Phillip and he ordered the boatswain, steward and an ordinary seaman to be flogged. The fourth seaman, a carpenter, was reprimanded. The women, who included Elizabeth Pulley, were put into irons. However, Clark records his displeasure at the lightness of the women's punishment:

> the Capt went on board the Commr. who order the men that the women wair with to be brought on board of him Sent the Carpenter the Boatswain the Steward and one of the Seamen being the four men that Elizh. Dudgeon Elizh. Pully Elizh. Thackly Sarah McCormick wair with Whome the Comr. flogd except the Carpenter and order the four Women to be keep in Irons all the Way -- if I had been the Commr. I Should flogd the four Whores also[28]

Little detail is known of this event other than what Clark writes. The heat below decks was unbearable, and foremost in most convicts' minds would be to try and keep cool. Phillip would have appreciated this, and his handling of the incident was consistent with his sensible treatment of the convicts during the entire voyage. He ordered that henceforth the crew would be flogged for such offences, but the women not. That is, the punishment should always be harsher for the marines and seamen than for the convicts, as the former were responsible for their own actions, while the convicts had to do what they were told.

At this stage of the voyage, intermittent winds meant the fleet made little progress. Phillip ordered that everyone be put on a reduced daily water allowance of 3 pt, not including 1 qt of water allowed for boiling peas and oatmeal. Surgeon White considered this overly strict and worried that dehydration due to excessive perspiration and a diet of salted beef could accelerate scurvy. Nevertheless, the prevailing weather conditions made it essential that water be rationed.[29]

The weather improved as the flotilla neared the equator. On July 18th, Surgeon White was informed that several marines and convicts on the *Alexander* were extremely ill. He boarded the ship and found that the bilge water (at the ship's bottom) was too high and putrid. Noxious effluent from the bilge had blackened the wood panels in some cabins, and even corroded the buttons on some officers' jackets. He recorded that 'when the hatches [to the convict areas] were taken off, the stench was so powerful that it was scarcely possible to stand over them'.[30] The stench would have been difficult for the crew but at least they could go on deck. For the convicts confined below deck, it was dangerous.

White was puzzled at how the bilge had got so polluted, especially as there were strict orders to pump out the bilge water daily. He sought the advice of Phillip, whom he greatly admired: 'Captain Phillip, who upon every occasion showed great humanity and attention to the people'. Phillip immediately sent Lt. King and Surgeon White back to the *Alexander* with instructions to neutralise the ship's bilge water with lime and to purify the ship by burning gunpowder. The problem was soon corrected, and the sick quickly recovered. And because the wind had swung to a favourable southeast direction, the daily water ration was increased back to 3 qt.[31]

About this time, Ralph Clark wrote that an infestation of bugs below decks on the *Friendship* had attacked everyone aboard.[32] Hot weather, storms, and an infestation of bugs – it is no wonder that Elizabeth Pulley was about to get sick. On July 24th, three weeks after she had been handcuffed to Elizabeth Thackery, Elizabeth Pulley was released and placed in leg irons. Clark recorded this in his diary:

> put also again Elizh. Barbor in Irons who was let out when Margt. Hall was Yesterday She being hand cuft with her -- hand cuft her with Elizh. Tackny and put leg Irons on Eliz Pully who was hand cuft with Eliz Tackny before[33]

Two days later, Elizabeth Pulley was found to be very ill, and the *Friendship* surgeon Thomas Arndell ordered her irons removed. Clark notes 'the doctor desired that Eliz Pully might be put out of Irons She being very ill having a blister on her'.[34] A week later, Elizabeth was obviously feeling much better, because she was reported for fighting with the usual four women and they were put back in irons.

> Capt Meridith put Elizh. Barbor and Elizh. Thackny in irons together and Elizh. Dudgeon and Elizh. Pully together -- the doctor having reported them well again Except Sarah McComick -- the damed whores the moment that the[y] got below fel a fighting amonst one a nother and Capt Meridith order the Sergt. not to part them but to let them fight it out which I think he is very wrong in letting them doe so.[35]

The day after this incident, the puppy *Efford* belonging to Clark went missing. It was suspected that the First Mate had thrown the dog overboard but there was no proof.[36] Because of his ill temper and arrogance, Clark was unpopular with most on board and the drowning of his dog was probably payback for some previous mistreatment of a crewmember.

On July 3rd, Sarah McCormick, who was a regular combatant of Elizabeth Pulley, became seriously ill and the doctor thought she would not survive the night. Clark's harsh commentary continued.

> She is now quit Speachless I am apt to think (God forgive) if it is not So, that She is eating up with the P[ox]. She is one of them that went throu the Bulk head to the Seamen – I hope She has given them a some thing to remember her -- never was ther a Set of greater rascals together than the[y] are -- the[y] are ten thousand times wors than the convicts and if the convicts had any thought to make ther escapt the[y] would assist them[37]

Despite this uncharitable diagnosis, Sarah lived, and later prospered in the new colony. Clark's opinion of all personnel aboard the *Friendship* was consistent, he criticised the crew and the convicts in equal measure.

At the end of July, it was particularly stormy. Rio de Janeiro was only 434 nautical miles (804 km) away and Phillip ordered the fleet to stay close together. On August 2nd HMS *Supply* leading the convoy signalled that the coast of Brazil had been sighted. But the winds were unfavourable, and it was not until August 5th that the fleet could safely enter the large harbour. As the flotilla approached the port, HMS *Sirius* saluted the harbour fortress with a 13-gun salvo, and the fort returned the same number. The next evening, August 6th, the fleet dropped anchor in the Rio de Janeiro harbour.[38] For Phillip this was familiar territory, and he very much looked forward to meeting up with old friends and naval colleagues.

Reaching Rio de Janeiro was greatly appreciated by all on board. The ships urgently needed food and water supplies for immediate consumption. Britain had excellent political relations with Brazil and Commodore Phillip was well known, so the purchase of provisions was expected to be straightforward. Phillip noted that the visit of Captain Cook in 1768 had received a much less favourable reception, and prohibitions were placed on Cook's landing. But Phillip's visit 'was polite and flattering to a great degree, and free from every tincture of jealous caution'.[39] In fact, this cordiality was to prove something of a hindrance. Whenever Phillip ventured ashore, he was promptly met by a troop of palace guards who insisted on escorting him. This somewhat hampered the business he had to conduct with merchants. Jacob Nagle, an Able Seaman on HMS *Sirius*, wrote in his diary that Phillip tried going ashore at different docks in the harbour to avoid the escort, as he did not wish to trouble the guards. However, every time that he landed, Nagle could see soldiers running to meet his small rowboat; they would then salute him and form an escort.[40]

The first purchases made in Rio were for large supplies of fresh meat, fruit and vegetables to be consumed aboard the flotilla. The fresh food helped combat the early signs of scurvy that had appeared among crew and convicts in the tropics, prevalent especially when water was rationed. The next priority on Phillip's victualing list was a wide range of general provisions required for the onward journey to the Cape and the new colony. These included seeds and potted fruit trees.[41] Phillip anticipated that a four-week stopover in Rio would be needed to replenish provisions in each ship. Deck and mast repairs also had to be made on HMS *Sirius* and HMS *Supply*.

Food in Rio was cheap and readily available, and the convicts and the marines were allotted a generous fresh food ration; 1¼ lb of meat and 1 lb of rice, plus vegetables. The marines and their wives also received spirits.[42] Lt. David Collins on HMS *Sirius* understood why fresh food was important.

> Great numbers of oranges were at different times distributed among them, and every possible care was taken to refresh and put them into a state of health and condition to resist the attacks of the scurvy, should it make its appearance in the long passage over the ocean which was yet between them and New South Wales.[43]

With the improved diet, Phillip observed that the convicts looked 'much healthier than when we left England'. In other words, the convicts had put on weight. Even so, illness among the weakest was omnipresent, and on the journey so far, 15 convicts and one marine's child had died. On the last leg of the voyage, five *Alexander* convicts had deceased; a total of 10 deaths on that ship alone.[44]

In addition to the supply of fresh food, the convicts' health benefited from being allowed to exercise on deck for long periods, day and night. Captain Hunter on HMS *Sirius* boasted that the general health of the 1500 personnel of the fleet exceeded that of any country town in Britain of a similar population.[45] Oranges were so abundant in Rio that most on board had a unique culinary experience – they were served *ten* oranges a day.[46] With such high intakes of Vitamin C, all signs of scurvy soon disappeared.

Minor repairs to the ships were soon underway, particularly on the leaking decks of HMS *Sirius*. The Rio authorities had allowed Phillip to pitch a tent on Enchados, an island in the harbour, to unload a few astronomical instruments to check the accuracy of his chronometer. Lt. William Dawes, an astronomer, was in charge of these measurements. Sailmakers were also landed on the island, along with tents made for the future settlement. These needed to be thoroughly aired.[47]

The miserable state of female convict clothing was still a worry for Phillip, and he wrote to Under Secretary Nepean in the Home Office; the letter would be sent on the next ship sailing back to England.

> The slops of the women not been send down before we sailed. ... With respect to the women's clothing, it was made of very slight material, most too small, and in general came to pieces in a few weeks. If materials are sent out, it will be much cheaper to Government, and the cloths will be better made[48]

He told Nepean that 100 sacks of the bread-substitute cassava had been purchased, and that the sack material, made from strong Russian flax, 'will be used hereafter in clothing the convicts, many of whom are nearly naked'. Bizarrely, at that same time Surgeon Smyth complained that seamen were spending their wages in Rio on clothing for the female convicts. He saw this as an appalling extravagance, which corrupted the morals of both parties.[49]

Seamen and marines who had completed their shipboard duties were granted shore leave. While they ventured ashore the convicts remained locked below decks in the tropical heat. Phillip and several of the officers even had lodgings ashore. On occasions naval and marine officers were introduced to the Viceroy – the Regal representative of Portugal and the Governor of Rio – and they received the same hospitality and courtesies given to Phillip. Ships' personnel visited all parts of town unescorted and made excursions into the country.[50] They were dazzled by the colour and splendour of the people and buildings, and especially by the religious processions on church feast days.

In far less salubrious surroundings, the Fleet Chaplain Reverend Richard Johnson performed divine Sunday service on two of the convict transports during their stay in port.[51] Following a long-held tradition of the Royal Navy, officers aboard HMS *Sirius* were regularly treated to musical evenings. After dinner, Surgeon George Worgan would play the pianoforte he had brought on board, and diners would join in the music and singing.[52] On occasions, Surgeon Smyth from the *Lady Penrhyn* was invited to dine with Captain Phillip, and to join in the entertainment.[53] These festivities would have been in stark contrast to the mournful chants coming from a slave ship anchored nearby. Smyth wrote that a ship had arrived carrying hundreds of African slaves 'At day light in the morning I awoke wt. their singing, as is their custom previous to their being sold or Executed. – They were all naked.'[54]

Below deck on the *Friendship*, convict Elizabeth Barber wrote (or someone else had written for her) a complaint to the Commodore about her punishment. Phillip asked Marine Major Ross to look into this disciplinary matter. When he boarded the *Friendship*, he 'found the complaint but fixious [*sic*]' and her punishment was continued.[55] The finding did not surprise anyone. Ross showed no sympathy for the convicts, either on the fleet or later in New South Wales and reputedly never decided in their favour.

On August 11th, Phillip ordered the transfer of six well-behaved female convicts aboard the *Friendship* to the *Charlotte* and be replaced with those 'whose [unruly] conduct was more exceptionable'. Phillip reasoned that those 'whose decent behaviour entitled them to some favour from those who were totally abandoned and obdurate'. [56] Elizabeth Pulley was not one of those transferred.

To instil more discipline, on August 13th, the Commodore and Major Ross visited each ship and spoke to all on board.[57] On the convict transports, he warned prisoners 'that in future any misbehaviour on their part should be attended with severe punishment, while on the other hand propriety of conduct should be particularly distinguished and rewarded with proportionate indulgence'.[58] Aboard the *Friendship*, Phillip asked Marine Captain Meredith to review the charges of the four women placed in irons. Ralph Clark wrote afterwards that the women were released having been told that if they caused further trouble they would be flogged like the men.[59]

Because of Phillip's intervention, Elizabeth Pulley was taken out of irons and after reading Elizabeth Barber's complaints about mistreatment he ordered punishments be investigated on all ships. He emphasised to the convicts that if they stayed out of trouble, their treatment aboard and in the new colony, would be just and humane.

On September 2nd, two days before the fleet departed Rio for Cape Town, Captain Hunter and Major Ross boarded the *Alexander*, Anthony's transport, 'to settle and examine the convicts'.[60] This followed a report to Phillip claiming that the *Alexander*'s crew and convicts were 'mutinously inclined' and had threatened Captain Sinclair and two mates. Sinclair seemed to have lost authority over his crew.[61] The issue in question is not clear but it may have been because of the crew's concern about the high incidence of sickness on the ship, and the 10 deaths that had already occurred. Presumably the report said that Sinclair needed to improve hygiene and sanitary conditions in the convict quarters in order to prevent further illnesses. No other record of the incident exists, but it is likely that the same cleansing procedures carried out on the *Alexander* in July were repeated.

Chapter 7

FEMALE CONVICT BEHAVIOUR

Clark displayed an arrogant intolerance of the women convicts aboard the Friendship. Early in the voyage, some sailors got into the women's quarters — but Clark blamed the women! Even if they were the "damned whores" he says they were, it is hard to imagine the women breaking through the bulkhead without assistance from the outside[1]

On the morning of 4 Sep 1787, after four weeks at anchor in Rio de Janeiro harbour, the First Fleet ships set sail for Cape Town. The stay had replenished the fleet's supplies and given the crew ample time to make crucial repairs to the leaking HMS *Sirius*. It had also been a very enjoyable month of relaxation and entertainment for the officers and marines. The convicts had not been so privileged, but at least their food was fresh and were able to exercise on the decks of the moored ships. The mood aboard the fleet was buoyant and optimistic as they prepared for the 3300 nautical mile voyage to the Port of Cape Town, on the southern tip of Africa. Nobody aboard was aware at this juncture just how important the provisioning in Rio de Janeiro would be to the success of the expedition.[2]

Upon departure a special tribute awaited Phillip. The fleet received a 21-gun salute from the Viceroy as the ships passed the port fortress 'the last compliment it was in his power to pay'.[3] Captain Hunter recorded the occasion in his diary.

> When the Sirius had got within about half a mile of Fort Santa Cruz, that castle saluted with 21 guns, which was answered by us with the same number; a very high and uncommon compliment, and such I believe as is seldom paid to any foreigner; but was no doubt meant as a suitable return to the attention paid by his Majesty's ship to the birth-day of the Prince of Brazil.[4]

Initially, sailing conditions in the South Atlantic were perfect for their eastern bearing but, within a few days, this changed. For the next week they were buffeted by violent storms, heavy squalls, thunder and lightning. Rough and powerful seas broke over the gunnels of the ships and all hatches had to be battened down to prevent water flooding below decks. The convicts were locked below in complete darkness and without fresh air. The dreadful stench of the bilge water and vomit permeated their cramped bunks. This, coming shortly after a month of placid waters and relaxation in the Rio harbour, was a most frightening and nauseating experience. A particularly heavy squall of wind and rain caused waves to dangerously roll the *Friendship*. The women aboard are recorded as having 'Read prayer and Sang Palms to themself'.[5]

After a week, the heavy weather abated briefly, and then returned again as heavy hail. Clark wrote that the *Friendship* was tossing heavily, and a great deal of water was below decks 'washt the marines out of ther beds and the Convict Women all the thing rouling about'.[6] In this storm, a number of the female convicts were hurt and bruised. Also of concern was that, only a month out of Rio, the supplies of fresh food ran low – rations for all on board were restricted mostly to salted meat.

Once more, Elizabeth Pulley was the subject of Clark's attention. On October 3rd she and Sarah McCormick were reported by Clark as claiming to 'be with child'. In fact neither was pregnant. It was either a ploy to curb Clark from threating to put them in irons again, or the early symptoms of scurvy. Clark diarised 'I hope the comr. will make the two Seamen that are the Fathers of the children marrie them and make them stay at Botany Bay'.[7] It was uncharacteristically generous of him to imply that it was not *all* the women's fault.

On October 4th, Phillip was informed that 30 convicts on the *Charlotte* were ill from scurvy and dysentery, and some were close to death. On the *Alexander* several of the sick had to be isolated from the healthy convicts. With the fresh food almost exhausted, the fleet desperately needed to get to Cape Town as quickly as possible.[8]

One week out of Cape Town there was another drama when the fleet became fog bound. With visual communications between ships lost, several convicts and seamen aboard the *Alexander* took this as an opportunity to overpower the ship before it reached Cape Town, and they had armed themselves with iron bars. John Powers, the convict who had escaped in Tenerife and been recaptured, had planned the mutiny. Once again, an informer thwarted the plan. Powers and four others were arrested and taken in irons to HMS *Sirius* and stapled to the deck. The informer was removed to the *Scarborough* for his protection.[9]

After the incident Surgeon Smyth predicted that there would be hangings when they reached Cape Town.[10] But Phillip maintained his abhorrence of hangings at sea. He knew from his years in the Royal and Portuguese navies that the sight of shipmates dangling from the yardarm fuelled hostility that would make it hard to achieve a trouble-free passage and a manageable colony. There was still a long and difficult voyage ahead and he needed to maintain crew morale and convict trust. Ships with so many prisoners and so few guards on board, had a better chance of success if the convicts were cooperative.

On October 12th Phillip reckoned from the calculated longitude that the Cape of Good Hope must be just over the horizon and sent the swift-sailing HMS *Supply* ahead to investigate. His calculations were correct, and the following day all eleven ships entered Table Bay on the Cape and dropped anchor directly out from Cape Town. Table Bay is on the northwest side of the Cape of Good Hope and relatively unprotected from the strong winds and heavy seas coming off the Southern Ocean. On entering the harbour, Phillip observed the same courtesy that he had shown in Rio and presented a 13-gun salute to the fortress. He was somewhat relieved when this was reciprocated. The fleet anchored in the harbour after sailing 3300 nautical miles in 5 weeks and 4 days without any separations or accidents.[11]

Cape Town would be the last port before the long passage, across relatively uncharted South Indian and Southern Oceans, to Botany Bay on a largely unknown continent. A thorough provisioning of the ships in Cape Town was vital to ensure the future success of the colony in New South Wales. Lt. King went ashore to enquire into the purchasing of the food and livestock needed for the last leg of the journey, but he received a very cool reception. The Dutch authorities informed him that food was in short supply owing to poor crops over the past two years, and there was little to sell to the fleet. The next day Phillip disembarked with some officers to investigate for himself. And, although port officials told Phillip there was a grain shortage, merchants confided to him that recent crops had been excellent. He was discreetly informed that supply would be possible, but the prices would be high.[12] The Dutch traders were determined to profit from the English, who had no alternate food sources to draw on.

Phillip was not unfamiliar with marketing produce from his farming days, and he explored available sources and bargained strenuously. Within ten days he had purchased most of what the fleet needed, admittedly at exorbitant prices. King was impressed by Phillip's abilities and wrote in his journal 'From having the honour of Governor Phillip's confidence I am very certain of what I am now assert, and I do firmly believe that a great sum might be saved Government by employing those young men, provided those who employ them keep their hands as clean as Mr Phillip did this'.[13]

As in Rio, fresh provisions were urgently needed for immediate consumption aboard the ships. No deaths had occurred on the passage to Cape Town, but 20 marines and 93 convicts were on the sick list. When Surgeon Smyth boarded the *Alexander*, he found many men dangerously ill with a putrid fever, a form of typhus. Surgeon General

White was also informed that there were at least 30 sick crew and convicts on the *Charlotte*, and that some were certain to die.[14]

With the availability of fresh provisions, those suffering from scurvy quickly recovered. The daily ration for convicts was 1½ lb of soft bread and 1 lb of fresh beef or mutton, together with a liberal allowance of vegetables.[15] Predictably, Ralph Clark on the *Friendship* viewed the ration as overly generous, writing 'You will Say not bad allowance for convicts and as much Greens as the[y] can make use of in there Broth – the[y] have been more treated like Children than Prisoners'.[16] In contrast, Lt. David Collins on HMS *Sirius* reported 'we had the satisfaction to see the prisoners all wear the appearance of perfect health on their being about to quit this port, the last whereat any refreshment was to be expected before their arrival in New South Wales'.[17]

While anchored in Cape Town Reverend Johnson preached every Sunday on each of the convict transports. And, as in Rio, marines and seamen were permitted shore leave. The settlement at Cape Town was relatively prosperous though much more subdued than the gaiety and charm of Rio. There were no taverns where officers could lodge, no festivals, no bright colours, and the food was expensive. It was also a foreboding place for the indigenous residents, who were clearly in fear of the Dutch authorities. Surgeon Smyth wrote 'There are many Gallows & other implements of punishment erected a long shore and in front of the Town' and were 'occupied by the mangled bodies of the unhappy wretches who suffered upon them'.[18]

Lt. Collins, who would be the Judge Advocate in New South Wales, had a professional interest in the dock scene. He viewed with horror the instruments for execution and torture: crosses for breaking men, gallows, spiked poles for impalements and breaking wheels for torture.[19] British punishment was severe, but the use of torture was rare. The last person in England to be broken on the wheel was in the year 1600, and human impalements were unknown.

The convicts could see the torture apparatus on the docks while exercising on deck. One can only imagine the dread that these would have conjured up. Were these punishments common in the places they were going to? The scenes probably fuelled all sorts of ghoulish tales aboard the ships, and the marines and crew would relish the embellishment of these stories, claiming that this was what awaited the convicts in Botany Bay.

The fleet's departure was delayed until the provisions being sourced outside of Cape Town were loaded. In the meantime the carpenters constructed stalls on the decks of various ships to hold 500 animals; cows, bulls, pigs, horses, sheep, hogs, goats and geese.[20] Some officers also bought animals for their intended farms in the new colony.

Surgeon Worgan observed that several ships now looked like 'little Noah's Arks'.[21] To accommodate *Noah's* animals and their fodder some convicts had to be moved to other transports. On October 27th, Ross instructed the master of the *Friendship* that all 21 female convicts should be distributed between the transports *Charlotte*, *Prince of Wales* and *Lady Penrhyn* to allow sheep pens to be installed.[22] Females on the *Friendship* would have had mixed feelings about the transfer, as close shipboard friendships and companionships were about to be lost. On the other hand they were overjoyed at escaping the attention of Lt. Ralph Clark. And, according to his diary, Ralph Clark welcomed the departure of the females as well:

> about 1 oClock Sent the Women convicts away as order thank god that the[y] are all out of the Ship – I am very Glad of it for the[y] wair a great Trouble much more So than the [men][23]

Soon after, Clark affirmed that he preferred the sheep to the women.

> thank God we have got Quite of the most trouble some Sett (the Women) and have Received 40 Sheep in there Room which I have not the least manner of doubt but we will find them much more agreable Ship mates than the (Ladys) were -- I never came a Cross Such a D.... Sett of B....... in all the course of my life than the[y] are -- the men cannot hold a candle to one of them & I am glad from the Bottom of my Soul that the[y] are gone for I was heartily tired of them[24]

Elizabeth and 12 other females were transferred to the *Prince of Wales*. Her friend Susannah Holmes and her son were moved to the *Charlotte* while Susannah's partner Henry Kable remained with the other male convicts on the *Friendship*. On October 28th, John Mason, the Captain of the *Prince of Wales*, entered into his logbook 'Received on board from the Friendship, 13 women convicts, with 12 beds'.[25]

The loading of livestock took even longer than anticipated. The squally weather in the open Table Bay made hoisting and securing the animals difficult. Phillip used the extra time for diplomacy. He gave a public dinner to honour some of Cape Town's officials and merchants, along with some of his officers. The Dutch governor had been invited, but an unforeseen event detained him. Chief Surgeon White wrote of the night 'Commodore Phillip had his band of music on shore upon the occasion, and the day was spent with great cheerfulness and conviviality'.[26]

With Elizabeth Pulley's move to the *Prince of Wales*, written details about her life on the fleet ends, and there is no further mention of her until disembarkation in New South Wales. While aboard the

Friendship, Clark's diary records sustained criticism of his female charges, and Elizabeth Pulley featured in many. However, while on the *Prince of Wales*, neither Marine Sergeant James Scott's diary, nor the captain's logbook, refers to her.

A number of the published histories on the First Fleet assert that Elizabeth Pulley's character, based on her reported behaviour aboard the *Friendship*, was disorderly and defiant. She is a key person in this history, and the evidence of her misconduct, and that of other female convicts, needs to be examined.

To begin with, are the contemporary records of Elizabeth's behaviour aboard the *Friendship* consistent with her earlier conduct ashore? Certainly conditions aboard the *Friendship* were difficult, but she had experienced worse on land and there is no record of previous uncooperative and insubordinate behaviour. On board she had her own bunk, albeit cramped, dark and uncomfortably hot, or cold. She ate regular meals, usually of better quality than in the gaols; she received routine medical care and presumably looked forward to a better life ahead. The support for life and limb was probably better than in most prisons and may even have been superior to those she experienced as a child servant. It is doubtful therefore that living conditions on board the ship would have led to increased recalcitrance.

Were there other factors on the voyage that caused Elizabeth's reported behaviour? The most common source of stress for females aboard the transports was the sexual harassment from the marines and the crew. There is little doubt that these pressures existed, but it would be odd if they alone should cause Elizabeth's reported misdemeanours. As a servant she would have known how to fend off unwanted males. Moreover, her conduct in later life was uneventful and law-abiding. In New South Wales she proved to be an obedient prisoner, a faithful wife, a successful settler and the caring mother of eight children, seven of whom survived childhood.

So were the accounts of her rebellious behaviour aboard the *Friendship* exaggerated? Our only knowledge of Elizabeth at this time comes from the writings of one person – Marine 2nd Lt. Ralph Clark. Of all the journals and diaries recording the First Fleet expedition, Clark's writings are the most provocative and the least reliable.[27] His accounts contrast with those of Marine Captain Watkin Tench and Surgeon Arthur Smyth, who recorded events aboard the transports *Charlotte* and *Lady Penrhyn*. Their records are insightful and balanced commentaries on the life on these ships and the activities of the convicts and crew.

The nature of Clark's diary entries raises serious questions about their reliability as a true historical record. On reading his diary, one is repeatedly struck by the emotional tone he adopts when describing the females.

> whome I had put in Irons ... this month for fighting ther was never three great whores living than they are.... the[y] are a disgrase to ther Whole Sex B.....s that they are I wish all the Women Wair out of the Ship... [28]

On 3 Jul 1787, Clark wrote that he would 'keep [them] in Irons all the Way -- if I had been the Commr. I Should [have] flogd the four Whores also'.[29] His diary is also riddled with abuse of the crew and the captain.

> I never met with a parcel of more discontent fellows in my life the[y] only want more Provisions to give it to the damed whores the Convict Women of whome the[y] are very fond Since they brock throu the Bulk head and had connection with them -- I never could have thought that there wair So many abandond wreches in England, the[y] are ten thousand time worse than the men Convicts[30]

The claim that Clark's entries are 'intimate, spontaneous and revelatory' accounts of what took place is odd and disappointing.[31] Such attributes might be levelled at the Samuel Pepys Diaries, but Clark's writings hardly qualify, and they definitely lack the equivalent assurance of authenticity.

There is a much less flattering interpretation of Clark's diary. Even in those blatantly misogynous times, his entries are much more than the private outpourings of a young man raging against females in his care. Clark's observations are, by any measure, excessive, demeaning and highly emotive. That some historians have accepted them as a factual record is worrying. His diary entries are the unsubstantiated ranting of a lonely young soldier who was in charge of shackled females on a male-dominated ship. What is more, Clark's untidy hyperbole was never intended for public viewing.

It is possible that Clark's emotional style resulted from his despondency at not being allowed to bring his family on the voyage. Phillip had refused his request that his wife Alicia and their young son accompany him, and this upset him greatly. Clark offered to pay their passage – the answer was always 'no'. Before sailing to Botany Bay, he had applied for a ten-day leave to be with his family, but this was also refused because they were soon to sail.[32] Clark's attitude to female prisoners aboard the *Friendship* was almost certainly affected by the lack of female companionship, and parallel entries in his diary dedicated to his wife appear to support this. Nevertheless, when he reached New South Wales, Clark lived with a female convict who bore him a child.

Questioning the veracity of Clark's diary entries is important historically. If there were a plethora of information about female convict life aboard the First Fleet, Clark's commentary would be a quirky, and largely overlooked, narrative of this epic journey. However, first-hand accounts of the life of female convicts on the voyage are scarce, and Clark's diary aboard the *Friendship* has assumed significance beyond its purpose. Without doubt, his writings have influenced the public perception of female behaviour on this and other convict voyages.

A number of historians have already questioned whether Clark's diary represents a faithful record of female convict life aboard the First Fleet. In their introduction to the publication of Clark's diary and letters, the editors P.G. Fidlon and R.J. Ryan, conclude that 'Reading his pompous criticisms of the moral laxity aboard the Friendship and knowing that Clark himself had a paramour (Mary Branham) might convey a sense of hypocrisy about the man'.[33] Fidlon and Ryan point out that Clark consistently displayed intolerance of the convict women aboard the *Friendship*.[34] Other authors have drawn similar conclusions. Tom Keneally, in his book, *The Commonwealth of Thieves*, writes:

> Ralph Clark gave later Australian feminist historians every opportunity of accusing him of rancour against the women convicts. He said of First Fleeter Rachel Early that she was 'the most abandoned woman that I ever knew or heard of', but that seems to be a definition that Clark applied to whichever woman he had last been required to punish.[35]

Keneally also points out that, when Lt. Clark is later transferred to Norfolk Island with Major Ross, his brutal treatment of convicts continued. He writes 'Clark's new posting gave him a tin-pot power, but it was also power of life and death over those that served time on Norfolk'. Clark's diary entries in Norfolk record a litany of convict floggings, many of them women. Keneally notes 'a growing coarseness of sensitivity in Clark's journal which is an index of the effects of flogging on the entire society', and 'Clark's voice is the voice of small-minded and savage authoritarianism'.[36]

The most unfortunate consequences of Clark's diary entries are that they have become a commonly accepted gauge of female convict morals aboard the fleet, and at the settlement. His diary is a veritable cornucopia for potboiler authors, such as Mary MacLaren, who write salacious fictional stories in the guise of history. MacLaren's books *The Four Elizabeths* and *Elizabeth's New Life* portray Elizabeth Pulley and her mother Alice as London prostitutes. This is complete nonsense. Elizabeth spent her entire youth in rural Norfolk, and her mother Alice lived her short life there as well.[37] The authors of such historical novels hide behind the caveat 'that all persons, places and events are fictitious' while having the audacity to use the real names of well-known historical figures and actual localities and events. Many other flawed pseudo-histories have drawn on Clark's writings to portray convict ships as 'floating brothels'; the convict women as 'prostitutes' who 'behaved like animals' and maintained that sailors frequently 'broke through into the female prison for another orgy'.[38]

Even today, Clark's diary entries continue to fuel cracking tales of lust and licentiousness aboard the early convict fleets. Such yarns had an enthusiastic readership in 18th century newspapers; after all, this was the behaviour expected of *society's rejects sailing into hell itself*. Our willingness to believe the worst of these deprived individuals has not diminished over the centuries. A recent BBC historical drama uses real names from the First Fleet and has a largely fictional storyline that is highly sexualised.[39] The untruths in this script could have been easily avoided without affecting the storyline – instead, it is just another pitiful TV soapie posing as history.

There is strong evidence that refutes the claim of prostitution on the convict transports, and on the *Friendship* in particular. In the 18th century soliciting was not an offence punishable by transportation and females so accused were, at most, liable to a short stay in the local gaol. The committal records of female convicts on the First Fleet bear this out – none is listed as being transported for prostitution.[40] The claims of *rampant debauchery* on the First Fleet arise almost entirely from a few diary entries written by an emotionally disturbed young soldier.

There may be a more sinister message embedded in Lt. Clark's diary and letters. Reading them in their totality leaves a clear impression that he was a deeply troubled person. He often declares his devotion to his wife, Alicia, in the same paragraph he rages against his female charges, claiming they are not punished enough. His diary entries are a disturbing blend of glorification and damnation, and they raise a serious question: did his aggressive attitude contribute to the females' misbehaviour? Or, to put it more bluntly, did Clark's harsh justice promote, even provoke, rebellion and misbehaviour among the females?

In today's vernacular, the ship *Friendship* was a restricted male-dominated 'workplace' where discrimination was entrenched and females required to be subservient. On board the other convict ships, male-female liaisons did occur, but nothing approaching those reported by Clark on the *Friendship*. Was it because the convicts and seamen on the other ships behaved differently? This seems implausible. The presence of the *Mercury* convicts on the *Friendship* may have incited a tougher regime but it is unlikely their influence would have been so pervasive.

There is yet another, more recent, perspective on the shipboard sexual misbehaviour claims. The basic social and sexual customs of those times were probably not that different from todays. The crowding of single men and women on a small boat for a long period can be expected to lead to sexual interactions. The naval authorities in England would have known this and advised officers to exercise leniency, and exact punishment only if there was general disorder. Watkin Tench on the *Charlotte* took this approach and, according to his records, good behaviour prevailed. This is important because Phillip had insisted on strict discipline on the transports. The sorts of misbehaviour recorded by Clark aboard the *Friendship* would have contravened the protocols Phillip had set. He was being kept well informed of convict behaviour by the captains and would have quelled repeated breaches. This suggests Clark's entries were, at the very least, exaggerated.

All the arguments above provide compelling reasons to doubt the extent of the reported female misbehaviour aboard the *Friendship*, and on the First Fleet as a whole. It would be unconscionable to allow the diary of a young, frustrated, clearly unworldly soldier to impugn the reputations of women who have no voice for their own defence.

Questioning the veracity of Clark's accounts is critical to authenticity of a First Fleet history. The occurrence of casual sexual relationships aboard the *Friendship*, and other transports, is not in question here. Such behaviour by young single people aboard a small boat (the *Friendship* was only the length of a cricket pitch) for months at a time is not unexpected. Elizabeth was a strong young woman who had made her own way since childhood; undoubtedly, she would make the best of a difficult situation. However, there is no evidence that she or others were involved in prostitution. Indeed, based on Elizabeth's and the other female convicts' court records, and their later conduct in the colony, the contrary is more likely to be true.

These are important issues. A precise and honest rendition of the early history of Australian colonisation requires a balanced and critical assessment of the sources of historically relevant material.

Chapter 8

LONG HAUL TO BOTANY BAY

It was natural to indulge at this moment a melancholy reflection which obtruded itself upon the mind. The land behind us was the abode of a civilized people; that before us was the residence of savages.[1]

On 10 Nov 1787, after a four-week stay in Cape Town, Phillip gave orders that the fleet would sail the next morning for Botany Bay, provided the weather was favourable. However, it would be another two days before fair weather permitted the flotilla to safely head out of Cape Town Harbour.[2] HMS *Sirius* did not give a gun salute to the harbour officials as the fleet departed. Marine Sergeant James Scott of the *Prince of Wales* suggested this was because the livestock aboard would have been spooked by the cannon noise.[3] It was more likely that relations with the Dutch officials remained frosty and a salute may not have been reciprocated. Phillip, as a representative of the British government, was not prepared to chance such an official slight.

Foremost on the minds of all aboard would have been the long 7000 nautical mile passage ahead through treacherous uncharted waters, with no possibility for replenishing supplies in ports on the way. This was a prospect that even the most experienced sailors were apprehensive about. Moreover, they were leaving behind the known world for an unchartered strange continent. Captain Watkin Tench recorded the mixed feelings of anxiety, trepidation and excitement among those on board.

> Soon left far behind every scene of civilisation and humanised manners to explore a remote and barbarous land and plant in it those happy arts which alone constitute the pre-eminence and dignity of other countries.[4]

As the Cape disappeared from view, David Collins diarised his mood.

> When, if ever, we might again enjoy the commerce of the world, was doubtful and uncertain. The refreshments and the pleasures of which we had so liberally partaken at the Cape, were to be exchanged for coarse fare and hard labour at New South Wales. All communication with families and friends now cut off, we were leaving the world behind us, to enter on a state unknown[5]

On the first five days of the passage easterly winds impeded the ships, and a large southerly swell buffeted them with heavy waves. The hatches had to be battened down and many aboard were seasick. The heavy conditions forced the fleet off its charted route and some ships had problems keeping up with the convoy. Even at this early stage of the passage there was concern that the drinking water supplies would run out, particularly with the heavy demands of the livestock. As a precaution, the water allowance per person was reduced to three pints per day and this included water for washing.[6]

Portrait of the diarist Marine Captain Watkin Tench.

Portrait of Colonial Judge Advocate and diarist Lieutenant David Collins.

On November 19th, Commodore Phillip informed the officers that he intended to divide the flotilla into two convoys of faster and slower ships. The former would sail ahead and arrive in advance to prepare a settlement area for the disembarkation of convicts. This plan came as a complete surprise to the other officers and was particularly criticised by Major Ross and Captain Hunter who believed a larger convoy gave greater security. But, unbeknown to them, the plan had already been discussed and approved by the Home Office Secretaries Lord Sydney and Evan Nepean.

Phillip explained that having the faster ships arrive earlier provided more time to locate the best site for the settlement before a general disembarkation. He pointed out that shelters would be needed for the sick and fresh vegetables had to be grown promptly to combat the ever present scurvy on such a long journey.[7]

Phillip would lead the first division in the swift-sailing HMS

Supply, and he transferred the Flagship status from HMS *Sirius*. The first division would comprise HMS *Supply* and the three fastest transports *Alexander, Scarborough* and *Friendship*. Major Ross was transferred to the *Scarborough* and Lt. Shortland to the *Alexander* to take command of the three transports in the first division. In the event that these ships could not keep up with HMS *Supply*, Shortland was instructed to make his own way to Botany Bay. The slower division, commanded by Captain Hunter on HMS *Sirius*, comprised the three convict transports *Lady Penrhyn, Charlotte* and *Prince of Wales*, and the three store ships *Borrowdale, Fishburn* and *Golden Grove*.[8]

Pelting rain and heavy gales, a first taste of the fabled fierce winds of the *Roaring Forties*, delayed the separation of the fleet. The seas were so rough that HMS *Supply*, the lightest ship in the fleet and the swiftest in light breezes, could not keep up with the convoy. Even with its storm sails set, HMS *Supply* floundered and was almost constantly taking in water.[9] In such punishing conditions there were further concerns that dividing the fleet was a poor decision. Surgeon Smyth even suggested that Arthur Phillip had lost his mental faculties.

> Had he conceiv'd the Idea, & put it in practice at leavg. Rio de Janeiro it might have succeeded in some measure but as it was now produced it was a mere abortion of the Brain, a whim which struck him at the time as the sequel will sufficiently evince.[10]

Smyth did not know that the Home Office had recommended that the fleet be divided, and Phillip had agreed with this recommendation.

On 25 Nov 1787, when the fleet was only 250 nautical miles east of the Cape, Phillip put his plan into action. Light winds and a calm sea permitted men and equipment to be moved between ships with minimum difficulty. Phillip boarded HMS *Supply*, taking with him Lt. King and Dawes and the valuable chronometer. Additionally, several sawyers, carpenters, blacksmiths and other mechanics were shifted from different ships onto HMS *Supply*.[11]

The transfers were made without mishap, and by the close of the day HMS *Supply* and the first division ships had separated from the rest of the fleet. By daylight of the next day HMS *Sirius* and her convoy had lost sight of the first division. From this point on, each division sailed independently, Phillip ahead on HMS *Supply* with three of the transports, and Hunter with his convoy of seven ships. Hunter had decided to take advantage of the stronger westerly winds of the Roaring Forties and took a more southerly bearing. He did not have a chronometer but as a veteran sailor he was an expert at traditional celestial navigation. During the Rio and Cape legs, Hunter had logged the ship's route using his own watch and checked this against the chronometer in order to calculate the latitude independently.[12]

The route chosen by Phillip took the first division through waters only mapped by Abel Tasman and James Cook. Driven by fierce gales, the heavily laden convict transport ships in both divisions tossed and rolled in the violent and cold southern oceans. High winds screamed through the riggings; waves were often over 10 metres high, and ships plunged and ploughed through interminable icy storms. The sea conditions were fearful for veteran sailors – for the landlubber convicts it would have been an experience beyond belief. Many incurred injuries when ships were breached by waves breaking over the bows. The waves were so enormous that the sight of other ships was often lost in the troughs and water pouring over the gunnels caused serious flooding between decks. Although the water was continually bailed and pumped out of the ships, the bilge level rose, and the stink was dreadful.[13]

Every movable item aboard was fastened down to prevent injury. Seasickness among crew and convicts was the worst it had been since they left England, and in the drenching storms they were cold and wet most of the time. In their dank confinement most convicts stayed in their bunks to keep warm, but their thin clothing offered little protection to the damp Antarctic cold. Despite these extreme conditions, Surgeon Smyth on the *Lady Penrhyn*, wrote that the convicts' health remained remarkably good.[14] This was not the case, however, on Anthony's ship, the *Alexander*, where many convicts had long-term health problems. This aside, Smyth praised the Naval authorities for providing suitable facilities for the convicts.

> Few Marines going out of England upon Service were ever so amply provided for as these Convicts are, & the Surgeons & Officers of the different Ships pay such strict attention to their keeping themselves & their Births well air'd & perfectly clean …. Therefore I must again repeat, (had the Convicts been all embarked in that perfectly healthy state wh. Government meant they shd. have been, & believed were) I firmly believe very few, if any wd. have died hitherto.[15]

In such massive seas, the livestock suffered more than the humans and many of the fowls perished. The cattle became terribly distressed and were injured when thrown off their feet in the violent storms. Hunter noted that HMS *Sirius* was unsuited to carrying such cargo, and little could be done for the animals, especially as the fodder ran low. The plant stocks purchased in Rio and Cape Town were also battered in the storms. Saplings and plants broke out of their containers and were irreparably damaged.[16]

The wild weather continued throughout December. The icy Antarctic winds and pelting rain particularly affected the seamen working in the rigging. Their clothes gave little protection against such extreme conditions. The cold was often so severe they were unable to perform their duties. By mid-December, both divisions had experienced snow, hail and fog, and their progress was necessarily impeded by the frequent use of the small storm sails.

Soon, scurvy was detected among the crew and convicts. Surgeon General White, aboard the *Prince of Wales*, noted that some females showed 'evident symptoms of the scurvy, brought on by the damp and cold weather we had lately experienced'. He attempted to keep sickness under control by administering essence of malt and some good wine. Only the sick convicts were given wine as antiscorbutic medicine, and White praised the Home Office for its foresight in providing it for this purpose.[17]

By the end of December some ships had run out of firewood, and the rations were distributed cold and uncooked. On Christmas Day officers on the second division ships had a small celebration, but not those on the first. Phillip's focus was on a speedy passage to Botany Bay and in his flotilla this holy day passed unobserved. Three days later, on December 28th, the Master of the *Alexander*, Duncan Sinclair, logged that his ship was scrubbed with vinegar to make it healthy, and that once the acrid smell had gone everyone felt much better.[18]

On 3 Jan 1788, the lead ship in the first division, HMS *Supply*, sighted the southern coast of Van Diemen's Land.[19] The accompanying three transports *Alexander*, *Scarborough* and *Friendship* were only two days behind.[20] Remarkably, on January 7th the second division ships also sighted the same coastline.[21] Almost as if in a long procession, though not in sight of each other, the eleven ships rounded the southeast tip of Van Diemen's Land and bore north towards Botany Bay on the east coast of the New Holland mainland.

The seas off the coastline of New Holland were unknown to Phillip except for the charts drafted by James Cook. Initially the progress of the first division ships was inhibited by northerly winds. The following second division ships had even greater difficulties. A wild local storm with severe lighting had within 30 minutes damaged every ship except HMS *Sirius*. The *Prince of Wales* lost three sails and spars. Surgeon Smyth observed that during the storm the convict women were so terrified that many were on their knees praying.[22] They now believed that they were truly at the *Ends of the Earth*, and that this might be the end of their lives.

Phillip had hoped the first division ships would arrive in Botany Bay at least two months before the second. HMS *Supply* was ahead of the three transports in the first division, but not by much. The unfavourable weather had slowed progress and it took them another two weeks to reach their destination.[23] At last, on 18 Jan 1788, HMS *Supply* sailed into Botany Bay and at 2:15 pm dropped anchor close to the Point Solander entrance. From this anchorage other ships could easily sight them.[24]

As HMS *Supply* had sailed into the Bay, several natives were observed running along the shore, brandishing spears. Phillip needed to know if the indigenous people were hostile, and that afternoon he and some officers landed in small boats on the north side of the bay and proceeded to inspect the land they had been sent to colonise. Lt. King records his first impressions as 'Just looking at the face of the country, which is, as Mr Cook remarks, very much like the moors in England, except that there is a great deal of very good grass and some small timber-trees'. They discovered areas of dark soil and grasslands but found little fresh water.[25]

The next morning, Saturday January 19th, the officers on HMS *Supply* were 'very agreeably surprized' when first division transports under Lt. Shortland's command, the *Alexander*, *Scarborough* and *Friendship*, arrived in the Bay. By 10 am they were moored nearby. Unknown to Phillip the second division ships were not far behind. Surgeon Smyth, sailing in the second division, described the exuberant feeling aboard 'The joy everyone felt upon so long wish'd for an Event can be better conceiv'd than expressed, particularly as it was the termination of the Voyage to those who were to settle at Botany Bay'. This was a feeling that the convicts certainly would have shared.[26] Captain Watkin Tench recorded the memorable achievement in his diary.

> To us it was 'a great, an important day,' though I hope the foundation, not the fall, of an empire will be dated from it.[27]

To his astonishment, the next day, Sunday January 20th, the seven ships of the second division sailed into Botany Bay. The crews on all ships rejoiced at concluding the long journey without losing a ship or suffering major loss of life. The second division had arrived so quickly that Phillip was unable to prepare a site to land the convicts. He later wrote to Lord Sydney, that HMS *Supply* had sailed 'very badly' and had not given him the advantage he had hoped for.[28]

It was remarkable that, after a passage of 7000 nautical miles, all the ships sailing different routes had arrived within two days of each other. The voyage had been a magnificent navigational achievement. To traverse uncharted oceans, in heavily laden small wooden ships without significant losses was a tribute to the Navy, and to Arthur Phillip and John Hunter. In a number of respects it is a sailing milestone unmatched in early naval history. Lt. David Collins narrated the achievement of the voyage that had taken them eight months and one week:

> This fortunate completion of it, however, afforded even to ourselves as much matter of surprise as of general satisfaction; for in the above space of time we had sailed five thousand and twenty-one leagues; had touched at the American and African Continents; and had at last rested within a few days sail of the antipodes of our native country, without meeting any accident in a fleet of eleven sail, nine of which were merchantmen that had never before sailed in that distant and imperfectly explored ocean.[29]

Collins also observed that whereas many convicts were diseased when they embarked in Portsmouth, 'we might be deemed peculiarly fortunate' that only 32 people died on the voyage.[30] The meticulous care that Phillip had taken to planning and providing food and medical supplies for the convicts contributed to the very low death rate. Many convicts had never eaten so well before, both in quantity and quality, or had such good medical care. During the voyage 22 children were born (12 convict and 10 marine children) and 32 people died (20 male and 3 female convicts), not including crew.[31] Eventually 1430 people disembarked: 542 male and 187 female convicts and 21 convict children. The true numbers may have been even higher because of uncertain crew counts.[32] Approximately 1500 personnel reached the shores of New South Wales aboard the First Fleet with a mortality rate on the entire voyage of about 2%.

Anthony Rope and Elizabeth Pulley were among the 729 convicts who had arrived safe and sound in a new country, and presumably were looking forward to starting a new life. From their ships' decks they could see on shore strange vegetation and wildlife. After eight months at sea – they had not been ashore during this time – they would have been desperate to stand on *terra firma*. The female convicts would have to be patient; they would not feel the sand between their toes for another three weeks.

Phillip had carried out a preliminary inspection of the Botany Bay shoreline, but a more comprehensive survey was needed. On January 20th, he and Captain Hunter were rowed to the south shore to assess its suitability for a settlement. Hunter records that they found little fresh water and no land suitable for intense cultivation.[33] In light of Sir Joseph Banks' recommendations, this was a major disappointment. However, James Cook's logs had mentioned another anchorage, Port Jackson, just north of Botany Bay, and Phillip decided that this would need to be explored before a decision could be made on the best settlement site.

LONG HAUL TO BOTANY BAY

A 1937 oil painting of the First Fleet arriving in Sydney Cove in 1788.

On January 22nd, Phillip, Hunter and a party of marines sailed in a small cutter out of Botany Bay, heading north along the coast to the entrance of Port Jackson in the hope it would provide a better harbour, and an area more suitable for a settlement. In case Port Jackson proved unattractive, Phillip ordered the land near Point Sutherland on Botany Bay to be cleared for a permanent landing. Under Ross's command, convicts from the *Alexander* and *Scarborough* were landed on the south side of the bay to clear land and cut grass for animal fodder.[34]

Phillip had little idea what to expect in Port Jackson; the report in Cook's 18-year-old log was brief. He was in for a pleasant surprise. When the cutter sailed through the narrow entrance to Port Jackson, on the afternoon of 22 Jan 1788, the sight was magnificent. They saw a large deep-water harbour surrounded by plentiful woodlands – it is a vista that still delights experienced travellers arriving in the harbour today. Phillip effused in his report that he 'had the satisfaction to find one of the finest harbours in the world, in which a thousand sail of the line might ride in perfect security'.[35] For two days, Phillip and Hunter explored the shore and saw several places that were well suited for settlement. Hunter recorded that the country was 'found greatly superior in every respect to that round Botany-bay'.[36]

They returned to the fleet on the evening of January 23rd, full of praise for the excellence of the harbour waters and the suitability of the shoreline for a settlement. The next morning Phillip gave orders for all ships to be prepared to sail immediately for Port Jackson. To their great astonishment, just as they were to weigh anchor, two ships flying French colours appeared at the entrance of Botany Bay.[37] The French ships *La Boussole* and *L'Astrolabe*, under the command of Captain de Lapérouse, were on a voyage of scientific discovery in the southern hemisphere. They had been prevented from entering the bay even earlier by heavy winds and strong currents.

France and Britain were no longer at war, but the competition to possess and control new lands for their empires continued unabated. Soon after the First Fleet had left England, de Lapérouse had been told of the Botany Bay expedition and was ordered to investigate where it went. Phillip was suspicious of the French presence in the area, and Paris naval archives show that he was justified.[38] He decided to ignore the usual exchange of courtesies with the French officers and sail to Port Jackson immediately to claim possession of this strategically important harbour.[39] Phillip may also have been reluctant to meet the French because of his involvement in intelligence-gathering activities in France; he was unsure just how widely this was known. Historian Alan Frost suggests that Phillip's failure to meet the French 'may reflect some fear that he might be known as a spy'.[40]

On January 25th, the entire First Fleet flotilla weighed anchor and attempted to sail through the bay entrance into the open ocean. The wind conditions were adverse, making it dangerous for the larger ships to traverse the narrow entrance and they were compelled to drop anchor. In the strong winds, only the nimble HMS *Supply* was able to pass through the entrance safely. Aboard HMS *Supply* Commodore Arthur Phillip proceeded to Port Jackson at full speed, leaving John Hunter to bring the rest of the fleet when weather conditions permitted.[41]

The possibility that the French knew of Port Jackson would have been a particular concern for Phillip, and he made sure that the British flag was officially unfurled on the harbour shore early the next day.

Chapter 9

A Colony at Sydney Cove

The behaviour of all classes of these people since our arrival in the settlement has been better than could, I think, have been expected from them.[1]

During their initial exploration of Port Jackson, Arthur Phillip and John Hunter had found a site for a new settlement much superior to that at Botany Bay. It was in a small cove on the southern shore of the harbour near a freshwater stream. On the morning of 26 Jan 1788, HMS *Supply* dropped anchor close to the cove and disembarked some convicts and marine guards to clear land near the water source. Soon after the British flag was raised, Governor Phillip took formal possession of the colony in New South Wales on behalf of King George III. The accompanying marines fired a *feu de joie* and gave three cheers. Phillip named the site *Sydney Cove* in honour of the Home Office Secretary, Lord Sydney.[2] It is interesting to note that when Thomas Townshend was offered the peerage, he considered the title Lord Sydenham. His decision to become Lord Sydney was fortunate for the later naming of Australia's largest city; *Sydney* has a distinctly better ring to it than *Sydenham*.

This formal declaration of a new British colony at Sydney Cove took place on the day after the two French ships had entered Botany Bay further south. Still anchored in the bay, John Hunter made a perfunctory courtesy visit to the French captains on January 26th, and then signalled the fleet to weigh anchor and set sail for Port Jackson. However, their departure was reminiscent of the earlier attempt, and the strong winds hampered the passage of the transports through the bay channel. The *Charlotte* was blown off course close to rocks, and the *Friendship* and *Prince of Wales* collided, both sustaining damage to their sails. Later, the *Charlotte* crashed into the *Friendship,* and the *Lady Penrhyn* nearly ran aground.[3] With crashing and banging and shouting resonating through the ships, the convicts below were probably scared stiff. Many would have thought they were about to be drowned within sight of their final destination. Although the shoreline was within view, scarcely any convicts would have survived if the ship sank, as few could swim.

After a flurry of mishaps and embarrassing manoeuvres, in full view of the amused French, all ships cleared the bay entrance and sailed north. At sunset they were safely moored off Sydney Cove in Port Jackson. That evening, Phillip mustered a party of officers on shore, where they repeated the flag raising ceremony and toasted King George and the success of the new colony.[4]

A 1937 painting showing Governor Phillip declaring the establishment of a British colony in New South Wales on 26 Jan 1788.

On the following day, the establishment of the new settlement began in earnest, and over the next week, men progressively disembarked and were assigned to clear land, construct storehouses and unload stores. One can imagine the exhilaration of the convicts when they stepped onto solid ground for the first time in many months. For those who had been imprisoned on hulks, perhaps it was after many years on water. The frenetic activity of a thousand sailors, marines and convicts spelt the end of a tranquil bush setting at Sydney Cove that for the indigenous people had existed for eons. The peaceful shoreline was transformed into a noisy, smoky, bustling camp. David Collins noted:

> the spot which had so lately been the abode of silence and tranquillity was now changed to that of noise, clamour, and confusion: but after a time order gradually prevailed every where. As the woods were opened and the ground cleared, the various encampments were extended, and all wore the appearance of regularity.[5]

A timber-framed canvas house brought from England was quickly erected on the eastern side of the cove and became the governor's temporary residence. It was located close to both the officers' tents and the majority of the convict huts that would later be constructed. Accommodation for the marine guards, male convicts, and the hospital were set up at the western side of the cove.[6] By the end of the first day, a number of tents had been erected, and some convicts and guards spent their first night ashore in the colony. In subsequent days the few livestock that had survived the rough voyage were unloaded to the east of the cove.

Within a week sufficient progress had been made erecting tents and huts that Phillip decided to disembark the female convicts from the transports *Prince of Wales*, *Charlotte* and *Lady Penrhyn*. On February 5th, the naval agent Lt. Shortland boarded the transports and issued new clothing to the women and children.[7] The next morning the female convicts, dressed in their new slops, were transferred by long boat to the shore. Elizabeth Pulley stepped onto solid ground for the first time in more than a year. It was a truly emotional occasion for the female convicts, whose elation was probably tempered by the uncertainty of what lay ahead. Most would have become accustomed to the shipboard regime, and, hard as it was, it was familiar and predictable. Surgeon Smyth witnessed the disembarkation:

> At 5 o'Clock this morng. all things were got in order for landing the whole of the women & 3 of the Ships Long Boats came alongside us to receive them ... abt. 6 O'Clock p.m. we had the long wish'd for pleasure of seeing the last of them leave the Ship - They were dress'd in general very clean & some few amongst them might be sd. to be well dress'd.[8]

However, the initial euphoria of landing was soon to be dampened by Sydney's fickle summer weather. Within an hour of the women coming ashore and being taken to their tents, a violent and prolonged storm struck the settlement area. Amid the thunder, lightning and heavy rain that raged for hours, a large tree in the middle of the camp was split open, killing some of the sheep and hogs penned beneath.[9]

Paradoxically that first stormy night ashore for the females, February 6th, has been depicted in some early historical narratives as *a drunken orgy*. There is little evidence to support this description. There is no doubt that some males welcomed the females ashore, presumably, while the marine guards were sheltering in their tents from the storm. Whether these were convicts, marines or seamen, or some of each, is not known. A gathering took place and little else is reliably recorded. Surgeon Smyth, safe aboard the *Lady Penrhyn* in the harbour, later wrote about the female convicts on their first stormy night ashore:

> The Men Convicts got to them very soon after they landed, & it is beyond my abilities to give a just description of the Scene of

> Debauchery & Riot that ensued during the night. .... The Scene wh. presented itself at this time & during the greater part of the night, beggars every description; some swearing, others quarrelling others singing, not in the least regarding the Tempest, tho' so violent that the thunder shook the Ship exceeded anything I ever before had a conception of.[10]

Since Smyth was on his ship in the harbour, his account must have been second-hand scuttlebutt and is likely to be highly exaggerated. Nevertheless, some modern-day descriptions of this party, based on his diary entry, refer to it as *a drunken orgy with convict couples rolling around in Sydney Cove's red mud.* Such accounts are bogus as there is no evidence of such behaviour, and no red mud exists anywhere near the cove. Moreover, the convict men had no access to alcohol. There were drunken sailors aboard Surgeon Smyth's ship because they had been given extra grog to celebrate the offloading of the convicts. Significantly, no other diarist, except the remotely located Smyth, mentions bad behaviour that night. If anything as licentious as this had happened in the settlement, Ralph Clark would have recorded it. Clark's diary entry on February 7th, details the storm and the farm animals 'Kild six Sheep 2 Labms and one Pigg belonging to Major Ross' but there is no mention of female misdemeanours on that day, or for several days thereafter.[11]

Historian Grace Karskens, writing about the night of February 6th, claims 'the orgy never happened' and debunks the orgy myth:

> ... it turns out that the orgy story dates, not from 1788, but from 1963, when the historian Manning Clark included it as 'a drunken spree' fuelled by 'extra rations of rum' in his *Short History of Australia*. After he re-read the sources properly, he quickly recanted. But it was too late, the story was out. ...... And with every retelling it just got raunchier. Robert Hughes was the originator of the modern version of the legend, for in *The Fatal Shore* (1987) he sites the action in the Rocks, with the lightning of a ferocious Sydney storm revealing couples bestially 'rutting' in the 'red clay' (there is no red clay in Sydney Cove). And in Hughes's version the sex wasn't consensual: 'the women floundered to and fro, draggled as muddy chickens under a pump, pursued by male convicts intent on raping them'.[12]

Karskens points out that the Zoologist Tim Flannery retells the orgy myth in his book *The Birth of Sydney* and Peter FitzSimons gives it another spin in the *Sydney Magazine* in 2005. Many histories of Sydney and early colonial Australia routinely include the orgy story. It has even been re-enacted for television as the documentary drama *The Floating Brothel*, and as a collection of comically shaking tents at the Botanic Gardens in *Tony Robertson Explores Australia*.[13]

The "foundational orgy" claim has no credibility, and it is absurdly unjust to label women as promiscuous sluts and men as rapists, when there is no written evidence of non-consensual sex.[14] Only one aspect of that stormy night is certain: those who met up were celebrating their first taste of freedom in months and had probably sought out each other's company. This would have been a natural thing to do. It is demeaning and absurdly high-handed to assume that the convicts were disrespectful of each other, or that they were unaware of social norms.

The female disembarkation was an important occasion for the new settlement, and it is apparent that Phillip avoided interfering in the females' newfound freedom; he understood how important this moment was to them. A somewhat philosophical Watkin Tench pondered in his diary after the female landing (his diary entry is not dated) on the future mixing of the genders in the settlement.

> While they were on board ship the two sexes had been kept most rigorously apart, but when landed their separation became impracticable, and would have been, perhaps, wrong. Licentiousness was the unavoidable consequence, and their old habits of depravity were beginning to recur. What was to be attempted? To prevent their intercourse was impossible, and to palliate its evils only remained. Marriage was recommended, and such advantages held out to those who aimed at reformation, as have greatly contributed to the tranquillity of the settlement.[15]

Tench was a fair person and his phrase 'their old habits of depravity' reflects the social schism that existed between the gentry and convicts. In keeping with the class prejudices of the time, many officers believed the lower classes devoid of common decency and respect. Such attitudes are also reflected in Surgeon Smyth's earlier comments. The hypocrisy of this was the well-known dalliances of the Royal heirs, the Prince of Wales and the Duke of Clarence. This was tolerated by "decent society" while the commoners were accused of depravity for relatively petty moral digressions. It was another example of one standard applying for the privileged and another for the rest.

Although precise details of what happened that first night ashore may never be known, the landing of the female convicts was a pivotal moment for Anthony Rope and Elizabeth Pulley. As far as it can be ascertained, this was the first time they had met. We do not know the circumstances of their meeting but is likely they recognised each other's Norfolk accent; a familiar voice from a distant place. Whatever the reason — loneliness or lust — they were attracted to each other and became partners. They never separated after that night, and their union was later formalised with a church marriage.

The morning after the female convict landing, on February 7th, Phillip proclaimed his commission to establish and to govern a new British colony before the entire assembled settlement.[16] At a military parade, the marines saluted the governor with their colours and fired a volley of musket fire, all accompanied by music from the marine band. The convicts sat on the ground as spectators and were encircled by guards. The formal dedication of the colony began with the Judge Advocate, Lt. David Collins, reading Governor Phillip's commission.[17] This was followed by a speech in which Phillip promised good treatment to deserving convicts.

> By the leniency of the laws, they were now so placed that, by industry and good behaviour, they might in time regain the advantages and estimation in society of which they had deprived themselves. They not only had every encouragement to make that effort, but were removed almost entirely from every temptation to guilt. There was little in this infant community which one man could plunder from another, and any dishonest attempts in so small a society would almost infallibly be discovered. To persons detected in such crimes, he could not promise mercy; nor indeed to any who, under their circumstances, should presume to offend against the peace and good order of the settlement.[18]

Phillip told the convicts and marines that he was prepared to forgive crimes committed on the voyage and since their arrival, but in the future bad behaviour would incur the full force of the law and good conduct would be rewarded. He then warned them that the stealing of livestock would be punishable by death, as it threatened the colony's very survival. Phillip also voiced his concern that only 200 out of 600 male convicts had worked in the past few days and that in this colony 'the industrious should not labour for the idle'. He stipulated that those who did not work would not eat, or verbatim, 'for the good Men, he promised, should not be Slaves for the Bad, their daily Labour should be much easier, on account of the Warmth of the Climate than the Common Labourer's in England, but that, they should perform, or Starve'.[19]

The governor warned the assembled convicts that unsanctioned intercourse between the sexes was an offence, as it encouraged a recklessness of manners that was damaging to society. If men attempted to enter the women's tents at night, the guards would fire upon them. However, legal marriages were encouraged, and newly-weds would get every assistance.

Phillip concluded his address by declaring an 'earnest desire to promote the happiness of all who were under his government, and to render the settlement in New South Wales advantageous and honourable to his country'. He told them to 'make the Day of their Transportation to this Place, the happiest Day they had ever seen', and declared the remainder of the day free of labour. Surgeon Worgan felt that Phillip's speech reflected his deep humanity but thought it wasted on 'reprobates' who would certainly try to take advantage of his kindness.[20]

How did the convicts react to Phillip's speech? Most would have given him a fair hearing because they respected him for his humane treatment and impartial justice during the voyage. Presumably Elizabeth and Anthony were just starting to grasp their new freedoms in the settlement – was Phillip promising much more, and were these really available to them? One would hope that Elizabeth appreciated that this was the first time that she had been offered the opportunity for a secure future. In England she had been treated badly, and the justice system had dealt with her harshly. She may have wondered whether the life Phillip offered was really open to her – it seemed almost too good to be true. Such thoughts would have raced through many of the convicts' minds. Elizabeth probably decided, there and then, to accept Phillip's promises at face value, and it can be justifiably claimed that she never looked back. Despite a court appearance following her marriage to Anthony – which ended in an acquittal – she never again fronted the judiciary. Phillip's better life in this new land had to be grabbed with both hands. Most female convicts would have thought the same, and few offended again.

What did Phillip's promises mean to the male convicts? Anthony Rope had led a hard, punishing life in England. The meritocratic rules that Phillip announced offered opportunities based on ability and hard work, rather than on social status. One may gauge from his subsequent behaviour that Anthony resolved to try and keep clear of the law. Court records show that he was not always successful, but his future misdemeanours were all relatively minor. The same record of endeavour and hard work applies to almost all of the First Fleet convicts.

Phillip's urging that couples marry was well understood. At the church service on Sunday February 10th, the second in the history of the colony, Reverend Johnson married five couples. Henry Kable and Susannah Holmes were among them.[21] The only sour note of this happy occasion was the diary entry of Lt. Ralph Clark. He questioned the motives of the newly-weds and accused some to 'have left wives and families at home'.[22]

The governor was true to his word about punishing men who entered the women's tents without authorisation. Several males were sentenced to 150 lashes for this offence, and a marine received 200 lashes for striking a female convict who refused to go into the woods with him. Clark continued his hostility towards female convicts by writing 'what a Seen of Whordome is going on there in the womans camp'. When three of his men were caught entering the female tents, he wrote 'going to these d[amned] B[itches] of convict women they will bring our men into manny Such Troubles'.[23] Apart from Clark's diatribe, the claim of rampant sexual behaviour among female convicts has little basis in fact. Official records show that incursions into the female tents were rare. At the end of February 1788, Watkin Tench diarised 'nothing of a very atrocious nature had happened' in the settlement.[24] Tench was a reliable chronicler of the colonial life, and he would have recorded any adverse sexual behaviour if it were conspicuous.

A government farm was quickly established on the high ground of Sydney Cove. Today it is the Sydney Royal Botanic Garden. Fresh vegetables and fruit were urgently needed, and the seeds, plants and trees purchased in Rio and the Cape were immediately planted. Phillip's personal servant, Henry Dodd, who had worked on his Lyndhurst estate in England, was put in charge of the farm. Growing fresh vegetables was a priority to combat scurvy, and although Phillip was fully aware of the seasonal differences in the southern hemisphere, the seeds were planted in mid-summer. But he saw no alternative – fresh greens were needed as quickly as possible. The vegetable seeds germinated, but the young plants soon withered in the summer heat. In any case the sandy soil at the cove was not fertile and there was no animal manure to enrich it. Fortunately Phillip and others had farming experience, and quickly ordered new crops to be sown at different localities around the settlement; on the hospital grounds, at Garden Island, and in large plots assigned to officers and marines close to the brickfields. Within a few months fresh vegetables were raised, but they were insufficient for the settlement's needs.

Finding local timber for housing was another problem for the colony. There was an abundance of large eucalypts encircling the cove but using them to construct wooden buildings proved very difficult. Unlike most European trees, eucalypts are exceedingly hard. Felling the large trees and sawing them into planks required much more effort than the tree-fellers and carpenters were used to. Furthermore, the tools brought from England were unsuitable for the tough timber, and the sawn planks warped and split as they dried out. When a large eucalyptus tree was felled, it would take several men three to four days to hew the timber planks and to remove the massive root system.[25]

Most of the terrain around Sydney Cove was rocky, with relatively shallow sandy soil, while the much-needed grain crops required deep fertile soils. If the settlement was to become self-sufficient, it was an absolute priority to find and establish better agricultural farmland. In early March, Phillip and other officers explored the upper reaches of rivers flowing into Port Jackson and discovered several areas with better soil and fewer trees. It was decided that these would be settled and cultivated in the following spring.[26]

A convict muster in February revealed that nine convicts had escaped from a work gang into the bush. They apparently trekked some 12 km south to Botany Bay and requested the French to take them on board their ships. The French had wisely declined. A few of the convicts survived the return trip, but the rest starved or were killed by Aborigines. David Collins noted that the escapes occurred when the overseer of the work-gang was a convict.[27] Marine guards often refused to act as overseers, stating that they were soldiers not supervisors. Phillip complained to Lord Sydney that many marine officers 'have declined any interference with the convicts, except when they are employed for their own particular service'. He wanted the marines to help with convict supervision, but Major Ross refused to let them do more than their duty as a soldier.[28] This was the first serious disagreement between Arthur Phillip and Robert Ross. Many more disputes were to come.

In February, dysentery and scurvy broke out in the settlement and several people died. Fortunately, Surgeon White, with the help of some enterprising convicts, had discovered that local native plants were high in Vitamin C and thus remedies for scurvy, and these were used to supplement the ration of salted meat. Even with these local cures, Surgeon Smyth reported that up to 100 patients remained in his care.[29]

The reluctance of marines to manage working gangs meant that trustworthy convicts were often put in charge. They were rewarded for this responsibility however it was far from popular because these convicts were treated as pariahs, and their orders were often ignored. Henry Kable, an acquaintance of Elizabeth at Norwich Castle prison, became a supervisor of female convicts. As his female charges had no official duties, this was a cushy job, and he relaxed while his convict mates laboured clearing land and building roads and huts. At this time Anthony Rope was working at the brickfields hauling material and loading the kiln. This was especially exhausting work.

Many of the road building and construction projects in the rapidly expanding colony required strenuous convict labour, but they were poorly managed. The government administration allocated work with little regard to convict skills. Phillip soon realised this was inefficient and ordered convicts be assigned jobs according to their abilities, as was the practice in English dockyards. Importantly, once convicts had finished their assigned labour, they were permitted to work for themselves. David Collins approved of the incentive of 'allotting a certain quantity of ground to be cleared by a certain number of persons in a given time, and allowing them to employ what time they may gain, till called on again for public service, in bringing in materials and erecting huts for themselves'.[30] The strengths and skills of convicts varied enormously – rural convicts were usually better labourers, while those from the urban areas fared better at the more technical tasks, especially if they could read and write.

All through this period the production of more food remained the core priority. But vegetable harvests from government farms were meagre and unreliable, and fresh food remained scarce. There was also a serious shortage of fresh meat, as few of the farm animals had survived the voyage and most were needed for breeding. Of those, lightning strikes had killed some, and the dingoes, convicts and Aborigines accounted for others. Contributing to the shortage, officers continued to slaughter their own stock for meat, without regard to husbandry needs.

On 11 Feb 1788, when the colony was two weeks old, the first criminal court was convened under the auspices of Judge Advocate David Collins. It comprised six officers or officials and included Reverend Johnson. To Phillip's annoyance and to Ross's delight, many marine officers refused court duty as it was 'thought a hardship by the officers, and of which they say they were not informed before they left England'.[31] The colony's court proceedings differed significantly from those in England because the governor had the authority to amend the punishments, he considered too harsh or too lenient. At the end of February, the criminal court passed judgement on four convicts who had robbed the government store. Stealing provisions was a very serious crime in the colony and the offenders were sentenced to death.[32] One of the men was hanged and the governor pardoned the other two just before their hanging. The stay of execution was granted after Phillip had received a petition from convicts begging that the men be spared. Phillip sympathised with the plea and the two men were banished to Bare Island in Botany Bay, as a temporary gaol until they could be sent elsewhere. The fourth offender was sentenced to 300 lashes but was later pardoned. The next day, Phillip pardoned another convict who had been sentenced to hanging. James Freeman was pardoned on the condition that he would become the colony's first public executor.[33] During the period 1788 to 1792, he performed 22 hangings of marines, sailors and convicts.

Marine officers were outraged at the governor's intervention in court proceedings, since, under military law, soldiers were liable to harsher sentences than civilians for the same crime.[34] Aggravating this apparent inequity was that marine privates usually came from the same social class as convicts, and military law was applied without remission or appeal. The marines saw the lighter civil sentences as a diminution of their status in the settlement and maintained that they deserved better treatment in courts than the convicts who they were guarding.

Among the Home Office instructions given to Phillip was the directive that Norfolk Island be settled as soon as possible. He instructed Lt. King to set up a farm on the island. On February 14th, HMS *Supply*, commanded by Lt. Henry Ball, sailed to Norfolk Island with nine male and six female convicts, some seamen, a surgeon assistant, and the newly appointed Commandant King.[35] After unloading the personnel and six-months supplies, HMS *Supply* returned to Sydney Cove, arriving back on March 19th. Lt. King would remain on Norfolk Island for two years supervising the cultivation of crops.[36]

Later in March, HMS *Supply* sailed for Lord Howe Island, which had been charted by Lt. Ball while returning from Norfolk Island. Sydney Cove was desperately in need of fresh meat to combat scurvy, and they planned to catch turtles that had been seen by Ball on the island. But the trip proved fruitless. They returned to Sydney Cove in late May after discovering that the turtles, previously seen in great numbers laying their eggs, were now all at sea. Scurvy was so bad in the settlement that nearly 200 people were unable to work.[37]

Within the government circles the competence of the governor was also being questioned. Marine Captain Campbell and Marine Major Ross, in particular, criticised Phillip's governance and court interference. They claimed the colony could not survive under such autocratic management. Campbell complained to his benefactor Lord Ducie in England that Phillip did not consult anyone on his plans for the colony.[38] Major Ross fully agreed, and in a letter to Under Secretary Nepean he complained that Phillip never consulted with him, or anyone else, on the intentions of the government. In addition, Ross claimed he was not treated in accordance with his commission as Lieutenant Governor.[39]

It was not long before the naval and marine officers started quarrelling. The hostility escalated when a court martial sentenced a marine private to either make a public apology or receive 100 lashes. Ross was outraged that a prisoner be allowed to choose his own punishment, so he sent the case back to the court martial, insisting that only one sentence be issued. The marine court of five officers, which included Marine Captain Tench, refused to review the sentence on the grounds that it was improper to alter the first decision. Major Ross promptly placed them all under arrest. When Governor Phillip was informed of the matter, he overturned Ross' order on the grounds that the colony had insufficient officers and needed all of them to be on duty.

Phillip then referred the matter by letter to the Royal Marine Headquarters in England. The delay that such a communication entailed gave Phillip a welcome two-year respite in which Captain Tench and the other officers resumed their normal duties.[40]

The colony's first official buildings, the hospital, storehouses and barracks had been constructed quickly from timber planks and shingles. But the governor had higher aspirations for official buildings, and he wanted them to be brick. As part of his advance planning for the settlement, Phillip had brought 10,000 bricks and 12 brick moulds from England as ballast on several of the ships.[41] Regrettably, the first houses built from these bricks were unsafe owing to poor mortar and did not survive heavy rainstorms.

Native clays suitable for making good bricks had been discovered inland from Sydney Cove. High quality sandstone was also close by, but initially there was no chalk or limestone for making mortar.[42] In mid-February, James Bloodworth, a London bricklayer, was put in charge of the colony's first brickworks at which hand-moulded bricks were being made. He supervised the convicts at Brickfield Hill, 1.6 km southwest of the camp, at the head of Long Cove (now Darling Harbour). On February 28th, Surgeon George Worgan recorded the activities on the colony's first brickfield:

> We have discovered a Soil in many Parts of the Country excellently adapted for making Bricks, and a Brick-Ground is already prepared, where 8 or 10 Convicts of the Trade are employed, and they say the Bricks are as good as those made in England.[43]

By that time Anthony Rope had joined the brickmaking gang responsible for carting brick materials, digging out kilns and firing bricks. It was backbreaking work. Limestone required for making brick lime had not yet been found close to the settlement, and a low-grade lime had to be made from oyster shells. Female convicts collected the shells from middens left by Aborigines on the adjacent beaches. These were crushed and burned to produce a lime substitute. But the poor quality of this lime meant that the governor's new brick residence, which started in May, needed extra thick walls, and took a year to complete.[44]

It is likely that Elizabeth Pulley was one of the female convicts employed in collecting shells for lime production, or making clay pegs to pin roof tiles, or sewing and mending uniforms for the officers and marines. Females were considered physically weaker than men and were not required to do construction jobs or work in the fields.[45]

In April 1788, Judge Advocate David Collins recorded the incidence of crime in the colony. There was some stealing, but he observed that convicts 'conducted themselves with more propriety than could have been expected from people of their description'.[46] Tench was also impressed by the demeanour and attitude of convicts.[47] Because of the lack of fresh greens and meat, and the rations being insufficient for those doing hard labour, the crimes mostly involved stealing food. Some convicts stole from others' provisions or gardens, and occasionally government stores were burgled, or stock killed.[48] This pilfering led to the establishment of a secure garden on Garden Island in the harbour, a mile from the cove.

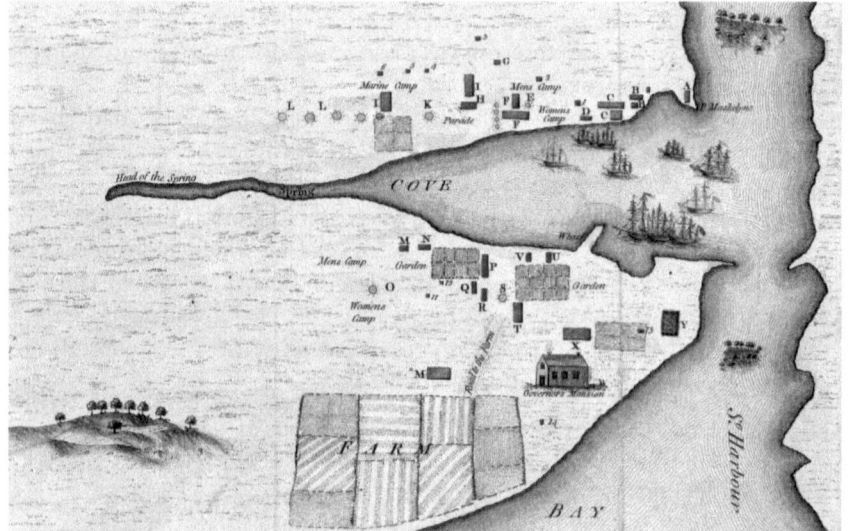

Sketch and description of the Sydney Cove settlement at Port Jackson made by convict Francis Fowkes on 16 Apr 1788.

The First Fleet ships were scheduled to return to England, and during April they were refitted for the voyage. Their imminent departure led to concerns in the colony that the struggling settlement would be isolated and abandoned. The returning ships were to take dispatches and reports to the Home Office, and convicts, crew and marines were also sending letters back to family and friends. Phillip knew that among these communications would be complaints about his governance from Major Ross and Captain Campbell.

A large number of convicts, especially those with wives and families, cherished the desire to return to England once their sentences had expired. However, they were unaware that the government had no intention of allowing emancipated convicts to leave easily and would not help them financially. Convicts had little money and their only chance of a return voyage was to become a sailor on one of the ships, which made it impossible for females and their children to accompany them. The departing ships created other difficulties. Some of the sailors had fathered children with female convicts, and their departure distressed the mothers who were now left as the sole breadwinners. Other women were upset because they would no longer receive a regular supply of tea and clothing from the sailors.[49]

The approaching winter was an incentive for the governor to build more substantial buildings, however, the settlement had only twelve trained carpenters. There were others on the ships, but they were busy refitting them for the return voyage. For Phillip's building projects to advance quickly he needed to find more skilled hands to speed up construction. The tenacious eucalyptus hardwood was slowing down building schedules, and most carpenters now preferred to work with the local cabbage tree because this pliable timber enabled much faster construction however, it was only really suitable for temporary shelters. The first huts were built in the style of those in rural England; one-roomed, timber framed wattle-and-daub walls and plastered with clay on the outside. The roof was thatched with reeds or grass. There was no glass, so a wattle stick lattice was used for windows.

In late April, Elizabeth and Anthony realised a baby was on the way, and they planned to get married as soon as they could. The usual practice in rural England was that couples wed when they had a place to live in. Anthony requested and received permission to build a hut, and his friend from the *Alexander,* James Price, had agreed to help. Wooden thatched-roofed huts in the colony usually took two men several weeks to build. Anthony was required to work on convict projects from 7am to 3pm each weekday and until 12noon on Saturdays, but outside those times he was allowed to work for himself. It is not known if he built his hut as part of ongoing government building projects or did the work in his free time; perhaps a combination of both. In any case, it would have been arduous. He and James laboured as convicts in the brickfields, and they would have been totally exhausted at the end of a day.

Anthony's hut was to be sited within the colony's convict encampment, so that Elizabeth could attend the women's camp for her work. Its precise location is unknown, but it was probably among the three rows of convict huts built on the east side of the cove, close to the governor's temporary house and new brick residence. Anthony worked hard and managed to finish his hut before most officers had moved into permanent housing. By late June, only four officers resided in huts; the others were still housed in tents.[50] Collins wryly noted that these huts 'formed a very good hovel' and 'were slight and temporary'. The huts were flimsy and, since the thatched roofs dried out quickly in the fierce sun, they often caught fire. The first huts were built with a fireplace which proved a serious fire risk, and in July, the middle of winter, an order was given banning fireplaces in thatched huts. Heavy rain also played havoc with the thatched wooded huts; the clay walls were regularly washed away in storms.[51] Nevertheless, simple as they were, the huts were considerably more comfortable than tents.

In early May 1788, the *Scarborough*, *Lady Penrhyn* and *Charlotte* were the first ships to depart the settlement. They planned to sail to China to load a cargo of tea for the East India Company and then return to England.[52] The cove residents watched the ships depart with remorse. Seeing them sail through the Heads heightened their sense of isolation and vulnerability. It also reminded many that individually they had little chance of seeing England again.

Surgeon Smyth was on board the *Lady Penrhyn* and, early in the journey, many seamen suffered badly from scurvy. The departing ships had little fresh food because of shortages in the colony. When they arrived in China, the crew had to be given extra shore leave to recover. The *Charlotte* and *Scarborough* did not arrive back in England until June 1789 and the *Lady Penryhn* in August 1789. They had been away for more than two years.

In mid-July 1788, the First Fleet ships *Prince of Wales*, *Friendship*, *Alexander* and *Borrowdale* departed Port Jackson under the command of Lt. Shortland.[53] It was assumed that they would sail to England as a convoy, making regular port calls to procure fresh fruit and vegetables. However, their plans went badly awry. Soon after leaving the colony, the ships encountered heavy seas and the convoy was separated. The *Prince of Wales* and the *Borrowdale* sailed together on a different route from the other ships, and the crews were soon affected by scurvy. The Captain of the *Borrowdale* and four sailors died; others were so ill they disembarked in Rio, and a new crew recruited. The two ships finally reached England in March 1789, before the *Charlotte*, *Scarborough* and *Lady Penryhn*, bringing with them the first despatches and reports from Phillip.

After the separation of the convoy, the *Alexander* and *Friendship*, the same ships that had transported Anthony and Elizabeth on the outward journey, met with disaster. When the ships failed to procure enough fresh provisions *en route*, crew members aboard became seriously ill. By the time they reached Borneo, 17 of the *Alexander* crew had died, leaving only enough sailors on the two ships able to sail one vessel; the unfortunate *Friendship* was scuttled in the Straits of Makassar. When the *Alexander* reached Batavia (Jakarta) the crew was so sick that only one man was able to go aloft, and seamen from other ships were needed to help set their sails.[54] A new crew recruited in Batavia enabled the *Alexander* to reach Cape Town. Its arrival coincided with that of HMS *Sirius*, which had left Sydney Cove three months after the *Alexander* and had already been in Cape Town for six weeks, purchasing vital provisions for the colony. By then the commander of HMS *Sirius*, Captain John Hunter, had already heard about the loss of the *Friendship*. The *Alexander* eventually reached England in May 1789. Hunter informed Phillip of the fate of the returning First Fleet ships some months later, when he returned to Sydney Cove.

One of Governor Phillip's keen interests was town planning. Not surprisingly, he favoured Georgian style buildings, which were in vogue across the George III's British Empire. The colony had a trained surveyor, Augustus Alt, but no architect. James Bloodworth, the brickfield supervisor, and the only convict with building experience, was assigned to design and build an imposing two-story, Georgian style, Government House. On May 15th the foundation stone for the house was laid on a prominent site overlooking the cove.[55] Today, its location is at the corner of Bridge and Phillip Streets, and the current Museum of Sydney has been built on and around its preserved foundations. The site is only 200 m from the water's edge at Sydney's bustling Circular Quay.

By July, Governor Phillip had prepared comprehensive plans for the future town at Sydney Cove. These led Watkin Tench to remark that the 'Extent of empire demands grandeur of design'.[56] The plans included a 200 ft (61 m) wide triumphal avenue running northeast towards the harbour entrance.[57] Unfortunately, Phillip's tenure in the colony was not long enough to see his plans for Sydney fulfilled, and subsequent building developments along the Tank Stream proved too difficult to later reverse.

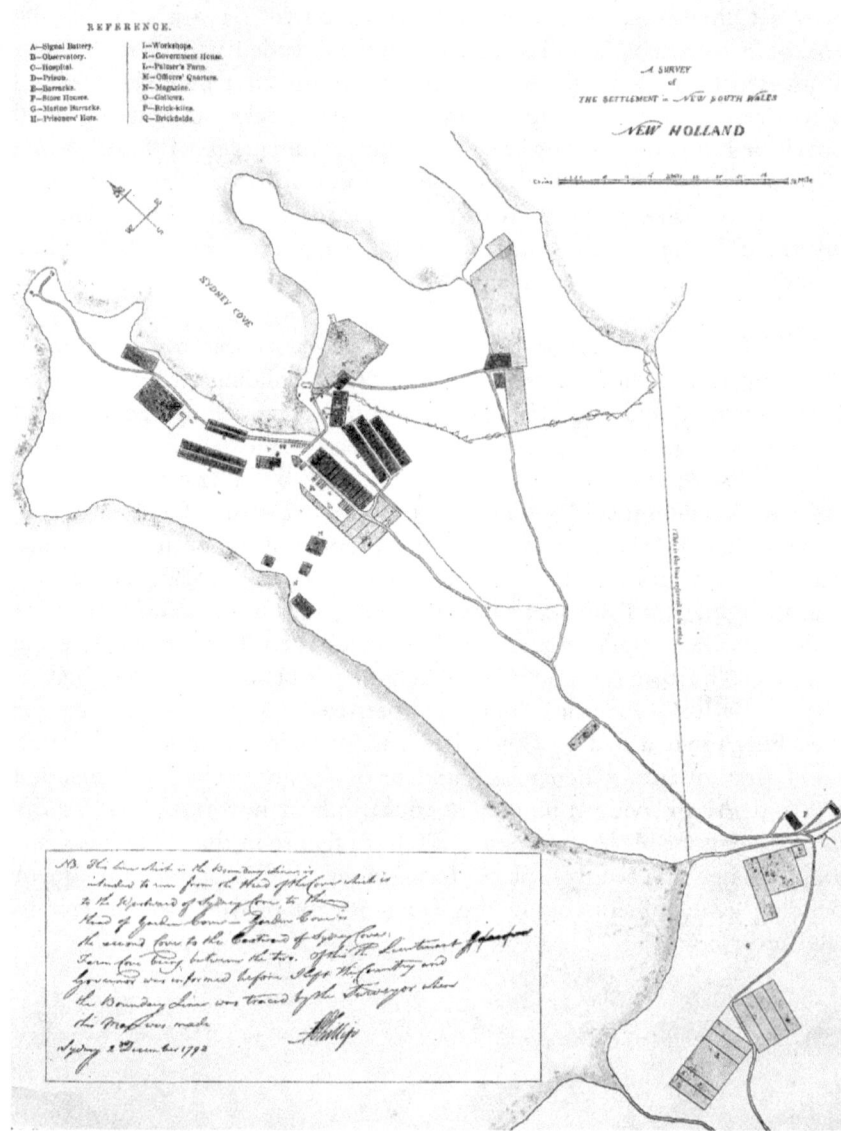

A survey map of the Sydney Cove settlement in 1792. On the east bank of the cove is Government House, surrounded by gardens, adjacent to barracks and three rows of convict huts. Opposite the huts, across the Tank stream, are the marine barracks. To the south, behind the gardens, are the Officer's quarters and magazines. On the western side of the cove are the prison, hospital, barracks and storehouses. The brick kilns are on the lower right end of the map. Below the kilns are the clay and sand pits, and the convicts' huts.

Chapter 10

A HEARTY WEDDING SUPPER

A fine She Goat belonging to one of Gentleman, was found Dead, and some of the Fleshy Parts cut off, and to Day two Men were taken up on Suspicion of having killed this Goat, and made a Pie of some part of it, but it appeared that they found the Goat dead, its Entrails torn out and otherwise mangled as if some Animal had been eating of it, and as it was at this time perfectly sweet, and one of the Men was to be married the next Day, they took the Liberty of cutting some of the Meat off, to make a Pie for the Wedding-Dinner.[1]

The small hut Anthony Rope had built during his free time was finished, and, by promises and persuasion, he was able to furnish it with a simple bed, chair and table. His marriage to Elizabeth Pulley had been delayed until the hut was ready, and they now set about organising their wedding. Anthony asked a shipboard friend, John Summers, to be his marriage witness. John had been on Anthony's hulk the *Justitia* and also on the *Alexander*. Elizabeth Mason would be Elizabeth's witness. The two had met on the *Friendship*. Mason had embarked in Plymouth with a baby boy who did not survive the voyage. In Cape Town, the two women were transferred to the *Prince of Wales* and became close friends. Mason would later share the Ropes' hut – shelter was scarce in the colony, and sharing tents and huts was not uncommon in the settlement.

The wedding ceremony was, by necessity, less traditional than it would have been in rural Norfolk, but Anthony and Elizabeth were determined to make it a memorable occasion. That it would certainly prove to be! Most female convicts had limited threadbare clothing. Fortunately for Elizabeth, one of her friends from the *Prince of Wales*, Frances Williams, had several dresses that had been given to her by her marine partner Robert Ryan, and she lent one to Elizabeth as a wedding gown.[2] This would have overjoyed Elizabeth, as her own slops were shabby, and she had probably never worn a store-bought dress before.

Some female convicts did own fine dresses bought for them in Rio and Cape Town by their sailor and marine friends.[3] The fact that Elizabeth had no special clothing of her own, supports the belief that she had not had any close liaisons on the voyage. Frances Williams and Robert Ryan were long-term partners and lived together in Sydney Cove, and later on Norfolk Island, raising four children. They remained together until Frances's death in 1801.

On Monday May 19th, Reverend Richard Johnson married Anthony Rope and Elizabeth Pulley in the Sydney Cove settlement under a large tree that was used to shade his church services. It was the 54th marriage in the colony. John Summers and Elizabeth Mason witnessed Anthony and Elizabeth sign the handwritten marriage document with marks.[4]

No 54   *By Banns*
The Solemnization of Matrimony between Anthony Rope & Elizabeth Pulley & married this 19th day of May one thousand seven hundred & eighty eight By me Rich. Johnson Chaplain

This Marriage was solemnized between us	Anthony Rope's	x
	Elizabeth Pulley's	+
And in the presence of	John Summers'	+
	Elizth Mason's	x

In today's Sydney central business district, an obelisk in *Richard Johnson Square* on the corner of Bligh and Hunter Streets commemorates where early colonial church services took place.

The wedding ceremony was a momentous event in Anthony and Elizabeth's lives. The now Mrs Elizabeth Rope, an orphan since the age of six, had a partner and protector. Moreover, she was pregnant and about to move into their own hut. For the wedding they had been granted short leave and the marriage took place on a Monday when many of their convict friends were working. Because of this, the newlyweds held the wedding supper on the following Sunday. Elizabeth invited Elizabeth Mason, Frances Williams and Frances' partner, Robert Ryan, and Anthony invited James Price and Samuel Day. Surprisingly, Anthony's marriage witness John Summers was not on the guest list. Catering for such a special occasion was difficult for the Ropes because of the food rations and other restrictions, and these constraints were to have serious repercussions.

The Ropes' wedding supper on Sunday May 25th is well recorded in the legal annals of the Sydney Cove settlement. For the supper, Elizabeth had prepared a 'sea pye', a meat pie topped with pastry. This pie would become "famous" not because of its traditional recipe, but for the non-salted meat it contained. Meat was hard to get in the colony, and virtually off limits to convicts. The pie served at the wedding supper was particularly rich in fresh meat, a rare ingredient that almost cost the newlywed Ropes their lives.

Five days after the supper, Anthony and Elizabeth were arraigned before Judge Advocate David Collins in a court enquiring into the disappearance of a goat belonging to Marine Lt. Johnston. Collins heard evidence from Joseph Hatton, Frances Williams, Elizabeth Mason and Ann Warburton (*aka* Daly). After the hearing, Collins committed James Price, Anthony and Elizabeth Rope and Samuel Day on the charge of theft.[5]

The Criminal Court of Jurisdiction sat the following Monday June 2nd in the presence of Judge Collins, Captain Hunter, Lt. Ball, Captain Meredith, Captain Tench, Lt. Poulden and Lt. Johnston. Theft of an animal was a capital offence in the colony, so this court appearance was extremely serious for Anthony and Elizabeth. The trial proceedings[6] opened with the charge sheet stating that James Price and Anthony Rope are accused of:

> That they on or about 24th Day of May last, with Force and Arms, twenty Pounds Weight of Goat's Flesh, of the Value of ten Shillings of the Goods and Chattels of George Johnston, Lieutenant of Marines, feloniously did steal, take and carry away.

Samuel Day and Elizabeth Rope were charged separately:

> That they on Sunday the 25th May last, twelve Pounds Weight of the said Goat's Flesh, of the Value of Six Shillings, being Parcel of the Goods & Chattels of the aforesaid Lieut. George Johnston, feloniously stolen, taken, and carried away as aforesaid, feloniously did receive and have, they the said Anthony Rope and Elizabeth Rope, then and there well knowing the said Goods and Chattels last mentioned to have been feloniously stolen, taken and carried away.

All four accused pleaded '*not guilty*'.

Marine Lt. Johnston told the court that a month prior a 'she-goat' cared for by convict William Roberts was sent to his plot outside the brickfields. Eight days ago, Roberts told him that the goat was missing and later he brought in the skin of the animal found near the brickfield. James Price was examined by the prosecutor and asked if the skin appeared to have been mangled by animals. Price answered, 'No – it appeared to have been skinned with a knife'.

William Roberts testified that the goat he was minding had been tied to a stake. Another convict named White had told him that he had seen the goat going up the path at sunrise with some of the rope still tied to her neck, but later could not find her. While looking for the goat Roberts met James Price, who told him where to find the skin of the animal. Price believed that some wild animals had torn the large holes in the skin. Roberts explained to the court that the holes in the skin appeared to have been cut with a knife, but no blood was found near the site. He recalled having seen Price at the time walking on Mr Johnston's ground, 'but does not remember to have ever seen Rope there'.

Joseph Hatton, who also worked at the brickfields, testified that on the Sunday afternoon Price came to the hut where he lived and asked the men to lend him an iron pot, which he took into the camp. Hatton said that: 'The next Morning, Price told the Men in the Hut, that they had a very hearty Supper at Anthony Rope's – that they had a very good Sea Pye made of Beef and Pork.' On Tuesday evening May 27th (two days after the wedding supper), Price had asked someone to bone some meat for his supper while he was working at the brickfields. About two or three pounds of fresh beef or pork meat was in a jar with some salted meat. When Hatton asked Price where he had found the meat, he said that this 'was not material'. Soon after Hatton had heard about the missing goat, he asked Price if the meat was from the goat, which he eventually admitted it was. Price told him that people at the brickfields had said where the dead goat lay. Hatton had heard from others that Price went out early Sunday morning and returned before breakfast and had asked who ever he encountered if there was blood on his clothes.

Next Elizabeth Mason was examined and told the court that on Sunday night there had been a supper at Anthony Rope's hut, where she also resided.

> The Supper there was a Sea Pye – that while it was eating, either Price or Rope asked, in general, if they knew what they were eating - that in replying in the Negative he said it was Kangaroo – that at the Supper there were present Price, Day, Rope, his Wife, a Marine, and a Woman named Williams – that there was some Beef and Pork in the Pye – that the fresh Meat was cut very small – that she did not see it come to the Hut, being out in the Morning and Afternoon of Sunday – that there did not seem much of the fresh Meat in the Pye – there was nothing else for Supper – that Eliz. Rope was not at Church on that Sunday Morning.

Frances Williams testified that the Ropes had invited her to a supper on Sunday night, May 25th, where a sea pie was served. Marine Robert Ryan came to the hut shortly after Frances and stayed until 8:45 pm. She believed the pie was made mainly from salt beef and pork, but it appeared that there was also considerable fresh meat in the pie. James Price testified that:

> He having assisted Rope in building his hut he was asked by him to come to his Home to Dinner, which was afterwards changed to Supper – that Rope not being able to get a Pot, he said, if his Comrades would let him, he would get theirs – that he got a Pot – afterwards Earl told him there was a black Sheep dead – he

> replied, but after it is the Black Goat by our Fields; they agreed with Rope to go and look for it – that they found it, that all the lower Part appeared as if it had been worried …. the entrails were all torn to Pieces – that Rope & he agreed to take Home what was left in it, that was fit for eating.

Anthony Rope defended himself by saying that he 'had nothing more to say in his Defence, than what Price had said'. Samuel Day said that Price invited him to the supper party. When Elizabeth Rope was asked to defend herself, she replied that she 'had nothing further to say than that she heard it was very much worried – & that she eat [*sic*] part of it'. Her evidence that the animal 'was very much worried' (that is, badly torn or lacerated) is important to the defence proposition that a wild animal, presumably a dingo, had attacked the goat. Joseph Haynes and James Brown testified that on Sunday morning May 24th, they were walking near the brickfields and 'saw something lying dead on the rock'. On closer inspection they saw an animal with horns that had the hind parts missing. Two crows were picking, and it seemed to be badly torn.

After hearing all the evidence, the court's verdict was: *Not Guilty – Acquitted*.[7] Judge Collins signed the acquittal papers, and the accused were released. For Anthony and Elizabeth it would have been a moment of enormous relief and probably a few tears.

At a time of strict rationing in the settlement, it was generous of the Ropes to invite anyone to a supper. Their food rations were small and the decision to share these with friends indicates how important the wedding celebration was to them. The scarcity of food meant that even regular meals had to be supplemented with edible native plants, fish, birds and kangaroos scavenged and caught close by. To find a dead goat with edible flesh was an opportunity that would not have been missed. The farm animals were regularly killed by dingos, but consuming this meat was illegal for convicts. Elizabeth must have known this and when the authorities were alerted, she would have greatly feared for her life and that of her unborn child. Even if the Ropes had no knowledge of where the meat had come from, the very act of using it in a pie, and consuming it, could have been enough for an unsympathetic court to condemn them to the gallows. The Ropes were fortunate that Judge Advocate Collins, and not Marine Major Ross, was presiding on this occasion. It was also particularly blessed that the trial was held in a court where convicts could call witnesses to support their case. In England, the verdict would have almost certainly been quite different. For the first time in their lives, the couple had been given a fair hearing.

Two days after the dead-goat-on-the-rock trial, Elizabeth,

Anthony and their friends had another reason to celebrate. On June 4th, the fledging colony commemorated the birthday of King George III. Phillip wanted this to be a memorable occasion for the whole colony and was determined that Sydney Cove should celebrate it in a way befitting a colony of the British Empire. It was a work-free day in which everyone was expected to participate.

At sunrise, HMS *Sirius* and HMS *Supply* fired twenty-one gun salutes and these were repeated at one o'clock and at sunset. The marines on shore fired three volleys with their muskets, and between each volley the band played the first part of *God Save the King*. As was tradition on such an occasion, Phillip revoked the punishment remaining for several sailors, and pardoned the four convicts he had reprieved from death and sent to Bare Island. The men returned to the Cove for the celebrations and were warmly welcomed by their friends. The convicts thanked Phillip for being a just and generous governor.[8]

As part of the celebration Phillip invited the naval and marine officers to dine with him. It was a gala evening with the marine band playing during the meal. After toasts and speeches, Phillip named the district in which the settlement resided as *Cumberland County* in honour of his Majesty's younger brother, the Duke of Cumberland. Its boundaries made it the largest county in the British Empire. He had also planned to lay a foundation stone on this day and to name the settlement *Albion* (the Roman name given to Britain because of the white cliffs on the coast of Devon), but the lack of progress in construction prevented it.[9] Later, Phillip changed his mind and named the settlement *Sydney*.

Several large bonfires were set ablaze for the King's birthday and the 'whole camp afforded a scene of joy'. As a special treat, every person in the colony received an allowance of rum. Anthony, Elizabeth and their friends would be among the celebrants gathered around the bonfires, singing and rejoicing. When Phillip visited the bonfires, the convicts drew up on the opposite side, gave him three huzzas (cheers), and sang *God Save the King*.[10] Phillip was quite rightly popular with the convicts, as Lt. David Blackburn, Master of the *Supply*, wrote in a letter:

> The Convicts (though they have Experiencd Every Indulgence from the Governor Whose Humanity & attention to them whilst at Sea & Since our arrival here Intitles him to their Esteem as their Best friend) in General Are a Set of Hardened Wretches.[11]

This had been a memorable day for everyone, and no doubt Anthony and Elizabeth would have heartily cheered Governor Phillip when he came to their bonfire. Sadly, while most were rejoicing, others used the opportunity to rob many of the huts and tents of food.[12]

In July, the convicts Henry and Susannah Kable launched the first civil action in the settlement. They sued the Master of the *Alexander*, Duncan Sinclair, for the loss of personal items in his charge during the voyage. These articles had been purchased in England from donations sent to them following the newspaper articles about baby Henry not being allowed to board the *Dunkirk*, and Sinclair had held these during the First Fleet voyage. When Henry and Susannah disembarked in Sydney Cove, most of these personal items had disappeared. The court ruled that the Kables be compensated £15.[13]

The importance of this trial is that Judge Advocate Collins' ruling set the legal precedent of ignoring English common law which maintained that felons were 'civilly dead' if they had ever been sentenced to death. A 'civilly dead' person was not allowed to hold property, give evidence, make contracts or sue in court. Although Arthur Phillip and David Collins were well aware of the English law, they had no official sentence documents to check Kable's convict status. A large number of the convicts in the colony had been given death sentences that were later commuted to transportation, and, had the English legal interpretation been applied, they would be barred from the commercial and legal affairs of the colony. Collins' decision to proceed with the case, and to find in favour of the Kables, cleared many legal obstacles for convicts to participate in the commercial development of New South Wales.[14]

In the months of July and August, the settlement experienced 'more inclement, tempestuous weather than had been observed'.[15] The rain was so heavy that the road to the brickfields became impassable and the brick kiln collapsed, destroying a large number of unfired bricks. Work at the brickfields was impossible and had to be closed for days. The rain also damaged the residential huts at Brickfield Hill and their repair required as much labour as their original construction.[16]

But the fierce storm was not life threatening and the routine of hard labour of convicts on weekdays continued unabated. On Sundays, convicts could work on their own huts and gardens. They were also allowed to explore the surrounding bush to collect native edible greens, such as wild spinach, celery, parsley, samphire, beans and berries. Convicts often ventured as far as Botany Bay to collect native foods, but only when armed soldiers provided protection.[17] Because Anthony and Elizabeth grew up in the country, they were experienced in scavenging local vegetation – in Norfolk they would have regularly collected and eaten wild fruits and herbs. Although Australian plants were entirely different to those in England, it would have been natural for them to gather wild produce to supplement their rations. Urban convicts were less familiar with this practice and their nutrition suffered accordingly.

By the end of the 18th century, the English obsession with drinking tea flourished even in the poorest households. Tea from China was available but scarce in Sydney, even for officers, and some enterprising convicts discovered that the plant *sarsaparilla*, a native ground ivy, was an acceptable substitute for tea leaves. Convicts and marines, who had no access to genuine tea, found it a 'very wholesome drink'. It produced a sweet liquorish-flavoured drink that served both as tea and sugar, and also proved to be a good treatment for scurvy.[18]

Another persistent problem for Phillip was the poor quality of convict clothing. Most were made from inferior textiles that deteriorated quickly for hardworking convicts. Consequently, replacement slops from by the government stores were in constant demand and soon ran out. In the first winter many convicts wore out their shoes and were forced to go bare-footed, and their thin clothing provided little or no protection against the colder weather.[19] Phillip had been a long term critic of the quality of convict clothing and had complained to the Home Office about this a year earlier when anchored in Rio. On September 28th, he wrote to Nepean 'The cloths for the convicts are in general bad and there is no possibility of mending them for want of thread; it is the same with shoes, which do not last a month'.[20]

There was also an urgent need for children's clothing, which had been omitted entirely from the ships' provisions. Elizabeth's baby was due at the end of October and needed infant clothes. Few children's hand-me-downs existed in the settlement, which meant that most baby clothes had to be made from discarded adult clothes. There were, however, some surprising benefits for an expectant convict mother in the colony. As a poor orphaned mother in England, Elizabeth may not have had access to midwifery care. In the settlement, a naval surgeon from the nearby barracks was available when needed, and she also had friends eager to help bring a baby into the new world.

In October 1788, the Rope's first child, Robert, was born. The next Sunday, November 2nd, Robert Rope was baptised by Reverend Johnson. The baptism took place during a storm of hail and lightning, under the same tree his parents had been married.[21] In keeping with family tradition, Robert was named after Anthony's brother, and his maternal grandfather, Robert Curtis. Conveniently, their close friend Samuel Day was married to Mary Bishop (*aka* Davis) following the baptism ceremony.

Over a century later, in 1895, Anthony and Elizabeth's grandson, James Toby Ryan, published his memoirs, *Reminiscence of Australia* and, in this book, he gave his version of the event.

> My grandfather and grandmother arrived with the first fleet in 1788, their son Robert being the first white male child born in

Australia. He was born in the Soldiers' Barracks, Wynyard Square, nine months and ten days after the arrival of the fleet in 1788.[22]

The claim that Robert Rope was the *first white child born in Australia* has appeared in several historical articles over the years, but it is unlikely to be true. It is possible that Robert was the first white male *conceived and born* in Australia, but a number of male babies conceived on the voyage were born in the colony before October 31st. Toby Ryan had grown up on a farm near his grandparents when they lived in Jordan Hill, today part of Llandilo. Here, his grandmother Elizabeth would have told him about Robert. It is impossible to validate the 'First Male Birth' claim because birth dates were not officially kept in the early years of the colony. Reverend Johnson recorded baptisms but not birth dates. In any case, if the parents were not Anglican their children were not baptised at all, and no official information on these births is recorded.

Phillip still did not have any official documentation on the crimes and sentences of the First Fleet convicts. He had the details gathered from convict interviews on the voyage, but without official information he was unable to declare if a convict's prison term had expired. In a letter written in July 1788 to Nepean, Phillip complained:

> I have no account of the time for which the convicts are sentenced, or the dates of their convictions; some of them by their own account, have little more than a year to remain, and, I am told, will apply for permission to return to England, or go to India, in such ships as may be willing to receive them.[23]

Until the official records had been received from Britain Phillip forbid convicts from leaving the settlement. This particularly annoyed convicts with short sentences, but Phillip had much more critical matters to deal with. Famine in the colony was a real possibility, and the rationing and preservation of supplies was now essential.

Finding new sources of food became Phillip's main preoccupation. Although considerable land had been cleared around Sydney Cove, most was unsuitable for growing wheat and barley. Livestock numbers were low and difficult to maintain, and the supply of local fish was unpredictable. The hunting of kangaroos and birds was possible but insufficient to meet the needs of the colony.[24] Before leaving Portsmouth Phillip had informed the Home Office that the colony would need supplies from England for at least four years before becoming self-sufficient, and that the First Fleet ships were only able to carry a two-year food supply.[25] Despite these shortcomings, Phillip remained optimistic, writing to Nepean that he expected the settlement to eventually become self-sustaining.

> I have no doubt but that the country will hereafter prove a most valuable acquisition to Great Britain, though at present no country can afford less support to the first settlers, or be more disadvantageously placed for receiving support from the mother country, on which it must for a time depend. It will require patience and perseverance, neither of which will, I hope, be wanting.[26]

A couple of months after this letter there were some encouraging agricultural successes. In the September spring weather, everything grew rapidly, and Governor Phillip's enthusiasm knew no bounds. 'We have about 20 acres of ground in cultivation, and those who have gardens have vegetables in plenty and exceeding good in kind.' Phillip was pleased with progress and even with the light sandy soil at Sydney Cove, 'it is, I believe, as good as what is commonly found near the sea-coast in other parts of the world.' He even praised the climate as being equal to the best in Europe, and that fruit trees had produced the first oranges, figs, grapes, apples and pears.[27]

But Phillip's enthusiasm was premature. The grain harvest proved to be too small to meet the colony's flour needs, and there was no seed stock for next years' crops. The settlement was also consuming more store provisions than had been planned for. In the face of rapidly diminishing stocks, Phillip reduced the food ration. When an inventory in October showed that provisions would last only one more year, flour rations were restricted even more.[28]

Etching of the Settlement on Sydney Cove, 20 Aug 1788, after a sketch by John Hunter.

The British Home Office anticipated the colony would phase out government food rations as soon as it produced its own food. On this assumption they planned to transport more convicts but less food provisions. Implementing this victualling plan depended, of course, on Phillip's reports on food production. With so few ships returning to England, the feedback had been intermittent and slow, and, at the moment, the colony badly needed more seeds, flour and livestock. In desperation, HMS *Sirius*, under the command of John Hunter, was sent on October 2nd to Cape Town to purchase critically needed supplies.[29]

Until HMS *Sirius* returned, Phillip focused on finding more arable land on which more grain and vegetables could be cultivated. On November 2nd, Phillip, accompanied by Surveyor Augustus Alt, two officers and a small party of convicts, sailed 20 miles up a major tributary of Port Jackson in search of new farming land. They found a fertile area close to what is now known as the Parramatta River. This they named *Rose Hill* in recognition of George Rose, the Secretary of the British Treasury.[30] The land at Rose Hill was lightly timbered, open country with a good loam soil. Shortly after this discovery, one hundred convicts led by Henry Dodd, and a detachment of marines, were sent to Rose Hill to begin clearing the land. The survival of the colony literally depended on their success.

On November 19th, the remaining First Fleet ships *Fishburn* and *Golden Grove* weighed anchor in Port Jackson and sailed for England.[31] The *Fishburn* had been waiting until its cargo of rum could be unloaded and properly secured in the settlement. The departure of two more ships reinforced the sense of isolation in the colony. HMS *Sirius* had already sailed for Cape Town to purchase provisions, leaving the little HMS *Supply* the only ship in the harbour. Captain Tench observed, 'Sequestered and cut off as we were from the rest of civilised nature, their absence carried the effect of desolation'.[32]

On their voyage back to England, the crew on the *Fishburn* and the *Golden Grove* suffered badly from scurvy. They replenished their fresh food at the Falkland Islands and stayed there for a month to allow the sick to recover. The ships arrived back in England in June 1789.

By Christmas 1788, Anthony and Elizabeth had been together for ten months. During this time they were often hungry, but the arrival of their baby Robert had given them a new sense of purpose. Because of food rationing Elizabeth gathered greens from their small garden and nearby bush to help nurture little Robert. Celebrating their first Christmas in the heat of summer would have felt strange to them, but not unpleasant. They had no nostalgia for the icy Christmases in England – the festive season was jolly for the wealthy but not for those who were cold and hungry. In the colony the Ropes had their own hut and every reason to be optimistic for the future. On Christmas Day, Rev. Johnson held a special service, and most convicts attended.

At the close of 1788, Judge Advocate David Collins, in his role as the governor's secretary, compiled the mortality statistics for the colony. He reported that since disembarking in Sydney Cove, 56 people had died from illnesses, Aborigines had killed four convicts, five convicts had been executed, and 13 convicts and a marine were missing.[33] Collins also recorded that, while there had been little illness aboard the fleet when departing the Cape, scurvy had raged with some virulence on arrival in Sydney Cove. The lack of fresh food was the main problem, but a shortage of medicine had also resulted in fatalities. Many convicts had deceased from long-standing illnesses contracted in England.

At the end of 1788, several of the colony's most prolific diarists ceased writing their journals and had returned to England. Fortunately, Captain Watkin Tench and Lieutenant David Collins remained in the colony and continued their meticulous recording of events until 1791 and 1797, respectively. Without these, and especially Collins' journals, our knowledge of daily convict life in the colony would be very limited indeed.

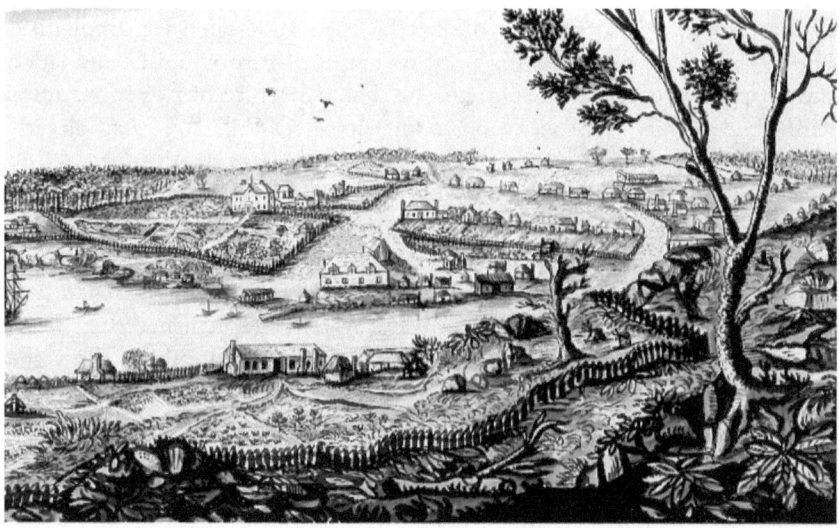

A 1789 sketch of Sydney Cove viewed from the Rocks at the rear of the General Hospital. Government House is seen to the upper left on the opposite bank of the cove among gardens. Rows of convict huts are located to the right of Government House.

Chapter 11

A Struggling Colony

We had long turned our eyes with impatience towards the sea, cheered by the hope of seeing supplies from England approach. But none arriving.[1]

Governor Phillip declared the first day of the year 1789 to be work free. To have a full day's break from hard labour would have been greatly appreciated by the convicts. Even so, the first year had been extremely hard for the settlement, and without adequate food the inhabitants had become increasingly resentful. They were not as yet uncooperative.

Judge Advocate Collins noted 'The ration of provisions, though still less by a pound of flour than the proper allowance, was yet so sufficient as not to be complained of, nor was labour diminished by it'. His report that only halve of the male convicts were employed in agriculture is surprising considering the urgent need for more food, and the government priority to make the colony self-sufficient. The remaining fit convicts were employed in essential public works: stores, houses, roads and wharfs. Sick or weak men could not work at all, and the marines, females and children were exempt from agricultural labour.[2] This meant that the entire food production effort in the colony rested on the shoulders of only 250 male convicts.

In early 1789, 110 convicts had been sent west 20 miles up the estuary river to cultivate new agricultural land at Rose Hill. To reduce food consumption in Sydney Cove, more convicts were shipped in March to Norfolk Island. The island now supported 94 people: 16 officers and marines, 50 male convicts, 23 female convicts and 5 children.[3] This meant the demands on the government stores in Sydney decreased but the loss of male convicts caused a shortage of skilled labourers for building projects. For some convicts this opened up opportunities, and since Anthony had some building experience with the construction of his hut and knew how to lay bricks from rural work in England, he sought to become a bricklayer. His recognition as a skilled worker is recorded later, when Watkin Tench lists Anthony as a bricklayer living at the Ponds.[4] This permitted him to work in his free time for money or extra food. Officers and settlers building houses or cultivating land hired skilled convicts, such as Anthony, to do this work.

Regardless of Anthony's improved status, the colony's court records show that he experienced the strict discipline imposed on convicts. On 11 Feb 1789, Anthony Rope and John Summers, his marriage witness, were sentenced by Judge Collins to receive 25 lashes for neglecting their work.[5] Although there are no details of the charge this was the usual punishment for tardiness or truancy. Perhaps he had overslept, exhausted from work or after a sleepless night with their crying baby. Such excuses were immaterial, as none was accepted – if a convict was late or failed to turn up, he was flogged. After the flogging, Elizabeth would have treated Anthony's bleeding back with salt water. The next day he would be back at work.

The reduced food rations continued to take a toll on the labour force. Without adequate sustenance or any incentive to improve their status, convicts only did sufficient work to avoid punishment. Judge Collins noted that convicts employed on public projects were 'barely exerting themselves beyond what was necessary to avoid immediate punishment for idleness'.[6] Whereas Governor Phillip always expected convicts to work hard in order to benefit themselves and the colony as a whole, it was unrealistic when the food rations were inadequate.

In early March 1789, the first serious conflicts between Aborigines and the settlement occurred. A convict working in the brickfields had gone to collect native sweet-tea leaves in nearby bush and was killed by Aborigines. His work mates were infuriated, and on March 6th sixteen convicts from the brickfields, without permission, marched to Botany Bay armed with work tools to seek revenge. They encountered Aborigines and, in the ensuing fight, another convict was killed and six were wounded. When the alarm was raised in the colony, a detachment of marines was immediately sent to the Bay, but they found only the body of the dead convict and a badly wounded boy.[7]

Phillip had strongly discouraged contact between the settlement and the indigenous people, and he was rightly furious at the encounter and the deaths. He believed these killings now posed a serious security risk. The following day he proclaimed that it was 'highly necessary to make examples of these misguided people, who had so daringly and flagrantly broken through every order which had been given to prevent their interfering with the natives as to form a party expressly to meet with and attack them'.[8] The 'misguided people' he refers to, are the convicts not the Aborigines. He immediately ordered that the uninjured convicts in the gang receive 150 lashes and wear shackles for a year. The wounded men in hospital received the same punishment after they recovered. The first seven men were punished in the presence of all convicts. Among those flogged was Anthony's friend, Samuel Day.[9]

It would have been difficult for Anthony and Elizabeth to watch this flogging; both had endured lashes themselves, though a lesser number. Even so, Anthony seems not to have learnt from his punishments. The following Monday, 9 Mar 1789, he was sentenced by Judge Collins to 25 lashes 'for neglecting to work where ordered'.[10] A likely reason to this sentence is that Anthony was upset at the treatment of the brickfields' men – all of whom he knew well. Remonstrating with his work mates about the punishment of the men and failing to stop when ordered probably led to the charge. Phillip would have given instructions that such protests should be quickly suppressed.

The administration continued to impose severe punishments for food theft. In early March, six marines were caught stealing large quantities of food, rum and tobacco from the storehouses they had been assigned to guard. While on patrol, they had copied keys to gain illegal access to the stores in Sydney and in Rose Hill. All six were sentenced to death and hanged. Phillip showed no mercy for people in authority who abused his trust, especially when it came to food supplies.[11] The severity of the punishments typified the edginess in the colony at this time. The food rationing affected everyone, from the governor down, and hungry people have short tempers. The lack of regular supplies from England eroded the optimism in the colony, and the anxious wait for ships seemed interminable.

In late afternoon Wednesday 6 May 1789, the mood of the Sydney Cove residents changed dramatically. After a 7-month voyage to Cape Town, HMS *Sirius* sailed back into Port Jackson to an exuberant and joyous welcome. The sighting of the ship caused shouts, screams and, no doubt, marine drums to resound across the harbour and many would have run to the cove shore. Aboard HMS *Sirius* was a cargo of 127,000 lb of flour, barley and wheat seeds, and medicine. Tench declared 'the day of famine was at least procrastinated'. The cargo increased the colony's food stores, but by much less than anticipated – the additional flour lasted only four months.[12]

The return of HMS *Sirius* rekindled hope that other supply ships were on their way. Everyone was particularly eager to hear news of the outside world from the *Sirius* crew, especially about what had happened in England over the past two years. The isolation had refurbished an interest in the 'Mother Country' even though few convicts had fond memories of their life there. The news of the tragic voyages of the *Alexander* and the *Friendship,* in which many seamen died of scurvy, would have shocked everyone. These men were well known; they were fathers, friends and lovers, and their loss would have been greatly felt across the settlement. It was also a fearful reminder of what could happen to them if they sailed back to Britain.

Thursday, June 4th, was King George III's birthday; an occasion to celebrate. The marines fired a salvo, and HMS *Sirius* and HMS *Supply* responded with a twenty-one-gun salute. The governor then entertained the officers in the new brick residence he had occupied since April. For the evening's entertainment selected convicts performed the first theatrical play staged in the colony. The play was a favourite of the period, Farquhar's comedy *The Recruiting Officer*. The performance was in a hut fitted out for the occasion, with 60 people 'of various descriptions' present to applaud the performers. It is unlikely that Anthony and Elizabeth were in the audience, more likely they and other convicts had witnessed the rehearsals of the convict players over the weeks leading up to the birthday performance. Seeing a play being acted out by their friends would have delighted everyone – it was a welcome 'escape from the dreariness and dejection' of their situation.[13]

On 5 Sep 1789, Anthony Rope and Susannah Huffnell witnessed the marriage of William Richardson and Isabella Rosson (*aka* Rawson).[14] William was a convict friend of Anthony's on the *Alexander*, and he now taught children under the supervision of Reverend Johnson. Both William and Isabella were educated and became teachers in the colony. In 1793 William was put in charge of the first schoolroom that was built next to the new St Philip's Anglican Church in Sydney Cove. They returned to England in 1810, and in 1812 gave evidence at the British parliamentary select committee on transportation.[15]

In November, when supply ships failed to arrive, stricter food rations were imposed with portions reduced by a third for men convicts, officers and sailors alike. No change was made to female rations, as they already received a third less than males.[16] The rations of overseers, and married men with children, were not reduced. Despite heavy losses from rats and caterpillars, the 1789 harvest at Rose Hill produced good crops of wheat and barley, and some oats, corn and flax. However, the grain yields were insufficient to meet the colony's flour demands or to provide seed for the next sowing season. The Norfolk Island settlement had a successful grain harvest and there was enough flour for six months of the Island's needs. Their vegetable gardens also did well.[17]

Regardless of the food shortages, Phillip remained positive about the long-term prospects of the settlement. He claimed that there was no better or healthier climate in the world.

> Of 1,030 people who were landed, many of whom were worn out by old age, the scurvy, and various disorders, only seventy-two have died in one-and-twenty months; and by the surgeon's returns it appears that twenty-six of those died from disorders of long standing, and which it is more than probable would have

carried them off much sooner in England. Fifty-nine children have been born in the above time.[18]

In June 1789, after the British government eventually received Phillip's dispatches, they responded quickly sending the naval frigate HMS *Guardian* with food, clothing, medicine and equipment.[19] At the same time, the transport *Lady Juliana*, the first ship of the second convict fleet destined to Sydney Cove, embarked female convicts in Portsmouth harbour. She departed in July 1789, two months before the HMS *Guardian* took a more direct route to Cape Town. HMS *Guardian* was already loading provisions in Cape Town when the *Lady Juliana* reached that port. Tragically, while *en route* to Port Jackson HMS *Guardian* struck an iceberg and was badly damaged. It took two months for the ship to limp back to Cape Town, only to be wrecked on reefs before it reached the harbour.[20] Some of the salvaged cargo was later conveyed to Sydney Cove on ships reaching Sydney in mid 1790.

Prior to the arrival of the transport *Lady Juliana* in June 1790, many Sydney residents were convinced that the British government had abandoned them entirely. The feelings of despair were so acute that some senior administrators considered the colony doomed. Major Ross condemned the whole enterprise and complained to Nepean in the Home Office that 'it will be cheaper to feed the convicts on turtle and venison at the London Tavern than be at the expense of sending them here'.[21]

Governor Phillip ridiculed such views and remained confident of the colony's ultimate success. Robert Ross openly criticised him, and the longer the wait for supply ships the harsher his condemnation. Minor issues led to heated arguments between the two men. The death of Marine Captain Shea, and the need to promote another officer in his place, sparked further conflict. Phillip recommended Lt. Johnston, the oldest Marine First Lieutenant, be promoted. Instead, without Phillip's knowledge, Ross offered the post to Lt. David Collins, on the proviso he gave up his post as Judge Advocate. Collins refused on the grounds that finding another candidate would be a serious problem for Phillip, and this would have left the colony in a legal limbo. Collins decided to remain both Judge Advocate and private secretary of the governor, as long as Phillip wished.[22]

Ross was furious and directed his hostility from then on at Collins' administration of the courts. At Ross's urging, Marine Captain Campbell declined to be a member of future criminal court benches, claiming this was not part of his military responsibilities and an additional hardship. Now Phillip was angry. He argued that officers of the Crown had no right to decline court duty and were obliged to serve when requested. The disagreements continued for weeks. Phillip eventually settled the issue, probably with Collins' help, by pointing out that the Royal Commission granted to Officers required them, by an Act of Parliament, to serve in the criminal court, if so called upon.[23]

The Ropes' hut was close to both the governor's house and the marines' barracks. Almost certainly they, and the rest of the settlement, would have known of the disputes. Quiet nights and flimsy timber huts provided little opportunity for privacy in the colony, especially if conversations were heated. In such a small community, gossip was a major pastime and there were few secrets among the residents.

Watercolour of Government House at Sydney Cove, painted in 1791.

In any case, the toxic differences between Phillip and the marine officers were about to become public. For some time convicts at the brickfields had been accused of most of the stealing in the settlement. Since the marines refused to police these thefts or to guard the stores and gardens, a watch of twelve trustworthy convicts was established. They patrolled at night with authority to arrest and secure anyone behaving suspiciously.[24] This proved very successful and stealing almost stopped. Not only convicts were stealing; others were also caught in the act. On one occasion, a marine soldier, who behaved suspiciously, was arrested within the convict's camp. This arrest caused another outburst from Major Ross who accused the governor of diminishing the role of the marines. It was a dangerous confrontation that threatened to destabilise law and order in the colony, and Phillip decided to disband the convict night watch.

Phillip later defended this back down in a letter to Lord Sydney and wrote:

> That it was an insult to the corps; if I wished to say anything further on that subject, he would wait on him the next day with two of his officers, giving me at the same time to understand that by the 5th Article in the Regulations given to the watch I had put the soldiers under the command of the convicts, and which Article, he hoped, would be withdrawn.[25]

Ross had agreed that the night watch had been effective in stopping the robberies, but he categorically refused to allow a convict patrol to arrest a marine. Phillip believed that when Ross 'had proposed bringing two officers with him, I desired, if he thought it necessary to see me with two officers, that all the officers at head-quarters might come with him'.[26] Fortunately the matter went no further. If this was intended as a challenge to Phillip, it was serious. A duel between the Governor and the Lt. Governor would have seriously harmed the already fragile security in the settlement.

Chapter 12

SECOND FLEET ARRIVAL

Our impatience of news from Europe strongly marked the commencement of the year. .... Famine besides was approaching with gigantic strides, and gloom and dejection overspread every countenance. Men abandoned themselves to the most desponding reflections and adopted the most extravagant conjectures. Still we were on the tiptoe of expectation. If thunder broke at a distance, or a fowling-piece of louder than ordinary report resounded in the woods, 'a gun from a ship' was echoed on every side and nothing but hurry and agitation prevailed.[1]

By the end of 1789, the shortages of food in the settlement had become so extreme that the prospect of starvation was tangible. The government stores were depleted and had far less than a year's provisions. Captain John Hunter recommended to Governor Phillip that a signal station be built on the South Head entrance of Port Jackson to inform the settlement when a ship was sighted at sea.[2] He thought this would help mitigate the palpable sense of fear and morbidity that had gripped the residents of Sydney Cove. The dominant sentiment in the colony was that Britain had abandoned them, and they had to fend for themselves.

Hunger, and the need to find other sources of food, now ruled the lives of all in the colony. Phillip had secretly discussed plans with his staff that, unless additional provisions arrived soon, many Sydney residents would have to be sent to another location where they could be fed. Over 100 inhabitants had already been moved west to the Rose Hill district where more grain was being grown, and reduced rations had helped. However, food consumption still exceeded the available supplies. Phillip realised he had no other option but to send another contingent of marines and convicts to Norfolk Island where there were better grain yields.[3] This also gave Phillip the opportunity to shift the uncooperative Major Ross, and his friend Lt. Clark, to Norfolk Island, and return Lt. King to Sydney. Ross would take over the Norfolk Island administration.

On 6 Mar 1790, HMS *Sirius* and HMS *Supply* sailed for Norfolk Island with 280 people on board, comprising 65 officers and marines, with 5 wives and children, 116 male convicts, 67 female convicts and 27 children.[4] Captain Hunter, commanding HMS *Sirius*, observed that the convicts sent to Norfolk were among 'the worst characters ever sent from Great-Britain'.[5] Once the ships reached Norfolk, King was to hand over the governorship to Ross and return on HMS *Sirius* to Sydney. Phillip had already decided that he would then send HMS *Sirius* to China to purchase more provisions for the Sydney settlement.

However, the transferring of cargo onto Norfolk Island proved a disaster. The rugged coastline made offloading goods difficult in strong winds and bad weather prevented the ships from discharging their cargo at Sydney Bay near the settlement. HMS *Sirius* and HMS *Supply* sailed to Cascade Bay on the northeast side of the island where they managed at low tide to disembark most passengers by longboat. After several attempts at offloading cargo, HMS *Sirius* was swept onto rocks, smashing her hull beyond repair. The crew survived but efforts to salvage the cargo proved futile. John Hunter and his crew were now stranded on the island and would remain there until February 1791.[6] A week later HMS *Supply*, with Lt. King on board, arrived back in Sydney with news of the wrecked HMS *Sirius*. The loss was a bitter blow to Phillip as the 20-gun warship ship was strategically important to the colony, and losing it left them almost defenceless. It also thwarted his plan to procure supplies from China. All hope for importing food now rested with the HMS *Supply*.

With the exodus of almost 40% of Sydney's residents to Norfolk Island, the remaining population now numbered only 591 people: 141 non-convicts with 60 wives and children, and 297 male and 70 female convicts and their 23 children.[7] The huts and gardens vacated by those sent to Norfolk Island were assigned to inhabitants whose huts were destroyed in recent heavy rains, and to convicts with no permanent housing. The sudden removal of so many people left an eerie sense of emptiness in Sydney. Collins wrote that 'the whole settlement appeared as if famine had already thinned it of half of its numbers' and 'every man seemed left to brood in solitary silence over the dreary prospect for him'.[8] The well-knit community formed over these past two years had been dismembered. Anthony and Elizabeth missed many of their acquaintances including Frances Williams, and her partner, marine Robert Ryan, and their baby girl. The absence of so many friends amplified to the feeling of isolation among those who remained.

Many marine soldiers were reluctant to go to Norfolk Island. Some convicts would have also complained, but they had little to say on the decision. The Ropes may have been concerned about being sent to Norfolk, especially when it was known that Major Ross and Lt. Clark were to be in charge of the island. Possibly the need for Anthony's building skills in Sydney had kept them off the transfer list. Convicts and marines alike knew that the discipline on Norfolk Island with Major

Ross in charge would be strict, and this proved to be the case. The Ropes, and other residents, wanted to be where Phillip was in charge.

On 17 Mar 1790, Elizabeth's seven-year sentence expired. Neither she nor the governor had papers to prove it, so nothing was done. She was just one of many convicts affected by the absence of official sentencing documents. Several complained to the governor that their sentence had expired and that, as free men, they should be paid for their work. But without official records, Phillip would not pay them or permit them to leave. He warned them that if they did not work, there would be no rations and they would probably starve.[9] This was 'truly distressing' for the convicts who had completed their sentence but were still being treated as prisoners. But most accepted the situation and worked for their rations. The one man who did protest was punished.[10]

As far as Elizabeth was concerned, not much would be gained if she had been declared a free woman, and there were more important matters to deal with until Anthony's sentence expired in March 1792. The entire focus of the Rope family's current existence was on getting food: queuing up for rations, picking wild greens and guarding their precious vegetable garden against theft. Little Robert had to be fed regular meals to stay healthy, and little else mattered.

On 27 Mar 1790, Phillip further reduced government rations. The smaller ration affected a convict's ability to do hard labour, and work now ceased at 1pm. The Ropes queued for their meagre rations between 1 pm and 3 pm every day and, if they had enough energy, they tended their vegetable garden.[11] Every possible source of food was exploited to stretch the diminishing supplies. Marines and trustworthy convicts scoured the nearby bush to shoot kangaroos and birds for fresh meat. In the evenings the government store sent out boats to fish in the harbour, and the catch replaced the salted meat.

Things got worse – the rations were cut further in April. Much of the government food distributed was at least 3-years old: 'Every grain of rice was a moving body from the inhabitants lodged within'. The salted pork was so dry that it shrunk to half when boiled, so instead it was toasted over a fire and the fat dripped onto a slice of bread or caught in a saucer of rice. The flour recently shipped from the Cape Town by HMS *Sirius* was fresh, and rather than making bread, it was often boiled up with greens to make porridge.[12]

Feeding the colony had become truly desperate by winter 1790. No supply ships had arrived from England, and food supplies had reached crisis point. The pressure on Phillip and his administration was now extreme and they drew up a raft of contingency plans – all of them were draconian. Phillip argued that a scheduled cargo vessel must have been lost at sea, and he remained confident that the colony had not been abandoned.[13] He was right, of course, but he did not know yet that HMS *Guardian* had been wrecked. Some of his officers agreed with him but others were convinced the colony had been left to starve. Surgeon White belonged to the latter camp:

> hope is no more, and a new scene of misery and distress opens to our view... a country and place so forbidden and so hateful as only to merit execration and curses, for it has been a source of expense to the mother country and of evil and misfortune to us ... In the name of heaven, what has the Ministry been about? Surely they have quite forgotten or neglected us, otherwise they would have sent to see what had become of us, and to know how we were likely to succeed.[14]

Phillip had no choice but to execute a supply strategy that would leave the colony totally undefended. HMS *Supply* would sail to Batavia to purchase provisions for the colony and charter a second cargo vessel to do the same. On 17 Apr 1790, HMS *Supply*, captained by Lt. Henry Ball, sailed for Batavia. On board was Lt. King, who carried dispatches from Phillip to the Home Office. In Batavia, King was to arrange passage back to England and deliver the letters.[15]

When Lt. Philip Gidley King was the Lt. Governor of Norfolk Island he cohabited with his convict housekeeper, Ann Inett. She had been sentenced to death in Worcester for stealing clothing; her sentence was later commuted to transportation for seven years. The couple raised two boys, named Norfolk and Sydney. When King returned to Sydney, the family came with him. However, as Ann's sentence had not yet expired, he sailed to England alone in 1790.[16]

The Batavia expedition of HMS *Supply* left the colony vulnerable, but Phillip was convinced that this was the only way to save the starving colony. When the little ship sailed out of Port Jackson, Watkin Tench wrote emotionally, '*In te omnis domus inclinata recumbit*' (Our frail state depends utterly on you).[17] Everything that could be done locally to produce food had been done – the procurement of provisions from an overseas source was now essential. In such distressing times, David Collins wrote that Phillip had 'from a motive that did him immortal honour' given his private store of three hundred weight of flour (152 kg) to the store, so 'that if a convict complained, he might see that want was not unfelt even at Government house'.[18]

Replacement clothing in the government store was exhausted as winter closed in. The marines' uniforms and shoes were in no better state than the convicts' clothing and many went about barefooted, even when on guard. For the marines, 'Pride, pomp, and circumstance of glorious war were no more'.[19] In the midst of the deprivation, the women kept up appearances by skilfully patching their own and the men's ragged clothing.

The short rations weakened the convicts and soldiers alike, and work requiring heavy labour became almost impossible. Nevertheless, some public building works slowly continued, and by late April, a guardhouse at the east end of the cove was completed. It was quickly put into use. The first inmates were several convicts who had been caught stealing from vegetable gardens. Food thefts had mushroomed across the colony. On short rations, many residents were so hungry that stealing food from gardens and houses became routine – as long as there was a vegetable standing, it would be picked. Even severe punishments failed as a deterrent. One thief was hung, several received 300 lashes and no flour ration for six months; others were chained together and forced to work on the roads.[20] The pangs of hunger ruled all, and nothing discouraged the widespread thieving. It was 18th century rural England all over again.

During the first two days in June 1790 a storm with heavy rain restricted work in the fields and fishing in the harbour. However, the next day, June 3rd, was a wet day that all in the colony would remember. Shortly after rations had been distributed, a shot rang out and a flag was raised at the South Head station signalling that a ship had been sighted. The residents went berserk. All who could ran to the shoreline or up the hill behind Government House to get a better view. Watkin Tench wrote of the reaction 'when the clouds of misfortune began to separate'.

> I was sitting in my hut, musing on our fate, when a confused clamour in the street drew my attention. I opened my door and saw several women with children in their arms running to and fro with distracted looks, congratulating each other and kissing their infants with the most passionate and extravagant marks of fondness. I needed no more, but instantly started out, and run to a hill where, by the assistance of a pocket-glass, my hopes were realised.[21]

Elizabeth would have been one of these women. With Robert on her arm, she excitedly hugged others as they jubilantly proclaimed that they had been saved – they were not forgotten after all. Elizabeth would have run to get Anthony who was probably working in their vegetable garden. Despite the wet blustery weather, everyone lined the harbour shoreline to cheer the large ship flying English colours as it entered the Heads. There were tears of joy in everyone's eyes as they kissed one another and shouted repeated hurrahs.

As the ship passed through the narrow harbour entrance there were cries from the anxious spectators that it could be wrecked on the entrance cliffs, and the cargo lost. The hungry residents were in agony and so was Arthur Phillip, who could wait no longer. With Surgeon White and Captain Tench, he commandeered a longboat and rowed out to meet the new arrival. They boarded the *Lady Juliana*, a convict transport with 222 convict women on board. She had left Portsmouth eleven months earlier and was the first of the five ships of the Second Fleet to reach New South Wales. The other four transports and one cargo ship in the Second Fleet would arrive soon after.[22]

Phillip was distressed to hear the fate of HMS *Guardian* from officers on the *Lady Juliana*, but he was consoled by the news that his requests of more supplies had been acted upon. Phillip later wrote to the new Home Office Secretary Grenville that if HMS *Guardian* had arrived as scheduled, it 'would have prevented the settlement from being thrown so far back that twelve months will not put it in the state it would have been at this time if the ship had arrived in February'.[23]

By evening, the *Lady Juliana* had safely anchored inside Port Jackson, and soon the much-needed food supplies, plus almost three-years of news and letters, were off loaded. The cargo included clothing for marines, medicine, sails and cordage, wine, blankets, bedding for the hospital, tools and agricultural equipment. There were also textiles for convict clothing. After years of stinting and salvaging, it would be possible to make new clothing. The old clothing would not be thrown away; it was be used for other purposes and children's clothes.

The choppy harbour water prevented the female convicts on the *Lady Juliana* from disembarking until June 6th. Two days prior to this, the Royal Birthday had been a double celebration. The settlement had its first full ration for many months and news of King George III's improved health was an added reason to celebrate. For the starving colony this was a joyous day, and, with news that other ships would soon follow, there was renewed optimism in the settlement. In keeping with the tradition for the King's birthday, the governor pardoned gaoled prisoners and those with corporal punishment pending.[24] Samuel Day, Anthony's friend, who had been punished for attacking Aborigines, was freed from his fetters.

Regrettably, the food provisions from the *Lady Juliana* proved much less than expected, and the ship's contingent had added more mouths to feed. It quickly became evident that the new food supplies would not support the colony for long, and only 1½ lb of flour was added to the weekly rations.[25] This was disappointing, but better than nothing. On June 9th, all work was suspended so that residents could attend a commemorative church service in which Reverend Johnson gave prayers for King George's further recovery from illness.[26]

SECOND FLEET ARRIVAL

A week later, the outpost at South Head signalled the arrival of another ship. It was the cargo ship *Justinian* and, excitingly, its cargo comprised only foodstuffs. Phillip promptly announced that a full ration would now be issued, and the normal working hours for convicts were to be restored.[27] The last three transport ships of the Second Fleet, the *Neptune*, the *Surprize* and the *Scarborough* arrived at the end of June. Apart from the *Lady Juliana*, on which only three women had died, the convicts aboard the Second Fleet ships had been treated terribly. Of the 1095 convicts (1006 male and 89 female) embarked on the Second Fleet in Portsmouth, 256 males and 11 females had died. This was a death rate of 24%, compared to a 2% death rate on the First Fleet. Convicts even died while being rowed ashore in Sydney; 486 convicts landed sick, and of those 124 later died.[28] The treatment of convicts on the privately run Second Fleet was the worst recorded in the history of transportation to Australia.

David Collins was disgusted at the condition of the convicts and wrote 'both the living and the dead exhibiting more horrid spectacles than had ever been witnessed in this country'. Watkin Tench demanded that the English government act immediately to prevent any reoccurrence, stating 'No doubt can be entertained that a humane and liberal government will interpose its authority to prevent the repetition of such flagitious conduct'.[29]

Phillip was appalled at the scenes of misery aboard the Second Fleet ships and protested strongly to the masters. He informed them that he would report officially to the Home Office in London about their treatment of convicts.[30] He wrote that the main reason for the high death rate was the gross neglect of prisoners' welfare by the private contractors, who were being paid for the *number of convicts embarking*, not for the number delivered alive. The ship's contractors had previously been involved in slave transportation to America and this was abundantly evident. The transports were overcrowded with convicts chained together and rarely allowed on deck to exercise. Although the ships carried adequate food supplies, convict rations had been kept small so that the excess food could be sold in ports for profit.[31]

Absurdly, the officers responsible for guarding the convicts had no authority over a ship's master and could not intervene even when they saw convicts being mistreated.[32] Phillip was furious at these reports and tried to have the ships' owners prosecuted. When his report on the Second Fleet's mortality rates finally reached England, the public was made aware of the horrors of the voyage. The master of the *Neptune* was charged with wilful murder but was acquitted. However, the damning reports submitted to the Home Office brought a swift response from the British government, and later fleets were more closely scrutinised.[33]

SECOND FLEET ARRIVAL

The arrival of Second Fleet convicts caused immediate problems for the colony. The hundreds of sick men placed a strain on the small hospital and medical resources. The ships also landed 100 convicts who, because of old age or chronic illness, could not work. Phillip later complained to the Home Office that the hulks and gaols in England seem to have retained the healthy prisoners and transported the sick. If this practise were to continue, the colony would be a burden to the mother country for years.[34]

The Second Fleet ships also arrived with a detachment of the newly formed New South Wales Corps. These soldiers had been sent to relieve the marine regiment, which was to return to England when HMS *Gorgon* arrived with the remaining NSW Corps members. One of the soldiers in the NSW Corps was Lieutenant John Macarthur. He and his wife Elizabeth were to become prominent members of the community.

Among the letters and documents brought on the Second Fleet ships, Phillip received the sentencing records of the convicts aboard the *Neptune*, *Surprize* and *Scarborough* but none for the women on the *Lady Juliana*. Bizarrely, the sentence records for the First Fleet convicts had still not been sent, and Phillip complained bitterly to Under-Secretary Evan Nepean about the absent documents:

> I have in my former letters requested the necessary information respecting the time for which the convicts sent out by the first ships were sentenced, and the intentions of Government respecting those convicts who, when that time is expired, may refuse to become settlers, and demand liberty to return to Europe. We have now near thirty under the circumstances, and their numbers will increase, as well as their discontents.[35]

The arrival of the Second Fleet ships had repopulated the settlement. Absurdly, the newly arrived convicts expected everything in the colony to be in 'a very prosperous state' and that 'plenty of conveniences were ready for their reception'. They found the very opposite.[36] Although the First Fleeters were disgusted at the cruel treatment meted out to the newcomers, they were not happy at having to make room for them in their huts. The poor health of these convicts also led to widespread concern about diseases spreading through the colony. Anthony and Elizabeth may have been required to share their hut with a newcomer and this probably would have worried them because of Robert. Nevertheless, they would have thanked their lucky stars at being on the healthy First Fleet and having Arthur Phillip as the fleet commander.

At the end of July 1790, a population muster was carried out at the settlements of New South Wales and Norfolk Island. It showed that the population of the colony had more than doubled to 2239 people, with three males for every female. This imbalance represented a problem for men in the colony, though many were already married with a family in Britain. The gender inequity was not helped by a preference of single females for the companionship of seamen or marines who had money and could offer them security.[37]

At the end of August 1790, all Second Fleet ships had returned to England, leaving no major vessel moored in Port Jackson. Life for the Sydney residents had improved – they received full rations, new clothing and new shoes in time for the winter weather. Previously, the governor had mandated that females should not be employed as labourers, though some were allowed to work on farms. With the arrival of new textiles, Phillip's administration instructed female convicts to make trousers and shirts for the government stores.[38]

With the onset of damp August weather participation in the open-air church services had dropped sharply. Reverend Johnson complained to Phillip about the reluctant participants, and he ordered that all inhabitants must attend church on Sundays. Without a good excuse, absentees had their flour ration docked.[39] Rain or shine, everyone became a regular churchgoer – the threat of starvation was certainly an effective way *to bring in the flock*.

In October, the much-loved little brig HMS *Supply* returned from Batavia with supplies of flour, rice, sugar, salt meat and medicine. The *Waaksamheyd*, a Dutch cargo ship chartered in Batavia, arrived in December with more provisions. In 1791 Governor Phillip hired the *Waaksamheyd* to transport Captain John Hunter and the crew of the wrecked HMS *Sirius* back to England.[40]

It was not appreciated yet by the Sydney Cove residents that the weather they experienced in the past two years was unusually mild and wet. The settlement was about to experience the flip side of the flood-drought cycle on the east coast. From June 1790 to September 1791, a severe drought set in. Coming from cool, damp England few residents had experienced a drought or the adverse effects of a hot summer on farming practices. With almost no manure to fertilise the fields and gardens, the fertility of the sandy soils quickly degraded, and the local grain harvest failed. The government farm in the Sydney area had always struggled because of sandy soil, and, without rain, it had to be abandoned. Food production was now concentrated in and around the Rose Hill district, with its more fertile land and reliable water supply.[41]

Phillip always maintained that if Rose Hill had been discovered earlier, it would have become the principal settlement rather than Sydney. The government farm in Rose Hill had been productive since November 1788, and under Henry Dodd's supervision, convicts produced most of the grain consumed by the Sydney settlement. Rose Hill also had abundant vegetable gardens. With the arrival of additional mouths to feed, farmland at Rose Hill needed to be doubled, and all newly arrived healthy convicts were sent to work there.[42] Farming efficiency was also helped by the arrival of skilled convicts and supervisors from the wrecked HMS *Guardian*.

In July, Phillip proposed a town plan for Rose Hill, and it would remain the layout of today's old section of the City of Parramatta. A 205 ft (75 m) wide main avenue, now George Street, ran for a mile (1.6 km), straight from the river wharf to the foot of Rose Hill. A house for the governor was built on the hill, and Phillip frequently visited the district.[43] Parts of the original residence still exist today, though the house has been enlarged and modified by successive governors.

Most of the new convicts sent to Rose Hill were employed clearing land and cultivating crops. When available, Sydney's construction gangs were also sent there to build huts and roads, with Phillip personally directing the works.[44] Although not mentioned by name, Anthony Rope was probably one of the 19 bricklayers and labourers sent to build a storehouse and huts in Rose Hill.[45] Bricklayers and carpenters were in much demand in the growing colony and Phillip pleaded with the Home Office to send out more skilled tradesmen.[46] Anthony appears to have been a good worker in Sydney, and this probably helped him obtain a much-valued bricklayer position.

In November 1790, Captain Watkin Tench noted when visiting Rose Hill to assess progress in its agriculture and building construction.

> The view from the top of the wheat field takes in, except a narrow slip, the whole of the cleared land at Rose Hill. From not having before seen an opening of such extent for the last three years, this struck us as grand and capacious. The beautiful diversity of the ground (gentle hill and dale) would certainly be reckoned pretty in any country.[47]

Tench claimed that the main street was so wide that Pall Mall and Portland Place in London should 'hide their diminished heads'. The governor's lath-and-plaster house was at the end of the street, with 32 huts built for single men on the main street. A cross street was lined with small huts for unmarried women and larger huts where 'convict families of good character are allowed to reside'.[48]

In the second half of 1790, the Rope family moved into one of these family huts. Loading up their few possessions, they would have taken the ferry called *The Lump* up the (now Parramatta) river to Rose Hill. The hilly terrain around the harbour meant that boats were the only efficient mode of transport. The Ropes would have greatly welcomed the move to Rose Hill where their new hut had an adjacent vegetable garden. The hut they built in Sydney was to be occupied by newcomers.

A view of Government House in Rose Hill. In 1790 the Ropes moved here and lived in one of the huts seen on the far left.

By November 1790, the Rose Hill population had doubled to 552 people. Its residents were considered well behaved and only 29 troops were assigned to guard the 450 male and 50 female convicts. Most convict women were employed making clothing, and the men worked clearing land, hauling brick or timber carts, and building roads. The 1790 muster of Rose Hill lists the skilled workers: 24 carpenters, 5 blacksmiths, 1 master brick-maker, 52 brick-makers, 1 master bricklayer and 28 bricklayers. [49] Anthony Rope was presumably one of the bricklayers, and no longer considered to be that of an unskilled labourer.

Governor Phillip had worked diligently to maintain good relations with the indigenous tribes of the area. In November of 1789, a senior male named Bennelong, from the Eora tribe in the Port Jackson area, was captured and brought to the settlement.[50] Here he quickly learned some English and developed a friendship with the governor and Judge Advocate Collins. However, after six months, in May 1790, Bennelong left the settlement without any warning.[51] This was of some concern to Phillip, who had no understanding yet of the nomadic lifestyle of Aborigines. Nothing more was heard of Bennelong until September 7th when he was sighted among a group of Aborigines feasting on a beached whale at Manly Beach. Anxious to talk with him again, the Governor, together with Lt. Collins and Lt. Waterhouse, sailed to Manly in the hope of a meeting.

The small boat was beached near the group and the party waded ashore without their muskets to emphasise the friendly intent of the visit. However, without any apparent provocation, one of the Aborigines launched a long spear at Phillip and lodged it in his right shoulder. The reason for the attack is uncertain, but it is likely the spear thrower believed he was about to be taken prisoner, just as Bennelong had been earlier. Bennelong, however, took no part in the attack. Phillip kept a small pistol in his pocket and discharged this to discourage the spear throwing. With the help of others, he struggled back to the boat, hindered by the long spear in his shoulder catching in the sand as he went. With great difficulty, Lt. Waterhouse broke the protruding spear off and the small boat headed back to Sydney in full sail. Phillip was bleeding profusely and few in the party expected him to survive. They reached the Cove within two hours and surgeons quickly extracted the spear, assuring the governor that the wound was not life-threatening. Phillip recovered quickly, and within a week he was walking about the settlement.[52]

Phillip decided to take no retaliatory action. When the Aborigines realised this, Bennelong and a few others sought a meeting with some of the officers. Once assured that there would be no repercussions from the incident, Bennelong began regular visits to the settlement, accompanied by some of his tribe. Through these visits Phillip was able to maintain good relations with the local indigenous people and they continued to fish and hunt in and around the Port Jackson waters unmolested.[53]

Chapter 13

FIRST SETTLERS

In the infant colony, those sent to maintain order and uphold the law might transgress, and those who had previously transgressed might become the guardians of society. Being one of great reversal, this situation offered the potential for individual redemption and improvement.[1]

The year 1791, the third anniversary of the young New South Wales colony, would bring major changes to the lives of all inhabitants and especially to the convicts and emancipists. The livelihood of unskilled convicts in the colony had thus far been one of serving out their sentences as labourers and servants of the government administration. This year many convicts would effectively break the chains of servitude by becoming settlers on their own land. They were about to experience an independence they could not have countenanced in England.

Moving to Rose Hill had been good for Anthony and Elizabeth Rope and their young son. Outside of his assigned convict hours, Anthony was able to do hired work to earn money or receive goods in exchange for his services. The Ropes were fortunate enough to have a hut adjacent to a vegetable garden that provided additional food when the government rations were unreliable. Their knowledge of wild native greens and berries also enabled them to supplement their rations, and to add extra Vitamin C to the diet of their fast-growing son Robert. Convicts from the later fleets were slow to appreciate the benefits of native plants and, in any case, many were initially too weak to forage in the bush. Some found it easier to steal food from fields or gardens than search in the bush or grow vegetables for themselves. It was essential to be vigilant for thieves, and the Ropes kept a very watchful eye on their valuable vegetable garden.

The unrelenting hot dry weather in early 1791 added to the Ropes' workload, and water had to be hauled from the river to keep their vegetables alive. When they first moved to Rose Hill, the countryside had been lush and green; the rolling hills and wheat fields reminded them more of England than the scrubby Sydney area. The recent heat and dryness had taken its toll on plants and people. Crops had withered and cultivating the hard dry land was exhausting. Although Rose Hill residents were on full rations, the arid conditions had reduced the availability of local produce. This meant an increase in food thefts. The ripe maize crops were regularly plundered, and punishments failed to deter the thieves. Collins observed that 'they now committed thefts as if they stole from principle'. The theft of maize incurred severe penalties: offenders had to wear a 7 lb (3 kg) iron collar with two spikes projecting from it. Often offenders were chained together and forced to perform hard labour. Collins had some sympathy for why people stole; he recorded that the stealing was only to procure food whereas crimes of violence were rare.[2]

The drought greatly reduced the quantity of flour available to both the Sydney and the Rose Hill settlements. In January, the weekly flour ration was replaced by rice.[3] Because food rationing applied uniformly across the entire colony – to convicts, marines, officers and the governor alike – there were no complaints of unfairness. Such an egalitarian distribution would have been unlikely in 18th century Britain during a famine – the upper classes would have insisted, and did, that the undeserving poor should starve. When Lt. Governor Francis Grose replaced Arthur Phillip, the colony would be reminded, to its sorrow, of the different entitlements of the privileged. Phillip's equitable rationing had kindled egalitarian practices in the colony, and this would remain a dominant part of the Australian psyche, despite the efforts of later leaders to remove its democratic origins.

In February 1791, close to her 29th birthday, Elisabeth realised she was pregnant again. This was at about the same age that her parents had died, her father at only 27 and her mother at 31. Elizabeth could remember the terrible conditions that the Pulley family had toiled under after her father died, and the widespread rural food shortages in Norfolk. The conditions at Rose Hill were not nearly as bad. Elizabeth was to live much longer than her mother, and see her children grow to adulthood.

In early 1791, Rose Hill had a population of about 550 people but only 16 children.[4] This meant that the young received extra attention from everyone and were often spoilt. Many convicts had left families behind in England, so seeing small children brought them both sadness and joy. The First Fleet arrived in January 1788 with only 54 children on board. Over 80% of the transported females were of childbearing age, between 15 and 45 years, so it is not surprising that a further 59 children were born to the colony by February 1790.[5] Child numbers surged with the arrival of later fleets, and by the end of 1791 there were 249 (half below the age of 2) in the colony, and 39 of them lived in Rose Hill.[6]

Because of the supposedly low food intake of convict women, the high birth rates in the early years of settlement have puzzled historians and medical scientists.[7] One explanation for the high fecundity is that the atrocious diets in English gaols had kept the women's body weight below that needed for fertility, whereas the adequate rations aboard the transport ships and at the settlement had reversed this. The prompt conception of baby Robert Rope was evidence of Elizabeth's robust health when she stepped from the *Prince of Wales* in January 1788.

Concomitantly, during the colony's "hunger years" (1789-1790), one might have expected female fertility in the settlement to drop. Diaries and letters from the first two years of the colony show that the above average birth-rate surprised the government administration. Watkin Tench credits this to the healthy climate:

> I ascribe the great number of births which happened, considering the age and other circumstances, of many of the mothers. Women who certainly would never have bred in any other climate here produced as fine children as ever were born.[8]

The Surgeon's Mate [name unknown] on HMS *Sirius* wrote 'Our births have far exceeded our burials; and what is very remarkable, women who were supposed past child-bearing, and others who had not been pregnant for fifteen or sixteen years, have lately become mothers'.[9] And marine John Nicol, from the Second Fleet, was astonished that 'old women' had new-born babies, 'There was an old female convict, her hair quite grey with age, her face shrivelled, who was suckling a child she had born in the colony. Every one went to see her, and I among the rest. It was a strange sight, her hair was quite white. Her fecundity was ascribed to the sweet tea'.[10] Of course, the stress of prison life and punishments made some convicts look prematurely old – grey or white hair was not really a gauge of age.

Replacing worn-out clothing and footwear was a constant burden for convicts. Most old timers had received their only pair of shoes from the government store when the Second Fleet had arrived eight months earlier. Anthony's shoes were falling apart, and he badly needed a new pair. In March 1791, the convict John Marrott offered to sell him shoes at a fair price. Believing they were Marrott's own shoes, Anthony bought them for cash, presumably earned from the sale of vegetables or from paid-for work. Such a transaction was illegal in the colony, as the governor had prohibited the on-selling of clothing in order to prevent their theft.[11] Anthony's purchase was indeed problematic; the shoes he had bought were stolen.

On 31 Mar 1791, at a hearing at the Rose Hill courthouse, John Beazley claimed that three weeks ago his shoes disappeared. The watchman John Ocraft, Anthony Rope and John Marrott were required to give evidence about the apparent theft. The court concluded 'Theft not proved, but Rope to receive 25 Lashes for buying a Pair of Shoes from Marritt [*sic*], and Marritt 25 for selling a Pair to Rope'.[12] The punishment was harsh but was considered necessary to reduce theft in the colony. This was the last time Anthony would be lashed, but not his last appearance in court. No doubt the flogging would have greatly upset Elizabeth, and Anthony's back would be sore for a week. Fortunately, life for the Ropes was about to get much rosier.

In March 1791, Governor Phillip issued the first colonial grants of land in the Rose Hill district to emancipists. The granting of land to ex-convicts – known as *emancipists* – was of special significance to the settlement. It was the first official action confirming that this was not a penal colony. The British government had understood that the most compelling inducement for ex-convicts to remain in New South Wales was the ownership of land. A land grant not only gave them an investment in the future, but it encouraged law-abiding participation in the colony's life and, most importantly, the farmed land contributed to food production. Without such an incentive, the Home Office believed emancipists would return to England and resume a life of crime. Governor Phillip's commission also gave him authority to discharge convicts from servitude and to issue land grants to those 'who shall from their good conduct and a disposition to industry, be deserving of favour'. A single man was to be granted 30 acres of land, a married man 50 acres, with an additional 10 acres for each child.[13]

The emancipist James Ruse, the marines Robert Webb and William Reid, and ex-superintendent of convicts, Philip Schaffer, were the first men to receive land grants. Ruse received 30 acres and the marines 60 acres each. Schafer was a German who had found his command of the English language inadequate to perform his duties, and he preferred to settle as a farmer rather than return to Europe. As an ex-superintendent his entitlement for a land grant was 140 acres.[14]

The land grant to James Ruse is worthy of special mention, as he was the first convict in the colony to receive one. When his term expired in August 1789 Ruse asked for his release and a land grant to become a farmer. Although Phillip was unable to verify his sentence length, he decided to help Ruse in order to ascertain how quickly an industrious man could support himself as a settler. With this in mind, in November 1789, Phillip ordered a hut to be built for Ruse on the 30-acre Experiment Farm near Rose Hill.[15]

By February 1791 Ruse was self-sufficient and no longer needed government rations. Because of this, he was given the title deed to the land. Ruse's success led Phillip to seek other energetic men and families in the Rose Hill area who could become productive and eventually go off-rations. Even prior to receiving the official sentencing records in July 1791, Phillip planned to let other convicts, who claimed their term had expired, become independent settlers.[16]

The expected food shipments from England still did not arrive with any regularly, and in April 1791 food rations were reduced again. Flour was the most sought-after item, as the stored rice was full of weevils, the salted pork 'ill-flavoured, rusty, and smoked' and the beef cured with spices that made it 'truly unpalatable'.[17] The smaller ration came into force at a time when the arid vegetable gardens were almost bare. Despite the meagre diets, the work hours required of soldiers and convicts remained unchanged. Captain Tench thought that the current suffering was less than experienced before the arrival of the Second Fleet.[18] As in previous years, the King's birthday was celebrated on June 4th, and everyone received an extra ration for the day. Convicts who wore iron collars as punishment for stealing maize were released.[19] To mark this day, the governor had two days earlier officially renamed Rose Hill to be *Parramatta*, the native name of the district.[20]

On 9 Jul 1791, the lookout at South Head signalled that another ship had been sighted. The following day the *Mary Ann*, the first ship of the Third Fleet, arrived in Port Jackson with 141 convict women and six children on board. Their voyage had been good and all aboard were healthy; only three had died. Within three months the remainder of the Third Fleet, eight transports and the naval ship HMS *Gorgon*, sailed into Port Jackson. The *Mary Ann* carried important correspondence from the Home Office informing the governor that henceforth convicts and food would be sent to the colony twice a year, and a periodic supply of provisions would be maintained until the colony was self-sufficient.[21]

Also, after an incredible three-year delay, the official sentencing records of the First Fleet convicts arrived on HMS *Gorgon*.[22] This meant that Elizabeth, now heavily pregnant, was officially declared a free settler. Anthony would have to wait another eight months before his release. With her newfound status, Elizabeth no longer needed permission to travel within the colony and she could go by ferry to Sydney without authorisation. Like many of the female convicts, Elizabeth had been in servitude for so long that the full meaning of freedom might have been hard to grasp. She could now go anywhere in the settlement, however, leaving the colony still required official permission. And, since she was married with children, this was unlikely to be allowed.

On arrival in Sydney Cove, Phillip had announced to the convicts that he would reward good behaviour, and convicts would be encouraged to start a new life in the colony. Now that the complete sentencing records had been received, he wanted to put these promises into effect. Phillip met with the convicts whose sentences had expired and offered them land grants if they were prepared to become productive farmers. He told those who were not interested in becoming settlers that they were free to return to England but there would be no assisted passage on a ship. Also, he reminded them that no man could leave the colony without his wife or children unless they had sufficient financial support.[23] Most of the unmarried convicts indicated their wish to return to England. The rest opted to become permanent settlers, and the Ropes were among them.

No doubt Anthony, Elizabeth and their friends had discussed the possibility of returning to England many times. Most emancipists could not afford the return passage, and crew positions on the departing ships were rare. In any case, only single males could work as a sailor on a returning ship; women and children had to pay. The Ropes had decided that the cost of returning was beyond their means, and, more importantly, nothing would be gained by going back to Norfolk. In England their lives had been dominated by poverty, deprivation and injustice. Why should it be any different now?

The farming successes of James Ruse were well known in the Rose Hill area, and with their rural experience Anthony and Elizabeth would have believed they could do as well. They decided to apply for a land grant. For Anthony, whose father had struggled to own land in Norfolk, the prospect of a grant was an unbelievable opportunity, and the determination to become farmers was now the focus of their lives.

In July and August 1791, Phillip allocated new land grants in the Parramatta district. Twelve emancipists were given land at Prospect Hill, which lay 6.5 km west of Parramatta. On July 18th, in the district called the Ponds, 3.2 km northeast of Parramatta, fifteen First Fleet men were given land where there were fresh-water ponds.[24] The Ponds allotment list includes the name of Anthony Rope. [25] All land grants were conditional on the farms being made productive. The grant recipient was required to live on the allotment and cultivate the land for five years or more. No taxes would be due for the first decade but, thereafter, an annual rent of 1s would be imposed. Any non-conformance with these terms would result in the forfeiture of the land.

The government provided grantees with initial assistance. They continued to receive provisions and clothing from the public stores, and medical assistance for 18 months from the day of settlement. To assist with land clearing and cultivation, each adult was given a hatchet, a tomahawk, 2 hoes, a spade and a shovel. To help start the farms, 2 pigs were promised to each settler, as well as seeds and grain for sowing and planting for the first year. A number of crosscut saws were shared across each settler group whose members were required to look out for one another. If someone fell sick, the rest had to assist for two days a month for up to two months, provided it involved no more than four days of work for each settler per year.[26]

The allocated farms were some distance from the Parramatta town site, reducing the likelihood of theft.[27] Even so, several muskets were distributed among the settlers to guard against scavenging convicts and hostile Aborigines, who had recently attacked settlers and burnt down their houses. For additional protection, several members of the NSW Corps would reside in each settlement district until sufficient arable land had been cleared.[28]

The 15 farms at the Ponds varied in size from 30 to 70 acres. The sentences of 12 of the 15 allotted convict settlers had expired – this included Anthony's friend, John Summers.[29] The sentences of the other three settlers, Thomas Kelly, John Petherick and Anthony Rope were still in effect, but they were allowed to work on their farms during their free time and on one full day a week.[30] Anthony, who was now 35 years old, received the largest land grant at the Ponds. It was eventually 70 acres; 50 acres as a married man and 20 acres for his two children (his second child Mary was born in late July).[31] *Rope's Farm*, as it became known, bordered on the west by Joseph Bishop's farm, on the north by William Field's and John Ramsay's farms, and on the east by Edward Varndell's land. The farm of Anthony's friend, John Summers, was 1 km to the northeast.[32]

The increasing frequency of ships bringing convicts to the colony had created a housing shortage, and Phillip wanted the new settlers to occupy their granted land soon after July 18th. The timing of this was awkward for the Rope family, as the birth of their second child was imminent. On 31 Jul 1791, their new baby girl, Mary, was baptised in Parramatta. Anthony and Elizabeth now had their own land and a daughter. The remoteness of their land meant that they had for the first time in their lives, independence and privacy. After so many years of incarceration it probably felt strange not to have an overseer giving orders, and to be able to wander freely on your own property.

However, they quickly realised that gaining freedom also meant increased responsibility and more effort to ensure personal security and sustenance. Anthony immediately set about erecting a hut with the timber from trees he had cleared from their land. This backbreaking work had to be carried out urgently as his wife and two children needed a roof over their heads. To be a pioneer farmer in virgin bush was exhausting work, which extended from the rising to the setting of the sun. At night they had no light except from an open fire, and until a metal or brick chimney was built into the hut, this was outdoors. There would have been few candles – they were too expensive.

And, as with all convict settlers still in servitude, establishing the farm was not Anthony's first priority – he still had to do assigned convict work. In those first months there would not have been enough hours in the day to accomplish what was needed on the virgin farm – the clearing, the timber making, the building, the soil tilling, the planting and the sowing of crops. Elizabeth would have helped where she could. Even with a baby to nurse, her support and physical labour would have been essential. Raised in rural Norfolk, the Ropes knew that farm work was demanding. The important difference now was that they were working for themselves, on *Rope's Farm*.

On each of the new Ponds allotments settlers were busy clearing their land. After cutting down the huge Eucalypts, the stumps and roots remained in the ground until they were grubbed or burnt out – all slow, labour intensive jobs. The land was then tilled ready for seeding using a spade and hoe. A plough was mostly impractical because of the roots, and, in any case, there were no harness animals for ploughs. The labour needed to start a farm caused some convicts to question their decision to become settlers, and many quit.[33]

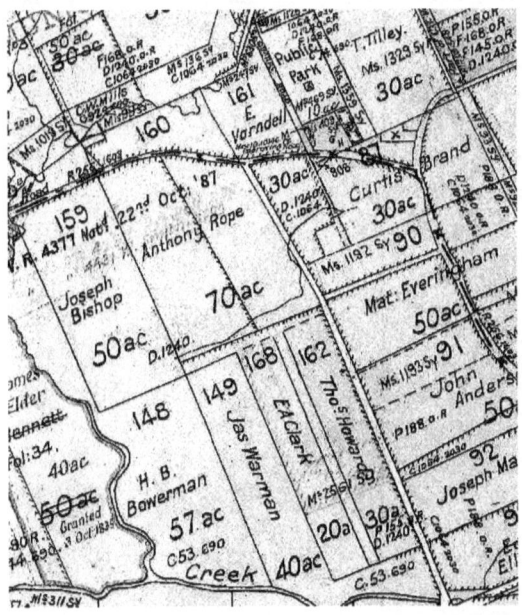

This extract of the 1900 Parish map of the Field of Mars shows the original land grants at the Ponds. Anthony Rope's 70-acre plot is north of the properties of Clark and Howard, which he later purchased.

Anthony, and two other convict settlers in the area, continued to work for the government until their sentence had expired. There is no record of what kind of work Anthony did, but, because the public building projects in Parramatta were an hour's walk from his land, he

147

may have been employed as a bricklayer. Outside his convict work hours Anthony cleared and cultivated his own land. At the end of June, the long-awaited rains broke a one-year drought. The relief was temporary, and further dry weather in August raised doubts whether a maize crop would survive if sown. The soil had become so dry that germination was unlikely without watering, and the heat had dried up the small lakes at the Ponds.[34] The settlers must have often wondered if establishing a farm on this new land was a waste of their strenuous efforts.

Finally, in September, the rains came in earnest and marked the true end of the drought. With good rainfall, gardens across the district produced an abundance of vegetables. Even the wheat crops, which had initially withered in the dry soils, were bountiful. Many farms had sown the more drought-tolerant maize, which gave even greater yields than the wheat.[35] Anthony and Elizabeth would have been overjoyed with their first farming successes. However, some settlers in the area were not so fortunate because a grub plague had eaten the young maize plants. These farmers had to replant their crops several times to get a harvest.[36]

Food rations and provisions for settlers were issued weekly at the government store in Parramatta. To fetch these rations the Ponds farmers had to walk into town every week. For many, these meetings were the only contact they had with those they depended on for their security and medical support. Anthony and Elizabeth were fortunate because they had each other and their children's company, but most single men, who made up the majority of settlers, had no companionship outside their weekly visits to Parramatta, and these gatherings became a much-anticipated social occasion. Since almost all settlers were illiterate, it was also an opportunity to catch up on news, to have someone prepare an official submission for them, or read or write a personal letter. The Ropes would certainly have needed these paid-for services occasionally.

Between August and October 1791, the remaining Third Fleet ships arrived in Sydney Cove and landed 1695 male convicts, 168 female convicts and 10 children. One of these ships, the *Queen*, had convicts transported from Ireland. They were badly undernourished and had been poorly treated. Mortality on the Third Fleet had been 11% (194 males, 4 females and 1 child died) – a dreadful record, but better than the 24% death rate on the Second Fleet. Over 30% of the convicts disembarking the Third Fleet's ships were sick and needed to be hospitalised.[37]

Several new detachments of the NSW Corps were aboard the Third Fleet as well. In late September, HMS *Gorgon* arrived. It brought provisions and livestock for the settlement, and Philip Gidley King. He came back to resume his old post as Lt. Governor on Norfolk Island, as soon as Major Ross departed.[38] King was accompanied by his new wife

Anna Josepha. His earlier *de facto* partner Ann Inett and their two sons Norfolk and Sydney still resided in Sydney. When King and Anna left for Norfolk Island, they took his eldest son, Norfolk, with them. King maintained regular contact with his previous family and made sure they were well provided for. In 1792 Ann Inett married the convict Richard Robinson, and they eventually lived comfortably in Sydney, returning to England in 1820.

With the arrival of new supplies on HMS *Gorgon*, Phillip ordered, somewhat prematurely, that full rations be resumed.[39] It was later discovered that the Third Fleet transports had substituted over a thousand tons of the promised provisions for copper, iron, steel and cord that could be sold in foreign ports, thus enabling ships' masters to buy cotton in Bombay on the return voyage to England. Moreover, the ships had brought only 9 months' food for the convicts transported, and nothing for the colony's residents. This meant that the full ration had to be suspended after 3 months, and the flour ration replaced with peas and oatmeal. Collins complained bitterly in a letter to his father 'that a Colony can never thrive, whose Vitals are so miserably destroyed as ours – if we enjoy the Luxury of a full Ration for a Season, it is taken away to make us taste the bitter Cup of Want, with more Severity'.[40] Phillip now had no other choice than to hire the transport ship *Atlantic* to sail to Calcutta and procure additional food for the colony.[41]

Avoiding hard labour was never far from the minds of convicts. In the early years of the settlement, convicts had fled into the bush but they either starved to death or were killed by Aborigines. A successful escape did occur in March 1791, when William Bryant, his wife Mary and their two children, together with seven First Fleet convicts, absconded in a small fishing boat and sailed north to Timor. They survived the perilous trip but were imprisoned there. Eventually, only Mary Bryant and four other convicts reached England. Mary's husband and children did not survive the escape, and the convicts who did were imprisoned until their sentences expired.[42]

The recently arrived Irish proved the most recalcitrant convicts and were soon plotting to escape. Some believed that China was just over the horizon, and that they could walk there. David Collins referred to this as the fantastic 'chimerical idea'.[43] In November 1791, 21 Irish convicts escaped into the bush and headed north to find China, or any other place where they did not have to work for the English. They thought that China was just across a river from New South Wales and here they would be granted refugee status. They got as far as the wide Hawkesbury River mouth at Broken Bay. Most were captured within weeks and brought back to the colony. Days later, several absconded again, and were later found dead. Coincidental with this breakout, 38 Irish convicts from the *Queen* downed tools at Parramatta and fled into the bush. At night they crept into town and stole from the local farms and gardens. They were caught quickly, and Phillip assembled all of the Irish convicts and warned them they would be severely punished if they continued creating work for the guards. He probably also told them just how far away China was. Despite occasional disturbances, Phillip was quite satisfied with the overall behaviour of the convicts.

> I can still say with great truth and equal satisfaction that the convicts in general behave better than ever could be expected, and that their crimes, with very few exceptions, have been confined to the procuring for themselves the common necessaries of life, crimes which it may be presumed will not be committed when a more plentiful ration renders those little robberies unnecessary.[44]

However, the administration was concerned about the large number of sick and disabled people arriving aboard the transports, and he complained to the Home Office about the debilitated inmates on the last two fleets. There were currently almost 400 sick in Parramatta and 192 in Sydney. Up to 100 convicts were so frail that they could 'not even pull out the grass needed as roof thatch', and, after their discharge from hospital, some convicts were so infirm as to be incapable of any hard labour.[45]

The new farms in the Parramatta districts were flourishing despite some grumbles from recent settlers. By early November 1791, 351 acres were planted with maize, 44 acres in wheat, 6 acres in barley, 1 acre in oats, 2 acres with potatoes and 4 acres with vines. The governor's garden of 6 acres was planted with wheat and maize. Over 80 acres of gardens in the settlement belonged to individual residents, and many outside plots were under cultivation. By the end of November, the barley crops had been harvested and the wheat was ripening well. With frequent rain in December, the maize harvest promised to be abundant, and wheat and barley harvests were better than expected.[46]

Captain Watkin Tench was due to return to England on HMS *Gorgon* at the end of 1791. On December 3rd he made his last visit to Parramatta and spent several days assessing its agricultural progress.[47] Tench walked through the small town and saw better gardens than he expected and observed that the convicts appeared to be flourishing. He noted that vegetation growth was at least one month behind that in Sydney and the 8000 vines in the governor's garden could expect grapes in the next season.

On December 6th he visited Prospect Hill, and then went to the Ponds to meet the settlers. Tench recorded that some areas at the Ponds looked 'desirable' (successful), and he praised John Ramsay's farm in particular. John and his wife, Mary Leary, had planted maize and had a well laid-out little garden. Ramsay told Tench 'he did not doubt of succeeding' and was looking forward to eating grapes from his own vines and sitting under his own fig tree. Tench doubted that many seamen would make good farmers, but this man 'bids fair to contradict the observation'.[48] He was correct; Ramsay proved to be a successful farmer.

Tench then visited the farm of Mathew Everingham. He had been sent to Rose Hill as a clerk's assistant at the government's farm, and later worked as a sawpit overseer. Tench questioned whether an attorney's clerk would make a good farmer, but Everingham was optimistic 'having youth on my side and pretty well inured to hard work and having an agreeable partner'. After some setbacks, Everingham also succeeded in his farming efforts.[49] Tench then visited the Hubbard and Kelly farms, reporting that they were managed better than most. Hubbard became a productive farmer but Kelly lasted less than five months. His farm was taken from him because of neglect, and in 1794 he returned to England.[50] Tench also visited the Rope's farm but made no record of it other than to note that Anthony was still 'a convict who means to settle here'. As close neighbours of Ramsay and Everingham, the Ropes would presumably have expressed an optimism about their future similar to that of the other successful farmers in the district.

Name	Trade	No. Acres	cultivated	[51]
Thomas Kelly	Servant	30	1½	
William Hubbard & wife	Plasterer	50	2¼	
Curtis Brand & wife	Carpenter	50	3	
John Ramsay & wife	Seaman	50	3½	
William Field	-	30	2½	
John Richards	Stonecutter	30	4½	*
John Summers	Husbandman	30		*
Edward Varndell	-	30	1	
Anthony Rope & wife, 2 children	Bricklayer	70	1	**
Joseph Bishop & wife	None	50	1½	
Mathew Everingham & wife	Attorney's clerk	50	2	
John Anderson & wife	-	50	2	
Edward Elliot	Husbandman	30	2	***
Joseph Marshall	Weaver	30		***

* They cultivate in partnership.
** A convict who means to settle here, is permitted to work in leisure hours.
*** They cultivate in partnership.

At the end of December, HMS *Gorgon* prepared to sail for England, and Major Ross and the marine regiment would depart on it. Not all marines were returning; 59 soldiers had accepted land grants to settle in

Parramatta and Norfolk Island. Most of these men had formed relationships with female convicts and wanted to stay.[52] David Collins had also considered sailing on the HMS *Gorgon* but the mere thought of spending months at sea with Ross had deterred him. Collins wrote to his parents 'Major Ross takes his Passage in that Ship – and with him I would not sail were Wealth and Honours to attend me when I landed'.[53] Collins added that he also did not want to leave Governor Phillip before a replacement Judge Advocate could be found. As Phillip's secretary, and living in the governor's house, Collins knew that Phillip was suffering from kidney stones and had sought permission to return to England for medical treatment. David Collins was loyal to the governor and was reluctant to leave without him.

Another of Phillip's admirers, the 33-year-old Marine Captain Watkin Tench, would be returning to England. In the context of this story, Tench's departure is a serious loss. His insightful diary entries, written between 1787 and 1791, are a rich historical resource. His journalistic abilities were first class, and he showed a real empathy for the convicts' situation. He was also a keen explorer and had spent considerable time on expeditions to the west and southwest of the settlement. He discovered that the Nepean River was a tributary of the Hawkesbury River. Watkin Tench must rank as one of the most important, though less known, chroniclers of early Australian history.

Only a week before HMS *Gorgon* sailed, Major Ross, who had only just landed in Sydney from Norfolk Island, fought a duel with Captain Hill of the NSW Corps. Two shots were fired but both missed. This was Ross' final effrontery to the Sydney Cove residents and to the governor, and almost everyone looked forward to him leaving soon. On 18 Dec 1791, HMS *Gorgon* departed.[54]

On board was a letter from Judge Advocate David Collins to Lord Grenville at the Home Office. He had changed his mind, and now sought permission to return to England as soon as possible.[55]

Chapter 14

PHILLIP'S DEPARTURE

[Phillip] *may be justly called, like the Monarch of Great Britain, 'The Father of his People'; and the Convict, who has forsaken the crimes that sent him to this country, looks up to him with reverence, and enjoys the reward of his industry in peace and thankfulness: – indeed, the kindness which we experienced from all around was such, that to have left the colony without a considerable degree of regret at parting from them would have shewn much ingratitude.*[1]

Despite early setbacks Arthur Phillip had remained steadfast in his belief that the Sydney Cove settlement would eventually become self-sufficient and prosperous. He knew from his farming experience that the New South Wales climate was suitable for growing all types of crops; the real challenge was to find and cultivate sufficient arable land close to the settlement. Phillip responded to the shortfall in provisions arriving from England by opening up large tracts of farming land in the Parramatta district and granting land ownership to convicts and emancipists who were prepared to become productive farmers. He was convinced that these settlers would make the colony independent of imported supplies before his governorship expired.

Phillip's last days in the colony were approaching fast. The kidney pains he had suffered for several years increasingly deprived him of sleep and were affecting his ability to govern. By 1792, he desperately needed to return to England for expert medical treatment. Much earlier in April 1790, Governor Phillip had requested the Home Office for leave to attend to his 'private affairs'.[2] His estranged wife Charlotte in England had been very ill, and because she was unlikely to live much longer, he was anxious oversee the future of their estate upon her death.[3] The Home Office knew nothing of these private matters, and it rejected his leave application because his leadership was considered essential to the struggling colony.

A year later, in March 1791, Phillip wrote again to the Home Office, informing them that for almost two years he had seldom been free from pain and requested a temporary leave of absence from the colony.[4] In November 1791, he told Lord Sydney that the violent pain in his left kidney was extreme.[5] A week later, in a letter to Joseph Banks, he stated, 'my health is gone, and I am worn out by a pain which affects the left kidney. It is no longer in my power to go about as I have done'.[6] There is no record of the precise diagnosis of Phillip's illness, but it was likely to have been a kidney stone. This complaint was an occupational hazard for veteran sailors who ate salted food for long periods at sea.[7] Kidney stones can lead to the most excruciating pain and there was probably little that the surgeons in the colony could do to alleviate it. Such acute pain would certainly have affected Phillip's sleep and prevented him from carrying out his duties as governor. Nonetheless, no approval for leave was forthcoming.

Arthur Phillip was a stoic man with considerable fortitude, and despite the acute discomfort he continued his daily duties. Watkin Tench's report on farming developments in the Parramatta district had reached him, and he would have been pleased to hear of the successes of the settlers.[8] Tench mentioned in his report that the settler Anthony Rope, a convict with three months left of his sentence, was determined to become a successful farmer. Phillip was true to his promise of rewarding hard work and good behaviour, and on 10 Jan 1792, he officially granted Anthony ownership of his farm.[9] This was a singular honour for a convict with two months left on his sentence, and Anthony and Elizabeth would have been consumed by pride and exhilaration at now being landowners. Shortly after this news, the emancipist Thomas Howard received a 30-acre land grant on an adjacent property, and the Ropes now had a neighbour on their southern border. Later, Howard's name would disappear from the records, and the Ropes were to eventually buy his land. Watkin Tench's survey of the Parramatta farms reinforced Phillip's conviction that the take-up of new land for grain production was the key to the settlement's self-sufficiency.

On February 22nd, with his Secretary David Collins, Governor Phillip signed and registered the Deeds for the 69 land grants that had been issued around Parramatta since 1791.[10] The first land deed was to James Ruse; the 55th was to Anthony Rope.

> In Pursuance of the Power & Authority vested in me as aforesaid, I do by these Presents Give & Grant unto Anthony Rope, His Heirs & Assigns to have and to hold for ever Seventy Acres of Land, to be known by the name of Rope's Farm, laying at the Ponds, the said Seventy Acres of Land to be had & held by him, the said Anthony Rope His Heirs & Assigns free from all Fees, Taxes, Quit Rents & other acknowledgments, for the space of Ten years from the Date of these Presents; Provided that the said Anthony Rope, His Heirs or Assigns, shall reside within the same, & proceed Improvement and Cultivation thereof, such Timber as may be growing or to grow hereafter upon the said

Land which may be deemed fit for Naval Purposes, to be reserved for the use of the Crown, & paying an annual Quit Rent of One Shilling after the expiration of the Term or Time of Ten years before mentioned.[11]

Governor Phillip, in the presence of George Johnston, John Palmer, John White and David Collins signed Anthony's deed. The Ropes now had the official deed document confirming the ownership of their land.

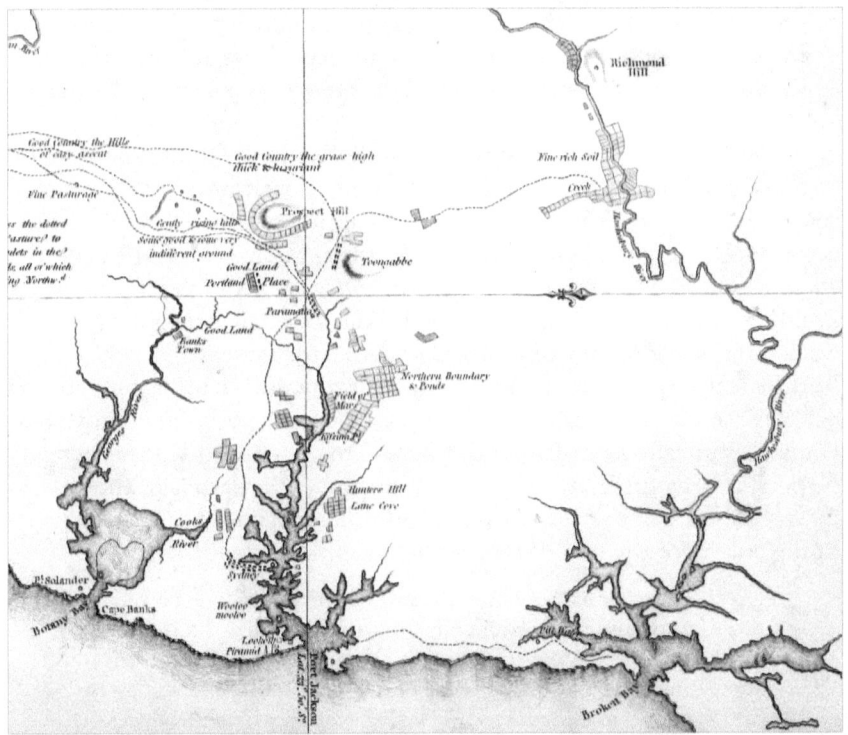

Excerpt of a 1796 map of the New South Wales settlement. In 1792, the Ropes moved from Rose Hill to the Ponds, a district seen in the centre of the map.

At the time the deeds had been issued, four of the settlers were successful enough to afford convict servants to help them. Conversely, four other settlers failed to meet the grant criterion of productivity. Two grants were forfeited because of a lack of crops, and two settlers had returned to England. These plots were granted to other settlers.[12]

Encouraging First Fleet convicts to become productive farmers remained one of Phillip's priorities, and he knew many of the settlers by name. His impartial and fair treatment of these men appears to have been a principal reason for the cooperation and good behaviour of the majority of convicts and marines who had arrived on the First Fleet. Collins contrasted this behaviour with that of Third Fleet convicts.

> To the credit of the convicts who came out in the first fleet it must be remarked, that none of them were concerned in these offences; and of them it was said the new comers stood so much in dread, that they never were admitted to any share in their confidence.[13]

First Fleet emancipists already saw themselves as the pioneers of the colony and, indeed, to be the founding community. These men and women now expected fair and equal justice to be a natural right – expectations that were still unattainable for most poor people in Britain.

On 14 Feb 1792, the raising of the flag at the South Head signal station announced the sighting of the convict transport *Pitt*. On board was Major Francis Grose, who had been appointed Lt. Governor of the colony and Commandant of the NSW Corps. Many of the 319 male and 49 female convicts transported on the *Pitt* were sick, though in better health than most recent arrivals. The food provisions brought by the *Pitt* were pitifully low, making it impractical to increase the rations.[14] Fortunately expansion of local food production had improved the colony's self-sufficiency, but it was still dependent on the provisions coming erratically from England. Major Grose wrote to Under Secretary Nepean shortly after his arrival and reported enthusiastically about what he saw in the colony. He obviously did not appreciate the past struggles of the colony or the lack of regular food supplies from England:

> ... to my great astonishment, instead of the rock I expected to see I find myself surrounded with gardens that flourish and produce fruit of every description. Vegetables are here in great abundance, and I live in as good a house as I wish for. I am given the farm of my predecessor [Major Ross], which produces a sufficiency to supply my family with everything I have occasion for. In short, all that is wanting to put this colony in an independent state is one ship freighted with corn and black cattle. Was that but done, all difficulties would be over.[15]

Grose's view that the colony was close to being 'an independent state' was mistaken. Phillip had already notified Nepean that the colony had been 'on a reduced ration since November, 1789' and required more provisions to be sent from England. He reminded Nepean that convicts could not work efficiently unless they were adequately fed.[16] This advice was heeded and the regularity of supply ships improved, mostly after Phillip had departed.

The colony's crop yields continued to increase but food yields failed to meet rising consumption, and further ration reductions had to be imposed. The rations were not as low as in April 1790 when there were deaths from malnutrition, but many of the convicts from the recent ships had landed in such an emaciated state that they were incapable of getting well on the meagre diet. Convict deaths still occurred daily in 1792; mainly among the terminally sick from the Third Fleet. Of the 122 male Irish convicts who had arrived on the *Queen*, only 50 were still alive in May 1792. This high death rate had put added pressure on Phillip to increase local food production. He ordered that every able-bodied man who could handle a hoe or a spade be sent into the fields. This was a critical time in the colony's bid for survival, and Collins wondered if 'the approaches of independence on Great Britain be something more than a sanguine hope or visionary speculation'. The weakest convicts were excused from hard labour and had to fish and kill game for those who were hospitalised.[17]

Richard Atkins, the newly appointed Registrar of the Vice-Admiralty Court and a Justice of the Peace, had arrived on the *Pitt*. He recorded his first meeting with Governor Phillip:

> [He] received me with his usual politeness, People may exclaim against him as much as they please, but I much doubt whether those who find much fault, would not run into much greater errors themselves; His situation is by no means a desirable one in point of duty.[18]

When the *Pitt* returned to England in April 1792, there were more than 30 ex-convicts on board either hired as seamen and carpenters or travelling as fully paid passengers. The loss of these fit males, many of them possessing skills needed in the colony, greatly concerned Phillip. He asked the Home Office to motivate 'a few intelligent farmers as settlers' to come to the colony.[19]

Improved access to fertile land, and a favourable growing climate, did not guarantee agricultural success, and Phillip saw that the energy, experience and determination of those cultivating the farms were of greater importance. He had observed that farmers from England took time to adapt to the different climate and seasons for planting, the soil variations, the effort needed to clear local trees, and the intermittent rainfall. In mid-April 1792, a deluge of rain with violent winds caused widespread damage to huts in and around the Parramatta farming districts. The rain was so heavy that housing in low-lying areas was destroyed, and rivers and creeks inundated fields and gardens.

When the Ropes' flimsy huts at the Ponds collapsed, they rebuild them in timber. More distressing for them was that a large portion of their crop lay under water. The unharvested maize had been beaten down and recently sown seeds were washed away.[20] Such losses threatened their survival much more than the damaged hut. But, along with the many other settlers in the area, they salvaged what they could, and started seeding again. They appreciated by now that being a pioneer farmer was hard, but the challenge of an erratic climate was worse.

Anthony made weekly visits to Parramatta to pick up rations. Elizabeth accompanied him when house and family allowed it, or if she wanted to help sell surplus garden vegetables to the store. Despite early dry weather and later heavy rains, most of the maize crop survived, and the harvest was better than expected. The Ropes kept some grain for seeding and bartered the surplus maize for articles needed by the family.[21] Anthony would have built or bought a wheelbarrow to help transport provisions back to the farm and their produce to Parramatta.

When it was possible on Sundays, the Rope family made the long walk to the Parramatta church. They were not particularly religious, but the church gathering was an opportunity to meet up and gossip with friends. In such a small, inter-dependent community these occasions were important to keep up with news in the colony, and everyone enjoyed the social aspects of these gatherings. Robert was now 3½ years old and Mary was close to 1 year. During the week Elizabeth and the children were confined to the house and vegetable garden, but when needed they helped in the field. Sundays were kept mostly for relaxation, socialising and playing with other children.

Despite the relative isolation, crops at the Ponds farms had to be protected from thieves. Some settlers reported that up to 15% of their maize was being stolen. Those caught stealing were flogged and sent to a government farm at New Grounds (later named Toongabbie). The latter banishment was more feared than the flogging, as it meant the loss of their huts and gardens, and isolation from the rest of the colony. Not only convicts were caught stealing; Aborigines had acquired a taste for ripe maize as well.[22]

At daybreak on 21 May 1792, Arthur Phillip and Richard Atkins visited the settlers at the Ponds on horseback (the colony had only eleven horses at the time). Phillip would probably have been in pain, but he was determined to see for himself how the settlers were faring. They welcomed his visit and proudly exhibited their farming achievements. This was Richard Atkins first visit to the district and diarised what he saw that day.

> At the Ponds are about 10 Settlers, each distinct from the other. Tho' they have not begun cultivating the Ground above 10 months, they are for the most part (and the whole might be with proper industry) very comfortably lodged, have plenty of vegetables, Indian Corn, for their families as well as to keep some

two some three Pigs, many have from one to two Acres of Ground under wheat and from eight to ten Acres cleared which will be ready for a crop next year. In short they are in every particular much better situated than they could possibly be in England. Indeed too much praise cannot be given to the Governor for (I may say) the paternal care and encouragement he give to all and each of them who deserve it. I have not but there are now some settlers who will in the course of three years make their lands fetch as much as many pounds, and that with the assistance at the first beginning of a spade, saw and hoe.[23]

Atkins was impressed by the agricultural progress and wondered whether the emancipist settlers would ever have had such an opportunity to prove their abilities in England.

Phillip attended Sunday church services and mingled with the settlers during his regular visits to Parramatta. He was always approachable, and as with any good "father" he listened to their stories and their complaints. The shortage of food meant the government closely monitored the success and failure of farms, and where possible addressed the settlers' concerns. There is little doubt that Phillip considered the efforts of the settlers more important to the colony's survival than the progress of the many other projects in the settlement. After all the government ration was possible because of the food produced by the hard-working farmers.[24] Most settlers were not yet self-sufficient or off-rations, but many expected to be soon.

By June 1792, deaths among the sick had fallen significantly. Hospitals now fed patients more fresh meat, fish and vegetables, and this speeded up recoveries. On June 20th, the long-awaited *Atlantic* store ship returned to Sydney from Calcutta, and, in August, the *Britannia* docked with more food and clothing provisions. Two more convict ships arrived shortly after. The supplies on these ships were meant to support 4000 people; the colony's population was about 4200. Phillip's insistence that incoming ships bring sufficient provisions to feed existing residents and the new arrivals had been being heeded, but not yet fully realised.[25]

The Home Office had not informed the governor of future plans to transport convicts. He also had no advance notification on how many convicts were *en route* to Sydney, or the future frequency of food shipments. Nevertheless, as his main concern was for the general health and wellbeing of the colony, he decided to reinstate full rations. This brave decision characterised his leadership. Phillip was resolute in his belief that the new colony should be supported by the 'Mother Country' until it was strong enough to be independent, and said so in his letter to the Home Office:

> It has, sir, been my fate to point out wants from year to year; it has been a duty the severest I have ever experienced. Did those wants only respect myself or a few individuals I should be silent; but here are numbers who bear them badly; nor has the colony suffered more from wanting what we have not received than from the supplies we have received not arriving in time.[26]

By August 1792 the sentences of 400 convicts had expired. These new emancipists were reminded that they were still subject to the laws and regulations of the colony. They were interviewed and each was asked how they would support themselves. Those intending to work independently were taken off the rations list, but once a week they had to report to the government their location and the name of their employer. Emancipists choosing to work on supervised public projects continued to receive rations. Anyone wanting to return to England needed to arrange for a passage on a ship, and for permission to leave the colony. Leave would be granted to those with a good behaviour record. The new emancipists accepted these conditions without protest, and, with few exceptions, their good behaviour was commended.[27] After full rations had been restored, Court Registrar Atkins noted a marked decrease in stealing. He diarised his surprise and admiration at the lawfulness of the residents:

> I should hope from a conviction that honesty is the best policy. Indeed I must say that considering they are people that have most of them forfeited their lives to their country they behave wonderfully well.[28]

In an effort to further promote good behaviour, all newly arrived convicts were now sent directly to Parramatta and not disembarked in Sydney. Judge Collins believed that Sydney had grown to possess 'all the evils and allurement of a seaport of some standing'.[29] He had apparently not spoken to Atkins who had a more favourable opinion of the locals.

By October 1792, Phillip's health had deteriorated markedly, and he decided not to wait for Home Office permission to leave. To the great concern of all at the settlement, the governor announced he was returning to England on the *Atlantic*.[30] Phillip was reluctant to depart before an official sanction, but with no major crises in the colony he believed that this was the right time. Although food security was still an issue, he was convinced that the settlement was on the verge of self-sufficiency. Moreover, Phillip was content that he had done his best, and, for most part, had achieved the objective of establishing a new British colony in New South Wales. In keeping with his general lack of interest in personal kudos, Phillip was more than willing to let future governors gather the bountiful fruits of the colonial tree he had planted and nurtured.

Since farmers were now accustomed to the soil types and climate, they had significantly improved their crop and livestock yields. By the end of 1792, the colony in New South Wales, excluding Norfolk Island, numbered 4203 people.[31] The farms in Parramatta and Sydney had 1703 acres under cultivation, 1186 acres of maize, 208 acres of wheat, 24 acres of barley, 121 acres of vegetables and fruit. There were also 23 cattle, 11 horses, 105 sheep and 43 pigs.[32]

Anthony Rope is recorded as having 4 acres in cultivation, 1 of wheat and 3 of maize.[33] These are small crops by today's standards, but since the land was cultivated by hand, it was a mighty effort. Moreover, during the dry periods, the crops were watered with buckets hauled from the nearby ponds. In fact, Anthony was doing better than some of his neighbours who had started their farms six months earlier. Other farmers had between 8 and 15 acres in cultivation, but they probably used assigned convict labourers. Anthony most likely could not afford assigned servants at that time and only had Elizabeth and little Robert to assist him – yet without that family effort, it would have been difficult to cultivate even 4 acres.

During his tenure as governor, Phillip issued a total of 95 grants for 3470 acres of land.[34] This was less than later governors, but he put stringent conditions on the recipients. Some emancipists were unwilling or unable to make such a commitment, probably because they had never set foot on a farm prior to reaching New South Wales. Many of the urban convicts, mostly from London, wanted to return to the city life they had left behind. Later, when Francis Grose came to power, many ex-convicts realised that returning to England was unachievable, and they settled in the new areas and became farmers.

One of Phillip's last actions as governor was to donate, from the public stock, a sheep to each married settler's family and a goat to unmarried settlers.[35] He wanted this to be an additional incentive for emancipists to take up farming rather than remain labourers. It was also his "thank you" gift to the settlers who had worked hard to save the colony from famine. The Rope family probably received their sheep when collecting their weekly rations in Parramatta. Anthony and Elizabeth would have heard the news of the governor's impending return to England with great sorrow. Phillip had been their benefactor and protector for almost five years and had given them the opportunity to create a new life and family.

On December 10th, Governor Phillip boarded the *Atlantic* and was farewelled by Major Grose, who would be the Lt. Governor of the colony until the next appointment was made. Accompanying Phillip on the voyage were two Aboriginal men, Bennelong and Yemmerrawanne. They had embarked 'voluntarily and cheerfully' to go with him to England.[36] The *Atlantic* weighed anchor at 3 am on 11 Dec 1792 and sailed out of Port Jackson accompanied by all principal officers of the settlement. Before reaching the harbour exit to the Pacific, the officers disembarked into long boats and gave the Governor three cheers; the ship's crew did the same.[37] Arthur Phillip was leaving a colony that he had almost single-handedly created and would never see again. Almost everyone in the colony was deeply saddened by his departure and, as subsequent administrations were to reveal, his leadership and honesty would be greatly missed in the coming years.

On 19 May 1793, Arthur Phillip arrived back in England almost exactly six years after he had sailed with the First Fleet from Portsmouth to the ends of the earth. On 23 July 1793, Phillip formally resigned as governor in a letter stating 'with the greatest regret that I ask to resign a charge which, after six years' care and anxiety, is brought to the state in which I left it… and hope that I may still be of service to a colony in which I feel myself so greatly interested'.[38] He recommended Lt. Governor Philip Gidley King as his successor as governor, but instead Whitehall selected the more senior Captain John Hunter.[39] Because the British government was preoccupied in the war with France, it would take another two and half years before John Hunter departed for New South Wales.

For the rest of his life Arthur Phillip maintained a keen interest in the New South Wales colony. He recommended competent officers such as John Hunter, David Collins, Philip Gidley King, Henry Waterhouse and George Johnston for promotion to high office, as well as lesser officers to positions of authority in the colonial administration. When in 1805 he was appointed as Naval Admiral of the Blue, Phillip continued to encourage the British government to be generous in its support for the colony and to safely transport convicts. He died in 1814 in the City of Bath and was buried in St Nicholas Church in the village of Bathampton.

Appropriately, on the bicentenary of his death in 2014, Arthur Phillip was ceremonially honoured in Westminster Abbey with a floor plaque of Sydney sandstone, engraved:

Admiral Arthur Phillip, Royal Navy, 1738-1814.
First Governor of New South Wales & founder of modern Australia.

Chapter 15

THE RUM CORPS
1793-1796

In infant colonies frequent differences of the mode of Governing, arise naturally from a change of the Governor; but, the very great difference between the present state of this, and its former one, is beyond conception; the meannesses practised by the Officers of the N.S.W. Corps exceeds all I could possibly suppose Usurers capable of.[1]

Within a month of Governor Arthur Phillip's departure the colonial administration regretted the absence of his steading hand. The new Lt. Governor, the 35-year-old affable and indolent Major Francis Grose of the NSW Corps, was in the colony ten months before taking up the reigns in December 1792. He quickly bowed to the demands of the NSW Corps for radical changes to the civil administration. It was not long before he gave the Corps absolute legal authority over all civil and military matters.

Between 1790 and 1791, Francis Grose had been responsible for recruiting the NSW Corps regiment in Britain and had profited from the selling officers' commissions. The Corps was not an attractive career choice for ambitious soldiers, and the men he signed on had invariably been rejected by established regiments, or were too old for active military duty, or were past criminals, deserters or mutineers. Since the primary role of the regiment would be to police a small remote colony, it was of little or no interest to professional soldiers looking for active service. These men preferred the famous army regiments based in exotic India, where there were opportunities to become wealthy in the employ of the East India Company. In short, the NSW Corps was not considered distinguished enough for serious soldiers. However, not all Corps recruits were interested in becoming soldiers. Some realised that the NSW Corps offered an ambitious man real opportunities for rapid advancement and wealth, and indeed, this turned out to be the case.

Judge Advocate David Collins thought the way the NSW Corps had been recruited was 'disgusting' because the sorts of men attracted did not have the best interests of the settlement at heart. In order to provide a 'counterpoise to the vices and crimes' Collins expected them to be chosen from the 'best characters', rather than men exhibiting a 'catalogue of our most imported vices'.[2] Future Governor John Hunter described the quality of NSW Corps soldiers in a letter to Home Office Secretary Portland:

> [They are] soldiers from the Savoy [a military prison] and other characters who have been considered as disgraceful to every other regiment in his Majesty's service, have been thought fit and proper recruits for the New South Wales Corps .... they are the most atrocious characters that ever disgraced human nature.[3]

The activities of the NSW Corps were already a concern in Phillip's time, but he had been able to keep a lid on their ambitions and ill-discipline. After Major Grose's arrival in February 1792, the Corps had sought special privileges and food rations.[4] Phillip had also deflected requests of Corps officers for large land grants and for convicts to work their land, by telling them that he had sought the advice of the Home Office. In the meantime, they were permitted to farm some land with the help of two assigned servants. Phillip's authority was always being tested, and in October 1792, without his approval, some Corps officers had hired a private ship to bring supplies from Cape Town for direct sale in Sydney.[5] Some Corps officers complained when he prohibited the importation of rum, and Lt. John Macarthur declared that he would no longer dine at Government House.[6] The Corps were restricted to relatively minor roles in Phillip's administration and, just as he had done earlier with the marines, he refused most demands for special privileges.

The day Grose took over the governorship of the colony, he abolished the civilian courts and transferred their magistrates to the authority of Captain Joseph Foveaux, the senior Corps officer at Parramatta. In effect this gave Corps officers legal authority over all civil and military matters. There is no evidence that Judge Advocate Collins vocally opposed these changes, but his diary entries show that he was definitely against them.[7]

Next, Grose abolished the equal-rations-for-all policy of Phillip and replaced it with two rations. Free people, watchmen and overseers would receive a larger ration than convicts.[8] But emancipists, who were now officially free citizens, would get the same ration as convicts. Grose had in a few days reimposed the privileges of the English class system on the young colony. He did this on the grounds that it would restore a better sense of order and rank in the settlement, and that the previous government had been overly generous to the convicts.

With his next action Grose did not attempt to hide behind the guise of good governance. In the same week Phillip departed he permitted the sale of alcohol to convicts – this had been prohibited to avoid drunkenness and disorder in the small fragile colony. Grose's decision went further than making alcohol available, it allowed the Corps to pay for produce or convict labour *in rum*. The consequences of this were immediate and tragic. Collins observed that 'the peaceful retreats of industry were for a time the seats of inebriety and consequent disorder'.[9]

Worse was to come. Grose appointed the most opportunistic officer in the Corps, Lt. John Macarthur, as Inspector of Public Works in charge of superintendents, storekeepers, overseers and convicts at Parramatta and Toongabbie.[10] He and other Corps officers aggressively sought to acquire the farm animals given to the emancipist settlers by Phillip. Grose thought emancipists incapable of farming and claimed their only ambition was to save enough money to return to England. The false rumour was circulated that the gifted animals were being killed and sold as meat – Grose decided that they needed to be "rescued" by the Corps. In reality, the Corps officers saw this as a way of acquiring the livestock at a low price and paying for it with rum. It is uncertain just how many sheep were purchased for two gallons of rum per head, though Registrar Atkins records that Corps Captain Foveaux in Parramatta acquired most of the livestock in the district.[11]

It is quite possible that the Ropes sold the single sheep they had received from Governor Phillip, but it seems much more likely that it was exchanged for a goat. A goat would be easier to raise and provided better milk for the children. And, of course, a goat might have been seen as a "good luck" token for the Ropes; it reminded them of their wedding supper and their subsequent success. Unmarried settlers would have looked upon the Corps' offer differently. They lived a hard lonely life on a remote farm with no prospect of finding a partner and selling animals for rum may have been difficult to resist. Access to spirits after years of deprivation and temperance would have been enticing to some as an escape from loneliness. Historian Grace Karskens writes 'Together with other 'stimulants' like tea and coffee, alcohol was a normal part of the diet, 'the use of which they had been accustomed in England from childhood'.'[12] The Corps officers understood the attraction well enough, and judging from the subsequent sale of farms, some settlers gladly accepted the rum payment and started on a downward spiral that often ended in debt, and the loss of their land.

By December 1792, the orderly life of convicts and emancipists that had existed under Phillip had been eroded – civil stability and order would not return to the colony under Grose's governorship. The trafficking of spirits was the main subject of David Collins' diary entries for January 1793. An American cargo ship anchored in Sydney Cove was selling alcohol to civilians, military officers and superintendents for resale mostly to convicts. Collins was greatly concerned about the effects a constant alcohol supply had on the population, stating that many men sold all that they owned for a drink.[13] Ominously, this was the dawn of the "Rum Corps reign" and it had Grose's full support.

To speed up the unloading of cargo ships, Grose directed the Harbour Commissioner to have the convict stevedores' work overtime, and to pay for this labour in rum. Collins was aghast and called this a 'serious evil'.[14] A shortage of hard currency, such as silver coins, helped encourage the trade in rum. The Corps argued that rum was a convenient currency substitute and the routine payment of wages in rum now became common. Even if residents resisted rum as a currency, it became increasingly difficult to get remittance in coins or in goods other than alcohol. Many convicts and emancipists were not given a choice.

In February 1793, Grose issued land grants to Corps officers for major holdings, in the Parramatta and Sydney districts, without any requirement that they be productively farmed. The first grants of 100 acres went to John Palmer and John Macarthur.[15] Grose explained to the Home Office Secretary Dundas that officers were the most reliable settlers, and he was encouraging their farming efforts.[16] Grose himself was not interested in farming and never took a land grant, but he knew that favouring the Corps would benefit him eventually. Grose saw the governorship as a stepping-stone to higher office and that he was just a temporary gaoler of a prison colony.

Phillip's grand plan to develop Sydney and Parramatta as the colony's major cities was abandoned. As Inspector of Public Works, John Macarthur transferred many of the workers from the public farms in Parramatta to the Sydney building projects. By the end of 1793, Sydney had grown with the addition of 160 huts and 5 barracks in a building development that extended almost to the brickfields.[17] The consequent reduction of the farm labour within the western districts almost brought grain production to a standstill and made the objective of self-sufficiency and food security more remote than ever.

The resale and trade in alcohol now became so ubiquitous that the Corps officers started to worry that not all the rum profits were flowing to them. They argued that the reselling of rum between convicts was making money for "the wrong people" and Grose took immediate action to protect the Corps' monopoly. He issued an order that convicts exchanging alcohol for other articles would be punished. The penalty for reselling alcohol without a licence was the confiscation of both the item sold and the alcohol, and the demolition of the offending person's hut. The Corps' control of the rum trade was soon restored.[18]

The deleterious effects of Grose's corrupt rule soon became obvious to outsiders. When Robert Murry on the ship *Britannia* visited Sydney Cove for the second time, he saw enormous changes. He wrote that he had never imagined it possible that Corps officers could trade so ruthlessly. He also noted 'since Governor Phillip left Port Jackson and the government of the colony has been in the hands of the military they have made several improvements in their methods of making money; this is chiefly done by buying corn and selling it to the Government'.[19] In Murry's opinion, only the convicts appeared to be industrious in the colony. He was appalled at their inhumane treatment at the hands of the officers, who laughed at the simplicity of the 'poor distressed wretches' and congratulated themselves on 'their own superior genius'. Murry observed that if a convict did not bow to an officer, he was punished for not giving respect. He wrote that 'Tyranny Oppressions and Fraud had arrived at their Meridian in Port Jackson under the Auspices of the Officers of the New South Wales Corps'.[20]

Sketch of an early settlers' slab hut. The style was popular and cheap and widely built until the 20th century. It is a typical settlers' construction, and likely to be the style of the farm houses the Ropes lived in at the Ponds, South Creek and the Nepean River.

Fortunately for the Ropes, farm life at the Ponds avoided most of the misery and corruption now common in towns. The farming tasks of tilling, sowing and harvesting went on as usual, but their interactions with the Parramatta community during the weekly trading visits had changed. The earlier sense of optimism and community had been lost.

Even the King's birthday on June 4th, a day when Phillip used to pardon convict misdemeanours and provide bonfire celebrations for all, no longer involved convicts. Grose invited selected Corps officers to Government House and everyone else was ignored.[21]

Drunkenness became rife in towns. Farmers were mostly isolated from these disturbances, but Elizabeth would have been worried about the safety of their two small children. Robert was now almost 5, and Mary 2 years old. However, even as remote settlers, the Ropes could not completely avoid the effects of alcohol. John Richards, who farmed in partnership with Anthony's friend John Summers, died at the age of 63 in August 1793 of intoxication – the first recorded alcohol-induced death of an emancipist settler.[22] The loss of a good friend and neighbour made the Ropes even more determined to resist dealing in rum.

A Corps Private John Love bought the deceased Richards' land two months later. It was re-granted in Love's name rather than recorded as being purchased, and this made it the first recorded grant to a low-ranked soldier.[23] The Home Office had never authorised the granting of land to soldiers of private rank, and according to regulations Richards' land should have been returned to the Crown, and then reissued.[24]

Grose's scepticism of emancipists' farming abilities was about to be seriously challenged. In September 1793, the colony's food supplies were greatly boosted by bumper harvests of maize and wheat produced by the small settlers. In contrast, harvests from the government's farms were poor, and the officers' farms had not yet developed beyond land clearing.[25] There is no record of the Rope's farming success but are likely to have produced enough grain for their own consumption and the next sowing. They always found eager buyers for their surplus harvest.

The settlers' bumper harvests were timely as the government food rations were due to expire in August 1793. Fortunately, the settlers managed to convince Grose, who was now aware just how important they were to the colony's food chain, that farmers were not self-sufficient for the entire year and the government ration was still badly needed. Anthony continued with his weekly walk to Parramatta and queued for the family's rations, sometimes accompanied by Elizabeth and the children. Under Grose's administration, the quality and quantity of store rations became increasingly unpredictable. Convict transports and supply ships, as well as American trading vessels, continued to bring provisions into the colony, but the rations distributed by the government stores fluctuated from oversupply one week, to none the next. When there were shortfalls, it was the smaller rations of the convicts and emancipists that were affected.

David Collins considered the quality of food rations distributed in December 1793 was the worst on record because unmilled grain had been substituted for the flour needed to make bread. There were few mills in the settlements and people had to line up day and night to mill their own flour.[26] The Ropes may have been able to mill their own by hand, or perhaps one of the farms at the Ponds had a mechanical mill that could be used for a fee. Bread was the most important part of the settlers' diet, and distributing unmilled grain was greatly resented.

The obligatory Sunday church services required by Phillip had virtually disappeared during Grose's administration, and probably so did the Rope family's participation. Grose was personally ambivalent about religion and permitted people to work on the Sabbath. He spoke unfavourably about Reverend Johnson who was pressuring his administration to build a church. The two quarrelled repeatedly about religion and the morals of the convict congregation. When Grose refused to build Sydney's first church, Johnson paid £67 from his own pocket to erect a simple wattle and daub church building that could hold up to 500 worshipers.[27]

In early January 1794, a year into Grose's maladministration, settlers at the Ponds became worried about rumours that the weekly food rations for settlers and their families were about to stop because the government stores had received too little of the latest harvest. Some of the farmers had been following the practices of grain dealers and had sold or bartered their crops privately. Much of this wheat was being used to distil spirits or brewed to make beer. Other settlers had sold crops privately to pay for alcohol and gambling, which had become another problem in the colony administered by Grose. [28] Fortunately, the prediction that government would cut rations proved false, or was repealed because of the outcry.

In early 1794, a new farming settlement was established on the banks of the Hawkesbury River, about 40 km north of Parramatta. Grose allowed 22 settlers to select allotments along the Hawkesbury River at what is now called Pitt Town Bottoms. The settler James Ruse was one of the first ex-convicts to receive a land grant close to Parramatta from Governor Phillip.[29]

On 7 Feb 1794, Elizabeth Rope, now aged 32, gave birth to a girl. On February 10th she was baptised as Elizabeth by Rev. Johnson in Parramatta. It is unknown if Elizabeth was strong enough only three days after giving birth to walk to Parramatta for the baptism. Several other farmers at the Ponds were now married, and there were other young children in the district. Because the Rope's 70-acre farm was large, Robert and Mary were relatively isolated from other children in the area. Robert was now old enough to do small jobs around the farm, such as minding animals and weeding the vegetable garden – the same tasks his father had done at that age in Norfolk.

In March 1794, two more cargo ships arrived in Port Jackson. Government stores were running low and the new provisions were greatly welcomed. Grose reinstated full rations, and at the same time instigated a review of local food resources. The current grain shortage had occurred at a time of good harvests and Grose believed settlers were withholding grain from government stores despite being offered a fair price. In a clumsy attempt to discourage this practice, he struck 63 settlers whose ration entitlements had expired, off the provision list.[30] Typically, Grose took no account of which of the farmers had actually been selling their grain privately.

The cessation of rations was a disaster for many settlers. The Ponds farming community would have met and discussed why they were being blamed for the food shortages, when the public farms were not. Also, there had been no government criticism of the poor productivity of Corps farms. The settlers saw this as the same prejudicial treatment tenant farmers had received in England when landed gentry affixed farm tariffs. Nonetheless, they realised there was little they could do in the present circumstances, other than to continue being productive farmers, to keep their heads down, and to stay clear of the Corps.

Paradoxically, there was a silver lining to not receiving rations. These settlers could now officially sell their grain to the highest bidder. This may have allowed the Ropes, and many of their neighbours, to achieve self-sufficiency. They could now sell their produce on the open market and use the money to buy other food they needed. However, the colony's "free market" was complicated and fickle. The prices offered by grain dealers fluctuated much more than those of the government store, and the cost of goods in rural areas also oscillated. An additional concern was that the buying and selling of grain invariably meant dealing with Corps officers, who insisted on paying in rum, not in cash.

Those on Norfolk Island also had to deal with the duplicitous Grose administration, and Lt. Governor King had problems with both the Corps and Grose. When King heard that the Sydney government store had only two weeks supply of wheat left, he offered, as stipulated by the Home Office, to provide them with grain from this year's bumper crop. King was furious when Grose claimed it was too expensive, and refused to take the grain, claiming that such a purchase would affect the private dealers' initiatives in the mainland settlement.[31]

When Major Francis Grose finally relinquished his governorship in December 1794, and left Sydney, there was little regret among the non-military personnel. Another NSW Corps officer, Captain William Paterson, was appointed as administrator until John Hunter assumed the governor's post in September 1795.[32] Under Paterson's temporary watch, the rum trade and monopoly of the NSW Corps continued unabated. He also promoted Lt. John Macarthur to the rank of Captain, and this enabled him to exert even more influence on colonial matters.

Somewhat unexpectedly, despite increased drunkenness and gambling in the community, some aspects of colonial life improved under Grose. Mortalities dropped from 189 in 1791, to 59 in 1794.[33] The likely reason for this was that sick convicts from the Second and Third Fleet had recovered under Phillip's improved medical care, and at Phillip's insistence the convicts on later transports arrived in better health. With increased food supplies from private ships and vegetables from local gardens, convicts became healthier despite the short rations.

Grose exhibited little vision or fairness, or, for that matter, any personal interest in government – he delegated most of his duties to subordinates. Grose's greatest disservice to the colony was that he handed over civil authority and control to fellow Corps officers. His belief that Corps officers would productively farm the land he had granted them was delusional, and his policy of favouring the military's dealings over those of the emancipist and convict farmers had long-term repercussions. The downturn in the colony's agricultural productivity had meant that the British government now needed to finance more ships to transport food to the colony at a time when England itself was on the brink of famine. If the settler-farmers in Parramatta and Norfolk Island had been supported and encouraged, they could have cultivated all of the grain and food needed by the settlement at a fraction of the cost to the Motherland.

But not everyone in the settlement was displeased with Grose's time in office. He had made many NSW Corps officers wealthy. The rum trade, the large land grants and the generous access to subsidised convict labour, had become the expected largesse of members of the Corps. These indulgences created long term administrative problems that none of Grose's immediate governmental successors would solve.

January 1795 marked the seventh year of Anthony and Elizabeth's arrival in the colony. In spite of strenuous efforts, their maize crop – which had initially looked promising – was poor, and the wheat harvest was not much better. They became increasingly aware that their low crop yields were due mostly to the soil being over-cultivated, and the lack of animal fertilisers. The manure from their few animals, and their own "night soil" was insufficient to benefit the depleted soils. A poor crop meant they had little grain for their own consumption and no seeds for next season's crop. Without a government ration, they had to purchase all their daily needs and money was short. Along with many settlers at the Ponds district, they borrowed money and hoped that they could pay off their debts with next season's produce.[34]

With repeated poor seasons, many settlers considered selling their farms and returning to Britain. They would not have known that English farmers were suffering from similar problems. While both the Grose and Paterson administrations had made it easier for emancipists to return to Britain, ship tariffs remained exorbitant and seaman's jobs scarce. Most settlers eventually realised that they had to stay put and look to other districts for farming opportunities. The land along the Hawkesbury River, opened up by Grose, offered better soils than those at Parramatta. The Ropes had heard that the new settlement at Mulgrave Place had a vista of green hills overlooking rich flat land. Moreover, a recently built road from Parramatta to the Hawkesbury River districts reduced the travel time from two days to an eight-hour walk.[35] The farms there spanned both sides of the Hawkesbury River, covering sections that became known as Windsor Reach, Argyle Reach, Upper Reach and South Creek. By March 1795, the population in those areas had risen to 385 people.[36]

The primary attraction of the Hawkesbury River region was dark fertile soil that promised better harvests. The region was also remote enough to avoid significant Corps interference, and this encouraged a steady exodus of new settlers from the Parramatta area. These migrants were soon to include the Rope family. Grose did grant land along the Hawkesbury to emancipists, though the allotments were small compared to the holdings his officers received. Despite government regulations fixing the size of land grants, he gave emancipists only 30 acres regardless of their marital status or children. Adding to this perfidy, anybody, including convicts who were still serving time, could get land with a slip of paper issued by the Corps commanding officer saying that the named person 'has my permission to settle'.[37] This was deemed sufficient authority to claim unoccupied land without a survey being undertaken, and let the occupier receive an assigned convict servant. Not surprisingly, low-ranking soldiers benefited most from the paper-slip grants, and because most of these grants were never surveyed, no title deeds were issued.[38] This later resulted in serious ownership disputes that Governor Hunter tried to solve.[39] When some settlers wanted to sell the unregistered land they had farmed for years, the "paper-slip authorisation" often proved to be insufficient proof of ownership.

On 7 Sep 1795, two naval ships, HMS *Reliance* and the venerable and much loved brig HMS *Supply*, arrived in Port Jackson. Aboard the *Reliance* was the new Governor of New South Wales, the returning First Fleet veteran, Captain John Hunter, aged 58. Also aboard was

Bennelong, the aboriginal who had accompanied Phillip to Britain. He was returning after his companion Yemmerrawanne had died in England. The naval officer Lt. Matthew Flinders and Surgeon George Bass were also aboard HMS *Reliance*.

The court Registrar and Magistrate Richard Atkins, who abhorred Grose's behaviour, was effusive about Hunter's return, writing 'How happy is it for this Colony that we have at last a Governor who will make the good of the community at large his particular care, abstracted from all party and dirty pecuniary views'. Atkins was convinced that Hunter 'will do every thing for the general good' but thought that reform would 'not easily be bought about, as the very people whose interest it is to prevent it, have the C. [Corps] ear'.[40] Judge Advocate David Collins was also greatly relieved that John Hunter had at last returned. He assumed that Phillip's policies would be reinstated, and the Corps' influences curtailed. Collins and Hunter knew each other well from the First Fleet days and, though Collins had received permission to return to England, he agreed to stay on as Hunter's Secretary.

Another good reason for David Collins to remain in the colony was his relationship with the emancipist Ann Yeats (*aka* Nancy Yates) with whom he had two children. Ann had arrived on the First Fleet transport *Lady Penrhyn*, the same ship as Elizabeth Pulley, and the two women knew each other well. In 1787 when the First Fleet was moored at Spithead Ann had become pregnant to a seaman and, shortly before reaching Botany Bay, had given birth to a son.[41] When the seaman returned to England, Ann Yeats became the mistress of David Collins and, in 1790, bore him a daughter, and, in 1793, a son. Until Governor Phillip's departure, Collins resided in the governor's house, while Ann and the children lived in a convict's hut close to the Ropes. It is highly likely that Ann's first-born son and Robert Rope played together. After Arthur Phillip left in 1792, Collins moved into a nearby brick house, which also served as his office.

Although John Hunter had received thorough briefings by the Home Office on conditions in the colony, he was shocked at what he found. When he left the colony in March 1791, it was struggling with low rations, but under Phillip's guidance it had become a stable and orderly community. He now found a lawless settlement verging on chaos. Hunter immediately embarked on reforms. He ordered a General Muster across the colony to give him a better understanding of the employment, food production and commercial activities in Sydney, Parramatta and the Hawkesbury. This revealed that Grose had granted 10,674 acres of land, and Paterson, 4965 acres. These were huge allocations compared to the 3389 acres granted by Phillip over a longer period. Hunter quickly uncovered the irregularities of recent land grants, but it took him another three years to cancel some and to rectify others. Many transactions were never sorted out. Hunter shared Phillip's belief that land ownership was the key to a productive stable society, and in subsequent years he issued the title deeds to 20,000 acres of land that Grose and Paterson had granted without ownership papers. Hunter's land grants over the years 1795 to 1800 totalled 28,279 acres.[42]

Throughout his time in the colony, Hunter carried a sketchbook in which he drew and painted the colony's birds, animals, flowers and people. He enjoyed exploring and drafted some of the first maps and charts of the colony. Shortly after becoming governor, Hunter received a report that a herd of cattle, lost in 1788, had been discovered west of the Nepean River. In October 1795, Hunter, Collins, Waterhouse and Bass went to see the reported herd, and found 38 cattle grazing on lush pastureland.[43] Hunter gave orders that the cattle should not be disturbed. He regularly visited this area over the years, and, in 1798, the number of cattle had increased to 170.[44]

The first major administrative reform to be instituted by Hunter was the restoration of civil control of convict labour. Convicts would now work for the government, not for the NSW Corps. This effectively closed the labour market controlled by the Corps for three years, and with it their profits. The Corps deeply resented the change, and they became less cooperative. Under Grose, each Corps officer had received the free services of 13 convicts, all fully provisioned by government. The original entitlement of an officer was two assigned convicts. Hunter did allow larger entitlements, but the assigned convicts had to reside at the farms where they worked and not in town. He also insisted that each emancipist receive one assigned convict, if requested. The Ropes did employ assigned servants from time to time but only when they had heavy labouring jobs the family could not handle. Extra farm labourers were a great help, but they cost more money than most settlers had.[45]

On the 22 Dec 1795, Elizabeth gave birth to a fourth child, John, named after his paternal grandfather. He was baptised on 2 Jan 1796 by Reverend Samuel Marsden, who arrived in the colony in March 1794, and had taken up an appointment in the diocese of Parramatta.

Captain John Macarthur continued to irritate the administration. The governor knew he had to circumvent the power Macarthur exerted in the colony, but it had to be done carefully. The Corps fully supported Macarthur's activities and they were responsible for law and order in the colony and Hunter needed some legitimate reasons to rein Macarthur in. The Corps were also exceeding their official responsibilities; a major incidence of malpractice would be needed to justify diminishing their non-military powers.

Hunter did not have to wait long. In February 1796, a carpenter foreman, John Baughan had a longstanding dispute with a Corps soldier. When the soldier left his guard post without his weapon to abuse Baughan to a fellow soldier, Baughan took the guard's musket and handed it into the Corps. The guard was imprisoned for abandoning his weapon. As retribution, some Corps soldiers went to Baughan's place, ruined his house and terrorised his wife. Baughan tried to defend his property but was held down and threatened with an axe. The soldiers left cheering that they had done 'something meritorious'.[46]

This vigilante action was the opportunity Hunter had been waiting for. He issued an arrest warrant for the Corps ringleaders, and the next day instructed Captain Paterson to instruct all the soldiers on civil law.[47] He also said the incident would be reported to the Home Office as a rebellion. Hunter's hand had been further strengthened because the attack had so alarmed the colony that many demanded the vigilante ringleaders be severely punished. Two days later, in his role as Magistrate, Surgeon William Balmain questioned Baughan on the attack. He declined to reply, presumably for fear of further retaliation. John Macarthur, acting on behalf of the Corps, asked Magistrate Balmain if he intended prosecuting the soldiers, and whether Baughan had been told to make his complaint. This implication led the magistrate to call Macarthur 'a base rascal and an atrocious liar and villain'. The exchanges flared and Balmain challenged Macarthur to a duel. Macarthur replied that, if Balmain persisted in the challenge, he would have to duel with the whole Corps. The duel never took place.[48]

This episode typified Macarthur's tactics. He never hesitated in using the Corps to fight his personal battles or assist in his commercial endeavours. A Corps threat of violence was not to be taken lightly, and, after receiving an apology and compensation, Baughan withdrew his allegations. Hunter had no option but to cancel the indictment against the soldiers. His decision to use restorative rather than punitive justice was weak, and he would later regret losing the opportunity to show his mettle. Hunter reported the whole issue to the Home Office and was to be later censured by Home Office Secretary Portland for not punishing the soldiers with the 'utmost severity', for threatening the safety of the government.[49]

One consequence of the Balmain affair was that Corps soldiers were now instructed to move from private huts back to the barracks.[50] When John Macarthur realised that his control of the Parramatta district was curtailed, he resigned as Inspector of Public Works declaring a loss of confidence in Hunter.[51] From then on, Hunter became his conspicuous enemy, and he cultivated discontent among the Corps officers. To offset this, Hunter, rather foolishly, slowed down his reforms. He did, however, persist in trying to reduce the rum trade by policing the licences needed for the distillation of alcohol.[52]

The King's birthday on June 4th was celebrated in a style reminiscent of Phillip's time, with gun-salutes, parties and the pardoning of prisoners under punishment. Governor Hunter was praised by the convicts for adhering to tradition and criticised by the Corps officers for extravagance. However, the food production had not yet recovered from the Grose years, and for many settlers the birthday celebrations were limited by the fact that they bordered on bankruptcy, and their crops had been pledged for two or more seasons to pay off their debts. Hunter realised it was difficult times for the settlers, and, in June, he ordered an enquiry into the state of small farms, and an assessment of the debt levels in the districts of Prospect Hill, the Ponds, Field of Mars, Eastern Farms and Mulgrave Place.[53]

The enquiry showed that there were about 250 small farms in these districts. The settlers had cleared 2747 acres of land, and owned 921 pigs, 30 sheep, 140 goats and 480 poultry. The total debt level was estimated to be £4419. Reverend Marsden and Surgeon Arndell, who conducted the survey, considered this estimate to be low, because many settlers were too ashamed to reveal their full debts. Collins' estimate of £5098 was probably closer to the real amount owing.[54] That would be over a million dollars today.

The 32 settlers in the Northern Boundary, the Ponds and Field of Mars districts had cleared the largest area of 723 acres, and owned 160 pigs, 22 sheep, 42 goats and 70 poultry. They claimed to have no debts, but it is more likely they were reluctant to admit them. One of the settlers at the Ponds, Edward Elliot, had resisted the Corps' offers to buy his livestock, and he owned all of the 22 sheep in the area. The enquiry reported the settlers in the Ponds as 'Many industrious; some few indifferent; a few bad'.

The report on the Hawkesbury settlers was not as flattering. It showed that the settlers' debts were mostly 'owing to a disposition to indulge in drunkenness' and their 'labour of a whole year had been thrown away for a few gallons of a very bad spirit'.[55] Settlers in the Hawkesbury area had 'a few industrious, and many worthless characters', and most were more in debt than in the other areas. And, because the fertile soil in the region required less effort to produce good harvests, the report suggested settlers were indolent due to their easy living. Unfortunately, this became an unfair stereotype image of Hawkesbury settlers for many years.[56]

Hunter quickly recognised that there was another reason for

debt and malaise in the farming communities. It was the purchase of farm produce with alcohol. This practice had prevailed for far too long in the farming districts and had eroded the will and the resources of many settlers. Hunter ordered that in future the government purchase most of the grain, and that retailers who were licensed to sell alcohol must not accept grain as a form of payment. Any breach would result in the cancellation of licences and the loss of the assigned convict labour entitlements.[57] Significant alcohol consumption and related violence still persisted, and Hunter had to assign civil magistrates rather than Corps officers to issue alcohol licences. He appointed Registrar Richard Atkins to John Macarthur's old post, the Inspector of Public Works. Hunter also decided that the dependency of settlers on government rations was counter-productive, and he cancelled the rations for those with land grants older than 18 months.[58]

A long-standing antagonism between Atkins and Macarthur persisted and was about to flare up again. A Corps Private had been charged with stealing turnips from the governor's garden in Parramatta. As the presiding magistrate, Atkins refused to name the accused soldier, believing that under military jurisdiction an overly harsh sentence would be imposed. The argument over who was authorised to try the soldier raged for months. It came to a head when Macarthur accused Atkins with a multitude of crimes: attempted fraud, intoxication and abuse of creditors, highway robbery, and writing a compromising letter. Judge Advocate Collins investigated these charges, dismissing them in favour of Atkins.[59] The now outraged Macarthur declared that for a civil charge to be made against a Corps soldier was an insult to the military. He wrote to the Home Office attacking Atkins, Hunter and the entire administration. He complained bitterly that Hunter was systematically reversing Grose's rulings. Macarthur was a prolific correspondent and, over many months, wrote long letters to Secretary Portland about Hunter and the state of the colony. He managed to convince Portland that he, and the Corps officers, had the best interests of the colony at heart, and Hunter had not.[60] The repercussions of these letters would take a long time to play out, and a much longer time to correct.

The neighbours on the south side of Rope's farm, Elizabeth Ann and Thomas Clark had decided to return to England. In September 1796 Anthony Rope purchased the 20-acre Clark farm.[61] There is no record of this sale, other than the fact that he later sold the land to someone else. The acquisition is surprising because of the money needed for the purchase. It is possible that Anthony borrowed this from another farmer, a publican or, even worse, the Corps. It was a brave investment, but in the long term it was successful. The Ropes remained the owners of the Clark property for over 25 years.

On 29 Sep 1796 HMS *Reliance* and *Britannia* departed Port Jackson for England. The ships sailed via Norfolk Island to take on board Lt. Governor King who was very ill and had been granted return leave. His wife and the two children born since their arrival on Norfolk Island accompanied him. His oldest son Norfolk returned to Sydney to be with his mother Ann Inett. Other passengers on the two ships included Captain Paterson returning on sick leave; the Rope's ex-neighbours, Thomas and Elizabeth Ann Clark; and Judge Advocate David Collins with Ann Yeats and their children. Collins carried despatches from Governor Hunter for delivery in person to the Home Office, and to Hunter's sponsor, Sir Joseph Banks.

David Collins had a wife waiting for him in England and had not resigned his office as Judge Advocate in the colony. There is no evidence that he planned to return to the colony, and he had gifted his 100-acre farm on the Hawkesbury River to Ann Yeats. Although Ann and the children went with Collins to England, they eventually returned to Sydney. In 1802 David Collins would be appointed Lt. Governor of Van Diemen's Land.

The return of David Collins to England in 1796 ended his remarkable diary entries about the life and events on the First Fleet voyage and the early settlement. In England he continued writing about the colony up to the year 1800 using letters sent to him by John Hunter. Both sets of diary entries were later published in separate volumes of *An Account of the English Colony in New South Wales*. These give unequalled personal insights into early colonial life.

As Judge Advocate and Governor's Secretary, David Collins was well liked and respected for his fairness and dedication. His personal diaries exhibit true journalism – he recorded events largely without interpretation or comment. Collins did occasionally try to explain the views of his colleagues, especially of the Governors and Lt. Governors for whom he acted as Secretary. In these writings one can sense that under Governors Phillip and Hunter he was prepared to make his own views known; under Grose and Paterson he was not. Collins' journalistic skills fail in only one respect. He wrote virtually nothing about himself, or his relationship with his partner Ann. His colleague and fellow journalist, Watkin Tench, did not hesitate to express his own views. Collins entries are unemotional, objective and informative and reveal nothing about the author. Despite several biographies on his life, David Collins remains largely an enigma.[62]

When David Collins departed Sydney, Richard Atkins became Acting Deputy Judge Advocate.

Chapter 16

FLOODS & DEBTS
1797-1801

The Rope family (the author's grandfather and grandmother) went afterwards to reside at "Tumble-down Barn" near Windsor, and from thence to William Faithfull's Estate, South Creek, between Shanes Park and Dunhaved, where the rest of their family were born, and from which they were afterwards married.[1]

Anthony and Elizabeth Rope had decided it was time to move to more fertile farmland. Their land grant at the Ponds required them to cultivate the property for at least five years, and on 10 Jan 1797 they were now permitted to sell their farm. Like many settlers at the Ponds, the Ropes were disappointed in the recent crop yields and believed that their intensively cultivated soil had lost its fertility. They were attracted to the farmland in the Hawkesbury River district where the soil was rich, and good harvests could be had for much less effort. The prospect of higher productivity was more important than ever for the Ropes who were now off-rations and struggling to keep ahead of food costs and their significant debts. The prices of staple goods had risen to an extent that small farmers without rations whose crop yields were poor could not afford to feed themselves. This forced some settlers to sell their farms to pay off large debts.

The claim in some histories that many farmers at this time lost their land because of alcoholism is unlikely to be true.[2] Some of the Rope's neighbours certainly had major debts, but these mostly arose from low crop yields and the high cost of living in remote areas. Grain sales records reveal that some farmers still accepted payments in rum, and for them the consequences were often grim. The likelihood of alcohol dependency certainly increased if a farmer was already heavily in debt. Unscrupulous traders were always prepared to offer generous cash loans at high interest rates. This often led to bankruptcy, and to the "fire sale" of farms. Through such nefarious dealings, many traders were able to rapidly increase their land holdings and wealth.

Anthony had borrowed money to buy the two properties

adjacent to Rope's farm, Thomas Howard's farm of 30 acres and Elizabeth Ann Clark's farm of 20 acres. He now owned 120 acres and was one of the largest landholders at the Ponds. The land was, of course, a valuable asset for the Ropes, but their loans needed to be serviced, and the capital had to be repaid as quickly as possible. In July 1797 Anthony sold the 70-acre Rope's Farm for £50 to John Larkam. The sale of Rope's farm enabled Anthony to pay off the loans taken out to buy the Howard and Clark farms, and to clear other debts. The Ropes leased their new land to tenant farmers and prepared to move their goods and chattels to the Hawkesbury district. Their leased land at the Ponds would, for some time, act as security against further loans and bankruptcy. If their farming venture at the Hawkesbury failed, they could always return to the Pond properties.

Before vacating their land, Anthony harvested the maize crop and sold the grain. They considered this to be a fair return for the hard work they had put into this year's harvest. The new owner did not agree, and Larkam sued the Ropes for a breach of the sale contract and demanded the return of the value of the missing crop. Without viewing the sale document it is hard to tell whether this was a misunderstanding on Anthony's part. The Criminal Court of Jurisdiction sat on 5 Jul 1797 in the presence of acting Judge Advocate Richard Atkins, Reverend Richard Johnson and Lt. William Kent. John Larkam stated that he had bought Rope's Farm for £50 'with crops', though no documentation has been found to support this. Perhaps such a condition was implicit in a verbal sale at that time. In any case, the court awarded the profits from the grain sale to the plaintiff.[3]

By mid 1797, the Ropes had moved to land near South Creek in the Hawkesbury district. The farming allotments there were first granted by Lt. Governor Grose and had spread along the Hawkesbury River from present-day Pitt Town to Richmond, and along the South Creek up to the junction with the Eastern Creek. By 1797 more than 600 people were living in the district.[4] The Rope family would have walked from Parramatta along the Old Hawkesbury Road to the South Creek. This is an 8-hour walk for an adult but for a family with small children and possessions, it would have taken at least two days. The only practical mode of transportation from South Creek to other parts of the settlement was by foot or by small boat.

For several years after 1798 there is little or no information about the Ropes' activities in the Hawkesbury district. Anthony's name first appears again in the 1800 General Muster of Mulgrave Place, an area encompassing the Hawkesbury and the Creek districts. Locating the land where the Ropes now resided is complicated for a number of reasons:

the deed to the land they purchased was never issued or recorded, and there are conflicting accounts of where the property sat between the South and Eastern creeks.

Toby Ryan, the Ropes' grandson, wrote in his memoirs of 1894 that after the birth of their son Robert, his grandparents 'went to live at Toongabbie'. Ryan also writes that Toongabbie was where his mother Mary was born.[5] Land records do not support this. They show that the Ropes were not in Toongabbie when it was opened up in December 1791; they had moved to their granted land at the Ponds in July of that year. Moreover, Toongabbie was initially a government farm where convicts were sent to do hard labour for committing crimes in the colony. Because of its poor reputation, the Rope family is unlikely to have considered moving there. The Hawkesbury district would have been much more attractive after they had decided to leave the Ponds. When Toby Ryan wrote his book in the 1890's the Ponds area had been amalgamated into a larger district called the Field of Mars, and this complicates the identification of old farm sites. Accurate survey maps were in general not readily accessible in 1890, and those showing farm allocations by name were only available in government offices.

Ryan also says that 'The Rope family went afterwards to reside at "Tumble-down Barn," near Windsor'. He added that this barn was on 'Marsden's old estate' between the South and Eastern Creeks.[6] Reverend Samuel Marsden was a much later landowner in this area. This places the Ropes' farm, at Tumble-down Barn, shown on an 1843 map of the area.[7] Ryan's recollection is consistent, geographically at least, with the Ropes moving to land on the peninsula, later known for its Tumble-down Barn, between the South and Eastern Creeks, just south of the river junction in a district known today as Riverstone.

In 1795, the Administrator of the colony, William Paterson, gave six Corps Privates land grants of 25 acres each on this peninsular.[8] In 1797 it seems that one or several of these soldiers had sold 30 acres of land to Anthony Rope, but there is no record of this sale. A likely explanation is that the Rope's had purchased land that the soldiers were not entitled to sell because of the grant time limit. Such a sale would have been verbal and unofficial, and no deed would have been issued. Some years later, in an 1811 court case about a loan, Anthony admitted that he had not received a deed for the land sale. The lack of a deed for their land would have been a continual source of concern for the Ropes.

Such land transactions did take place frequently although they were not recognised officially. To further complicate the ownership of this land, in November 1799, Governor Hunter issued deeds for the same six 25-acre properties to Sergeant William Sherwin of the NSW Corps, after he had purchased the land from the original owners.[9] In

1803, the 150-acre property was sold to Reverend Samuel Marsden.[10]

Records of these sales reveal that the farmland occupied by the Ropes had been sold from under them, first to William Sherwin and then to Samuel Marsden. Several Corps Privates had obviously managed to sell their allotments twice. Despite all this, the Ropes remained on their South Creek property until late 1805, when they moved to the Nepean River district. Neither Sherwin nor Marsden occupied their land during this period, and the Ropes farmed the land as squatters, albeit having paid money for that right. Much of this is supposition, but it is the likely explanation based on existing records.

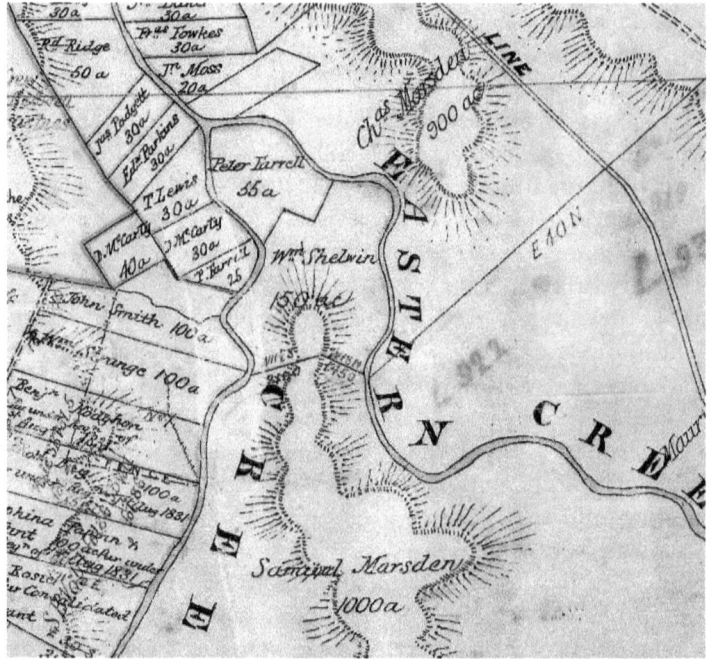

Part of an early (date unknown) St Matthew parish map showing the land allotments between the South and Eastern Creeks of Peter Farrell and William Sherwin. The Ropes lived from 1797 to 1805 in the same area, known as Tumble-down Barn.

When the Ropes moved from the Ponds in 1797 to the timbered plot on South Creek, they faced immediate and pressing challenges. Anthony, at the mature age of 41 years – the average lifespan was then only 45 – set about building a slab hut from timbers hewn from his trees. The hut had just one or two rooms in which all activities of the household took place, the cooking, sleeping, child rearing and socialising. A contemporary map of the area shows their allotment was in a remote corner of the Hawkesbury district, with no neighbours to the south and only one to the north. In 1794, Joseph Burdett had been granted 30 acres between the South and Eastern Creeks, and two months after moving onto his land he was killed by Aborigines. In December 1799, Governor Hunter re-granted Burdett's land, plus an additional 25 acres, to Corps Corporal Peter Farrell.[11] The Rope and the Farrell farms were for some time the most isolated properties in the Hawkesbury district. Without a boat, many neighbouring farms along the substantial South Creek were inaccessible in winter. In summer, South Creek was reduced to small pools in some places and could be crossed on foot.

In general, little is known about the daily lives of female emancipist settlers in the colony, but it can be predicted with some certainty from existing records. Just as it is in today's rural communities, the support and resilience of wives, mothers and daughters were essential to the success and survival of most farming settlements. The women would have worked as hard, and in some cases, harder, than the men. Throughout history pioneering women have shown enormous resilience and fortitude – to succeed in these remote bush areas these were essential attributes. And because they were less susceptible to the temptations of alcoholism and gambling, females were often the bankers in a family. Indeed, without their frugality and insistence to save money in the good times, many more settlers would have undoubtedly failed.

It is reasonably safe to assume that Elizabeth, having lived all her life in rural communities, accepted, and perhaps even enjoyed, the remote farming existence. Of course, she may have thought wistfully about the more comfortable lives that others had in Parramatta and Sydney, but she and Anthony were creating their own little bush paradise and were members of a friendly, close farming community. At least they were free to do as they pleased, with no Corps soldiers interfering in their daily lives. To be in charge of her own destiny gave Elizabeth a sense of security that she had never experienced in England. As a strong young woman of 35, she was dedicated to sharing the running of the farm with Anthony. It was hard work and from time to time they needed to employ assigned convict labourers to clear tree roots, till the soil and plant crops, but because employing men was costly, they did most of the work themselves. Elizabeth also cooked and minded the children. As a team, the Rope family managed a workload that few single settlers could.

When Anthony had finished their wooden hut in early 1797, they began clearing the land, tilling the rich soil and sowing maize and wheat seeds. Elizabeth also established a large vegetable garden. Their first harvests were small but sufficient, and they would have celebrated their success. Robert was now old enough to work with his father in the fields, and Mary helped Elizabeth with domestic chores around the house and the vegetable garden. It would have been unremitting toil from dawn to dusk. But in the evenings Anthony and Elizabeth had each other, and the children gave their lives purpose and kept them entertained. Soon, there would be another addition to the family – Elizabeth knew by the end of 1797 that she was pregnant again.

Establishing the farm at South Creek had been very gruelling for the Ropes but they anticipated better harvests than those at the Ponds, and for less effort. These expectations were, however, about to be tested. It was not widely understood by the new settlers that the low-lying land along the South Creek regularly flooded after heavy rain in the western mountains. These rains turned the Hawkesbury River into a wild torrent, flooding all the adjacent rivers and creeks. Two years on, settlers were to experience the downside of living and farming in a low-lying fertile valley.

None of the Rope children had any schooling and, like their parents, they could neither read nor write. This was not unusual for working families at the time. The colony had several private schools in Sydney and Parramatta, but few settlers could afford them. Besides, farmer's children older than six were needed to assist their parents or be employed elsewhere to bring in money. Moreover, education in most farm districts was impractical simply because of distance – the nearest school to the Ropes would entail a few hours travel by boat down the South Creek. The only books likely to be in the Rope household were those with illustrations. An educated neighbour might occasionally visit and read to the whole family. This would have been a very special treat. Settlers who did have books would sometimes read aloud to large groups, adults as well as children, in local meeting places or around a fire. Such shared literary events were eagerly anticipated in farming communities, even when attendance involved considerable travel by foot or by boat.

Governor Hunter directed much of his efforts into increasing food production. He was well aware that the cost of hired labour, the high price of staple goods, and the unfair usury practises in the colony were threatening the settlers' existence. He approached the farming community and asked them to suggest solutions to these problems. It was probably the first time in the colony's history that the settlers had been invited by the governor to express their views as a group, and to have their petitions considered in person.[12]

In January 1797, Governor Hunter received the written statements from the settlers about the 'excessively exorbitant' of free labourers, and how this limited productivity. He asked that selected representatives from each district meet regularly and decide what were fair wages.[13] Two months later, agreement had been reached on fixing the labour charges and on the appropriate penalties for breaches of these rates.[14] In June 1797, Hunter reported to the Home Office that unfair trading of goods and grain was not just confined to Corps officers, but also to public servants. He recommended that the superintendents and storekeepers who spent more time trading goods than on their official duties, be dismissed.[15]

In January 1798, on receiving a further petition from settlers, Hunter wrote to the Home Office that the prices charged to settlers by traders were 'out of all reason exorbitant'.[16] Because of the high profit margins on goods purchased by merchants from ships, their retail prices were much higher than in government stores. Moreover, the government stores had little stock because retailers had paid ships much higher wholesale prices. Hunter sympathised with the settlers, suggesting 'that their distresses be considered, and that some means be devised for relieving them in the purchase of such European articles as they require'. He told Home Office Secretary Portland that unless this was stopped, the farmers would not be able to produce enough grain for the colony.

> The settlers are so frequently ruined, their crops mortgaged, their persons imprisoned, and their families beggared, and falling back upon the public store to prevent starving through the heavy debts they contract, ... their ground by this means becomes useless for the want of strength to work it.[17]

Hunter wanted settlers to be as financially independent as possible, and he requested the Home Office to send additional officers to help accomplish this task. A month later, in February 1798, he visited the settlements and met with the farmers, observing that because of 'the frequent bankruptcy of some of our oldest settlers' they were much distressed, and he asked for written statements of their hardships.[18]

Reverend Marsden and Surgeon Arndell were ordered to go to the farm districts and encourage the settlers to write down their grievances. In these statements, the farmers accused the traders, dealers and publicans as being 'the engines of our destruction' and claimed that the colony was now 'infested with dealers, pedlars, and extortioners it is absolutely necessary to extirpate them'. They were also infuriated that wealthy merchants claimed tea and sugar were luxuries 'a settler ought not to aspire to'. To the settlers this was a 'most egregious error', since many of those who purchased tea, ate very little meat, preferring instead to employ more farm labourers, with whom they shared these luxuries.[19]

The retailers naturally refuted claims that large debts were due to high prices. They argued that most loans taken out to consume alcohol, and that this had brought about the settlers' ruin. Marsden and Arndell disagreed, claiming it was the cost of general commodities.[20] The settlers were buoyed by this report, believing that the governor would now address these inequities. Farmers from the Field of Mars district hailed Hunter as "the angel from heaven" who would abolish these evils.[21]

Marsden and Arndell also recorded that, of the 73 farmers settled by Governor Phillip, only 21 remained on their land by March 1798. Of the 16 original settlers at the Ponds, only four were still living on their farms. The rest had sold their farms, or rented them out to tenant farmers, in order to settle debts. The farmers who remained were all very poor. However, Marsden and Arndell stated that 'It may be proper to observe that ye first settlers were considered as men of general good character' and that creditors had taken too many farmers to court to recoup their money. They added that 'Unless some speedy and salutary measures are adopted to save the falling landed interest, it is our joint opinion ye expenses of government and the distress of the farmers will duly accumulate'. The report concluded that the problems facing small farmers were usually not of their own making.[22]

Farmers expected Governor Hunter to act promptly on this damning report. They were disappointed – the settler's grievances had been heard and understood, but the influence of the NSW Corps was still powerful, and Hunter's resolve weakened. He instead recommended to the Home Office that a public store be established where European articles could be bought at a reasonable price. He suggested that such a store would undercut the retailers and allow the settlers to buy goods with produce from their farms.[23] In November, the Home Office replied and reprimanded the governor for not acting on this matter earlier, since he had already received the authority in August 1797.[24]

Other malpractices adversely affecting settlers continued to flourish. When the smaller farmers wanted to sell their grain, the larger landholders prevented sales by falsely claiming the granaries were full. Farmers then had to sell at a lower price to someone with enough influence to have the grain stored. It also became common practice for grain dealers to use false weights when buying settlers' produce. In an attempt to circumvent this, the weights used by dealers had to be proofed by the government.[25] This slowed the practice, but, without the cooperation of the Corps, fraudulent practices were not eliminated.

Government records clearly show that Hunter wanted to govern justly, but the Corps officers responsible for implementing his orders largely ignored his directives. The Corps maintained the pretence of good order by paying lip service to official edicts, but where possible avoided their execution, unless, of course, they suited their own business interests. Hunter was obviously aware that his authority was being undermined, but he apparently lacked the strength of character, or the ability, to enforce his authority. Faced with such conspicuous opposition from the Corps officers, Hunter delayed, or entirely postponed, matters requiring his attention. Several influential people in the colony communicated this to the Home Office, complaining that Hunter's governorship had become ineffectual.

There was a great deal to admire about John Hunter both as a person and a naval officer. He had been a first class Post Captain in the Royal Navy, an outstanding mariner and navigator and Arthur Phillip's right-hand man in the first years of the settlement. But a naval command was quite different to running a government; naval orders were executed without hesitation or severe punishment ensued. No such penalties applied to his orders as governor, especially when policed by the Corps. Hunter strived to do many admirable and worthwhile things during his governorship but he was simply unable to cope with the politics inherent in his position, particularly against the ruthless behind-the-scenes manoeuvring that John Macarthur was so expert in. With the Corps' backing, Macarthur effectively had "the majority vote" on all colonial decisions. And, unfortunately, because the Corps administered law and order in the colony, Hunter believed that unless he trod cautiously the security of the colony would be threatened.

Surprisingly, in early 1797, Hunter had secretly lobbied the Home Office to replace the NSW Corps with a contingent of regular marines. Government orders were set in train to have a detachment of marines embark on the next transport to New South Wales.[26] Tragically for the colony, the orders were cancelled owing to the priorities of the war with France, and the regiment was stationed elsewhere. The Irish Rebellion further impeded the possibility of a new military contingent being sent to the colony in 1798. The Home Office had other pressing matters and Hunter's request to replace the NSW Corps was forgotten.

John Macarthur, however, had a much more receptive ear within the Home Office. He wrote frequently to the Duke of Portland about Hunter's interference in Corps matters, avoiding any mention of his main concern that the Corps officer's profits were being eroded. Macarthur was a prolific correspondent and something of a bush lawyer, and his views on what was good for the colony would have been in stark contrast to that of Hunter. He complained about excessive government spending, the granting of land to settlers who were lazy and incapable of farming it, and of moral degradation in the colony, where 'vice of every description is openly encouraged'.[27] For Macarthur, these problems were just the tip of the iceberg, and he hammered all of them home to Secretary Portland. Governor Hunter was largely unaware of the contents of Macarthur's letters until the Home Office demanded a response to the allegations.

Despite of his administrative distractions Hunter continued to pursue his love of exploring, and he encouraged the careful mapping of the coastline of New South Wales. In the first years of the settlement, little was known of the east coast 30 km north of Port Jackson. It had not yet been established that New South Wales and the west coast of New Holland were part of the same continent. In 1795, George Bass and a group of men had attempted to cross the Blue Mountains but were forced back by a lack of provisions. Hunter funded attempts by Lt. Matthew Flinders and Surgeon George Bass to chart the New South Wales coastline. In 1797, Bass mapped parts of Victoria, and in 1798 he and Flinders sailed along the northern coast of Van Diemen's Land, proving that it was separated from the mainland. At Flinders' suggestion, Governor Hunter named these waters *Bass Strait*.

On 1 Mar 1798, Elizabeth, aged 36, gave birth to a baby girl on their remote South Creek farm, with probable help from neighbours. Three months later, on June 26th, baby Sarah was baptised by Samuel Marsden in Parramatta's first church, a makeshift construction of two timber huts.[28] Anthony had taken his whole family to Parramatta, first by boat on the South Creek and then on an eight-hour walk along the old Parramatta Road. Before they set out, the Ropes harvested their crops and took the grain to the store in Green Hills (today called Windsor). Because of the width and depth of the South Creek – in places it was 10 metres wide and several metres deep for most of the year – it is highly likely that the Ropes owned, or had easy access to, a small rowing boat. Without this the Rope family could not have left their farm for much of the year. In Parramatta, their daughter was blessed, and afterwards the Ropes probably collected the rent from their two tenant farmers at the Ponds. They also took the opportunity to meet old friends, such as John Summers, who was still living at the Ponds. It was a visit that Elizabeth would not make again for many years.

At their South Creek farm, Anthony had built a small jetty for shipping future grain harvests to Green Hills. Their land was now partially cleared of timber and the tasks of sowing and harvesting grain became routine. In early January, the land was manually tilled before sowing maize to be harvested in March; and from April to May wheat grain was sown, this cropped in November-December. Another crop of maize, planted in October, was harvested at the end of the year.[29]

In the summer months of January to March in 1799, the colony experienced a severe drought. The creeks in the Hawkesbury district dried up and the summer heat led to fierce bush fires in the Parramatta and Sydney areas. In late March the drought ended with days of heavy rain, and the ensuing overflow from the vast Nepean-Hawkesbury catchment area roared down the Hawkesbury River and connected waterways. The river rose 50 ft (15 m) and was so powerful 'it carried all before it'. This happened so quickly that the settlers along low-lying parts of the Hawkesbury River and South Creek were quite unprepared for the floods. Storehouses, huts, crops and animals were swept away. Although only one life was lost, many people needed to be rescued from the tops of their houses and trees by the few boats in the district, and their farms were devastated.[30]

The farmers on the banks of the South Creek had more reason than most to bemoan their losses. They lived on the lowest part of the district that had been inundated in smaller floods in 1795.[31] As the Ropes' farm was on a low bend between the South Creek and Eastern Creek, their crops and pigs were lost, and the roof of their hut was probably their refuge during deluge. It would have been a truly frightening time for the Rope children. Elizabeth had faced danger before, but now she was afraid for her family.

When the floods receded, the Ropes were confronted with a landscape of utter devastation. They immediately set about recovering as much as possible and rebuilding their small hut; the whole family pitching in and keeping alert for the many snakes sheltering in the debris. By April, the farm had been mostly cleared. The loss of their maize crop was especially upsetting as this was their financial mainstay and provided fodder for the surviving pigs. On the positive side, the heavy mud from the flood improved soil fertility, and maize seeds were sown as soon as possible. A good crop was expected to follow, provided the flood was a one-off. The settlers had not yet fully appreciated that the remarkable richness of the area was a result of regular flooding, just as it was in Egypt's fertile Nile Valley.

By 1800 the farmers in the Hawkesbury area had become the colony's main grain producers. This meant that the heavy flood losses were a severe blow to the viability of the colony as a whole. Most of the farms belonging to Corps officers were closer to Parramatta, and their losses from flooding were comparatively light. The losses of the farmers on the Hawkesbury, who were almost exclusively croppers, were the heaviest. But they were a hardy and optimistic lot – with such variability in weather conditions they needed to be. By November many reported that their crops were 'bending beneath the weight of the richest ears of corn ever beheld in this or indeed any other country'.[32]

But nature owes no favours. Just before harvesting was due, heavy gales flattened the wheat crops. The Ropes and many small farmers in the area were now destitute. The wind damage caused the price of flour in the colony to rocket to new highs. However, to the astonishment of the farmers whose crops partially survived the storm, the prices offered by the government store were 20% lower than for last year's harvest. Hunter wanted to keep food prices low, following the criticism of the Home Office for not doing so previously. He also demanded that outstanding debts had to be paid before grain would be received into the stores. The outraged settlers refused to put their wheat on the market until their returns properly reflected the shortage in supply. They maintained the boycott for three months until there was a flour crisis in the colony and Hunter agreed to match last year's price.[33]

To justify backing down on the wheat prices to the Home Office, Hunter requested some supporting submissions from the settlers that claimed the low grain prices were 'intolerable'. At the time, merchants were selling goods in the Hawkesbury area at prices double those in Sydney. A report submitted to Hunter estimated that the cost of growing 25 bushels of wheat to be £13 5s 9d, whereas it could only be sold for £12 10s.[34]

By 1800 the settlements of Sydney and Parramatta had grown in size and prosperity to a level that Arthur Phillip would have found hard to believe. The districts in New South Wales had a population of 5100, of whom 1931 were serving convicts. The number of children in the colony had risen from 54 in 1788 to 832 in 1800. Despite the recent floods, the Hawkesbury remained the preferred farming area. Few of the 829 cattle and 5676 sheep in the colony belonged to small settlers, but they owned half of the 3088 goats, and 81% of the 2390 pigs. Settlers were the main grain growers, harvesting 76% (42,757 bushels) of the colony's wheat.[35]

In February 1800, the Hawkesbury settlers presented another petition to the governor complaining about high prices in the district. They omitted the usual diplomatic niceties and made their case as eight emphatic bullet points. The petition represented 181 settlers, of whom, 173 signed.[36] Anthony would have been one of them. The settlers bluntly said that not enough had been done to rectify their situation. Hunter disagreed, claiming he had been more than supportive of the settlers. Realising that perhaps they had gone too far, the settlers wrote another more temperate petition, and this was received more favourably. Hunter assured the settlers that he would rectify any aggravation within his power.[37] But it soon became apparent to the settlers that the governor was no longer prepared to act on their complaints, or he had decided that fixing the inflated prices was impossible.

In March 1800 the Hawkesbury flooded again. The river burst its banks and flooded crops in the basin ready for harvesting.[38] Anthony

FLOODS & DEBTS 1797-1801

and Elizabeth's land and hut were inundated. They would have to start from scratch again, only this time the money they had saved from the last harvest had been spent. Bankruptcy and famine loomed over the community and some settlers decided they were fighting a losing battle against nature and gave up. But within a month, the Ropes had cleared the land of flood debris and replanted wheat and maize seeds. Along with most settlers in the area, the Ropes had to go into further debt to buy seeds for the replanting.

The Hawkesbury floods occurred just when there was about to be a change in governors. On 15 Apr 1800 the transport ship *Speedy* docked in Port Jackson with Captain Philip Gidley King on board. Dispatches from the Duke of Portland recalled John Hunter to England, and appointed Captain King as governor. The letters from Macarthur and others to the Home Office had destroyed Hunter's reputation.[39] However, the lack of political strength and leadership had also led to John Hunter's downfall. The Home Office had not received his written defence of the charges made against him before they had appointed Philip Gidley King as his replacement.

Portrait of John Hunter, the colony's second governor (1795-1800).

Portrait of Philip Gidley King, the colony's third governor (1800-1806).

Captains King and Hunter had been colleagues on the First Fleet, and knew each other well, but the handover of government was not smooth or swift. The 63-year-old incumbent governor had no intention of departing quickly and pressed a claim to command the new warship, HMS *Buffalo* (that had not yet arrived in Port Jackson) for his return to England. Hunter remained governor for another five months, during which time his relationship with Captain King deteriorated badly.

While waiting for the handover, King reported to the Home Office that a feeling of 'vice, dissipation, and a strange relaxation' had invaded the colony. Alcohol 'that fiery poison' was everywhere, in the cellars of the 'better sort of people' and with the 'blackest character among the convicts'.[40] King predicted that his duties during the next five years would be laborious and highly discouraging. He also noted that the prices for the common necessaries were even too high for *him* to pay, and that many other disagreeable issues had been left for him to sort out.

In July 1800, a General Muster of all residents, land and livestock in the colony was conducted. Anthony Rope is recorded as having 8 pigs, 10 acres of wheat crop and 5 acres planted with maize, and that the Rope family was 'off store' (no government rations).[41] The muster records show (incorrectly) that the land at South Creek had been *granted* to Anthony, and that 70% of the Hawkesbury farmers had over 6 acres under cultivation – which, by John Macarthur's assessment, would have qualified them as industrious.[42] Since Anthony had 15 acres cultivated, he had easily met Macarthur's meritorious criterion. It was a major achievement to clear, hoe and plant such a large area even with the help of an assigned convict labourer, though there is no record of a resident servant in this muster. Elizabeth and the children Robert, 11, and Mary, 9, would have been Anthony's main help in the fields, and during the seeding and harvesting, neighbours may have lent a hand. The settlers in this area pulled together in order to survive and prosper.

By midyear a rumour was circulating in the Hawkesbury district that the government was not going to buy this year's grain crops, and King, who was not yet governor, made strenuous efforts to refute it.[43] A lack of a market for their grain would have meant the total ruin for small farmers. King was involved in other issues as well. Following instructions from Britain, he stepped up the campaign to eradicate the rum trade. His first step was to impose strict regulations that forbade government workers to trade in alcohol.[44] There was fierce opposition to these reforms, and he wryly commented that 'the greater their rank is the more I shall be the object of their resentment'.[45]

Finally, on 25 Sep 1800, the 42-year-old Philip Gidley King was installed as the third Governor of New South Wales. On September 28th, John Hunter embarked on the HMS *Buffalo* to return to England. Hunter had been an honest and faithful servant of the Crown and the colony, but he struggled in his role as governor. His recall was probably necessary, but the strong censure from the Home Office was undeserved. Few men could have maintained strong governance in the colony when the power lay in the hands of the military, and Hunter was simply not one of those.

The political fragility of the colonial administration would persist for years and could only be solved by decisive action from the Home Office.[46] When Hunter reached England, he requested a public inquiry into the charges made against his administration, but Home Office Secretary Portland refused to see him. Two years later, in an attempt to clear his name, Hunter published his own account of his administration.[47] His service as Governor of New South Wales was eventually acknowledged with a pension grant. He continued his interest in the colony long after his departure. In 1807, he became a Rear Admiral and, in 1810, was promoted to Vice Admiral. He died in 1821 at the venerable age of 83.

The new governor and his wife Anna, and their son and two daughters moved into the governor's house. King was determined to solve longstanding problems in the colony. Based on the demographic data of the 1800 Muster, he issued a series of governmental edicts designed to remove the principal abuses of previous administrations. First, he limited the number of servants assigned to Corps officers, or civil personnel, to two convicts. Next, he prohibited anyone other than administration officials going aboard incoming cargo ships, and insisted the government have first choice on purchasing imported goods. Private retailers were only permitted a 20% mark-up on the remaining goods.[48] He also established public warehouses that sold imported articles at a low profit. These controls immediately reduced retail prices.

King knew that these changes would irritate the Corps officers, but he had learnt from Hunter's demise to keep the Home Office informed of his actions. He also forwarded the responses of residents, both good and bad. Regular and detailed communications with England was needed to counter the letters sent by Corps officers critical of his actions. He inundated the Home Office with statistics on everything; people, land and livestock, finance, purchasing, prices of goods, labour prices, employment, weekly rations, provisions in the storehouses as well as incoming ships' cargo and what was purchased. King's style was decidedly managerial. He kept abreast of the demographic and production figures that enabled him to monitor fiscal success and anticipate issues that his opponents would try to use against him.

On 6 Jan 1801, the settlers on the South Creek sent a petition to Governor King requesting his indulgence in assisting with their high debts. The petition was largely in response to requests from the administration edict that government loans should be repaid, or debtors would face immediate prosecution.[49] Anthony Rope was one of the 19 settlers on the petition. The Ropes, and many other settlers, had taken out loans following heavy losses from floods. This was a necessity to replace seeds, stock and homes lost in the floods. They requested King's compassion in averting the loss of their farms, and their consequent imprisonment and ruin. They pointed out that the successive floods of 1799 and 1800 had left them 'helpless spectators only of our stacks, Barns, Houses and stock swimming down the current'. They reminded the governor that an earlier successful petition had permitted an extension on their loan terms, but, just when the current wheat crop was ready for harvesting, the most recent heavy rains and floods had washed away any hope of meeting these obligations.[50]

A sketch showing the extent of the 1816 flood in Windsor. On the right is the flooded South Creek with only the rooftops of farmhouses visible above the water.

The petitioners complained that to add to 'our misfortune our Creditors also request their dues and threatening to sell our Farms and throw us in Gaol if we do not or cannot immediately pay them'. They hoped that 'with another season which by hard Labour, Diligence and frugality so we cultivate once more, by doing which and trying all we can hope with the blessing of Providence to be able to pay our debts'.[51] King was greatly concerned about the effects of these successive disasters in a region producing most of the colony's grain. He assured the settlers that the administration would look into their concerns favourably.

Illustration of the plight of families in the 1867 Hawkesbury flood. The Ropes would have been in the same situation in the 1799 and 1801 floods when they had been rescued from their rooftops or from floating debris.

Before the government could act on the petition, yet another flood in 1801, the *third in four months*, swept through the district. The Hawkesbury River rose 40 ft (12 m) and the flood was so extensive that it drove settlers from their land. To survive, many people had to hang 'in trees and pieces of floating wood, until the floods subsided'.[52] The Rope family avoided drowning by sitting on the roof of their hut. Their grandson, Toby Ryan, recalled the flood 93 years later. He wrote that while walking to Windsor, he passed by the Tumble-down Barn:

> where their grandfather and mother, uncles and aunts resided at the time of the great August flood, and who were rescued from the barn loft, where they had taken refuge for three days and nights, by that heroine, Margaret Catchpole.[53]

The plight of parents and children sitting on a roof for three full days in the cold, wind and rain would be extreme – it was probably more frightening than the voyage from England. Eventually, a neighbour would have heard their shouts and rescued them by boat. Toby Ryan's account of this being 'the great August flood' is unlikely to be correct. The only Hawkesbury flood *in August* was in 1809, and by then the Ropes had moved to Jordan Hill in the Castlereagh district. The famous emancipist, Margaret Catchpole, did eventually reside in the Hawkesbury area, but not until much later; she only arrived from England in December 1801. Catchpole was subjected to the 1806 and 1809 floods, and had sat on a roof, but there is no evidence of her rescuing anyone. When the Ropes moved to Agnes Banks in Castlereagh in 1805, she worked on neighbouring farms as a midwife and nurse. Later, Catchpole owned land at Agnes Banks, facing Castlereagh Road.[54]

Governor King eventually declared the devastating 1801 floods a natural calamity. He reported to the Home Office that the Hawkesbury settlers were 'exhibiting such a state of woeful misery that is but seldom seen or heard of'. They had lost their clothing, houses, wheat and corn harvests and nearly all of their animals. King saw this as a disaster for the entire colony; over half of its grain and most of its pork meat came from the Hawkesbury. Without this produce, the colony faced a major food shortage, and King seriously considered sending ships to India to supplement the grain supply.[55]

After recovering as much as they could from their flooded farms, 82 settlers from the Hawkesbury pleaded with the governor in another petition.[56] They told him that successive floods over two years had destroyed almost everything they owned, and they were greatly in debt. They asked King to delay creditors from demanding loan repayments and to stop the threats of gaol. Following previous floods creditors had forced defaulting settlers to put their farms up for sale, and they were sold for only a tenth of their value. King acted swiftly and gave settlers a one-year's suspension of any civil court action by creditors.[57] Despite this reprieve, many settlers were so disheartened by their losses that they gave up cultivating their farms and worked for the settlers who persevered. Anthony was in the latter category, while there was still strength left in his body, he would stay a farmer. He and Elizabeth remained determined to create a better future for their growing family.

In 1801 the Ropes had their sixth child, Susannah. Elizabeth was by now 39 years old. The work needed on the farm following the floods meant that they had no time to travel to Parramatta for a baptism, and, in any case, it was no longer affordable; putting bread on the table came first, the baptism would have to come later.

In July 1801, another muster was carried out in the colony. A General Order was issued requesting all females and children in the Hawkesbury region assemble at the Government House on July 5th in Green Hills. All male settlers who held land by grant, purchase or rent were assembled on July 17th at Green Hills and were required to bring the deeds of their granted land.[58] The only way for the Ropes to reach that location was to sail down South Creek. Although Anthony did not have a deed for the land, he was recorded in the muster to have *purchased* the land.⁵⁹ They are shown to have 30 acres land, of which 8 had been cleared; 2½ acres had been sown in wheat and 6 acres in maize. The Ropes owned 8 pigs, held 4 bushels (102 kg) of maize and were in debt to the government. The entire family, 2 adults and 5 children, were no longer receiving government rations. The listing of only 5 children means that young Elizabeth had died prior to the muster. Her death was probably not officially registered because the closest cemetery and church was in Parramatta. The cause of death is unknown but it likely to have been connected to the floods or subsequent diseases. The young Elizabeth would have been less than six when she died and was probably buried in an unmarked grave on, or near, the Rope's property.

To help repay their debts, the Ropes decided to rent out part of their South Creek farm to John Dunn, an Irish emancipist who arrived in the colony in 1796. The subdivision of farmland became a necessity for many settlers badly affected by the floods to keep creditors at bay. Settlers deeply in debt sold their entire farm. In an attempt to remain farmers, some settlers kept just enough acreage to feed themselves and their families.⁶⁰

In contrast to the exhausting, hazardous lives of the Rope family, Henry and Susannah Kable, Elizabeth's Norwich Castle prison friends, lived comfortably in Sydney Cove. Henry was clever at finding good jobs, such as the supervisor of female convicts, and in 1791 when he became a member of the colonial night watch. Always on the lookout for business opportunities, Henry had struck up friendships with Corps officers, and they later secured him a post in the military administration. Lt. Governor Grose had gifted him two land grants in Sydney, 30 acres in 1794 and 15 acres in 1795.⁶¹ Shortly after this, he was appointed as a Constable and Nightwatchman.

In August 1796, Matthew Farrel was shot by the night watch. Henry Kable was charged with his murder but was found not guilty. In 1796, Kable was made Chief Constable and Gaoler of Sydney Cove. From 1798, he owned a tavern in the Sydney Rocks area opposite the gaol where he was Chief Constable. While performing these duties, he pursued several financial ventures with Corps officers. In 1799, Kable was indicted for providing the metal sheeting to build an illegal alcohol still, and for warning distillers that an inspection was imminent. The case was dismissed in court. He later invested in emerging boat-making and seal-slaughtering industries.⁶²

The 1800 Muster shows Henry Kable as Chief Constable with three convict servants, having 55 acres in wheat, 100 acres in barley and 40 in maize, 100 pigs, 7 goats, and 3 horses.⁶³ Remarkably, but not surprisingly, the wealthy Kable family still received rations from the public store. Public servants and military personnel were eligible for food rations independent of their income or wealth. In stark contrast, the struggling Ropes had not received rations since 1794. It is unsurprising that farmers battling to eke out a meagre living saw the entitlements of persons of influence, as a great injustice. When Governor King regulated trading from ships and restricted alcohol importation, Kable would have almost certainly been among those opposed to this reform. In 1802, Governor King dismissed Kable as Chief Constable for behaving poorly in the execution of his duties.[64] Along with John Macarthur, Henry Kable was later complicit in the Rum Rebellion, and strongly supported Governor Bligh's dismissal.

Alcohol was still being shipped into the colony in large volumes, but, because of the latest government controls, many ships left without clearing their cargo. In the first six months of 1801, the restrictions prevented the landing of 36,000 gallons (163,660 litres) of spirit and 22,000 gallons (100,000 litres) of wine. Although King restricted alcohol importation, he encouraged the purchase of 'dry goods' from ships at a regulated price.[65] The crackdown on the rum trade and the regulation of imported goods, met with strong resistance from the Corps, since it struck at the very heart of their business model. It meant that a clash between Captain John Macarthur and Governor King was inevitable.

In July 1801, Governor King reversed a court sentence committing Lt. James Marshall to one year in prison. He had been found guilty of assaulting Captains Macarthur and Abbott during an investigation into a theft. The governor referred the matter for trial in England, on the grounds that the court had refused to consider Lt. Marshall's objection to Corps officers sitting on the bench. Macarthur vigorously objected to this interference. King duly reported these objections to the Home Office and predicted correctly that 'One thing I shall remark, that the arts and intrigues of a man you have heard so much about (I mean Captain McArthur) will one day or other sett this colony in a flame'.[66] This prediction was well founded.

Macarthur considered the referral of the trial to England as another insult to the Corps and demanded that all officers boycott the governor's social invitations. When the Corps' senior officer, Colonel Paterson, refused to agree to this request, Macarthur threatened to destroy him by revealing his personal correspondence. Paterson had had his fill of this irritating subordinate and challenged him to a duel, which took place in September 1801. In the duel, Paterson received a severe wound and was expected to soon die. Macarthur was arrested but was released when Paterson recovered. In an attempt to defuse the situation King decided that he would send Macarthur to Norfolk Island as the

Corps Commandant. But Macarthur refused the appointment and demanded to be court martialled by his fellow officers. King knew that Macarthur held too much power in the Corps to have him tried in the colonial court, and preferred that the matter be dealt with in England.[67] King made it very clear to the Home Office 'that if Captain McArthur returns here in any official character it should be that of Governor, as one-half the colony already belongs to him, and it will not be long before he gets the other half'.[68] In a letter to Secretary Portland on 14 Nov 1801 he revealed his frustration at Macarthur's conduct, and that he had ordered him to leave the colony. King assured the Home Office that the opposition of Corps officers was not shared across the community.

> I have a pleasure in assuring your Grace of the general regular behaviour of the inhabitants, and wish I could say as much of those whose support I ought to have, instead of the opposite tendency their conduct has shewn.[69]

In mid-November 1801, John Macarthur sailed to England on the ship *Hunter* (a fitting coincidence of names perhaps). Before departing, he purchased 1400 sheep and left his wife in charge of the farm.[70] The popular Elizabeth Macarthur, and her farm supervisors, not her husband, were mostly responsible for the sheep breeding at their Parramatta farm; a historical fact that is not widely appreciated.[71]

Governor King sent dispatches to the Home Office on the ship *Anna Josepha*, giving full details of the charges against John Macarthur. However, when this ship docked in England the governor's submissions had vanished from the dispatch box. An associate of Macarthur aboard the *Anna Josepha* was almost certainly responsible for the theft, but no inquiry was held into their disappearance. The loss of Governor King's evidence gave Macarthur a clear advantage in the enquiry, and he was not court-marshalled. He was severely censured for bad conduct and released.

In 1805, Captain John Macarthur would return to the Sydney settlement in triumph.

Chapter 17

GOVERNORS KING & BLIGH 1802-1806

> *We beg to observe that had we deputed anyone, John McArthur would not have been chosen by us, we considering him an unfit person to step forward upon such an occasion, as we may chiefly attribute the rise in the price of mutton to his withholding the large flock of wethers he now has to make such price as he may choose to demand.*[1]

After John Macarthur's expulsion from the colony in November 1801, Governor King set about addressing the remaining obstacles that prevented his administration from efficient and fair governance. Many trade malpractices persisted in the colony, and the NSW Corps remained in control of the rum trade. He knew his reforms would generate further friction with the Corps, but King was determined to eradicate the alcohol trade and monopolies once and for all. The governor was well aware that Corps officers would keep Macarthur informed of the reforms, and they were now inclined to rebuke him in public.

King responded by isolating the military where possible from his administration and developing stronger links with the progressive emancipist and free settlers in the community. He reinforced this by pardoning large numbers of well-behaved and productive convicts, creating, in effect, an influential "emancipist block" within the colony. His government maintained that all emancipists were 'as Free and Susceptible of every Right as Free Born Britons as any Soul in this Territory'.[2] The pardons granted were at two levels, conditional and absolute. A conditional pardon cancelled sentences but obliged emancipists to remain in the colony. An absolute pardon permitted an emancipist to return to England if he or she so wished.

King granted more pardons than any previous governor. Arthur Phillip had granted 26 pardons, John Hunter 36, and Philip Gidley King 78. Many of the new emancipists played an important role in the colony, and, in effect, became the governor's political backers and advisors. They did not, however, join the civil service or the military.[3] One of the men to receive a full pardon was the convict Henry Fulton, who was born in

England and ordained as a minister of the Anglican Church of Ireland. Fulton was implicated in the 1798 Irish Rebellion and sentenced to transportation for life. King gave him a pardon in 1805, and he was appointed a colonial chaplain. Fulton became a strong ally of Governor King, and later a friend of Governor Bligh. Over the years, Fulton consistently supported the Hawkesbury settlers, and became the Rope family's chaplain in the newly established Castlereagh Church.

The Irish Catholic priest, Father James Dixon, was another political prisoner to receive a conditional pardon from King. Because of his involvement in the Irish Rebellion, Dixon was sentenced to death in 1798, commuted later to transportation for life. After his pardon in 1803, he was allowed to administer the Holy Sacrament, provided he and his congregation strictly obeyed the governor's orders. Later, two of Anthony and Elizabeth's sons-in-laws, Thomas Frost in 1815 and John Ryan in 1821, were granted conditional pardons. King also initiated a ticket of leave system, which awarded temporary freedom for a defined period to convicts who exhibited good behaviour and were able to support themselves. [4] A ticket of leave allowed convicts to seek employment within a specified district, but the holders were not permitted to leave that area without a magistrate's permission.

Governor King's generous concessions for small farmers provided the price stability and predictability needed to increase grain production. The new regulations he imposed on retail prices, wages, working hours, financial arrangements and assigned convicts, particularly benefited settlers. He also tried to reduce forgeries by introducing printed forms for promissory notes. Unfortunately, these were not widely accepted. After repeated complaints from farmers about the unreliable shipment of produce from the farming districts into Sydney, King made sure that the transportation of grain from the Hawkesbury was properly policed.[5] The settlers were appreciative of his help, and in 1803 he was sent a letter with over 200 signatories, thanking him 'for the many fold blessings we freely enjoy from your determined, just, and salutary Government'. The settlers were particularly grateful that King had suppressed 'the infamous and ruinous monopolies'.

> You have, by the extirpation of that great evil, rendered our lives comfortable, our circumstances easy, our families happy, and given a prospect to our children of becoming useful members to society, which otherways must have had no other opening into the world than a life of trouble, and in all probability a life of infamy. You have, by your impartial and just Government over those under your command, brought to us that sense of liberty which we never felt before. By your administration of justice, the

rich, the poor, the free, and the bond, enjoy the same privileges as if in our mother country, where no distinctions are made.[6]

Through King's leadership the colony had finally become self-sufficient. His promotion of freedom of expression and better communications led, in March 1803, to the establishment of the colony's first newspaper, *The Sydney Gazette and New South Wales Advertiser*. The editor was the emancipist George Howe.[7] *The Sydney Gazette* became the official government publication for orders, laws and regulations.

Between 1801 and 1803 the circumnavigation of the island continent *Terra Australis* (otherwise known as New Holland) was completed, and this exploration verified it was a single landmass. Lt. Matthew Flinders on the *Investigator* had sailed around the continent and charted its shoreline. This occurred at a time when the French were engaged in a similar survey. Alerted to the presence of the French ships, Governor King advised the British in 1802 to establish a settlement in the Port Phillip area of Bass Strait.[8] Within weeks of receiving this advice in London, Captain David Collins, the previous Judge Advocate of the New South Wales colony, was appointed Lt. Governor of Port Phillip.

In late 1802, two French ships, *Geographe* and *Naturaliste*, under the command of Captain Nicolas Baudin, sailed into Port Jackson for refitting, provisions and water. While in Sydney, they were entertained by Governor King who spoke good French. The French officers were 'completely astonished at the flourishing state ... [of] this singular, and distant establishment'.[9] They had anticipated a struggling village, but found a town with substantial buildings, a stone clock, windmill, hospitals, schools and prisons, warehouses, barracks, stores and shipbuilding in the dockyards.

The visitors also noted that many ships from different parts of the world were anchored in the vast harbour. What impressed the French most was the abundance of agricultural products. The 'immense and useless forest of Eucalyptus' had been transformed into productive fields, pastures and orchards. Baudin was staggered at the advances the English had made over the previous 12 years and wrote (in French) that it 'was difficult to conceive how they have so speedily attained to the state of splendour and comfort in which they now find themselves'.[10]

When the French ships sailed out of Port Jackson to resume their expedition, it was reported to King that someone had heard that the French intended establishing a settlement on Van Diemen's Land.[11] King quickly arranged for a fast vessel to overhaul the French ships and determine their intentions. He was assured that this rumour was baseless. Nevertheless, King remained suspicious, and, in August 1803, he sent Lt. John Bowen with 49 other men to establish a small settlement on Van

Diemen's Land at the Derwent River.[12]

When Lt. Governor David Collins reached Port Phillip on 9 Oct 1803, he disembarked some convicts, settlers and stores at Sullivan Bay (near Sorrento), but was disappointed at the lack of timber and water close to the settlement site. When Collins complained about the poor soil at Sullivan Bay, King recommended moving the settlement to Van Diemen's Land. Collins promptly reloaded the ship and sailed to a site on the south coast of the island that was named Hobart Town after the Colonial Office Secretary Lord Hobart.[13] Port Phillip remained unoccupied for the next 31 years. In October 1804, King's deputy, Corps Commandant Col. William Paterson, was commissioned to establish a settlement on the north coast of Van Diemen's Land at Port Dalrymple.

Irish convict uprising at Castle Hill on 5 Mar 1804, showing Major Johnston and 25 Corps privates firing on the armed rebels. Twelve rebels were killed.

On 4 Mar 1804, 330 Irish convicts working at the government farm in Castle Hill, 11 km north of Parramatta, attempted to overthrow the local authorities. Many of these men had been participants in the 1798 Irish Rebellion and they wanted to return to Ireland to fight for an Irish Republic. The rebels, led by Philip Cunningham, raided houses in the Castle Hill area for weapons, and planned to enrol another 300 men in the Hawkesbury district, before marching on Parramatta and Sydney. On hearing of the insurrection Governor King proclaimed martial law. A company of soldiers, commanded by Major Johnston, confronted the rebels at Vinegar Hill, 16 km south of the Hawkesbury, and offered them the governor's mercy if they surrendered. They did not, and the soldiers opened fire, killing 12 men and wounding many more. The ringleaders were arrested at gunpoint.[14] Following a brief court hearing, the eight rebel leaders were hanged, and nine others were sentenced to between 200 and 500 lashes. Many men were sent in chain gangs to the re-established Coal River settlement to dig coal and to cut cedar.[15]

Following the uprising convict security was strengthened, and it became a painful memory for many Irish residents in the Nepean and Hawkesbury districts. Toby Ryan, son of an Irish convict and grandson of Anthony and Elizabeth, referred to the uprising on the first page of his book, written 90 years later, as 'The first incident of note related to him by his people was the open rebellion'. He wrote that harsh punishments were 'too common in those barbarous days'.[16]

By early 1805, Hawkesbury farmers had mostly recovered from the successive major floods and prospered from several good harvests that enabled them to repay their debts. On the Rope's Farm at South Creek, the 16-year-old Robert was now a young man who worked at his father's side on the farm. His brother John was only 9 years old, but he could help with sowing, planting and harvesting. In 1805, Elizabeth, aged 43, gave birth to their seventh child, a boy named William. The remoteness and farm duties did not allow him to be baptised in Parramatta. By now Rev. Marsden had bought a large plot at South Creek, and this included the land that the Ropes believed they owned. The Reverend was well known for his animosity towards convicts and emancipists, and if he had been aware of their presence on "his land", he would certainly not have been pleased.

The Ropes' neighbours had changed over the years. Dennis McCarthy and John Kenny were two Irish farmers on the western side of the South Creek opposite Rope's Farm. McCarthy share-farmed the 40-acre plot with fellow Irishman John Dunn, who had previously rented land from the Ropes.[17] On 27 Mar 1805, Anthony and Elizabeth were witnesses in the court case in which McCarthy sued Kenny.[18] A 500-bushel stack of McCarthy's wheat had been burnt after Kenny had set fire to grass on his land. The fire had escaped and travelled to McCarthy's wheat stacks, destroying the entire harvest. From their side of the creek the Ropes had observed the fire spreading. In the court case, when called by the plaintiff, Anthony told the court what he saw:

> ... the defendant on the day stated set fire to the grass on his own farm in three different places, and that shortly afterwards the wind rose considerably, its direction towards the stacks which in about an hour after were on fire, and were totally consumed.[19]

Elizabeth affirmed his statement and added that the distance from McCarthy's stacks to the spot set on fire by Kenny was no further than 30 rods (150 m). Patrick Ducey stated that, 'Anthony Rope was assisting in extinguishing the flames, and repeatedly declared, that the third fire kindled by the defendant had done the mischief'. Dennis McCarthy was awarded damages of £64, half of the amount he sued for.[20]

In June 1805, John Macarthur returned from England. He had not been court-martialled, as requested by Governor King, but had resigned his Corps commission and obtained a land grant of 5000 acres from Lord Camden, the new Colonial Office Secretary (the Home Office had been renamed the Colonial Office).[21] The location of the grant was not specified, but Macarthur requested it be at *Cowpastures*, which was the finest land yet discovered in the colony. Governor King had been protecting the *Cowpastures* plains – the land where wild cattle grazed on the west side of the Nepean River and intended the cattle to be a future government herd. He objected to the selection of this valuable property, and made the grant provisional, pending clarification from Lord Camden.

Considering John Macarthur's past behaviour it seems odd that he would be awarded a major land grant. H.V. Evatt writes, that Macarthur was closely associated with members of the Colonial Office at a time when corruption was rife in Britain. He also suggests that Lord Camden may not have investigated the theft of Governor King's despatches to the Colonial Office on Macarthur, partly because 'Camden's private secretary was hand in glove with Macarthur'.[22] Despite the damning case against Macarthur he had been given the 'provisional' grant of *Cowpastures* and requested 20 convicts on full rations to farm it. However, the governor, undoubtedly with some considerable pleasure, refused the latter stating that the colony was short of assigned convicts.[23]

Sometime in 1805 the Rope family left their farm on the South Creek and rented a 48-acre farm from James Badgery on the Nepean River. The reason for the move is unknown but was probably because of the repeated flooding. The loss of another harvest to floods would have been devastating for the family, financially and emotionally. Also, without a land deed to prove ownership of the South Creek land, the Rope's decision to move, before being evicted, was probably a wise one. With increased land demands from new settlers, Governor King had in 1803 offered grants of land allotments in the district of Evan, along the Nepean River. These grants were in areas known as Agnes Banks, Castlereagh and Birds Eye Corner. In May 1803, the free settler James Badgery received a grant for 100 acres at the junction of the Grose,

Nepean and Hawkesbury Rivers. The following year the grant was increased by 39 acres.[24] James Badgery offered 48 acres of his land at the Nepean River for lease, and the Ropes decided to take it up, expecting the new land to be less prone to flooding. This was optimistic, as the land was close to three rivers, and near the Yellow Mondays Lagoon, known today as Agnes Banks.

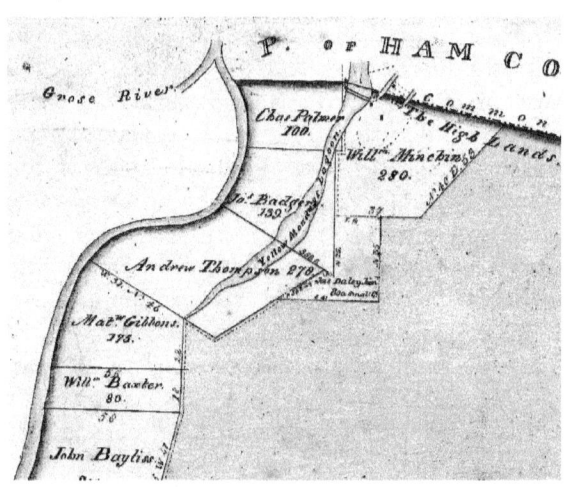

Part of a 1820 Castlereagh Parish map showing the land grantees at Agnes Banks. These were along the Nepean River on the left of the map.
In 1805 the Ropes had leased land from James Badgery, probably close to the Yellow Mondays Lagoon in the centre of the map.

The Rope family loaded their few possessions into a boat and rowed and sailed up the Nepean River to Badgery's Farm.[25] The property had not been previously cultivated, so they were starting from scratch again. Anthony and the boys built a bark hut as their farmhouse, and immediately began clearing the trees and tilling the land by hoe. They were experienced farmers by now and the sowing and planting of wheat and maize was soon underway. Their neighbours at Agnes Banks were a mixture of educated free settlers, military men and emancipist. By now, the distinction of class and rank among pioneer settlers had been blurred. In these remote areas all farmers faced the same problems with weather and seasons, and eventually friendships, marriages and shared hardships eroded most social distinctions.

The Ropes immediate neighbours, and their landlords on Swilly Farm, were James Badgery and his wife Elizabeth. The Ropes' neighbour to the north was Charles Palmer, who arrived in 1802 to teach at the newly established orphan school in Sydney. After receiving a 100-acre land grant in 1803, Palmer became a farmer instead, remaining on his farm for the rest of his life. Their neighbour to the south, Corporal Joseph Bayliss had received a land grant in 1803, but he apparently never farmed his land. The Ropes' eastern neighbour was another military man, Adjutant William Minchin. He received a 280 acre grant in 1804.[26]

An 1809 painting of the confluence of the Nepean, Hawkesbury and Grose Rivers. In 1805 the Ropes leased a farm from James Badgery at the junction of these rivers.

Under King's astute administration, the colony's agricultural production and building construction – activities that had so impressed the French three years earlier – flourished. Sheep had been imported from Bengal in 1793 and the Cape in 1796, and these had been crossbred to produce fine wool. Coal mining, as well as whaling and sealing had become profitable enterprises. In 1805 the *King George*, a locally built whaling vessel owned by Simeon Lord, Henry Kable and James Underwood, was launched in Sydney. By the end of 1805 the wealth of the colony had grown to an extent that the per capita income was at least as high as in Britain.[27] The New South Wales settlement population was now 6980 people; every third was a convict and every fourth a child. With better food more pregnancies carried to full term, and, with a lower incidence of childhood diseases, children reached adulthood in greater proportions than in England.[28] However, the gender imbalance remained at one female to three males.[29]

The year 1806 started badly for settlers. In March, after a week of heavy rain, the Hawkesbury and Nepean Rivers rose 50 ft (15 m) inundating the low-lying lands and flooding many farms, including the Ropes. Farmers, and especially Andrew Thompson and Thomas Biggers, used their boats to rescue almost 300 people from roofs, trees and straw rafts. The drowning of five people was attributed to a mistaken belief that the huge floods of 1801 could not happen again.[30]

Anthony and Elizabeth had been relatively fortunate; the damage to their farm was not as severe as further north. If they had remained at South Creek, where water had risen 8 ft (2.5 m), their losses would have been far greater. Because of a small hill, *The High Lands*, next to *Badgery's Farm*, the Rope family had avoided any personal harm.

In total, over 42,000 acres of farmland in the Hawkesbury, Nepean and South Creek districts had been flooded, destroying most wheat and maize crops, and drowning 4000 pigs.[31] Small farmers suffered extensive losses, but their never-say-die spirit prevailed, and they maintained that 'One good Crop will repay two bad ones'.[32] Even so, the repeated crop losses were threatening the very survival of the colony, and King arranged for the importation of grain from overseas.

In May 1806, the prominent emancipist Andrew Thompson became a neighbour of the Ropes when he purchased the bordering farm from Joseph Bayliss. Thompson already owned several properties on the Hawkesbury and South Creek, where he leased most of the land to tenant farmers. Thompson owned several boats that were used to transport goods along the Hawkesbury and Nepean Rivers to Sydney. By the time he became the Rope's neighbour at Agnes Banks, Thompson was the largest grain grower in the colony, employing 29 convicts and 94 free men on his various properties.[33] Because of his outstanding rescue efforts during the 1806 floods, King gave him a permit to establish a brewery on the banks of the South Creek in Green Hills.[34]

Although the governor allowed a brewery to be built, he remained committed to eradicating the illegal distillation of spirits. On 11 May 1806, the government offered rewards to anyone reporting the use of alcohol stills. The offer stated that a convict informant would receive a reward of £10 and a conditional or absolute pardon. Other informants would receive livestock to the value of £28 to £56.[35] The rewards led to the confiscation of many private stills and heavy penalties on distillers.

Soon after the reward announcement, convict James Craig told authorities that he had seen the free settler Robert Crumby using a still at South Creek. Under cross-examination, Craig disclosed the names of other men involved in the distilling. One of them was Anthony Rope, who was said to have received a copper kettle from a John Smith. On 19 Jun 1806, the court ordered Robert Crumby to pay a fine of £50 for having an illegal alcohol still. The case against Anthony Rope was, however, deemed unproven.[36] James Craig, who had informed on them, received a £10 reward and a conditional pardon, and almost certainly had to leave the district.

In August 1806, five months after the flood, a General Muster at the Nepean shows that Anthony was renting 48 acres land from James Badgery.[37] On this land the Ropes were cultivating 4 acres in maize, 18 acres of pasture, 26 acres in fallow and had no livestock. They held 1 bushel of maize and 6 bushels of barley. The Ropes now had 6 children, all off-ration and employed one free farm hand. The use of a farm labourer indicates that Anthony had been able to save enough of his flooded crop to remain self-sufficient. He was probably too poor to own livestock, or to replace any that he had lost in the flood.

Philip Gidley King had become governor in September 1800, and his term of office was about to close. In July 1806, only one month before the arrival of his successor, he received notice of his recall to Britain.[38] The decision of the Colonial Office to replace the popular governor had not been expected in the colony, and the announcement caused some concern. The persistent opposition of the NSW Corps had in 1804 led King to request temporary leave to visit England and respond to Macarthur's complaints to the Colonial Office.[39] It is possible that the Secretary Lord Hobart had interpreted this request as a resignation. More likely, however, is that King's leave request was used as an excuse to act upon John Macarthur's criticisms, and to replace the governor. King was staggered at the injustice of the dismissal, especially considering his administration's successes. However, there were also medical reasons for him wanting to return to England; he was suffering from severe gout that badly needed specialist treatment.

On 6 Aug 1806, Captain William Bligh RN, arrived on the ship *Sinclair* to become the fourth Governor of New South Wales. Bligh's daughter Mary accompanied him, and HMS *Porpoise*, commanded by Mary's husband, Lt. John Putland, escorted the *Sinclair*.

On the recommendation of Joseph Banks, the British government had commissioned William Bligh as governor with a salary of £2000 a year, twice that received by King. William Bligh had joined the Royal Naval as a boy. In 1776, at the age of 23, he was appointed master of HMS *Resolution* as part of James Cook's third and last voyage. In 1787 Bligh was Commander of HMS *Bounty* and led an expedition to Tahiti to procure breadfruit for the West Indies. The reluctance of seamen to resume naval duties after five months in Tahiti ultimately led to a mutiny, in which Bligh and 18 others, were cast adrift in a 7 m open boat. Bligh's skilful seamanship enabled them to reach Timor after 41 days at sea.[40] On return to London, Bligh was court-martialled for the loss of HMS *Bounty*, but acquitted. There were allegations that Bligh's tyranny had led to the mutiny, but others claimed he was no harsher than any other naval commander of those times.

This brief history of Bligh's leadership experience is relevant, as he was about to face serious disobedience in the colony. The Corps officers had displayed rebellious behaviour towards past governors. Bligh was fully informed about this and would have been confident that he was capable of handling these military buffoons. Bligh had a deserved reputation for steely determination, discipline and being absolutely unmovable when he believed he was right. Bligh often used strong naval language and certainly did not tolerate insolence or disobedience. His patron, Sir Joseph Banks, was familiar with his authoritarian nature, and regarded a 'severity of discipline' as necessary for the task ahead.[41]

William Bligh was happily married man of 52 years of age, with five daughters. His wife Elizabeth had not considered accompanying him to New South Wales because she had an absolute phobia of the sea and would not even step onto a ship moored safely in the harbour. Their daughter Mary was to be the colony's First Lady, and she would play an important role in his governorship. Mary's husband, Naval Lt. John Putland, was in the early stages of tuberculosis when he left England. It was hoped that the warmer climate in New South Wales would help his illness, but he died eighteen months later in Sydney.

The official welcome for William Bligh, when he stepped ashore in Sydney, was somewhat less grand than he had expected as the new governor. It was delayed by the late arrival of a contingent of the NSW Corps, who were to escort him ashore. Protocol demanded that arriving governors, who represented Royal authority in the colony, be received with appropriate pomp and ceremony, but Bligh's reception was decidedly low key. In any case he appeared nonplussed. He would have been well aware from Colonial Office briefings that the Corps opposed his appointment, and that his tough reputation had preceded him.

Just for that reason, Bligh and King quickly established a cordial relationship, and the transfer of power went smoothly. King informed Bligh of all the current governmental challenges and listed the obstacles the Corps were likely throw up to avoid their resolution. The bulldog spirit in Bligh was probably relishing the prospect of the battles ahead. Before the official handover, Captain Bligh accepted three land grants from Governor King. And, on taking up office in August 1806, Governor Bligh's first action was to grant King's wife, Anna, 790 acres of land between the South Creek and another creek (subsequently named Ropes Creek). This farm bordered on the 2340 acres land that Governor King had granted to his children, as a means of future security.[42] The Ropes were to be the neighbours of the large King family estates.

On 13 Aug 1806, Philip Gidley King and his wife and their four children, boarded HMS *Buffalo* for their voyage back to England. However, King's gout became so severe that he was forced to disembark, and their departure was postponed. The King family convalesced in Parramatta for six months until the gout was less inflamed. In February 1807, they departed on HMS *Buffalo*.

Governor King had been an efficient and popular administrator, and particularly well liked by the Hawkesbury settlers. He achieved much in the colony, but his continual disputes with the Corps and John Macarthur had worn him down and tarnished his reputation in the eyes of the Colonial Office. The small settlers greatly appreciated King's support after floods and lauded him as being responsible for the improved economic health of the colony, and for improvements to the judicial and civil administration of the colony.

By the time King and his family reached England, after a nine-month voyage, his health had deteriorated. He applied to the Colonial Office for a much-deserved pension but died on 3 Sep 1808 before it was granted. He was only 49 years old. Three of his children would eventually return to New South Wales, and his wife Anna returned 24 years later to be with her children. Philip Gidley King had made a major contribution to the establishment and growth of the early colony, both as a member of the First Fleet, and Governors of Norfolk Island and New South Wales. King failed to fully restore his reputation in Britain, but, like the well-intentioned John Hunter, his energy and abilities are acknowledged in the annals of early Australian history.

On 14 Aug 1806, a day after William Bligh became governor, he was presented with a written welcoming address signed by Major George Johnston for the military, Judge Advocate Richard Atkins for the civil service and John Macarthur on behalf of the 'free inhabitants'.[43] Bligh gladly accepted the tribute, but after it was published in *The Sydney Gazette*, 135 settlers from Sydney and 244 from the Hawkesbury sent a separate welcoming letter to Bligh.[44] Anthony Rope was one of the men who signed the Hawkesbury Settler's Address. The letter pointed out that Macarthur had presented his address to the governor on behalf of free inhabitants without their support or authority. The letter confirmed what Bligh had been told in England of Macarthur's egoism and conceit.

> Yet they consider the Act of John McArthur, Esq., in signing for them "the Free Inhabitants," without previous application or authority, public or private, to be such an invasion of their Rights and Privileges as British Subjects as to call for their pointed animadversion, and authorize us to say that had a Public Meeting been held they would by no means have authorized Mr. McArthur to have signed such Address to Governor King as appears in the Second Paper.[45]

Bligh had arrived in the aftermath of the 1806 flood, and the settlers' letter and welcome was an attempt by the farming community to initiate a fruitful relationship with the governor. His response was prompt. Bligh immediately put in place measures to relieve the flood distress by distributing food to those who had none and promised that government stores would buy their crop after the next harvest. Although his actions were similar to that of Hunter and King, they were rapid and more forceful. He fixed the price of wheat sold to the government store and guaranteed the same price for next seasons if sold as payment for an outstanding government debt.[46] This encouraged settlers to plant larger crops that when harvested could be used to repay their debts.

Next, Governor Bligh replaced most of the current government officials, many of them Corps officers, with his own appointments. The Corps officers were livid. In October 1806, he issued new port regulations that tightened the government's control over incoming ships, their cargoes, crew and passengers, including the prohibition of alcohol. Heavy fines were to be imposed if convicts escaped on these ships.[47]

Over subsequent months, Bligh visited the areas most affected by the floods. He met with the small farmers and developed a fondness for these "industrious settlers" on the Hawkesbury. He considered them the backbone of the colony, and within a short time the settlers became his most loyal supporters. Bligh paid less attention to the graziers on the large estates, who used their land for livestock, or to traders in Sydney, of whom he said were 'in general, and particularly those from Prisoners, are not honest, have no prudence, and little industry, besides being burthened with debts; great chicanery is used in all their dealings, and much litigation'.[48]

Bligh strongly believed the immediate economic future of the colony lay in food production, not in the development of the wool trade or overseas trade, or even in manufacturing.[49] He gave assistance to settlers who lacked the skills and knowledge to be successful farmers and became a farmer himself. In early January 1807 Bligh purchased land near Pitt Town on the south bank of the Hawkesbury.[50] Here, under the supervision of Andrew Thompson, the Ropes' neighbour at Agnes Banks, Bligh established an experimental farm to educate farmers in methods of soil conservation and improvement.

Sometime in late 1806 or early 1807, Anthony and Elizabeth Rope, and their large family, were on the move again to new land on the South Creek, 20 km south of where they had previously farmed. It is possible that their well-connected neighbour, Andrew Thompson, had given them information about farmland available for rent further up the South Creek, where the King and Bligh families had recently received land grants. At that time Anna King had already establish an estate, called *Thanks*, between the South Creek and the future Ropes Creek.

Once again, the Rope family packed their farm tools, pots, pans and rudimentary furniture, and sailed down the Nepean-Hawkesbury River to the mouth of South Creek. They then trekked or sailed south, past their old farm at Tumble-down Barn, to a new farm at Jordan Hill.

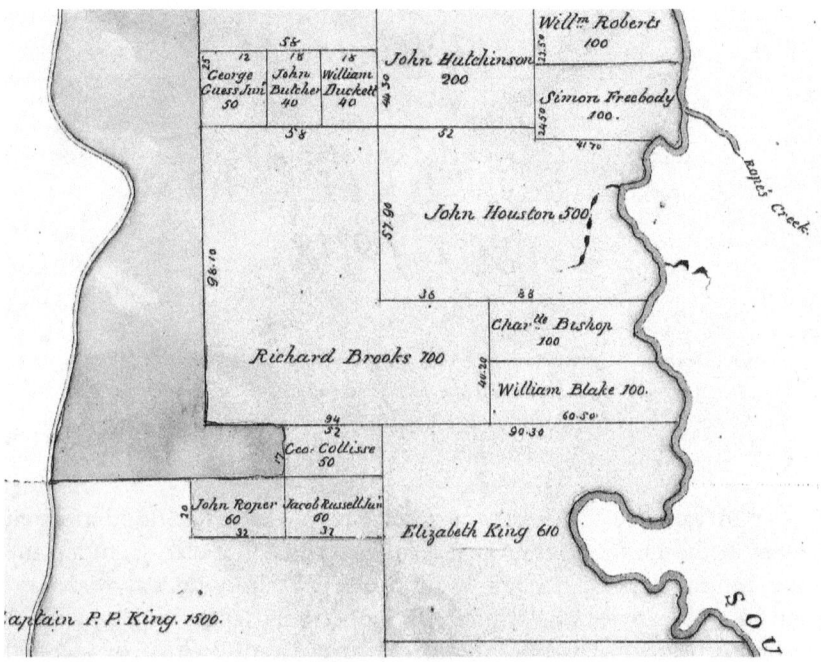

Part of the Londonderry parish map showing the land grants of John Houston and Richard Brooks, later purchased by William Faithful. From 1806 the Rope family lived on the estate of 'Jordan Hill' bordering the South Creek to the right. Rope's Creek flows into the South Creek on the upper right side. John Rope's first land grant is in the left corner, labelled as 'John Roper', next to George Colliss' land.

Although most land and muster documents over the next 20 years record the location of their new farm as Windsor, Evan or Castlereagh, the 1828 census shows the Ropes renting land at Jordan Hill. Toby Ryan writes that his grandparents moved:

> to William Faithfull's Estate, South Creek, between Shanes Park and Dunhaved [sic], where the rest of their family were born, and from which they were afterwards married.[51]

The Ropes leased 20 acres of farmland from their absentee landlord, Lt. John Houston, whose 500-acre farm was called *Jordan Hill*.[52] After Houston died in 1814, the land was sold to William Faithful, who had received permission to exchange a grant in the Liberty Plains area for better land on the South Creek.[53] The precise locality of the 20-acre plot on this estate is not known, but the Ropes seem to have been one of the earliest tenants. It is likely their farm fronted onto the South Creek. This is where they would stay for the rest of their lives.

Chapter 18

THE RUM REBELLION
1807-1808

But Governor Bligh was not to be diverted from his good intentions. He had undertaken the Herculean task, and he was fixed in his determination to lay the axe at the root of so monstrous an evil.[1]

In early 1807, Governor Bligh efforts to assist flood-affected farmers in the Hawkesbury gained him enormous popularity among the settler community. On 29 Jan 1807, the Hawkesbury district presented Bligh with a letter of thanks for his 'unbounded attention', and more support than anyone had before him 'in this dreadful Crisis of General Calamity'. Some 156 settlers, most of whom were the larger landholders, signed the letter. As evidence of their gratitude, they promised: 'We have subscribed all the Grain we can possibly spare from our own support to be carried to the Public Stores at your stipulated price, rejecting far greater prices in money which we could receive from the present Market Sale'. They also pledged that in the event of any future grain shortages, they would supply their produce at a fixed price.[2]

Bligh was in complete agreement with his predecessor King on the unsuitability of locating John Macarthur's land grant at *Cowpastures*, and on 7 Feb 1807 he wrote to Secretary William Windham in the Colonial Office recommending this allocation be changed.[3] However, Windham was about to be replaced by Viscount Castlereagh as Secretary, and he did not respond until December 1807, and by then Bligh was no longer in charge.[4] Castlereagh agreed with Bligh's assessment and suggested Macarthur be granted land elsewhere. He advised that no further land grants be made west of the Nepean River in order to protect the wild cattle. While these delayed exchanges with the Colonial Office took place, Macarthur badgered Bligh on the *Cowpastures* allocation, and this led to many heated arguments. *Cowpastures* was the jewel in Macarthur's grazing empire; he would not let it go without a fight.

From the start of his governorship, Bligh, like his predecessor, was determined to eliminate the iniquitous rum trade. On 14 Feb 1807, he published a General Order prohibiting 'the exchange of spirits or other liquors as payment for grain, animal food, labour, wearing apparel or any other commodity whatever', and banned importation of alcohol stills. Severe penalties were imposed for violations of these regulations. Convicts faced 100 lashes and 12 months of hard labour, while emancipists incurred a £20 fine and a three-month prison sentence. A free person was fined £50 and lost privileges. Part of the fines would be paid to the informant.[5]

The new alcohol restrictions proved effective. They almost eliminated rum trading and collapsed the Corps' trading monopoly. The Corps was especially upset by the reward offered to the informant. It meant that a convict or an emancipist could "dob in" a soldier or trader and be paid for it. This infuriated Macarthur who argued that the regulations were unjust because the rum trade was a well-accepted local practice that had benefited the business community and the colony. There were no altruistic reasons for his protests; he simply wanted to protect his and the Corps' profits. Consistent with his opposition to past governors, Macarthur disagreed with any regulation that affected his business enterprises, or those of his friends. And, because Corps officers were part of his commercial cabal, he knew that none of his actions would be subject to a legal challenge, or to the possibility of arrest.

Sentiments beyond the business community strongly supported the new rum trading restrictions. The farmers understood how they would improve grain transactions and reduce the price of commodities in remote areas. On 25 Feb 1807, 546 Hawkesbury settlers sent a letter to Governor Bligh supporting his efforts and pledging their loyalty in the event of any future difficulties.

> Beg leave to return our sincere thanks for your wise and unwearied Solicitude over the Public Welfare at all times, ... under a just, equitable, and gracious Government, which we, imprest with the strongest desire to support with our Lives, as also a bounden duty in all loyal Subjects, have willingly, according to Your Excellency's Order, enrolled our names for the Defence of the Country, in which we will readily participate at all times of need, but sincerely hope that your Excellency, in your wisdom, by judging from the real and presumptive proofs exhibited in this Country now and for many years past by those disaffected People, of their relentless and incorrigible spirit of Rebellion, Murder, and Atrocity, keeping liege Subjects in constant alarm, that you will be graciously pleased to dispose of the Ringleaders and Principals so as to prevent future Conspiracy amongst them, and to restore public Tranquillity.[6]

The signatories to the letter were mostly landholders and included Andrew Thompson who supervised Bligh's farm. Tellingly they also included ex-military men with land grants, along with freemen and emancipist farmers. Anthony Rope's name is not among them.

The Ropes land was now at a remote location, and they may not have appreciated the seriousness of the political storm brewing in the settlement. News from boatmen coming from Sydney eventually reached the small communities, and included the latest scuttlebutt on the tussle between the governor and the Corps. For most settlers, restricting the power of the Corps would be seen as positive, and, from the Ropes' perspective, government edicts were welcomed if they made the grain sales easier. On their new farm at Jordan Hill, Anthony and the boys had already cleared the land and sown their first crop. Money was needed to establish the new farm, and Anthony sought additional paid employment on adjacent farms.

The neighbouring property was *Elizabeth Farm*, one of the five King family estates that encompassed 3130 acres in the area. These farms were on both banks of the South Creek, close to where the Ropes now lived. The Rope's Farm was directly opposite Anna King's, and bordered, to the south, the lands of her children Maria and Phillip Parker King. To the south of Jordan Hill were Elizabeth and Mary King's farm adjacent to the land of Bligh's daughter, Mary Putland. While the King family resided in England, Rowland Hassall acted as the agent for the estates. Hassall had been a missionary in Tahiti and now lived in Parramatta. He visited the area regularly, and they became friendly with him – this proved beneficial. Anthony would be offered construction work on the King estates, and three years later, his 15-year-old son, John Rope worked for Hassall in Parramatta.

In May 1807, Rowland Hassall's accounts show that a stockman's house and stockyard had been built on Elizabeth King's farm, and Anthony Rope was one of the main builders. On 23 May 1807 he was paid £8 9s 4d for the timber construction of the house.[7] An archaeological examination of the area in 2008 revealed remnants of a timber building on the highest point of Elizabeth King Farm, and that it probably had a brick chimney.[8] It is likely that Anthony, as a known brick maker and bricklayer in the area, had made bricks there to build a chimney. In such an isolated place in 1806, he would have needed to find local sources of timber and clay – transporting building materials to such a remote location was difficult and expensive. Anna King's 790-acre farm straddled a small creek and during the construction work Anthony crossed this many times, and it became known locally as *Ropes Creek*. The origin of the name is uncertain; it was probably initially a nickname separating it from the many other small waterways in the area. But the name endured and was first published as 'Rope's Creek' in *The Sydney*

Gazette on 29 Dec 1821.⁹ For almost 200 years it has remained the official name of this waterway.

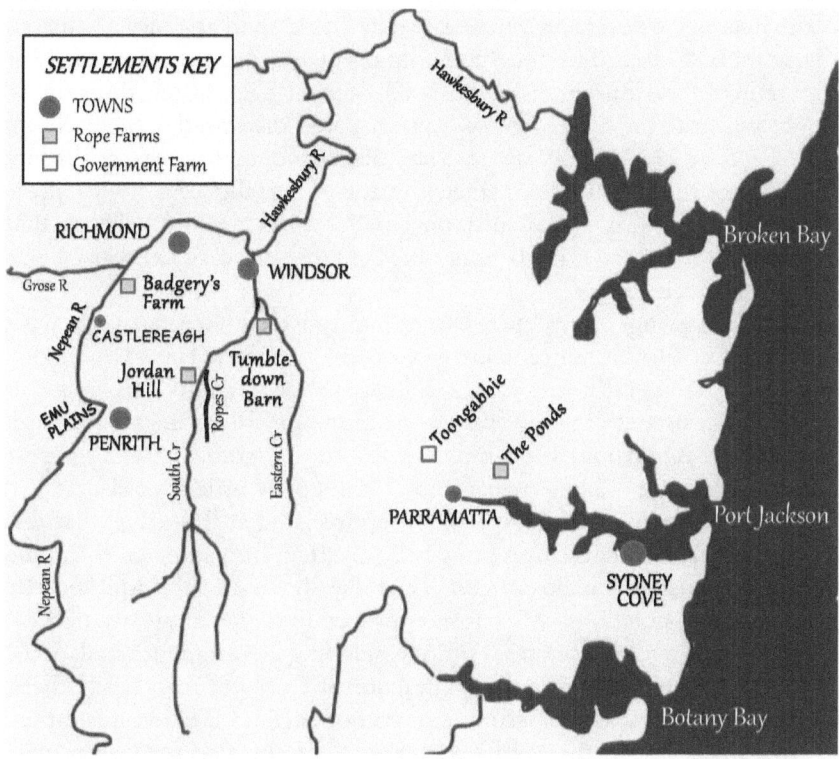

Localities in the colony where Anthony and Elizabeth Rope lived. The map also includes towns where the Ropes traded and shows the location of 'Ropes Creek'.

The money Anthony earned constructing the stockman's house was greatly needed. It bought seeds, pigs and new clothing for the growing family, and to pay off their debts. In the following years it is likely, though there is no documentation to confirm it, that Anthony carried out other construction and labouring jobs on the adjacent farms. He was, by then, recognised as a skilled builder.

Governor Bligh was determined to streamline his administration and reduce the bureaucracy. He decreed that the term 'currency' be only applied to money and not to barter in goods, and that all promissory notes must written as payable in 'Sterling money'.¹⁰ This decree did not affect old transactions, as many notes made in quantities of wheat remained unpaid. After the 1806 flood, the wheat prices varied between the low government-store price of 7s 6d per bushel and the high open market price of 20s. In July 1807 John Macarthur sued Andrew Thompson, Bligh's farm overseer and the largest grain grower in the colony, over a promissory note made out in bushels of wheat. At the court hearing, Thompson refused to pay more than the store value of the note, but Macarthur sought the much higher open-market price for the grain. Macarthur lost the case. His appeal against the decision to Bligh, who sat on the Court of Appeals, was dismissed.[11] In his book *Rum Rebellion* H.V. Evatt wrote that Bligh's judgement was a 'distinct setback to those who had taken advantage of the scarcity to press unexpectedly onerous demands on small settlers'. Evatt believes that Macarthur might have deliberately brought on the case 'to test Bligh's courage and tenacity'.[12]

Following this rebuff, Macarthur refused, once again, to visit Government House and encouraged others to follow suit. The colony started to split into pro- and anti-Macarthur factions. In spite of mounting resistance in the business community, Bligh insisted that all government regulations be complied with, to the letter. As with his past commands, those "sailing on his ship" should obey orders, or else!

The enemies of Bligh had not appreciated at this stage, that this naval Captain still had a lot more salvos to fire in his campaign to rid the colony of business malpractices. Thus far, he had only attacked the conspicuous violations of current procedures; he now wanted to eliminate unlawful *interpretations* of long-standing government regulations.

The first of these was the practice of Corps officers, and others, assigning convicts to work for them without telling the administration. D'Arcy Wentworth, the Surgeon in charge of the Parramatta hospital, had for some time directed invalid convict patients to work illegally on his farm. Instead of returning a recovered convict 'to Government labour or to the poor Settlers from whom they came', he or she was put to work for him for months before their discharge.[13]

Bligh was informed of this practice, and he immediately ordered Wentworth to send convicts to their original workplaces, which were mostly small farms. Wentworth had aristocratic family connections but was known to ignore legal niceties if it suited him. He arrived in 1790 with the Second Fleet, having been acquitted of three counts of highway robbery and only escaped conviction on a fourth charge by declaring that he was going to serve as an assistant surgeon in the NSW colony.

In July 1807, Wentworth was charged with misusing the labour of sick convicts for his private advantage. He was nonplussed by the summons because he knew that allies would be sitting on the court bench, and the case would be heard before a weak magistrate, Judge Advocate Atkins. He was right. Although the court found him guilty, Atkins sentenced him to only a public reprimand.[14] Bligh was furious and two days later suspended Wentworth from hospital duties until he received advice from the Colonial Office about the charges. Wentworth sought permission to go to England to argue his case, but Bligh refused.[15] The suspension of such a prominent member of the colonial society raised shackles among the professions and caused many letters to be sent to the Colonial Office alleging government misconduct.

In this, and other actions, Bligh made clear his intent to protect the less advantaged in the community from the illegal practices of those in privileged positions. Some historians of this period have judged Bligh's support for settler community as being vainglorious. This seems unreasonable. The blatant misuse of assigned convict labour had become a major problem in the colony, and Bligh should not be criticised for wanting to stamp out the practice. The court action against D'Arcy Wentworth demonstrated that Bligh was prepared to prosecute anyone, independent of their social rank, violating government regulations. It was a startling, and most unwelcome, wakeup call for the elite in the colony.

Open disrespect for the governor now became conspicuous in the business community. In August 1807, Henry Kable, and his business partners Simeon Lord and James Underwood, wrote a letter to Bligh seeking permission to move goods directly from one ship to another in the harbour. This was contravention of regulations, and their poorly written letter was seen as derogatory and insulting to Bligh's authority.[16] Permission was denied. The three men were arrested, gaoled for one month and each fined £100. This incident led Bligh to write in a letter to Colonial Office Secretary Castlereagh that some ex-convicts had not benefited from servitude. Emancipists had become wealthy through nefarious dealings, and Bligh found them the most troublesome people in the colony.[17]

Although the growth and sophistication of the Sydney settlement had astounded the visiting French in 1802, William Bligh was not impressed by the quality of buildings when he arrived in 1806. He claimed that Sydney was 'sinking into decay' and its public buildings and storehouses were 'in a state of dilapidation'.[18] The Sydney settlement under Governor King had grown quickly and Arthur Phillip's town-planning scheme was mostly ignored. A large area behind Government House and St Philip's church was originally zoned as a public domain or crown land but various governors had granted short-term leases on parts of this land. Despite regulations limiting leases to five years, King had given new leases for 14 years shortly before departing.[19]

In July 1807 Bligh sought to improve the vista of Sydney and correct the lease irregularities. He made many of the leases invalid and issued orders to demolish houses that had been built without a lease or a grant. John Macarthur was among those challenged as he had a plot of land near St Philip's church. Many other powerful allies of Macarthur found themselves in a similar situation. Other land was offered as compensation, but these prominent landholders were not about to give up their cherished central properties without a fight. Macarthur built a fence around his leasehold, using soldiers from the NSW Corps, but Bligh stopped the fencing because it enclosed a public well.[20] A long dispute about leases fuelled more letters to the Colonial Office complaining about Bligh's intransigence.

The principal reason the business community considered Bligh unfair was that previous governors had requested but *not insisted* that building regulations be adhered to. Both Hunter and King had attempted similar reforms, but most residents had, with Corps' help, ignored them with impunity. They now had a governor who actually meant what he said – the business community in the colony were on a steep learning curve. By the end of October 1807, Bligh started to feel reasonably confident that people were listening, and he wrote to Joseph Banks that the colony had recovered from a 'most deplorable State'.

> Indeed I can give you every assurance of its now raising its head to my utmost expectation. The Public Buildings carry an aspect of their value and private homes the pride of their inhabitants, – poor as they are yet they are neat, and the town altogether is become what has not been seen before in this Country.[21]

Another malpractice on Bligh's "hit list" was the bias of the law courts. Appointees to the court benches were often, because of personal connections, prejudiced in their decisions. Bligh advised the Colonial Office to change the regulations controlling criminal and civil courts in the colony to be identical to those in England. In particular, there should be an Attorney General, a qualified Judge and a trained lawyer or solicitor. Bligh distrusted Judge Advocate Atkins, whom he described as a 'disgrace to human Jurisprudence'. He requested Atkins be replaced.[22]

Bligh also requested much more fundamental changes be made to the enforcement of law and order in the colony. He wanted the Colonial Office to disband the NSW Corps or send them to India, saying 'Whatever soldiers are here let them be soldiers, and not those who are without exception engrafted with convicts'.[23] Two weeks later, Bligh wrote a letter to Secretary Windham, warning him that the Corps might become 'a dangerous militia' if the soldiers were not removed from the colony to do regular military duties elsewhere. He reminded the Colonial Office that a governor 'must be determined and firm in his measures, and not subject to any control here'.[24]

In late November 1807, there was a whiff of insurrection in the air. Bligh's insistence on absolute compliance to the laws of the colony had certainly heightened opposition to his administration in trading and military circles. In England, upper echelons of government were also concerned about Bligh's rigid reform agenda. Letters from business leaders in the colony lobbied the Colonial Office to replace Bligh with the former Lt. Governor Francis Grose, who was now a general in the marines. The Corps would certainly have welcomed Grose's nomination – he had been most generous to them previously.[25] Fortunately for the colony, the Colonial Office did not agree.

In December 1807, John Macarthur was in court again because a convict had escaped the colony on one of his ships. To deter escapes, ships' masters had to lodge bonds that were forfeited if a ship assisted in the escape of a convict. In this instance, a convict had escaped to Tahiti on the ship *Parramatta*, partly owned by John Macarthur. When the *Parramatta* returned to Sydney it was impounded. Macarthur not only refused to pay the fine, but he refused to feed the ship's crew, forcing them ashore in breach of landing regulations. Macarthur would not respond to the charge and said the government could keep the ship. He abandoned a ship worth £10,000 rather than paying a fine of £900.[26]

Bligh believed that Macarthur was directly implicated in the escape and referred the matter to Judge Atkins, requiring that he defend himself in court.[27] When Macarthur declined, Atkins issued a warrant for him to appear before the magistrate court on 16 Dec 1807. Macarthur ignored the warrant and 'fell into a great rage', saying that if the constable came again, he should be well armed 'for he would never submit until there was blood shed'. He declared that the governor and justice officers would 'soon make a rope to hang themselves' and called the governor a tyrant.[28] Macarthur was arrested, given bail, and committed for trial on 25 Jan 1808. However, John Macarthur was a past master in deflection and obfuscation, and when released on bail he demanded that, before his trial, Judge Atkins repay him £82, a personal loan borrowed 15 years earlier. The original loan was £26.[29] Atkins promised to do so, but later reneged on the payment. It was a decision that Macarthur would soon use against him.

The year 1808 opened with the colony in high tension. Bligh was strongly supported by the settlers, but he faced influential opposition in the towns. The rumour circulated that Bligh now 'preferred sitting down with an Hawkesbury settler than an officer'.[30] It was also claimed by his opponents that Bligh's robust language and nautical manners appealed more to the rough settlers than to the "civilised" residents of Sydney.

Bligh's farm overseer Andrew Thompson was coordinating support among the Hawkesbury settlers and the prospect of Macarthur removing Bligh reinforced their determination to stand by him. On 1 Jan 1808, Thompson wrote to Bligh that 'from a fidelity and strong attachment to your Excellency, which nothing can shake or alienate'. A letter signed by 833 settlers, including Anthony Rope, assured Bligh that they were bound to him and would risk their lives and properties to support his government.

> [We] express the fullest and unfeigned Sense of Gratitude for the Manifold, Great and Essential Blessings and Benefits we freely continue to enjoy from Your Excellency's Arduous, Just, Determined, and Salutary Government over us, happily evinced by the present plenteous and flourishing State of this Country, rapidly growing in Population, Opulence, and all Improvements calculated by a Wise and Patriotic Government to make a large Colony of People happy and rich in all their internal Resources. And, while enjoying such inexpressible Benefits from Year to Year under Your Excellency's Auspicious and benign Government, We feel and hold ourselves gratefully bound, at the risque of Our Lives and Properties, at all times, as liege Subjects, to support the same.[31]

The letter also made two requests of the governor. First, that they be permitted to trade directly with visiting ships, and second, that the courts adopt 'trial by elected jury' as in England.[32]

The settlers were convinced that an armed revolt in the settlement was a real possibility but, surprisingly, especially considering his past experience in such situations, Bligh did not. The letter, which was widely circulated, would have concerned Bligh's opponents because it showed that many settlers and Sydney residents supported his actions. For the Corps, the written requests for freer trade and trial by jury were also alarming; if Bligh agreed to such changes, their legal and commercial power would be greatly diminished.

The night before Macarthur's trial over the *Parramatta* escape charge, the acting Commandant of the NSW Corps, Major George Johnston, hosted a dinner party. Johnston claimed that, after the sumptuous evening with plentiful alcohol, he fell out of his chaise on the way home and suffered minor injuries. Evatt observes 'Thus, on the day before Macarthur's trial, the anti-Bligh alliance was sealed in a little blood and a great deal of rum'.[33] John Macarthur was probably present, though in a later enquiry he swore he was not, and that he had an alibi. The court met on 25 Jan 1808, with Atkins and six military officers on the bench. At the opening of the trial, Macarthur demanded with 'a great Torrent of Threats and abusive Language' that Atkins retire as judge because he intended to sue him over the unpaid debt, and he must therefore be considered biased.[34] Atkins withdrew from court, stating that the proceedings should not continue without him. In his hurried exit, he left his court papers behind. The other members on the bench ignored Atkins' absence and illegally released Macarthur on bail.

The next day, January 26th, the 20th anniversary of the foundation of the colony, the jurisdictional impasse had to be resolved. Bligh ordered that Macarthur be re-arrested and gaoled, and he asked Major Johnston to come to Government House. Johnston declined, claiming he was disabled by his fall.[35] The governor then summonsed the court bench members who had granted bail to Macarthur to Government House and ordered the return of court papers that were now illegally in their hands.

It became apparent to Macarthur's supporters that the governor was about to charge the six court bench members, Captain Kemp, Lt. Brabyn, Lt. Moore, Lt. Laycock, Lt. Minchin and Lt. Lawson, with treason. The mood among the Corps officers now became hostile. And, when Surgeon John Harris falsely reported that 'an insurrection of the inhabitants was to be feared', Major Johnston miraculously recovered from his injuries and ordered that Macarthur be released. This reversal of Bligh's arrest order was deemed to be the first act of a rebellion.[36]

Immediately on his release, Macarthur prepared a petition calling on Major Johnston to arrest Governor Bligh and to take charge of the government on the grounds that 'The present alarming state of this Colony, in which every Man's Property, Liberty, and Life is endangered'.[37] The arrest petition was a hastily prepared note and was initially only signed by Macarthur and six other men. The process by which the document was drawn up, and when it was signed, before or after Bligh's arrest is still disputed. In its final version, 151 Corps officers and Sydney residents signed the arrest petition. Some residents, who added their names to the petition *after* Bligh's arrest, claim it was done at the point of a bayonet and only after constables had gone from house to house seeking signatures. Bligh later declared, not surprisingly, that the men named on the petition were 'inhabitants of all descriptions, some of which are the worst class of life'.[38]

On the 26 Jan 1808, with Macarthur's arrest petition in his hand, Major Johnston led a Corps regiment of some 400 men on the short march to Government House with colours flying and accompanied by a band playing the march *The British Grenadiers*. Immediately behind the troops was a group of notables that included John Macarthur, Simeon Lord, Henry Kable and D'Arcy Wentworth. Inside Government House, Bligh celebrated a 20th anniversary dinner with his magistrates, the Provost Marshal Gore and the Chaplain Henry Fulton. The soldiers surrounded the building, and Bligh and his guests were arrested.[39]

The resistance of Bligh's daughter Mary, who had only recently lost her husband to tuberculosis, delayed the soldiers briefly. Ignoring her own safety, and with 'extreme anxiety to preserve the life of her beloved father prevailed over every consideration', she blocked several inebriated soldiers carrying fixed bayonets. It was observed 'She dared the traitors to stab her to the heart, but to respect the life of her father'.[40] Reverend Fulton stopped the soldiers from forcing the hall door and was eventually arrested by soldiers who came through another entrance. Initially, Bligh could not be found and had escaped into a secure inner room to conceal and protect important official and sensitive papers. Corps officers allege that he was found "hiding under the bed in terror", a surprising claim considering Bligh's meritorious military service and tenacious character. Evatt's explanation is that:

> Bligh also hoped that, during the night, he might be able to escape and seek the assistance of the settlers in the Hawkesbury district who were his supporters almost to a man, so that he might rally behind him all the loyal forces in the colony. In such circumstances and for such purposes, concealment is no evidence of cowardice.[41]

That night the Corps celebrated their takeover of government with alcohol, bonfires and burning effigies. The few officers and men not part of the rebellion and faithful to Bligh were insulted and feared for their lives. Macarthur, the hero of the day, paraded the streets.[42]

Major Johnston assumed command of the colony as self-appointed Lt. Governor, and a swag of reprisals soon followed. In early February 1808 Johnston made the Surveyor General Charles Grimes the Judge Advocate and ordered that Macarthur and the six officers be retried. Predictably they were found not guilty.[43]

In the days following the trial, all public officers were dismissed. This included the past Judge Advocate Atkins, the court magistrates and Chaplain Fulton. Andrew Thompson, Bligh's farm overseer was removed as the Hawkesbury Chief Constable. Simultaneously the civil and criminal courts were replaced with military courts. Several men who opposed these measures were required to leave the colony. Provost Marshal William Gore, who had gaoled Macarthur, and the emancipist attorney George Crossley, who had advised Bligh in Macarthur's prosecution, were convicted and sentenced to the Coal River coalmines for seven years.

By mid 1808, most of Bligh's supporters had been removed from the government, and John Macarthur was appointed to the position of Colonial Secretary. This position enabled him to oversee the business dealings of the colony and the decisions of Johnston.[44] William Bligh was placed under house arrest in Government House. Johnson offered him a return to England on the first ship departing Port Jackson, provided he pledged not to attempt to reassume authority in the colony. Bligh refused to leave unless certain conditions were met, and that his papers confiscated by the rebels on his arrest were returned.

THE RUM REBELLION 1807-1808

Watercolour painting of Government House at Sydney Cove in 1807. Governor Bligh and his daughter Mary were held here under house arrest in 1808.

Bligh remained under house arrest for almost a year. The prospect of an ill-equipped settlers' army trying to rescue him were remote, and he discouraged any plans for it. Bligh was quite prepared to wait on the response of letters he had secretly sent to England. He fully expected the British to soon restore him to his lawful position.

Within days of the rebellion, the settlers at the Hawkesbury suffered retribution from the rebels for backing Bligh. Johnston ordered that all debts owed to the government store had to be immediately repaid.[45] The small farmers who had lost everything in the floods carried most of these debts, and Johnston was now intent on subjecting them to his version of martial law. It is not known how much the Ropes owed the government store, but certainly most of the farmers on the Hawkesbury and Nepean badly affected by the 1806 floods, had substantial debts.

The consumption of alcohol in the colony very quickly returned to the pre-Bligh and King levels, and John Macarthur was at the centre of the trade. On 8 Feb 1808, the rebellion supporters met in Sydney at the St Philip's church, of which Henry Fulton was no longer chaplain. At the meeting, Macarthur's business partner, Garnham Blaxcell, proposed that donations should be collected to send John Macarthur to England to explain Bligh's maladministration and to justify his overthrow. The money collected was also intended to cover the cost of a sword to be presented to Major Johnston for his 'wise and salutary measures which he adopted to supress the tyranny which ruled this Country', and to pay for the silver plate to be given to the officers who sat at the bench at Macarthur's trial. Messer's Lord, Kable and Underwood promised £500, but others were not forthcoming. No Corps officers donated, and only £1000 was raised. In the end, the promised money was never paid.[46]

Commissioner, John Palmer, who had been dining with Bligh when the rebellion took place, was arrested and all of the government store papers, accounts and keys were seized. Palmer remained loyal to Bligh and later embarrassed the rebels by refusing to modify entries in the store accounts that would implicate Bligh in misappropriation of funds. Macarthur threatened him that 'immediate measures will be resorted to, which, it is hoped, may bring you into a more temperate frame of mind'. In the ensuing year Palmer reported to the Colonial Office on the activities of the rebels showing that government cattle were given to Macarthur's supporters and to some settlers as payment for grain. He also reported on the renewal of land leases, the issue of large new grants to rebel supporters and the removal of rum supplies by Corps officers.[47] Palmer requested leave to return to England but was gaoled for three months the following year. Eventually he would go to England with Bligh as his chief witness against the rebels.

Within months of the rebellion, deep divisions appeared among the rebels' ranks because promised rewards had not been paid and were unlikely to be. There were rumours that the Hawkesbury settlers planned to assassinate John Macarthur and that they were willing to sacrifice lives to accomplish this.[48] In April 1808, hopes soared for the reinstatement of Bligh when some of the wealthier settlers openly objected to Macarthur being appointed Colonial Secretary. Letters were written to Lt. Colonel Paterson in Van Diemen's Land and to Johnston requesting that Paterson return to Sydney to re-establish legal government and 'restore tranquillity to the colony'. In the letters, they claimed that Macarthur was the source of constant quarrels among the officers, and that he had 'violated the law, violated public faith, and trampled on the most sacred and constitutional rights of the British subjects'. The writers pleaded for Macarthur's removal 'We most earnestly pray that the said John Macarthur may be removed from the said office of Colonial Secretary, from all other offices, and from all public councils and interference with the government of this colony'.[49]

Johnston ignored the letters. Paterson did not respond either. He had heard that Lt. Colonel Joseph Foveaux would soon return to New South Wales to take up the governorship of Norfolk Island and believed that he would sort things out. Paterson had duelled with Macarthur in 1801 and loathed him. The rebellion is unlikely to have happened if Paterson had been the Corps commandant at the time. For this reason Johnston and Macarthur feared that the settlers' letters might provoke Paterson into trying to restore Bligh as governor. However, for the time being, Paterson was enjoying his post in Van Diemen's Land, and was quite content to let someone else sort out this distant mess.

For family reasons, the rebellion year 1808 would also prove to be difficult for the Ropes. In 1807, at the age of 15, their eldest daughter, Mary, left home to work as a servant for Thomas Hobby and his wife, Ann, in Green Hills. For a young uneducated female this was seen as a good placement, and the Ropes would have been pleased Mary had found a position in a prosperous household. The Hobbys had arrived in the colony in 1799 and Thomas commanded the NSW Corps contingent at the Hawkesbury settlement. After a dispute with Governor King, he retired on half pay in 1803 from the Corps and was appointed to the civil court. In 1805 he resigned from the Corps, and by the following year he owned 250 acres in the Hawkesbury district.[50]

On 17 Feb 1808, the 16-year-old Mary Rope gave birth to a boy named Thomas. The child's father was Mary's employer, Thomas Hobby, who had had no children with his wife Ann. After the birth Mary and the child remained on the Hobby farm. This was difficult at several levels. The two families lived in the same district but socially and politically they were worlds apart. The Ropes had pledged to fight for Bligh, whereas Hobby supported the Corps. This issue would have been an additional barrier, and it is unlikely that there were family exchanges. Perversely, at the same time, fellow Corps officers shunned Thomas Hobby because of his association with ex-convicts.[51]

On 24 Mar 1808, Mary's mother Elizabeth, aged 46, gave birth to Elizabeth Ann. Farm work prevented travel to Parramatta for a baptism; this was delayed until Governor Macquarie had built a church in the district. Three years later, on 15 Sep 1811, Elizabeth Ann was baptised in the St Matthew's church in Green Hills, now called Windsor.

About 1808, or perhaps even earlier, the Rope's oldest son, Robert, also left home. He now worked at Andrew Thompson's tannery, close to Green Hills and east of South Creek, in an area today called Pitt Town. Thompson, the Rope's former neighbour at the Nepean River, was a farmer with a brewery in Green Hills, and his tannery manufactured leather from seal and kangaroo skins. Anthony had probably spoken to him and arranged for the employment of his son.

On 28 Jul 1808, six months after the rebellion, Lt. Colonel Joseph Foveaux returned to Sydney. The arrival once again raised Bligh's hopes of reinstatement, and he asked his supporters Commissary Palmer, his Secretary Griffin and Chaplain Fulton to have discussions with Foveaux. But the talks were fruitless. Foveaux was unsympathetic to Bligh's predicament.[52] He had been originally commissioned to transfer the inhabitants of Norfolk Island to Van Diemen's Land. Foveaux was a capable administrator, but his previous administration of Norfolk Island had been difficult, when he imposed severe punishments on Irish convicts following a thwarted rebellion.[53]

Within days of arriving in Sydney, Foveaux took over the colony's administration as Lt. Governor. He distanced himself from the rebels in the community, and appointed Lt. James Finucane as Colonial Secretary in place of John Macarthur.[54] However, Foveaux was convinced that Bligh had mismanaged the colony, and wrote to Paterson that 'Captain Bligh has been acting on a settled plan to destroy and ruin the better Class of Inhabitants'.[55] Foveaux adhered to the Corps' ideals and did not question the right of the privileged to rule over the majority. During Foveaux and Finucane's time Bligh remained under house arrest, and the rebel governance continued.

In August 1808, Bligh secretly informed the Colonial Office Secretary Castlereagh that Macarthur, Blaxcell and Kable had taken large quantities of goods from the public stores without payment and were regularly removing articles for their own use. Macarthur and Blaxcell had each taken two millstones, and Kable one, at a time when Hawkesbury farmers were unable to produce flour because of a lack of millstones. Macarthur, Blaxcell and Kable owned ships and were stealing quantities of ropes, metal, canvas, sails and clothing. In addition, soldiers had stolen store clothing intended for convicts, and as a consequence they were 'almost left naked'. Bligh was appalled at Macarthur's brazen dishonesty. Ammunition was removed and shipped to South Sea Islands and used as barter for pork that was used to undermine the Hawkesbury settlers' pork prices and increase Macarthur's meat trading profits.[56]

In late August 1808, Anthony and Elizabeth heard that their 19-year-old son Robert had been charged with murder. John Brazil, a servant of Andrew Thompson of Red House Farm, had been found shot with a musket. It was suspected that Brazil had gone with some accomplices to rob the pigsty of Robert Richie on South Creek. In the dark Brazil had been mistaken as a servant of Richie and shot dead by one of his accomplices. Robert Rope worked at the Thompson tannery and shared a hut at Red House Farm with John Brazil and Mark Eivers. On the night of the murder Rope and Eivers had been found asleep in their hut. It was claimed that Rope was in the habit of carrying a musket to protect his master's property, and that this musket had been recently discharged and blood spots found on Robert's trousers.

On 2 Oct 1808, a criminal court was convened at which Robert Rope and Mark Eivers pleaded *not guilty* to the charges of wilful murder.

The defence stated that 'both produced good general characters', and for want of sufficient evidence, they were summarily acquitted.[57] It is not known if Anthony attended the trial, but if he did it would have been a sharp reminder that with the current martial law in place, one's life hung by a delicate thread. There was now little sympathy in the colony for emancipist families and had Robert had been found guilty, he definitely would have been hanged.

The demanding life of small farmers in the Hawkesbury district went on as usual, but without any recognition by the government for being the breadwinners of the colony. The focus of the rebel government was on increasing the wealth and commercial success of its supporters. Foveaux continued to show open animosity towards Bligh. During this period the settlers secretly kept Bligh informed of administrative irregularities in the settlement, such as bartering with alcohol and the legal system's bias against farmers. Surgeon Martin Mason wrote to Bligh that the court was now 'fortified with villains' who lied under oath to protect their patrons, but the settlers continued to support him:

> The settlers collectively, and without exception (excepting a few who are employed as agents and pedlars, directly or indirectly, for the present magistrates and officers), are to a man decidedly in your favour, and highly approve of your administration ... wish to express their loyalty and gratitude.[58]

In 1810, Mason would sail with Bligh back to England to be one of the witnesses in the Johnston trial.

In secret, a number of Hawkesbury settlers sent a petition to Secretary Castlereagh in England on 4 Nov 1808, stating that the colony faced disaster. It emphasised that, since the overthrow of legal government, the courts were corrupt and farmers no longer received cash for their grain, and consequently were unable to repay debts or support their families. In effect, Corps monopoly meant that many farmers could not grow sufficient grain to survive. They pleaded with Castlereagh to reinstate Bligh, adding that, while only a few of the larger landholders had signed this petition, many more wanted to but had been prevented by a 'system of terror'.[59]

The principal author of the petition was a settler, George Suttor. He was a passionate Bligh supporter and for organising this petition and defying a general muster, Foveaux imprisoned him for six months. In 1810, when Bligh returned to England, he took George Suttor with him as one of his key witnesses against the rebellion.[60]

Chapter 19

BLIGH DEFIES THE REBELS
1808-1810

In one sense, the life of Bligh is a tragedy, but a tragedy in the grand manner. He was the victim of two mutinies, one at sea, the other on land. In neither case was he the victim of his own tyranny. The objective of the Bounty mutineers was immediate return to the Lotus Land of Tahiti. In the case of Bligh's New South Wales administration, the thought of forcible rebellion was probably suggested by the fact of the prior Bounty mutiny. It is only a child who would reason that, because there were two mutinies against Bligh, he must have been guilty of conduct justifying both.[1]

On 1 Jan 1809, Col. William Paterson arrived on HMS *Porpoise* from Launceston to assume control of the rebel government. Paterson had been reluctant to take up this post because he knew it would be perverse administratively and politically. As a past commandant of the NSW Corps, he understood better than most the pressures that would be brought to bear by both the Corps and the business community, as well as by the emancipist settlers requesting the re-establishment of a just government. Doubtless Paterson would have much preferred the simpler life in Van Diemen's Land, but he was now duty bound to enter the fray.

Paterson's arrival, almost a year after the rebellion, raised hopes in the Bligh camp that legitimate government would be re-established.[2] At the very least the governor expected the return of his personal papers and property. Moreover, he assumed that Col. Paterson would have the good sense to respond positively to his request that no person be allowed to leave the colony until instructed to do so from England. Paterson failed to do any of these things.[3] A disappointed Rev. Fulton records that Paterson was unwell from excessive drinking. In fact, he was drunk for most of the day, showing 'imbecility when sober and stupidity when drunk'.[4] Because of this, Macarthur and Foveaux were able to manipulate him while remaining in the background, and made sure Paterson acted on their demands.

The settlers who had requested Paterson to come back and assume office were mortified. When their grievances and requests were completely ignored individual farmers and groups sent letters to the

Colonial Office praising the Bligh administration and pleading that it be reinstated. The rebels removed some of these letters from outgoing ships, but others were conveyed personally to England and reached the Colonial Office. They protested vehemently about the Corps officers' behaviour 'the more settlers were ruined the cheaper they could purchase estates; the less grain grown by the settlers, the better prices they had for their own'. They pointed out that prices had skyrocketed, as had the profits of unscrupulous dealers, and that the law courts were no longer safe places to lodge complaints about unfair trading. Justice now served the rebel interests, and often the complainant ended up in prison.[5]

The growing support for Bligh within most non-establishment circles was a serious worry for Paterson and the rebels. They feared, now, more than ever, that Bligh would be reinstated by the British. Another concern was that loyal naval officers aboard HMS *Porpoise*, which was commanded by Captain Porteous, would act on Bligh's authority as "Commander of all Royal Navy ships in the South Pacific" and attempt to release him. Since Bligh's arrival 1807, he had retained HMS *Porpoise* in the region to act as the principal naval support for the colony. Bligh was prepared to board HMS *Porpoise* and leave, but only when Paterson met his demands that his papers be returned, and certain individuals accompany him to England. These demands were refused, and Bligh remained confined to Government House. He had however instructed Captain Porteous not to leave the area without his permission.

Paterson was aware of Bligh's communications and attempted to eliminate the threat of HMS *Porpoise* by sending it to help transport the inhabitants of Norfolk Island to Van Diemen's Land. But Bligh ordered Porteous to stay put. Paterson countered by threatening to either send Bligh by small ship to England or place him in prison. Bligh was not easily intimidated, and he flatly refused to relinquish his naval command or to voluntarily leave the colony. On 30 Jan 1809, Bligh was removed from Government House and taken under guard to the military barracks in a one-horse chaise, with his daughter Mary running behind. Mary remained with her father in the barracks' prison.[6]

With Bligh imprisoned, Corps officers tried to loosen his control on HMS *Porpoise* by bribing Porteous and other naval officers with large land grants. They accepted the grants but remained loyal to Bligh. Paterson next threatened Bligh with a forced expulsion on the convict transport *Admiral Gambier*. This ship was soon to take John Macarthur and Lt. Col. Johnston to England. Sharing a ship with such companions was unthinkable for Bligh, and he furiously objected. Eventually it was agreed that Bligh could leave for England on HMS *Porpoise* provided he did not interfere in any colonial matters, and that, until his departure, he and Mary could return to Government House under house arrest.[7]

On 20 Feb 1809, after almost 13 months confinement, Captain William Bligh boarded HMS *Porpoise* as its commander, in readiness for the return to England. When the Bligh entourage left Government House and passed its guardhouse, the Corps officers ignored him, but Bligh observed that 'the Privates of the Guard turned out of their own accord, touching their Caps'.[8] One of the clauses in the Paterson-Bligh pact was that John Palmer could return with Bligh to England, along with several other supporters. Belatedly, Paterson had a change of mind about releasing men to be witnesses in a future court case and refused permission for Palmer to leave.[9]

By mid-March HMS *Porpoise* was still in Sydney harbour waiting for the pact conditions to be complied with. The Hawkesbury settlers took this opportunity to present Bligh with a letter of gratitude for his 'firm, upright and impartial administration'.

> We no sooner began to feel the benefits of your administration and see your benevolent plans than our spirits began to revive, and our hopes to brighten, that by industry we would be able to support our families in comfort, improve our farms, and leave our children with a prospect of supporting themselves by a similar conduct.[10]

As governor, Bligh had protected the settlers and their property, but now they were subject to widespread abuses. He met with their spokesmen and privately assured them he would remain in the area until he had received explicit instructions from the Colonial Office. To emphasise that he had not lost all his influence in the colony, Bligh issued a proclamation to all ships' masters in the port, warning people connected to the rebellion not to leave the colony, and listing the names of all Corps officers, and of 15 civilian and public officers.[11] The men who distributed Bligh's proclamation were later imprisoned and fined by the rebel administration.

Bligh's actions unnerved the rebels and they now demanded that he 'should be kept as a hostage' and that the pact be cancelled. Bligh was informed that the Corps would soon board HMS *Porpoise* to arrest him again.[12] Believing this was likely, Bligh abandoned his insistence that Palmer accompany him and prepared to sail. On 17 Mar 1809, HMS *Porpoise* weighed anchor and sailed out of Port Jackson. However, instead of setting a course through the Bass Strait for England, Bligh sailed to the south of Van Diemen's Land. He intended keeping his word to the settlers and to remain in the area. Paterson had reneged on their pact by not letting Palmer leave, and that cancelled Bligh's obligation to him.

Back in Sydney, the rebels were incensed and concerned at the sedition claims in Bligh's proclamation to ships' masters. At the request of Lt. Col. Johnston, Lt. Governor Paterson arranged for several rebel leaders to sail for England promptly so as to support their case for Bligh's overthrow. On 28 Mar 1809, a group of rebel supporters, including George Johnston and John Macarthur, sailed on the *Admiral Gambier*, intending to arrive in London before Bligh did.[13]

HMS *Porpoise* had instead sailed to Van Diemen's Land and on 29 Mar 1809 docked in the Hobart Town harbour, where Bligh requested that Lt. Governor David Collins support his cause. Surprisingly, and infuriatingly for Bligh, Collins refused. However, Bligh was not a man to accept "No" easily, and he pressed Collins for official recognition. The relationship between the two naval colleagues strained, and eventually exploded. When Bligh returned to HMS *Porpoise*, Collins forbade any contact with the ship, and refused to supply the crew with provisions.[14]

Intriguingly, but perhaps predictably, some of the settlers who had been forcibly transferred from Norfolk Island to Van Diemen's Land supported Bligh and secretly rowed fresh food out to the ship. Collins punished several for doing so.[15] Bligh reacted to his exile with his usual resolve and bravado. HMS *Porpoise* blockaded incoming vessels to Hobart Town and required them to provide provisions for his ship's crew.[16] This remained in place until the ship returned to Sydney in January 1810. In March, two months after Bligh left the Hobart waters, David Collins suddenly died, aged 54. It was a sad early death for one of the First Fleets' most prolific diarists. Collins was a hardworking, trusted colleague of Arthur Phillip and, as Judge Advocate, served with honesty and dedication the difficult role of Australia's first senior judicial officer.

The year 1809 began ominously for the colony, politically and economically. Continuous rain at the end of 1808 severely damaged crops, and the harvested grain was insufficient to feed the colony. The rebel administration resisted paying farmers cash for their crops, preferring barter instead. While some farmers managed to pay off their debts, most incurred losses, and grain merchants continued to make handsome profits.[17] The barter system seriously discouraged settlers from growing larger crops, and this contributed to lower grain yields and a food shortage in the colony. The following grain-growing season was equally unfavourable, with the prospect of another poor harvest looming. But this was only the beginning of the settlers' misfortunes. In 1809, the colony endured two devastating floods. The Hawkesbury River flooded in May and in August, and most of the Green Hills and South Creek farms were inundated, with five people drowned.[18] The grain and animal losses further exacerbated the existing food shortage.

The floods also placed a massive strain on the facilities and resources of the Hawkesbury district. Farmers and townspeople worked together to try and save lives, properties and buildings. As with past floods, the two prominent farmers in the district, Andrew Thompson and Thomas Biggers, coordinated rescues using their boats. Thompson's farmhouse and tannery, where Robert Rope was working, was inundated.[19] It is probable that Robert helped in the boat rescue efforts, and perhaps this experience led to his later decision to become a sailor. For his rescue efforts Andrew Thompson received a 1000-acre land grant from the rebel government. Sadly, his strenuous efforts appear to have adversely affected his health, and he died a year later.

The Ropes were spared the 1809 floods. Their South Creek farm was a considerable distance from the main floods and no major losses were reported in their area. To assist the flooded farmers, Lt. Governor Paterson sent 120 convicts from Sydney to help clear the debris. The government also tried to reduce the grain shortages by removing the monopoly on grain sales. Paterson requested that those with gardens raise more vegetables to reduce food shortages, and he imposed a ban on the export of bread, flour or grain.[20] However, these measures gave little relief to struggling settlers in remote areas, where the food shortages and prices ballooned. Predictably, there were no settlers' petitions or pleas to the government for flood relief, as had been in Hunter, King and Bligh's time. The settlers understood that such pleas were futile with the rebel administration, and may well result in a fine, or even a prison sentence.

With William Bligh and John Macarthur out of the colony, Paterson was able to relax for much of the time in Parramatta and let Lt. Col. Foveaux run the colony's affairs from Sydney. During Paterson's administration in 1809, the number of land grants issued rose sharply; 403 grants totalling 67,475 acres.[21] Up until 1806, only 85,000 acres land had been granted. Arthur Phillip had granted 3389 acres over five years, and Bligh, who did not believe in free land grants, issued only 2180 acres.[22] Governor Macquarie was later to comment that Paterson had been 'such an easy good natured thoughtless man that he latterly granted Land to almost every person who asked them, without regard to their Merits or pretensions'.[23]

The land grants in 1809 went mainly to rebel supporters, friends and ex-soldiers. Paterson also used land grants to buy-off opponents. A small, but nonetheless generous, grant of 100 acres was given to ex-Corps soldier, Edward Field, whose daughter Maria, later married John Rope, Anthony's second son. The former Corps officer, Thomas Hobby, father of Mary Rope's boy, received 640 acres at Mulgoa, and Henry Kable obtained a half-acre grant in Sydney, 300 acres in Minto and 300 acres on the Nepean.[24] In January 1810, the next governor, Lachlan

Macquarie, rescinded most of these grants, and the land was returned to the Crown. Anthony appears to have been a man of strong loyalties; he had declared his allegiance to Bligh, so the offer of free land grants to rebel supporters did not entice him to switch sides.

The news of the New South Wales rebellion and Bligh's arrest reached London in September 1808. The British government did not treat it as a matter of great urgency – it had much more critical matters to deal with than the governance of a distant small colony. Britain was fighting the Peninsula War in Spain and trying to contain Napoleon's dominance of Europe. Nevertheless, the Colonial Office did understand the seriousness of the matter, and in December 1808 Brigadier General Miles Nightingall was appointed as the new Governor of New South Wales. At the same time, Lt. Col. Lachlan Macquarie was appointed Lt. Governor and placed in command of the 73rd Highland Regiment of Foot, which was to be sent to relieve the NSW Corps. In April 1809, General Nightingall fell ill, and the former Lt. Governor Francis Grose volunteered to replace him. Fortunately for the colony, Lachlan Macquarie was also nominated, and he was commissioned to be the fifth Governor of New South Wales.[25]

At the end of May 1809, Lt. Col. Macquarie, his wife Elizabeth and the 73rd Regiment left England on the store ship *Dromedary*, escorted by HMS *Hindostan*. On 28 Dec 1809, the two ships arrived in Port Jackson. Macquarie had been instructed by the Colonial Office to reinstate William Bligh as governor temporarily before taking over the position. On hearing that Bligh was on HMS *Porpoise* moored in Hobart Town harbour, Macquarie thought it appropriate to assume the governorship on 1 Jan 1810. The timing deprived Bligh of the satisfaction of being briefly reinstated.[26]

The appointment of Lachlan Macquarie as governor introduced a new energetic era in the colony' governance. The British government had at last listened to the complaints of ex-Governors Hunter, King and Bligh, and appreciated the parlous state of the military and politics in the colony. They instructed Macquarie to arrest Major Johnston and send him back to England for trial. John Macarthur 'the leading Promoter and Instigator of the mutinous Measures' was to be arrested and charged with criminal acts against the government and tried in the colony. The entire NSW Corps Regiment, including Lt. Col. Foveaux, was to be recalled to England and then disbanded. Col. Paterson was to be permitted to return to Van Diemen's land if he wished. All papers belonging to William Bligh were to be restored to him.

Macquarie was instructed to implement ambitious reforms that would restore confidence, improve morals, encourage marriage, promote education, prohibit the use of alcohol and increase agriculture. Castlereagh's instructions recognised that these measures had failed in the past because of the lack 'of Example and Co-operation in the higher Classes of the Settlement'.[27] This advice was not dissimilar to that given to Bligh and previous governors but, with the disbanding of the NSW Corps, Macquarie was expected to have a better chance of success.

On arrival, Col. Foveaux informed the new governor that his superior officer Col. Paterson in Van Diemen's Land had ordered him to take over the colony's administration. Macquarie accepted this excuse at face value, and briefly engaged Foveaux to help the new administration. Within days of taking office, he reinstated the public officers who had been dismissed since Bligh's arrest. Macquarie cancelled all land grants and leases made by the rebel government, and any convict pardons made during the rebel rule were revoked. The trials and investigations after Bligh's arrest were declared invalid and all convictions were quashed.[28] Judge Advocate Atkins was ordered to return to England.

When Macquarie inspected the government facilities and buildings, he found the government stores almost empty and many public buildings in a state of ruin. Despite the serious faults in the rebel administration and other inequities, he deemed it appropriate to prohibit settlers from taking legal action against rebel officials, unless they had committed specific acts of oppression or injustice. The other misdemeanours would be punished in due course.[29]

William Bligh returned to Sydney on HMS *Porpoise* three weeks after Macquarie's arrival and was received ceremoniously. HMS *Porpoise* fired a 13-gun salute when Bligh disembarked, which was reciprocated by the guns of the 73rd Regiment. On shore, Governor Macquarie and Lt. Governor Maurice O'Connell welcomed Bligh personally. A contingent of the 73rd Regiment accompanied William and Mary to Government House, where they dined with the governor and his wife. It was a far cry from their recent experiences in the same building. Within a week, Bligh had been handed back his seized documents and other possessions. The governor personally presented Bligh with his confiscated ceremonial sword.[30]

However, Bligh found that several important documents were missing from his personal papers; Johnston and Macarthur had taken them to England to help argue the case for the rebellion. Bligh remained in the colony for a further four months while he compiled detailed evidence of the mutinous behaviour of the rebels.[31] This was a tedious task but was considered essential for the trial in England. Macarthur and the Corps had done everything possible to destroy his reputation, and he was determined that their allegations be refuted with well-documented evidence. More than his good name was at stake here. All future posts for him in the Royal Navy depended on the successful court martial of the rebels, as did the granting of his government pension.

Portrait of William Bligh, the colony's fourth governor (1806-1808).

Portrait of Lachlan Macquarie, the colony's fifth governor (1810-1821).

By the end of April 1810, Bligh was ready to return to England. A few days before departure, he was totally surprised when Lt. Governor Maurice O'Connell proposed marriage to his daughter Mary. Bligh had been unaware of their growing friendship over the past few months. Maurice and Mary were married on May 8th, and the new Mrs O'Connell remained with her husband in Sydney.[32] William Bligh sailed out of Port Jackson on 12 May 1810 on HMS *Hindostan*, as part of a three-ship squadron with HMS *Dromedary* and HMS *Porpoise*.[33] Also aboard HMS *Hindostan* were 22 men who would be witnesses for the Crown in the court martial of Lt. Col. Johnston. They included Commissary John Palmer, Provost Marshall William Gore, Reverend Henry Fulton, plus three Sergeants and five Privates of the NSW Corps. This cross section of people indicates the breadth of support for Bligh in the colony.[34]

A number of soldiers from the disbanded NSW Corps had requested to remain in the colony with their families. Macquarie granted them a temporary stay pending a decision from England, and the rest embarked on the three ships. Col. Paterson and his wife boarded the HMS *Dromedary*, but he died *en route*, and was buried at sea.[35]

Shortly after William Bligh's departure, Governor Macquarie reported to Secretary Castlereagh about the feeling in the colony.

> But, in justice to Governor Bligh, I must say that I have not been able to discover any Act of his which could in any degree form an excuse for, or in any way warrant, the violent and Mutinous Proceedings pursued against him on that occasion, very few complaints having been made to me against him, and even those few are rather of a trifling nature. On the other hand, there cannot be a doubt but that Governor Bligh's administration was extremely unpopular, particularly among the higher orders of the People.[36]

The last comment reflects a conviction in the colonial establishment that Bligh was unsympathetic to the wishes of 'the higher orders of the People'. It was these same characteristics that endeared him so much to the settlers and the lower classes. One also wonders if Col. Foveaux, who worked closely with Macquarie in the initial days of his governorship, had influenced his views on Bligh. Later in his tenure, after repeated conflicts with the "higher orders of people" in the colony, Macquarie would have thought quite differently about Bligh's uncooperative reputation. There is no doubt, however, that William Bligh was a blunt opinionated man who vigorously opposed anyone who disagreed with him. He had little time for the fripperies and subtleties of society; he lived by simple rules and expected others to do so as well. Despite the colony's small size and isolation, it had strict social protocols and etiquettes, and the veteran mariner's language and brusque manners probably shocked upper-class sensitivities. For people who knew him well, Bligh's social crassness was more than offset by his courage, his honesty, and a generosity to those he thought deserved it. Few leaders, then or today, could rise above the indignities and pressure he had been subjected to, and fought so strongly for what he believed in. In a very real sense Australia's egalitarian society and fair judicial system survived because of Bligh's determined spirit. He had fought against entrenched opposition and won.

The naval squadron with William Bligh aboard reached England on 25 Oct 1810, and he and his supporters immediately prepared for the court martial of Lt. Col. Johnston that was to begin in May 1811. Though Bligh was not a defendant in the court proceedings, the Johnston defence team made every effort to portray him as the cause of the mutiny, a tyrant and a coward. A propaganda cartoon depicting Bligh hiding under his bed at the time of his arrest was widely circulated and published. The cartoon implied that Bligh was cowardly and therefore not fit to govern. [37] This was damaging because cowardice was considered the worst possible trait for an officer or a gentleman. Although these accusations were made by mutineers and refuted by his extensive record of courage and bravery in the Royal Navy, they hurt

Bligh, and unquestionably influenced the court proceedings.

On 2 Jul 1811, the court martial concluded that Johnston was guilty of mutiny and sentenced him to be cashiered from the military. This was a ridiculously light sentence for such a treasonable offence. It was in effect a dishonourable discharge, without pension, for a crime that usually led to a hanging sentence. The record of the court martial conclusions attempts to justify the inadequacy of the sentence for such a serious charge.[38] The token punishment assigned to Johnson would have considered that the act was non-violent, but the sentence mostly reflected the prejudice of the court martial bench towards the integrity and reputation of William Bligh, the victim of the treason. In any case, George Johnston was permitted the following year to return to the New South Wales colony as a free settler.

John Macarthur never faced court in England and managed to avoid prosecution in the colony by a self-imposed exile. He would have understood the consequences of returning all too well. A lengthy term in prison at the very least. The British government dropped charges against Macarthur, and he was allowed to return to New South Wales in 1817 with the caveat that he did not become involved in public affairs.

The minor penalties imposed on Johnston and Foveaux are unlikely to have satisfied William Bligh. While the courts had clearly vindicated him and his government, the sentences imposed on the rebels were unusually light. From all accounts, Bligh shrugged off his disappointment and moved on. In 1812, Bligh was promoted to Rear Admiral of the Blue, and in 1814 to Vice-Admiral of the Blue. In 1812, he was invited to give advice to the Parliamentary Select Committee on Transportation, and a year later was granted a full government pension. Vice-Admiral Bligh died on 7 Dec 1817, aged 63.

What can be said about the contribution of this controversial man to the fledgling colony? The Hawkesbury settlers regarded him as a person of courage and honour; a heroic fighter against what they saw as a corrupt system. He was considered 'one of them', who had fought for their cause and had been arrested as a consequence. Portrayals of Bligh's character vary greatly in contemporary history, ranging from a fractious troublemaker to inspirational leader. But all assessments agree that Bligh's actions were always honest. He strived to do the right thing by the colonialists who battled the hardest, however, he appeared unable, or unwilling, to rally the entire colony to his causes. Bligh either lacked, or undervalued, the political and diplomatic skills needed to convince the businessmen that his goals would lead to a successful prosperous colony. His blunt edicts were uncompromising, and this outraged the trading community who expected some give and take in government transactions – in any case, since Hunter's time they were accustomed to get what they wanted. Bligh's rigid no-compromising reforms came as a real shock, and those most effected believed they had no option but to fight against them.

In modern times, the support or damnation of the Bligh governorship seems to be divided along ideological lines. One right-wing opinion is that the rebellion 'was caused not by rum but by the code of honour, which set out how gentlemen should behave. Governor William Blight was overthrown by the powerful people of Sydney because he was no gentleman'.[39] Those in the opposite corner, claim that Bligh's battles with Macarthur and the Corps were to protect the underprivileged, and to preserve democracy and equality. Overall, the latter camp appears to have many more historical facts on their side.

The commonly cited negative traits of Bligh are difficult to reconcile with our knowledge that he was a devoted family man and was considered something of a hero by most of the small farmers. Some settlers named their newborn sons after him and the use of 'William Bligh' or 'Bligh' as forenames for boys born in that era are evidence of this admiration. One example of this is William Bligh Turnbull, who was born in 1809 in Windsor, and is the ancestor of a former Prime Minister of Australia, Malcolm Bligh Turnbull.[40]

Unquestionably Bligh's character has been blighted by quite a few historical half-truths. In his memoirs Toby Ryan writes that Rev. Fulton 'remained as chaplain to Bligh, but this tyrant quarrelled with his parson and deprived him of his living, but when Macquarie arrived he was reinstalled'.[41] This is not correct. Macquarie did re-instate Fulton, and it was Johnston who suspended him for supporting Bligh during the rebellion. Fulton remained loyal to Bligh but declined preaching to Corps officers.[42] Toby Ryan's characterisation of Bligh probably came from his mother, Mary Rope. Before Mary married the Irish convict John Ryan, she had two children with Thomas Hobby, a retired Corps officer who vigorously opposed Bligh, and supported his arrest.

The earliest writings damning Bligh were written by the colony's educated elite who supported his overthrow. The written opinions of the illiterate emancipists went largely unrecorded, but the few surviving letters and petitions show their determined support and admiration. Probably the most learned and detailed analysis of William Bligh's governorship is that of the socialist politician, lawyer and historian, H.V. Evatt.[43] In his book *Rum Rebellion* Evatt reveals that he is an unapologetic admirer of Bligh. This is not surprising. Knowledge of Evatt's own character, and his fierce battles in the Australian Labor Party and Australian Parliament, leads one to suspect that he and Bligh would have been the very best of friends, had their lives coincided.

Chapter 20

Macquarie & Equality 1810-1815

But in My humble Opinion in Coming to New South Wales they Should Consider that they are Coming to a Convict Country, and if they are too proud or too delicate in their feelings to associate with the Population of the Country, they Should Consider it in time and bend their Course to some other Country, in which their Prejudices in this Respect would meet with no Opposition. No Country in the world perhaps has been so Advantageous to Adventurers as New South Wales. The Free Settlers, who have Come out as Adventurers, have never felt their dignity Injured by trading in every way with Convicts, even while they are such, but, further than it suits their Interest to have Intercourse with them, they would rather be excused.[1]

The appointment of Lachlan Macquarie as governor in January 1810 brought much needed stability and efficiency to the colonial administration. With William Bligh's reputation reinstated, the settlers had hoped that Macquarie would follow a similar policy of assisting small farmers to increase food production in the colony. However, although Macquarie gave assurances of his support for this policy, his actions by no means matched those of the Bligh administration. The governor's first priority was to try and heal the serious rifts still in the community, and he avoided overt favouritism, initially at least, to any particular sector. In his hands, the colony's overall economy began to recover from the mishaps of the rebel administration.

Nevertheless, Macquarie made it clear that grain production was a priority for the government, and the free and emancipist settlers quickly understood this. Most importantly, with the removal of the New South Wales Corps from the marketplace, the financial rewards to farmers who cultivated large crops rose sharply. Fair-trading became the norm and grain prices were stable and predictable. Macquarie made sure the government civil servants and the court officials treated everyone equally, independent of their social status or occupation. His policies eventually enabled people from all sectors of the community to be promoted into important positions in the administration, and he insisted that emancipists in the community be given the same social and business opportunities as free settlers.

It was not long before Lachlan Macquarie realised that some 'better members of society' were excluding emancipists who had become successful through hard work and entrepreneurship from legitimate recognition in the colony. Such unjustified discrimination clashed with his Scottish and military upbringing, and he was determined that it be stamped out. As early as April 1810, Macquarie appointed the emancipist farmer-industrialist Andrew Thompson as a Justice of the Peace and Magistrate in the Hawkesbury District. Thompson was the first ex-convict to become a Magistrate, and Simeon Lord, another emancipist, was the second. Lord was appointed as Magistrate on the Sydney court benches. These appointments were strongly criticised by wealthy free settlers and civil officers, who argued such men had no place in respectable society, and that granting them positions of power would corrupt the social order. Macquarie believed these criticisms were made by people who had only recently achieved social standing in the colony and did not want this diluted by nouveau-riche emancipists.[2]

Reverend Marsden was one of the most outspoken opponents of Macquarie's encouragement for widespread social equality. Marsden's views on the importance of social distinctions were in stark contrast to those of the governor, and he became a persistent critic of all aspects of the Macquarie administration. When Marsden refused to join a trustee board of which Andrew Thompson and Simeon Lord were members, Macquarie considered it an act of civil disobedience.[3] Like Bligh, Macquarie was a military man who had little tolerance for dissent. He was hostile to those opposing his egalitarian efforts, maintaining that equality was essential to the harmony of such a diverse community.

Andrew Thompson gained wide acceptance in the community for his courage, honesty and fairness as a magistrate, and became a regular dinner guest at Government House. Unfortunately his health deteriorated rapidly following his heroic rescues in the Hawkesbury floods and he died in October 1810 at the age of 37. He was one of the colony's wealthiest settlers with an estate worth in excess of £20,000 (over £2 million today). Thompson, who was unmarried, bequeathed a quarter of his estate to Governor Macquarie for recognising his abilities, and a quarter to his friend and fellow emancipist-magistrate Simeon Lord.[4] The remaining half was to be equally divided between his brother, and four nephews and nieces in Scotland. Bizarrely, they never accepted the inheritance – perhaps believing that benefiting from a transported criminal's honest earnings would taint their good name. Their refusal to benefit from Thompson's estate is a telling example of 19th century propriety and prejudice, befitting a Charles Dickens tale. Andrew Thompson had been an honest, industrious and successful young man, of whom any family would have been proud if they had known of his achievements and good deeds.

De facto relationships among emancipist couples had become *de rigueur* in recent years and Macquarie was determined to raise the moral standards of the community. He set out to actively encourage marriage, and made church attendance mandatory for convicts, just as it had been under Phillip. Macquarie reduced the number of licences for public houses to sell spirits and beer and increased the alcohol tax. At the same time, he capped the prices of grain and meat. The cost of shipping grain from the Hawkesbury was fixed, with the government paying any excess charges. Those settlers with a land grant, but no means of paying for livestock, received cattle, sheep or goats from the government stock, on credit or as payment for their grain.[5] Macquarie saw this assistance as part of his grand rehabilitation plan.

> With such assistance from Government, and the steady exertion of industry on the part of the settlers themselves, the Governor is fully convinced that they may very shortly become as happy, thriving, and prosperous a people as any other throughout His Majesty's extensive foreign dominions.[6]

Macquarie regarded many of Sydney's buildings as shabby. He was convinced that fine buildings on well-planned streetscapes enriched the whole community, promoting social order and morality. He wanted roads to be 50 ft wide with a footpath on each side, and a neat fence in front of each property. Macquarie announced that any house obstructing his plans would be removed at government expense, and all future buildings would require government approval.[7] With these community objectives in mind, Macquarie embarked on a massive public works program for which he is well known today. By any measure, it was a far-sighted effort that, by 1822, culminated in 265 new buildings and a vast network of new roads and bridges.

During 1810, the Rope family doubled their farming efforts on the upper South Creek. Anthony and Elizabeth, now 53 and 48, strived for greater prosperity by planting, seeding and harvesting larger crops. Anthony was still paying off loans taken out as promissory notes, and wherever possible he and the children took on additional work outside the farm. Without this extra income the prospect of the debtor prison or a farm sale was never far off, as it was for many of the neighbouring settlers. On 18 May 1810, 'Mrs Rope' is recorded buying a 1 lb (½ kg) of tea at Rowland Hassall's store in Parramatta; a luxury that cost £1. Two weeks later, Elizabeth purchased more tea at £1, and two days later she bought one sheet of writing paper for 3d.[8] This indicates that the Ropes had a good harvest and were able to afford the high cost of tea. But Elizabeth would certainly not have gone to Parramatta three times in two weeks to procure such items, even if someone had offered to drive her there in a cart. It is probable that Rowland Hassall, the farm agent of the adjacent Anna King's estate, had brought these to her on his regular visits to the area. Since Elizabeth and Anthony could not write, one wonders what the writing paper was for. Perhaps they were planning a submission, written by someone else, to the governor for a land grant.

View of the King Estate *Dunheved* on South Creek. Anthony and Elizabeth Rope farmed on the other side of the Creek.

The June 1810 transaction records of Rowland Hassall's Parramatta store show that Anthony Rope received £10 from Mrs Anna King for picking and husking 400 bushels (almost 10 tonne) of maize.[9] Processing such a large crop must have involved the Rope children, John, aged 14, Sarah, 12, Susannah, 9, and William, 5. The King estates straddled both sides of South Creek and were only a short walk from Ropes' farm. The family would have needed to work from daybreak to dusk to get the husking job done and, over the years, the little team probably took on additional contract harvesting jobs. The Ropes' work on the King's farms is typical of the additional efforts needed by early settlers to keep the wolf from the door.

Most owners of big estates in the Hawkesbury district did not live on their farms. Overseers ran these estates, employing large numbers of assigned convicts and farm labourers. The owners often built private roads, wide enough for carriages and wagons, for easy access to their farms. Over time, these roads became the main transport routes, particularly for residents on the upper South Creek, which became too shallow for heavy boats in summer. It was the custom at that time for roads and fields in these farming districts to be identified by the settler's names. One example is the stretch of land leading to Anthony Rope's leasehold in Jordan Hill, on the upper South Creek, which was known as 'Rope's Paddock'. Toby Ryan mentions this in his memoirs that he and his father John, years later, were held up by bushrangers when walking from Parramatta to their farm in Jordan Hill. This was next to his grandfather Anthony Rope's farm. The bushrangers let them pass unharmed, and they went 'via the Putland road, through Dunhaved [sic] and Rope's Paddock'.[10]

By the end of October 1810, Anthony and Elizabeth's 15-year-old son John had left home and gone to work at Rowland Hassall's store in Parramatta. On 25 Oct 1810, John signed, with a cross, a 12-month contract for £20 a year with weekly rations. His responsibility was to look after the animals at the Parramatta property, and to do any other work required. Provided he gave a month's notice, John could leave after one year, otherwise, the contract could be extended for another year. On the same day that he signed the contract, John bought two yards brown cotton for 11s, and thread for 1s. This material was for making new clothes. A month later, John Rope is recorded as a 'Sheppard' who bought a pair of shoes for 16s.[11] His expenditure of almost two months' wages on new clothing was a big step in the life of young John – it was probably the first new clothing he had ever owned.

On 6 Nov 1810, Lachlan Macquarie and his wife Elizabeth with a group of colonial officers, set out on a seven-week inspection tour of the colony. They visited rural areas and large farming estates and surveyed land proposed as new settlement districts. On November 7th they visited the flood-prone area of the Georges River, and, on the higher ground, Macquarie founded a town he named *Liverpool* in honour of the Earl of Liverpool, the new Secretary at the Colonial Office. On November 28th the group arrived at South Creek and visited the Rope's neighbours at Mrs Anna King's farm, now supporting 700 cattle.[12]

These visits convinced Macquarie that some farms and residences should be moved away from flood-prone areas to avoid further loss of lives, animals and crops.[13] But he also appreciated that the low-lying river flats were too fertile to be abandoned entirely. On 6 Dec 1810, at a dinner in the Hawkesbury district, he gave his now-famous speech announcing that five new townships would be established on high ground above the flood plains. A new town, named *Windsor*, would replace the current village of Green Hills; the village at the Richmond district would become the town of *Richmond*; the Nelson district was to be called *Pitt Town* 'in honour of the immortal memory of the late great William Pitt, the Minister who originally planned this Colony'. The Phillip District was to have a town named *Wilberforce* to honour MP William Wilberforce, the famous British opponent of the slave trade. And, most importantly for the Rope family, there would be a new town in the Nepean and Evan districts called *Castlereagh* to honour Lord Viscount Castlereagh, the past Secretary of the Colonial Office.[14]

Watercolour painting of the settlement at Green Hills (Windsor) on the Hawkesbury River in 1809. Anthony Rope would have brought his grain by boat to the storehouses and embarked here when sailing to Sydney or Port Macquarie.

In early January 1811 Macquarie went from Windsor to inspect the intended site for the township of Castlereagh. He observed that the grounds 'are beautifully situated, fronting and overlooking the Nepean River, and having a full view of the lofty Blue Mountains to the westward of that river'. A great square in the centre of the town was marked out and the name 'Castlereagh' was painted on a board nailed to a high post erected in the centre. The surveyor pegged out the principal streets and located a cemetery about a ¼ mile northeast of the square. [15] Sometime later, blocks of land were allocated within the town grid. Macquarie believed that the settlers on the Nepean would eventually want to live on the Castlereagh hill rather than the river flats. He would be disappointed. For the Ropes, moving to a house in Castlereagh was not an option since it was over 9 km from where they farmed.

After a flood in March 1811 in the Hawkesbury area, Macquarie urged the Nepean settlers to establish houses and farms on the higher ground of Castlereagh.[16] But the settlers were reluctant because of a lack of water in summer, and most settlers preferred to stay close to the river where the cleared and cultivated land was also more fertile. In any case, the planned town site of Castlereagh was too far for most farmers to walk to their fields. For all these reasons, the plan was unsuccessful. The Castlereagh cemetery, however, to the northeast of the town centre, was used until 1880, and is the final resting place of many early pioneer families, including the graves of Anthony and Elizabeth Rope. Today this small heritage cemetery in its rural bushland setting, on the outer edge of the Penrith suburb of Cranebrook, is the only visible remains of Macquarie's grand plan for the township of Castlereagh.

Macquarie's steady honest administration led to steady growth in prosperity for the colony, even though many farmers still had major debts accrued during the rebel administration. The livelihoods of these farmers remained insecure. On 18 Apr 1811 Anthony Rope was called before the Court of Civil Jurisdiction to repay a promissory note to William Baker for £48 12s 6d. The court records show he 'acknowledged the note, which he says was the purchase money for a certain farm, of which he has never had the deeds. Defendant has had possession of the farm ever since'. He was ordered to repay the said amount.[17] There is no information about the location of the 'certain farm', but it is almost certainly the 'Tumble-down Barn farm' occupied by the Ropes from 1797 to 1805. This is the land that Anthony purchased from two Corps soldiers, without bill of sale or deeds, and the Ropes later occupied. Such a large repayment would have been difficult. Most likely it involved new smaller loans using his Ponds' farms as collateral, and/or money earned by taking on extra work in the area. It seems likely the Ropes retained their two properties at the Ponds, Howard's farm and Elizabeth Clark's farm, to earn rent from the leases. However, these lands also provided collateral to obtain future loans at good rates. Farmers then, and today, routinely borrowed money to buy grain seeds for the next season.

A year later, on 9 Mar 1812, the eldest Rope son, Robert, aged 23, married the convict Ester Mary Gamble, aged 15, in St Matthew's church in Windsor. Ester had arrived on the transport *Friends* only 5 months earlier. She had been sentenced to death in the Old Bailey in July 1810 for stealing lace worth £54. The sentence was later commuted to transportation for life because of her age.[18] Over the next two years, Ester gave birth to two boys, but sometime in 1814 she and Robert must have separated. Very little is known of Robert after this date, though the name of 'Robert Rope', seaman, appeared on 20 Jun 1818 in the

Hobart's ship departure list of the *Duke of Wellington*, bound for Mauritius.[19] Toby Ryan claims that in 1823 Robert enlisted as a seaman on a whaling ship built by Captain Grosvenor at Richmond. Whaling was a lucrative industry and crew earned good wages. The Ropes heard nothing of Robert over these years, and this would have saddened them greatly – he was their much-loved first child. In 1860, long after the death of Anthony and Elizabeth, the family heard that Robert had drowned in 1835 in Van Diemen's Land.[20]

On 11 Jul 1812, Anthony and Elizabeth's daughter Mary, now 21 years old, gave birth to a girl, Eleanor Ann. The father was again Thomas Hobby. Mary had now been living in the Hobby household for five years, and it is likely that there was considerable friction between Mary and Hobby's wife Ann. In the previous year, Thomas Hobby Senior had been promoted to be the Coroner of Windsor.[21] In 1814 he also became the assistant to the Surveyor William Cox who was to construct a road over the Blue Mountains. In Hobby's absence Mary and Eleanor moved back to the Rope's farm, leaving their 6-year-old son, Thomas, to grow up in his father's house. Young Thomas was raised in a literate wealthy household that was quite different to the Ropes' farm.

In later years, a serious rift developed between the 20-year-old Thomas Hobby and his father when he was charged with stealing a saddle and a bridle and appeared before the Windsor Quarter Sessions. His father was a juror at the Quarter Session and, soon after this, retired from his position as coroner.[22] Details of the sentencing have not survived, but it seems that Thomas was sent to prison. A year later, Thomas junior married Marcella Kennedy, and leased 640 acres in Roxburgh near Bathurst, and a further 2560 acres at Cox's River. In 1833, Thomas Hobby senior died at the age of 59. In his will, Eleanor Rope was acknowledged as his daughter, and after the death of his wife Ann, Eleanor inherited the farm at Fish River with 350 head of cattle. His son Thomas was not mentioned in the will. After this family rejection, Thomas' life went rapidly downhill. Within eight months he was accused of stealing cattle and was imprisoned. He escaped prison and was caught. On 4 Feb 1834 Thomas was found guilty of selling 16 cattle that he had herded to Sydney for Mr. Glennie and was transported to Van Diemen's Land for life.[23] In May 1834 he sailed there with his wife Marcella and their two children on the *Admiral Gilford*. In June 1835 Thomas was fined £1 for drunkenness and outrageous behaviour and sentenced to work for 12 months in a convict gang constructing a road from Grass Tree Hill to Richmond. Within a year of doing hard labour he died at the young age of 28.[24]

In 1812, the British Government set up a Parliamentary Select

Committee enquiring into the transportation of convicts and the efficacy of this punishment. The committee addressed the strong criticisms of the British penal system by vocal and powerful reformers. Among those appearing before the Committee were the former Governors John Hunter and William Bligh, Commissary John Palmer, Rev. Richard Johnson and the explorer Captain Matthew Flinders. The Committee looked into issues as diverse as the trafficking of alcohol in the penal colony, health standards, commodity prices, land grants, treatment of convict women and punishment regimes in the colony. When the Select Committee asked Admiral Bligh what the general conduct of ex-convict settlers was in comparison to free settlers, he replied 'some were equally good with [as] the free settlers with respect to industry'. He thought that the ex-convict settlers and 'the convicts unite one with another, and get on very well'. Bligh was not as magnanimous on the question of whether emancipists should be admitted into society, entertained at Government House or nominated as magistrates. He thought that this was 'not to be expected until after generations, when they deserve it'.[25] The Report of the Select Committee recommended that fewer tickets of leave be issued, and that governors should grant less pardons. However, it supported Macquarie's claim that 'long-tried good conduct should lead a man back to that rank in society which he had forfeited, and do away ... all retrospect of former bad conduct'. The report concluded that the humanitarian principles of Macquarie's policies were in general beneficial. It recommended that the ratio of women in the colony be improved by granting permission for the wives of convicts to accompany their husbands to the colony.[26]

Back in the colony the emancipist Anthony Rope was once again entangled in the legal system. In 8 Jan 1813 he was before Judge Advocate Nicholas Bayly at the Court of Civil Jurisdiction on a charge of not paying a promissory note.[27] The plaintiffs, Timothy Warren and John Gandell, both butchers in Sydney, claimed that Anthony Rope of South Creek had drawn a promissory note on the 29 Nov 1809, and that a balance of £25 remained unpaid. The court ordered Anthony to pay the debt forthwith, plus the additional court costs of £4 2s 2d. Anthony paid this promptly, presumably by taking on additional work building, harvesting or working on boats. There is no information on the nature of the loan, but since the rebel administration gave no flood support to the settlers, most farmers carried major debts and loan exploitation was rife. It appears that the plaintiffs had taken over a promissory note of an earlier farm-related loan. Lenders and businessmen often made good profits by buying up discounted promissory notes, and then pursuing debt collection – a practice that settlers had routinely complained about to Governors King and Bligh.

In late June 1813, Macquarie finally received the Report of the Select Committee on Transportation from Britain. He agreed with the reforms to the colonial law courts and trial by jury but, in a letter to the Colonial Office about his social recognition of emancipists, he vehemently disagreed that 'petty and Grand Jury Men ought to be Free'.

> It has been My Invariable Opinion, and Upon that Opinion I have Acted ever since I Came to this Colony, that, Once a Convict had become a Free Man, either by Servitude, Free Pardon, or Emancipation, he should in All Respects be Considered on a footing with every other Man in the Colony, according to his Rank in Life and Character. In Short, that no Retrospect Should in any Case be had to his having been a Convict. This being My decided opinion, it is hardly Necessary to add that they should take their Turn of being Jury Men in Common with Persons resident in the Colony, who have never been Convicts.[28]

He also rejected the recommendation limiting a governor's ability to grant pardons, or tickets of leave. He wrote to the Colonial Office that the withdrawal of this power would 'greatly retard the Improvement and Prosperity of the Country'. Macquarie did not waver in his promotion of convict advancement and their admittance into society, and it remained a key objective during his time as governor. He wrote bitingly to the Colonial Office that free settlers who were opposed emancipists having equal social standing *should reconsider coming* to a 'convict country' at all.[29]

Financial dealings in the colony continued to be inhibited by the lack of an acceptable and ready means of exchange. Until early 1814, settlers, such as the Ropes, had no consistent means of paying for goods other than with a multitude of foreign coinage and by barter – this ragtag financial system had partly fuelled the iniquitous rum economy. The New South Wales colony badly needed a currency of its own.

To avoid the obstacles placed before previous governments, Macquarie made in late 1810 a comprehensive and well-planned proposal to the Colonial Office, for the establishment of a colonial bank with the power to issue currency. Disappointingly, this was seen in Britain as premature and somewhat dangerous. One can envisage English civil servants being aghast at the very thought of "convicts running a bank", and the proposal was rejected out of hand. Instead, 40,000 Spanish silver dollars, worth £10,000, were sent to the New South Wales colony from India, arriving in late 1812. To prevent their re-export, the coins were over-stamped and a hole punched in the centre. These rebadged coins, the 'holey dollar' and the centrepiece called the 'dump', were the colony's first official currency. The dollar was set to a value of 5s, and the dump to 15d giving a combined value of 6s 3d. These coins remained in circulation from the beginning of 1814 to 1829.[30]

In early 1814 another severe drought occurred that caused widespread grain and livestock losses, particularly among small crop farmers. The consequent scarcity of grain led Macquarie to request the farmers who usually sold their grain privately, to deliver their grain surpluses to the government stores. Furthermore, he required settlers who had received cattle from the government on credit, to sell their grain to the administration or be sued for neglect of payment on their debts.[31] Rev. Marsden was asked to read out a General Order to this effect during his church service. He refused, presumably because of his ongoing dispute with Macquarie over social equality. Macquarie saw this as disrespectful of the government and reminded Marsden of his ecclesiastical duty to ensure an orderly society. The Governor told him that if the duty of reading the Order was too onerous, he should raise the matter with the Archbishop of Canterbury.[32]

Predictably, government's intervention into the grain market actually contributed to the shortages. When harvests were poor, farmers traditionally expected higher prices, just as they accepted lower prices when there were surpluses. And, as they had done with Governor King, they withheld their grain until Macquarie increased the price to twice that of the previous year. Even then, the meagre yields meant that the colony only had enough grain for six months. Macquarie justified his price reversal to the Colonial Office as being more prudent than importing grain from outside the colony, particularly as overseas grain was always infested with weevils. Subsequently the standard price of grain was raised for the next season as well.[33] This was a win for the small farmers such as the Ropes, and it also boosted Macquarie's reputation in the community. The grain price standoff gave Macquarie a much better sense on how to exert governmental influence on the settlers and the economy. He never forgot this lesson and from then on knew which administrative levers to pull, and what players to influence in order to keep "the ship of state" on course.

The year 1814 would prove a busy one for the growing Rope family. Their little farmhouse was crowded; their second eldest son John had returned from Parramatta and daughter Mary now resided in the house with her two-year-old girl. Three generations now lived under one roof and in all likelihood, Anthony had either added another bedroom to their house, or built a separate hut for the older children. This willingness to share their house, food and presumably income indicates a real closeness within the family. The first priority of Anthony and Elizabeth was the wellbeing of their children and a commitment to giving them everything they had missed as youngsters themselves.

The Ropes' second son, John, aged 19, had applied for a land grant, and on 30 Jun 1814, he received notice that he had been granted 60 acres of land.[34] Anthony may have also applied for a grant at the same time but was unsuccessful, most likely because of his advanced age. In any case the Ropes would have been delighted at John's success. The land grant was to the southwest of Jordan Hill and on some of the early maps the land was mislabelled as belonging to 'John Roper'.[35] The new land was a short walk away from his parents' farm, making it ideal for the father and son to help each other. But the surveying of John's land still needed to be done before he could cultivate it, and bureaucracy in the survey office meant serious delays in the issuing of official boundaries and land deeds.

John remained at his parent's home until he was married, and his virgin bush block stayed uncleared. Unlike the later Governors Brisbane and Darling, Macquarie allowed settlers to occupy their granted land prior to the official survey. Many settlers farmed their land before a deed was issued, and, in some cases, even sold their land without a deed. Undeeded transactions were often subject to ownership disputes, and, after his father's experiences with this, John delayed clearing his land for another 14 years.[36]

The Rope's leasehold at Jordan Hill was about to change as well. After the death of John Houston in 1814, William Faithful took over the 500 acres in exchange for a land grant he had received at Liberty Plains. Four years later, Faithful bought the neighbouring 700 acres from Richards Brooks, bringing his estate at Jordan Hill to 1200 acres. Over the years Faithful gradually increased his land holdings, and eventually became one of the most prominent settlers in the Richmond area. Toby Ryan writes that William Faithful was a good landlord, and highly respected by his tenants.[37]

In October 1814, a General Muster was held at Windsor. All free men in the district assembled at the public stores in Windsor on October 17th, and all free women gathered on October 20th starting at 6 am, but children under the age of 15 were not required to be present.[38] To attend the muster, Anthony and Elizabeth would have walked at least 4½ hours along the Northern Road and the Londonderry Road to Windsor. The Londonderry Road was also their route to the new town of Castlereagh. If they were lucky, a neighbour may have given them a ride to Windsor on a cart drawn by a horse or an ox. The muster lists Anthony Rope as a landholder in Windsor, with a wife Elizabeth, six children and granddaughter Eleanor. Except for Robert, all their children were living at home and received no rations from the public stores.[39]

The 1814 muster data shows that the 26-year-old settlement had a population of 13,116 inhabitants of which 1765 were convicts (13%). The gender imbalance remained at 5 men to 2 women.[40] Agricultural productivity over the past nine years had risen sharply – horse and sheep numbers had increased fourfold and cattle sixfold. The number of animals held by small farmers in the Hawkesbury district had dropped since 1805, to half the pigs and a quarter the goats. These decreases were almost certainly due to the recent floods and droughts, and, without fodder, the pigs had been sold for meat. Interestingly, most land was being used to raise cattle and sheep rather than grain. Macquarie was incensed at this, and suggested graziers should give more to the 'general welfare of the country' rather than the 'lazy object of rearing of cattle'.[41]

The 1814 muster reinforced Macquarie's belief that small farmers were the mainstay of the colony's food supply, producing the bulk of grain, vegetables and fruit, while earning only a pittance of the profits. Because of the meagre returns for their hard work, Macquarie lauded the settlers' robust optimism, and admired the easy cooperation between free and emancipist farmers. The settlers lived by simple rules and expected that everyone in the community receive equal treatment.

The muster record also reveals the most popular first names in the colony. The most common male first name was 'John' (1 in 5 males), followed by 'William', 'Thomas' and 'James'. These four names accounted for almost half the male population, whereas the name of 'Anthony' was rare – only seven men had this name (0.2%). One in five adult females were called 'Mary', followed by 'Elizabeth' and 'Ann'. Every second female had one of these three names. When combined with the names 'Sarah', 'Jane', 'Catherine' and 'Margaret', almost three quarters of the female population were accounted for.[42]

Reverend Henry Fulton returned to the colony in 1812 after the court martial of Major Johnston in London. Two years later, in April 1814, he became the Chaplain of Castlereagh.[43] His parsonage was a large two-story brick house built on a 400-acre glebe block in the southwest corner of the town. A schoolhouse was constructed close by and although a new church was planned for the town centre, it was never built. Instead the school served as the Castlereagh chapel. This was the first church service the Ropes could attend in years, being within 1½ hours' walking distance. The chapel soon became the centre and meeting place of the small Castlereagh community, with Henry Fulton as its spokesperson.

In June 1814, Fulton advertised in the *Sydney Gazette* that a Castlereagh Classical Academy would teach Latin, Greek, French and English, grammar, writing and mathematics. The school was for boys 'intended for Commercial, Military, or Naval Pursuit' at an annual fee of £50 per annum for tuition and board.[44] It was far too expensive for most settlers, whose children remained uneducated. The government had already established charity schools in Sydney, Parramatta, Richmond and Windsor, but not in Castlereagh. Across the colony, school participation gradually increased, but it was not compulsory. Nine years later the Castlereagh school became a public school with eight pupils and included girls. At least three of the Ropes' grandchildren Toby Ryan, George and Henry Frost were educated at the Castlereagh public school. The school closed in about 1827; by then a larger public school had been established in Penrith.

The constant disputes between Lachlan Macquarie and Samuel Marsden came to a climax in 1814 over the level of punishments being meted out by colonial magistrates, and that Marsden's sentences were the harshest. The governor issued an official statement in *The Sydney Gazette* that limited the number of lashes that a magistrate could administer.[45] Marsden took offence at the caveat that magistrates, who sat at the bench alone, could not inflict over 50 lashes. Marsden routinely issued sentences of several hundred lashes – there were good reasons why he became known in the colony as the 'Flogging Parson'.[46]

An 1824 watercolour painting of Windsor viewed from the south. The road in the foreground crosses the South Creek, a tributary of Hawkesbury River. The Ropes travelled this route from their farm to sell their produce and to attend musters.

The search for more agricultural land continued and, following the crossing of the Blue Mountains by Gregory Blaxland, William Lawson and William Wentworth in May 1813, a road from the Nepean River through the mountains began construction in July 1814. William Cox and George Evans, assisted by Thomas Hobby and a large number of convict and free labourers, worked on this difficult route. All men were volunteers who had responded to the substantial rewards being offered for the road's completion. These included land grants and livestock for free men, and emancipation or tickets of leave for convicts.[47] While most workers were labourers, convicts owning a horse and cart were employed to haul provisions and tools from the Nepean River at Emu Ford to the road gangs. Among the haulers was 28-year-old convict Thomas Frost, who had arrived on the *Indian* in 1810.[48] In 1807 Frost had received the death sentence for stealing gold coins to the value of £99. This was later commuted to 14 years transportation. The 101-mile long mountain road was completed on 14 Jan 1815 in a remarkable 27 weeks, without a single loss of life or serious accident. Later, the Western Road connecting Parramatta to Emu Ford was built, and this led to rapid population growth in the Emu Ford area rather than Castlereagh. Emu Ford eventually became the City of Penrith.

The summer of 1814-15 was very hot and dry, and maize crops across the colony suffered badly.[49] It was a disappointing harvest for the Ropes, and a family wedding came as a welcome diversion. On 14 Mar 1815, Sarah Rope, 17, married Thomas Frost, 29, at the Castlereagh church. Two months later Thomas Frost received a pardon for his work on the cross-mountain road.[50] Thomas and Sarah became tenant farmers in the Castlereagh district and had twelve children. Much later, in 1843, Frost admitted that he had had a wife in England, and that she had just died. In 1844, he and Sarah were remarried by Joseph Holgate in the Penrith Israelite Church where Thomas was also a preacher.

The population of Rope's farm continued to grow. On 12 Jun 1815, daughter Mary gave birth to another boy, George – the father was not named. Anthony and Elizabeth did everything possible to support their daughter and her two children. There were now nine people crowding their small home: Elizabeth and Anthony, their five children, John, Mary, William, Susannah and Elizabeth Ann, and their two grandchildren, Eleanor and baby George.

Macquarie continued to insist on equality in the colony. Early in 1815 he announced that non-convict residents were permitted to trade directly with ships docked in the harbour.[51] This was greatly welcomed by farmers, who had been asking for these rights since 1808. Macquarie also gave notice that imported articles would no longer be sold in government stores. The changes reduced the monopoly of the commercial traders and importers in Sydney, but they remained a potent force in the colony and exerted considerable political influence. Opposition to Macquarie's reforms came from the Judge Advocate, Ellis Bent, who arrived on the same ship as the governor in 1810. Initially Bent worked well with Macquarie but in 1814 major disagreements arose between the two over the status of the judiciary. This coincided with the arrival of Bent's older brother Jeffery as the first Supreme Court Justice to the colony. Ellis fell under the influence of his brother's conservative views, and they sided with Marsden in opposing the governor's efforts to advance emancipists. In particular, Jeffrey Bent opposed Macquarie's insistence that emancipist attorneys be allowed to serve in the Supreme Court. He blocked the first sitting of the Supreme Court for five months while waiting for lawyers from England to arrive. Macquarie declared this action 'frivolous and ridiculous'.[52] He insisted the first sitting of the Supreme Court to take place in May 1815, and that the two emancipist attorneys, Edward Eagar and George Crossley be permitted to participate. Crossley had worked for Governor Bligh prior to being sentenced by the rebels to seven years labour in the Newcastle coalmine. However, Justice Bent refused to let these men speak to the court, declaring that he would never allow the court 'to be disgraced by the Practice of such Men. If they attempted it, he would Severely punish them'.[53] Macquarie was furious that Jeffery Bent had defied public policy and wrote 'the Charitable Hope that Men transported hither would be found worthy of being restored to a Participation in those Rights and Privileges from which by their former Convictions they had been justly Suspended'.[54]

As for past governors, the constant undermining of government policies by the conservative establishment threatened to thwart Macquarie's objectives. In July 1815, the governor had enough of the senseless opposition and threatened to quit. He told the Colonial Office that either he, or the Bent brothers, should leave the colony.[55]

The last thing the British government wanted was another rebellion, so they recalled the Bent brothers.[56] Ellis Bent died before the Colonial Office decision arrived, but his brother Jeffery returned to England. This was the first serious attempt to dislodge Macquarie, and it had failed. The establishment, Rev. Marsden included, continued to complain about Macquarie to the Colonial Office and this would have later consequences.

Chapter 21

PROSPERITY FOR EMANCIPISTS 1816-1821

I am perfectly Satisfied in My own Mind that the best and Most Useful Description of Settlers are the Emancipated Convicts, to the Exertions and Industry of whom are to be attributed the present improved State of the internal Resources of the Colony.[1]

Disputes over promissory notes led to more court actions in the colony than any other matter. On 17 Feb 1816 Anthony Rope and his son-in-law Thomas Frost appeared before the Governor's Court regarding the non-payment of a promissory note due to Sir John Jamison.[2] Sir John had returned to Sydney from England in 1814 to administer the large Regentville Estate he had inherited south of Emu Ford crossing. His father had left the colony to be a witness in the Lt. Col. Johnston's court martial and died in England in 1811. In the court hearing, Jamison claimed that a promissory note drawn up with Rope and Frost on 14 Mar 1815 at Regentville was for £65. Only £15 had been paid, despite assurances that the balance would be forthcoming. No details of the initial loan or the repayment schedule were given. However, as no further records on this matter can be found, the loan was presumably repaid. Anthony was not the only person in the colony to cross swords with Jamison. Governor Macquarie had him on his secret list of enemies, as 'intriguing & discontented'.[3]

The repayment of such a large loan would have been difficult for the Ropes. Their farm was doing well but £50 was a great deal of money (about $7500 in today's currency). Moreover, their 25-year-old daughter Mary was about to be married, and the wedding celebration planned for August 1816 would be costly. On the other hand, Mary leaving to wed the 19-year-old convict John Michael Tobin Ryan would help reduce the Rope's household expenses. The Irish-born John Ryan was an educated man who had worked as a printer in London. In July 1814, he and two other men were found guilty in the Old Bailey of stealing a handkerchief valued at 3s. For this, all three were sentenced to transportation *for life*; a ridiculously excessive sentence even in those times. Stealing an article valued at over 1s was now a capital offence, and since Ryan was Irish, no mercy was shown. He was put on the hulk *Retribution* at Woolwich and then transported on the *Indefatigable*, arriving in Port Jackson in April 1815. Within four days of arriving, Ryan was sent to the Windsor district, and between 1816 and 1818 he worked as an assigned servant to a farmer in the Castlereagh district.[4]

On 6 Aug 1816, John and Mary married in the Castlereagh Chapel, and with Mary's daughter Eleanor they moved to his assigned farm. Mary's youngest child George stayed with his Rope grandparents, who would raise him for the next decade. In 1818, Mary gave birth to James Tobias Ryan, and five more children quickly followed. In 1818 John Ryan received his ticket of leave and this enabled the family to rent a few acres of land on the Nepean River from William Bowman, where they remained until 1821.[5]

John Ryan knew the benefits of education, and he had a teacher reside in his house to school the children. The eldest child, James Tobias (Toby), was a keen student, and in 1825 he was sent for a year to Chaplain Fulton's public boarding school in Castlereagh. Toby had a good education – by the standards of those times, at least – and he went on to become a successful businessman, butcher, grazier, publican, auctioneer, and racehorse owner. Toby Ryan became one of the richest men in the district, and in 1852 he built an impressive house at Emu Plains on the western side of the Nepean River where he entertained the leading politicians and dignitaries of the day. This house is one of the few of this period surviving in Penrith today.

At the age of 42, Toby Ryan entered politics and was elected in 1860 as the representative of the Nepean district in the N.S.W. Legislative Assembly. He held this seat for 12 years. Most of Toby's political and commercial achievements occurred after the death of his grandparents, Anthony and Elizabeth Rope. Had they been alive, they would have been proud of the success and the high position that their grandson had achieved in colonial society – for a family to progress from illiterate felons to the wealthy political class in two generations was noteworthy. However, in the late 1860s Toby Ryan's rising star dimmed somewhat. He suffered badly financially from the flood damage to the Nepean toll bridges that he had invested in and was declared bankrupt in 1871. He lost his Legislative Assembly seat and became a Sydney publican and won contracts to asphalt streets in the city. Later he ran a boarding house and, in 1895 published his memoirs *Reminiscences of Australia*. In 1899, Toby Ryan died aged 81.[6]

Macquarie's determination to have emancipated convicts fully accepted into colonial society continued unabated, and he praised the emancipists to Colonial Office Secretary Bathurst while condemning unproductive graziers.

> What are generally denominated Gentlemen Settlers, or Settlers of the first Class, Come out here Miserably poor, depend principally on the Indulgences granted them by Government, and very Seldom attend to Cultivating their Lands or Increasing the Internal Resources of the Colony, giving up the whole of their time to the Rearing of Cattle or Shop-keeping; and now, after Seven Years Experience, I am perfectly Satisfied in My own Mind that the best and Most Useful Description of Settlers are the Emancipated Convicts, to the Exertions and Industry of whom are to be attributed the present improved State of the internal Resources of the Colony.[7]

During this difficult period of his governorship, when Macquarie was unfairly criticised and isolated, he better appreciated and admired the stoic resilience and generosity of the emancipist settlers. It contrasted with the incessant complaints from other quarters. The unproductive graziers, who included Samuel Marsden, refused to recognise the importance of small farmers to the colony. Their attitude was consistent with the class distinctions of the time where priority was usually given to the big landholders and social elite. Macquarie viewed Marsden's stance as outright hypocrisy; he preached love to his parishioners but opposed advancement for the less well off in his flock.[8]

A number of the government's opponents wrote letters to prominent conservatives in Britain and pointed out that Macquarie was cultivating a "privileged criminal class" in the colony. This was, of course, a complete nonsense, but it struck the right chord with British conservatives. One of them, Henry Bennet MP, was a strong critic of the current penal transportation system. Another was the previous Judge Advocate Jeffrey Bent, who had earlier opposed Macquarie and had been recalled. Both Bennet and Bent used these complaint letters to support their case for harsher penal sentences and mounted a campaign in Parliament questioning Macquarie's ability to govern. Their actions eventually led to the appointment of John Thomas Bigge to head up a commission enquiring into all aspects of the government administration.

In Sydney, Macquarie was being attacked on other fronts. As with past governors, the military was proving increasingly uncooperative. Since early 1814, the 46th Regiment, commanded by Lt. Governor George Molle, had been responsible for the security of the colony. Molle and his officers resented being posted to a prison colony and accused the Macquarie's administration of being too lenient on the emancipists. Molle often disagreed with the government's actions, and Macquarie's intolerance of criticism contributed to the friction. In effect, the military tried to exclude emancipists from their society, and, until the 46th Regiment was replaced three years later, their officers resisted implementing any policies that promoted emancipists.[9]

In Britain, the social instabilities that followed the Napoleonic Wars had severe ramifications for the legal system. Over 160,000 returned soldiers and sailors entered the workforce at a time of high unemployment, and the resulting civil disruptions led to increased property crime and a demand for better policing and harder punishments. Concomitantly, the public increasingly saw the existing convict transportation system as ineffective, and Macquarie's treatment of convicts as far too generous. The politicians wanted the sentence of transportation to be feared by the criminal class, and to be a deterrent against stealing. In the first years of transportation to New South Wales, this had been the case, and the number of convicts transported per year never exceeded 1000.[10] After the Napoleonic wars, this increased to 2000 in 1817, 3350 in 1818, and 4000 in 1820.[11] The trickle of convicts being sent to the antipodes had turned into a veritable flood!

This convict surge placed significant strain on the New South Wales settlements, financially and administratively. To cope with the influx of new convicts, Macquarie initiated a range of public works programs, constructing new buildings, roads and bridges. As soon as the convicts disembarked, the administration selected the men with special skills for government projects. Contractors and estate owners in the major settlement areas had second choice, and as many as possible of the remainder were sent to small settlers as assigned convict servants. Unfortunately, the convict influx occurred in years of flooding and poor crops when settlers usually needing labourers were unable to afford them.

Settlers normally employed assigned convicts by application to a magistrate. It is likely that Anthony Rope had at various times used an assigned servant, as did his son John and his son-in-law Thomas Frost. Under the regulations promulgated by Governor King in 1804, anyone with an assigned servant must feed and clothe him and pay £10 a year in wages.[12] The wage requirement was waived if masters rewarded assigned convicts in kind. In such cases, they were allowed to use a small part of the masters' land to grow grain and raise pigs in their free time. However, abuses eventually led to changes in the employment of convicts. Wages had to be paid if the servant preferred money, with a deduction of £3 for supplied clothing, and settlers who no longer needed a servant had to return him or her immediately to the administration.[13]

The convicts on the First Fleet were predominantly from the poor rural parts of England that had high unemployment. These convicts had farm experience and were well suited to the work for settlers. In later years, a higher proportion of convicts came from cities. They had mainly artisan or factory skills unsuited to labouring, and this caused problems on the farms. Some free settlers gained a reputation for harshly treating the assigned servants who were unfamiliar with farm duties. Emancipist settlers, who had suffered servitude themselves, usually avoided inflicting punishment – they simply returned them and asked for someone more suitable.[14] Inevitably, this meant that convicts preferred to be assigned to ex-convicts, who offered fairer employment, better treatment and greater freedom.[15] In 1818, John Rope returned a convict who had stolen from a fellow servant after one month but did not inform the authorities of the theft. For this the convict would be flogged, and John knew about the harshness of this from his parents. The thief was only named after he had been returned multiple times to the government without emancipist settlers revealing the reason.[16]

In 17 Feb 1817, Chaplain Fulton married the Rope's second son John aged 21 to Maria Field aged 15 in the Castlereagh Church. Both signed the wedding certificate with a cross. Maria was the daughter of the former NSW Corps Private Edward Field and the convict Elizabeth Mitchell. John moved out of the Rope farm, but not having received the deeds to his granted land, he rented land in the neighbourhood.[17] In the previous year John had successfully purchased a cow from the government's herd and was given a credit for 18 months to be made in cash or in wheat.[18] The cow cost £20, a small fortune – this much money could buy almost 20 acres of land. John and Maria Rope were to have 10 children, but only 7 would live beyond the age of one.

Promissory notes continued to cause problems in the colony and payment disputes over notes clogged the civil courts. Nevertheless, without proper banking facilities, they remained the mainstay of most financial transactions. In 1810, Macquarie had unsuccessfully proposed that a 'Government Colonial Bank' be created.[19] By 1817, promissory notes had become such a burden for business that Macquarie independently created the colony's first bank, *The Bank of New South Wales*. Australia's own bank notes, valued at 5s, 10s, £1 and £5, and paper tokens for 1s and 2s6d, were printed by the *Sydney Gazette*'s newspaper office. The circulation of the notes and prohibition on issuing promissory notes opened up a capitalist economy in the colony.[20]

Despite his effective and stable administration of the colony, Macquarie's reputation at the British Colonial Office was severely damaged. He had been in New South Wales for eight years, much longer than any previous governor, but the steady stream of letters sent to London by disgruntled exclusives were now being listened to. Macquarie realised that he had lost the confidence of the Colonial Office, and on 1 Dec 1817 he resigned. He concluded his resignation letter with a list of the twelve men who he knew to be complainants 'in the rank of Gentlemen, in this Colony, whom I look upon as my secret tho' not avowed Enemies'. The enemy list included Sir John Jamieson and five of Governor Bligh's long-standing enemies who had been involved in the rebellion and his arrest. Number one enemy was Rev. Samuel Marsden, whom he labelled as 'Discontent, Intriguing and Vindictive'.[21] John Macarthur, who had returned to the colony in late 1817, was not on his list. Macarthur had stayed in the background and worked behind the scenes against Macquarie, but he was preparing to become politically active again. Macquarie had submitted his resignation as governor to the Colonial Office but would stay at the tiller until this was accepted and his successor had arrived from England. He would remain in charge of the colony for another four years.

At the end of September 1817, the Rope family's newest neighbours, Lt. Phillip Parker King, the eldest child of Philip Gidley King and his wife Anna, arrived in New South Wales with his wife Harriet. Lt. King had been assigned to lead an exploration and hydrographical survey of the parts of the Australian coast not previously mapped by Captain Matthew Flinders.[22] While Lt. King was away surveying the Australian coastline over the next five years, Harriet largely managed the estate, especially after Rowland Hassall resigned in 1819 owing to illness. The Rope family would have known Harriet and probably did contract work for her.

Increasingly, the continent of which New South Wales was part of became known as 'Australia' in official communications and documents. Captain Matthew Flinders was the first to adopt this name in the 1814 publication of his charts and journal of the exploratory voyage. The use of *Australia* for the colony rather than *New South Wales* first appeared in *The Sydney Gazette* in 1816. After that, the name 'Australia' was widely used.[23] A year later, Governor Macquarie introduced it into his letters to the Colonial Office and on 21 Dec 1817, he recommended that henceforth the continent and colony be called 'Australia' rather than 'New Holland'.[24]

The first *Australia Day* celebration was held on 26 Jan 1818 to commemorate the 30th anniversary of the colony. The official celebration of this day paid tribute to Arthur Phillip 'whose virtues and talents entitle him to the grateful remembrance of his Country, and to whose arduous exertions the present prosperous state of the Colony may chiefly be ascribed'. In recognition of the anniversary, a 30-gun salute was fired.[25]

The disputes between Macquarie and Marsden came to a head in early 1818. Rev. Marsden was summonsed to Government House where Macquarie accused him of conspiracy and 'malicious attempts to injure' his character. Macquarie said Marsden was the 'Head of a Seditious low Cabal' and that he never wanted to see him again, except on public duty.[26] Afterwards Marsden tendered his resignation as magistrate, which Macquarie declined. However, when Marsden subsequently sentenced his own servant to 50 lashes and 12 months in double irons in a chain gang, for being insolent, Macquarie deemed this totally inexcusable. Three months later, *The Sydney Gazette* announced that Reverend Samuel Marsden would no longer be a Magistrate and Justice of the Peace.[27]

In 1818 the Anthony Rope decided to sell his long-held land at the Ponds. It is likely that he needed money to settle debts, and, because promissory notes were no longer allowed, a banker probably advised him to sell his land rather than borrow more money. On 1 Jul 1818, Anthony sold the 30-acre Howard's farm at the Ponds to John Bowman for £30. This included the house, outhouse buildings and other improvements. Both Anthony and John had settled in the Hawkesbury district and knew each other well. Close friendships were critical to the early remote settlers since they bolstered the chances of survival. Four years later, Anthony sold the 20-acre Clark's farm at the Ponds also to John Bowman, but the land value had risen, and he received £30.[28]

On 10 Aug 1818, Reverend Fulton sought permission from the governor for Susannah Rope, aged 17, to marry convict John Bradley, aged 30. They were married in the Castlereagh Church on September 7th. Both signed the marriage certificate with a cross, and Susannah's sister and brother-in-law, Sarah and Thomas Frost, were witnesses. In 1814 John Bradley, a soldier stationed on the Isle of Leon in Spain, had been court martialled and sentenced to transportation for life for stealing 300 Spanish dollars and deserting his post. Bradley arrived in Port Jackson aboard the transport *Baring* in 1815 and was immediately sent to the Windsor district to work as an assigned government servant.[29]

After the wedding, Susannah accompanied her husband to the assigned farm. Their first child was born five months later, followed by two more children. In 1819 John Bradley was appointed Constable to the district of Evan and received his ticket of leave.[30] He was now able to do paid work but was not allowed to leave the district without a magistrate's permission. In 1820, Bradley was made District Constable on the 1300-acre Chapman's Farm.[31] With the help of Reverend Fulton, Bradley petitioned the governor a year later for a conditional pardon. Fulton wrote on the petition that Bradley had been a servant of his for 1½ years and a constable for 4 years, and that 'his conduct was sober, honest and industrious'. The pardon was refused.[32] This was not unexpected since conditional pardons were usually only granted to 'lifers' after they had been in the colony for a decade.³³ Bradley had been in the colony for only six years and had to wait before petitioning again.

The General Muster of November 1818 records that Anthony Rope held 15 acres of land: 5 acres of wheat, 3 acres of maize, ½ acre of barley, ¼ acre of oats, ¼ acre of peas or beans, ½ acre of potatoes and ½ acre garden & orchard. He also had 6 pigs and 8 bushels of maize. The household included Anthony, 62, Elizabeth, 56, their two youngest children William, 13 and Elizabeth Ann, 10 and grandson George, 3. The crops of peas, beans, potatoes as well as fruit and vegetables from their orchard and garden indicate that they were marketing their products to provide additional income for the family.³⁴

The better harvest for South Creek farmers in 1819 helped them overcome the significant crop losses due to floods in previous years. The industry of the settlers during these testing times impressed Macquarie greatly, and he had fixed a high price for wheat in 1819 despite pressure from the British government to lower it. He argued that he needed 'to give the poorer Class of Settlers time to recover from their more recent Losses'.³⁵ The September 1819 General Muster in Windsor shows that many settlers in and around the Hawkesbury had increased in prosperity. The Ropes now had 13 acres of crop under cultivation, 5 pigs and had stored 10 bushels wheat and 8 bushels of maize. The 63-year-old Anthony was still a fit and strong individual. He may have employed an assigned servant or free farm labourer from time to time, but with his son William, he did most of the manual work.³⁶

For at least three years, the British government had been examining the effectiveness of convict transportation as a deterrent to property crime. In September 1819, the Colonial Office sent John Thomas Bigge to Sydney as a Commissioner charged with investigating the present state of the colony.³⁷ The Colonial Office questioned if transportation was a cost effective punishment. Bigge was told never to forget that transportation was intended as a 'severe Punishment' and as such 'must be rendered an Object of real Terror to all Classes of the Community'.³⁸ Secretary Bathurst believed that transportation had worked initially because of the perceived remoteness of the colony, but that this was no longer dreaded and nor was the punishment. Bigge was commissioned to find out whether a 'System of General Discipline, Constant Work, and Vigilant Superintendence' should be reinstated to make the sentence much more frightening. The instructions given to Bigge implied that Macquarie was the cause of disciplinary problems.

> If therefore, by ill considered Compassion for Convicts, or from what might under other circumstances be considered a laudable

desire to lessen their sufferings, their Situation in New South Wales be divested of all Salutary Terror, Transportation cannot operate as an effectual example on the Community at large, and as a proper punishment for those Crimes against the Commission of which His Majesty's Subjects have a right to claim protection.[39]

The British clearly had never wanted the dregs of society to see the shores of the Mother Country again.

By mid-September 1819, Governor Macquarie was still waiting for a reply to his resignation letter. Secretary Bathurst had written to Macquarie asking him to reconsider his resignation, but this letter never reached the colony. Only five days before Commissioner Bigge's arrival, Macquarie received a letter telling him of the enquiry into his administration, and of the imminent arrival of the Commissioner. Not knowing Bigge's brief, Macquarie expected a favourable attitude towards his successful administration He was to be disappointed. The Commissioner, as per his instructions, was opposed to the humanitarian treatment of convicts and the advancement of emancipists. This came to the fore when Bigge disagreed with the appointment of the emancipist surgeon, William Redfern, as magistrate. Macquarie refused to reverse this decision and appealed to Bigge to treat the emancipists fairly, and to show a 'Sense of Moral Feeling'.

> Avert the Blow You appear to be too much inclined to Inflict on these unhappy Beings (if You make them so!); and let the Souls now in being as well as Millions yet unborn, bless the Day on which you landed on their Shores, and gave them (when they deserve it) what you so much admire Freedom![40]

Macquarie maintained that one of the important functions of the colony was to rehabilitate and reform convicts, and he was absolutely appalled at Bigge's opposition to this. The battle lines between the two men could not have been more clearly drawn. Macquarie supported egalitarian policies for emancipists, while Bigge believed a criminal record could never be erased, and that convicts should never be part of civil society. Bigge claimed an emancipist magistrate would endanger the community.

Macquarie's health was failing, and the Commissioner's criticism increased his desire to leave the colony. After a decade of leadership, he was weary of defending what he saw as self-evident rights. He also wanted to return to England to refute the slanderous accusations made by MP Henry Bennet in the House of Commons. Macquarie had been badly hurt by Bennet's apparent dishonesty. Marsden's correspondence had led Bennet to claim that the 'real situation of this colony' was the 'flagrant example of misgovernment, and the almost entire failure of the experiment as place of reform' and was 'little better than a deposit of all the vices and crimes which have been, and are the scourges of the more civilized inhabitants of the mother'.[41] In a well-written reply to the charges laid by Bennet, Macquarie defended his policies and the people of Australia. He wrote 'this country should be made the home, and a happy home, to every emancipated convict who deserves it'. Macquarie now clearly considered himself an Australian and wanted to defend the reputation of its people. It is no surprise that the free settlers, emancipists and convicts considered him 'a friend and protector'.[42]

Macquarie saw himself more as an *improver* than a *reformer* – he wanted to create a harmonious society. To achieve this, he directed his administration to serve everyone equally, strive to improve public infrastructure, and make health and education facilities accessible to all. Macquarie may not have considered himself a reformer, but his policies were visionary, and before their time. It is no wonder that the Conservatives in both the colony and in Britain saw him as a radical, and someone who needed to be reined in quickly. In February 1820, Macquarie tendered his written resignation for the second time.[43]

In November 1819 the French ship *L'Uranie*, commanded by Captain Louis de Freycinet, sailed into Sydney Cove during their expedition to circumnavigate the globe. On board was the writer, artist and explorer Jacques Arago. He was impressed by the 'curious spectacle' when sailing into Port Jackson – amid a novel vegetation was a flourishing city of sophisticated European architecture. Argo wrote:

> Farther on we see country houses, that remind us of the elegant seats in the environs of Bordeaux. .... Every thing is turned to advantage, every thing is rendered useful, round this superb habitation... Spacious buildings assume the place of smoky huts; an active and intelligent population is now in motion, and eager in pursuit of pleasure. ... Obscure paths become broad and level roads: a town arises — a colony is formed — Sydney becomes a flourishing city.
> Magnificent hotels, majestic mansions, houses of extraordinary taste and elegance, fountains ornamented with sculptures worthy the chisel of our best artists, spacious and airy apartments, rich furniture, horses, carriages, and one-horse chaises of the greatest elegance, immense storehouses —would you expect to find all these, four thousand leagues from Europe? I assure you, my friend, I fancied myself transported into one of our handsomest cities.[44]

In 1820, Commissioner Bigge travelled to all parts of the colony interviewing residents about their concerns. At these gatherings he collected evidence on government misdemeanours and heard views on how the colony should be administered in the future. These meetings gave John Macarthur ample opportunity to persuade Bigge on the benefits of business monopolies and private development, concepts that, not surprisingly, suited his own investments. Once Macarthur had Bigge's confidence, he proposed that the colony's transportation systems be expanded to help the sheep industry, and that farm productivity be organised around large privately owned estates. Instead of consulting Macquarie about the wisdom and workability of such suggestions, Bigge communicated only with the major landholders and business leaders. John Macarthur and John Bigge became, as Macquarie would later recall, 'intimate associates and most frequent visitors'.[45] As a leading sheep farmer, Samuel Marsden also promoted the wool industry and praised the economic and moral benefits of the assigned convict system. He proposed that convicts be assigned to wealthy graziers without any cost to them. Such proposals were similar to the organisation of convict labour in America – which was only one step away from slavery.

John Macarthur had previously told Macquarie about his ideas, but the governor was not interested. In any case, Macquarie was not about to hand over the colony's economic development to self-serving graziers who were only marginal players in the colony's food economy. But he had underestimated the influence Macarthur and Marsden had on Bigge, although he knew that Macarthur had been asked to draft a plan for the future of Australia. In this plan, the export of fine wool played a dominant role in the economy. The era of the Sheep Barons and their stations would come in time, but in the 1820s increasing food production needed to be the first priority of the colony.

Macarthur's plan also proposed that convicts be punished by their masters rather than by magistrates and recommended that the quantity and quality of a convict's food be dependent on their work and good behaviour. He suggested that farming estates be at least 10,000 acres in size and that new land grants be given only to "men of character" who had the necessary skills and capital.[46] In many respects, Macarthur's plan reflected the views of the landed aristocracy in rural England, and promulgated aspects of the Britain's 18th century Enclosure Acts. It also promoted the system favourable to the owners of large estates in the American eastern states, and in the West Indies, where the use of slave labour was ubiquitous.

All this advice to Bigge ran counter to Macquarie's focus on improving food production. The small settlers had shown themselves to be the most efficient farmers in the colony, and Macquarie was determined that they should not be disadvantaged by the ambitions of the large graziers. If Macarthur's plan came into effect, most existing settlers would not have land to farm and never be eligible for land grants. Such an outcome would have well suited Marsden and Macarthur and they did not disguise their intentions – they advocated that the wealthy free men of the colony should run the economy, not the government, nor the uneducated ex-convicts.

The ultra-conservative nature of these proposals was designed to appeal to the class-conscious Bigge, and he was clearly impressed. At this point in the process, Macquarie realised that his social reforms were in serious jeopardy, not only from the local elites but also from Bigge and Bathurst in the Colonial Office. However, Macquarie was not in this fight alone. He knew that he had large numbers of supporters in the colony. They were small farmers, emancipists and less-vocal members in the business community, and they had been overlooked by the Bigge enquiry. The political awareness of smaller farmers had matured since the Bligh rebellion, and settlers expected to be treated fairly and equally. Their voices would not be easily ignored, and any attempt to reverse their rights, either from within or without the colony, would meet with fierce resistance.

In Macquarie's opinion a government had a moral duty to act in the interest of all citizens, not just the privileged few. These were early glimmers of democracy in Australia, and John Macarthur and the British Tory politicians considered it dangerous. In a letter to Bigge in February 1821, Macarthur made another attempt to manipulate his opinion:

> this democratic feeling has already taken deep root in the Colony, in consequence of the absurd and mischievous policy, pursued by Governor Macquarie and as there is already a strong combination amongst that class of persons, it cannot be too soon opposed with vigour.[47]

The Commissioner departed for England in February 1821, and in July 1822 his report was considered by parliament.

By late 1820, Macquarie had heard that his resignation had been accepted, and he awaited the arrival of his successor.[48] Between 1810 and 1819, Macquarie had granted 352 absolute and 1164 conditional pardons to convicts.[49] The new emancipists took for granted that their civil rights would be fully restored. This was not the case, as rights were still limited by the *1815 New South Wales Act*, passed by the British government, which decreed those persons freed by a governor's pardon, rather than by Royal Decree, could *not seek a personal action in law or acquire, retain or transmit property*. The Act applied to emancipists and their freeborn children, and if strictly applied, it would deprive the majority of people in the colony of land titles, and their ability to sell land, houses or other property.

It was essential that the *N.S.W. Act* be put to the test. In August 1820 Judge Barron Field ruled on the property ownership of the emancipist Edward Eagar – in affirming the Act, it confirmed the worst fears of the emancipists. However in recognition of the precedent it set, the finding was delayed for a year to allow for clarification from England.[50] In October 1821, Edward Eagar and William Redfern sailed to England with a petition to King George IV and the British parliament. Macquarie fully supported the petition and provided strong recommendations.[51] The petitioners called upon His Majesty to reverse the finding and restore their legal rights. Signed by 1368 people, the petitioners pointed out that through hard labour they had converted an unproductive wilderness into a thriving colony that was now an important part of the British Empire. To emphasise the consequence of the Act, the emancipists stated that over 13,000 ex-convicts and families would be affected, whereas only 2500 people had come freely to New South Wales. The emancipists and their families held the majority of investments in shipping, trade and commerce, three times the area of cultivable land, and twice the number of sheep and cattle of free settlers. The overall wealth of the emancipists was nearly double that of the rest of the community.[52] The efforts of the petition delegation proved successful, and the British Parliament nullified the *N.S.W. Act* in 1823.

The Rope family had greatly benefited from Macquarie's land policies and humane treatment of convicts. John Rope was granted 60 acres land in 1814 and Sarah Rope's husband, Thomas Frost, received a 50-acre land grant in 1820.[53] Mary Rope had applied twice unsuccessfully for a land grant. When her husband applied in September 1821 for a conditional pardon, he received both the pardon and a land grant for 80 acres.[54] In considering an application for a pardon Macquarie largely ignored a petitioners' criminal record and based his decision mostly on recent behaviour. He wanted recent good conduct to be rewarded and give convicts every opportunity to make a fresh start.

Lachlan Macquarie planned to return to England in 1821 and toured all of the settlements including those in Van Diemen's Land and Port Macquarie. Everywhere he went he was received with great warmth and respect. Inhabitants presented him with farewell letters, presents and speeches praising 'the mildness, the equity and the wisdom' he had shown and 'the comfort and happiness' he had given to all inhabitants during his long administration. Hawkesbury settlers particularly regretted his departure and expressed their admiration in a written address.[55]

Macquarie was most gratified by the warmth of his reception. It reassured him that, despite the British government's criticisms, the colonialists appreciated his time in office. He reported this with great satisfaction to Secretary Bathurst – someone who had never given his government credit – emphasizing that the economy was progressing well and the farmers were in 'a state of perfect tranquillity' after the best harvest since the beginning of the colony.[56]

Three years earlier, surveyor John Oxley had discovered a good harbour 390 km north of Sydney during his inland explorations. He named it 'Port Macquarie' after the incumbent governor, and the location was selected to become a new penal settlement for convicts who had committed crimes in the colony.[57] With its thick bush, tough terrain and long distance from Sydney, it was an ideal place to put recalcitrant inhabitants. In November Macquarie visited the port as part of his grand tour of the colony.[58] The visit was personally rewarding, but the timing proved unfortunate.

Without Macquarie's knowledge, the new governor, 48-year-old Sir Thomas Brisbane, and his family, was due to arrive in Port Jackson when he was in Port Macquarie. Brisbane was a Major General in the Scottish army and had been recommended by the Duke of Wellington, under whom he had served. The new governor appears to have been attracted to the post primarily because of his interest in astronomy. He knew the location would be ideal for observing stars in the southern hemisphere with his telescope.

At the inauguration of Sir Thomas Brisbane as governor, on 1 Dec 1821, Lachlan Macquarie opened his speech with the words, 'Fellow citizens of Australia', and went on to describe the growth of the colony since he had arrived in 1810. He concluded with the prediction that Australia in less than 50 years would 'be one of the most valuable appendages belonging to the British Empire'. His speech made clear that he had done everything possible to advance the colony's wellbeing and prosperity, and he would leave the office proud of his administration's achievements.[59]

During Macquarie's eleven years in office the population of the colony had almost tripled to 29,783 people. The number of convicts made up half of the population with 46% (12,608 males and 1206 females). Only 5% of the inhabitants came freely to the colony, 18% of the population were ex-convicts (5312), 6% were born in the colony and 25% were children (7224).[60]

On 12 Feb 1822 Macquarie and his family left government House for the transport ship, *Surry*. The military regiment escorted his party to the waterfront, where flags were flying and vessels in the harbour were decorated. The festooned streets of Sydney were lined with crowds cheering the governor, and newspapers reported genuine sadness at his departure. When Macquarie boarded the *Surry*, a 19-gun salute rang out in his honour. *The Sydney Gazette* newspaper captured the sentiments of those present, reporting 'Australia saw her Benefactor, for the last time, treading her once uncivilized and unsocial shores and felt it too; – the parent and the child must endure the parting pang!' Macquarie had spent eleven years living 'amongst these poor attached People', and he was deeply moved and humbled by the occasion.[61]

Macquarie arrived back in London in July 1822, about the same time that Commissioner Bigge's first report was submitted to the Parliamentary Select Committee. Bigge tabled a second report in 1823. As anticipated, both reports were critical of Macquarie's policies, and the eventual acceptance of the findings led to major changes to the British penal system. Macquarie's lenient and generous treatment of the convicts and emancipists ran counter to a government that wanted more punishment than rehabilitation. Bigge recommended increasing penalties to a level where even the hardest criminals in Britain would fear transportation. He reversed Macquarie's policies on convict assignments, emancipist rights and public works expenditure. New South Wales was now to be a *penal*, not a *free*, colony.[62]

In London Macquarie made a determined effort to salvage his reputation with the Colonial Office, and to secure a pension. The pension was eventually granted in 1824, but he had little time to benefit from it. Lachlan Macquarie died on 1 Jul 1824 at the age of 62.

As with other active governors, Macquarie had become a victim of the political pressures exerted by conservatives in the colony and in Britain. Macquarie never received the accolades he justly deserved from his country of birth for his diligent and intelligent governorship. Most of the colonialists in Australia recognised the brilliance of his leadership, energy and his fairness as Governor of New South Wales. He remains a legend today, and was aptly named a 'Father of Australia'[63]

Such sentiments were massively amplified when Bigge's reforms started to be implemented. It was during Brisbane and Darling's tenures as governor that the song about Macquarie, the old Viceroy, echoed through colonial inns and taverns, in defiance of the authorities:

> *Macquarie was the prince of men!*
> *Australia's pride and joy!*
> *We ne'er shall see his like again;*
> *Here's to the old Viceroy!* [64]

Chapter 22

CURRENCY LADS & LASSES 1822-1825

> *Our Currency lads and lasses are a fine interesting race, and do honour to the country whence they originated. The name is a sufficient passport to esteem with all the well-informed and right-feeling portion of our population; but it is most laughable to see the capers some of our drunken old Sterling madonnas will occasionally cut over their Currency adversaries in a quarrel.*[1]

Governor Thomas Brisbane was a reserved educated man whose leadership style was in marked contrast to his predecessor. Macquarie had been inclusive and gregarious, and he had entertained and involved as many inhabitants as possible in his administration and in his building projects. The new governor was not inclined to include emancipists in his affairs, and they definitely did not sit at his table or be considered for official posts. Indeed Brisbane seemed not to be interested in any of the colony's residents, free or emancipist. The contrast in leadership styles went further; whereas Macquarie attended to administrative minutiae at all levels, Brisbane delegated most decisions to his officials.

One such official was the Colonial Secretary of New South Wales, Major Frederick Goulburn, who had arrived in 1820 during Macquarie's tenure to be in charge of official records.[2] Initially Goulburn had little influence on government policy, but in the new administration this changed. Once Brisbane had settled into the role of governor, he spent long periods in Parramatta with his telescopes searching the sky for new discoveries, and he was quite content to let Goulburn transact the daily government business in Sydney.

Goulburn's free rein to run the colony would soon be curtailed. There were concerns in the community about the extent of his official duties, and some questioned Goulburn's competency. The policies being enacted at that time were largely a result of the Colonial Office's decision to apply the recommendations of the 1822 and 1823 Bigge reports. Brisbane had been instructed to implement the major Bigge reforms and enforce stricter convict discipline. The New South Wales colony should be a place to fear, not one of rehabilitation and opportunity for convicts.

The first Bigge recommendation was to revamp the assigned convict servant system. In keeping with Macarthur's advice to Bigge, the practice of paying convicts directly for work was abolished, and servants were assigned to settlers according to the size of their farm or business. The new system gave convicts almost no free time or personal reward for their labours, but it did lower the labour costs for landholders and employers. A week after taking office, Brisbane invited settlers to apply to Goulburn's office for the assignment of convict servants. Preference was given to those who had previously maintained convicts at no expense to the Crown. Convicts with mechanical skills, the most desired farm workers, were no longer automatically assigned. They could only be employed through weekly payments to the administration.[3]

The servant assignments were coupled to a reorganisation of the land grant system, and the number of convicts allocated depended on the area of land being cultivated. Brisbane ordered that for every 100 acres of land received by grant or by purchase, one convict servant must be 'fully maintained'.[4] On larger properties convict servants were assigned for the entire term of their sentence, and the master was entitled to all of the convict's labour time. This ended the practice of allowing convicts to work for themselves after servant hours. Convicts no longer received a wage, with the master paying the government a fee for their medical care, religious instruction, and the maintenance of good order. Those needing labourers to clear their estate of timber, or to harvest grain, could apply to the Colonial Secretary for convict gangs. The fees charged for gangs depended on the work performed and could be paid for in grain delivered to the government store. Servants were assigned to small settlers without the land-area provision, and they paid the government for the work, not the servant.[5]

The government benefited financially and administratively from the new policies, but they were regressive for convicts who now received no extra money to feed themselves or their families. The permanent assignment of convicts to large farms also acted as a disincentive for farmers to help servants obtain a ticket of leave. In any case, new government regulations placed stricter conditions on the granting of tickets of leave and pardons. Convicts now had to serve the greater part of their sentence before applying. Under Brisbane, sentences were only reduced for outstanding behaviour.[6] However, Governor Brisbane resisted following the Colonial Office's reforms to the letter. He often applied less severe policies and tried to respond in a sensible way to local conditions, individual needs and special circumstances.

Another reform on the Colonial Office's list was to increase the number of magistrates in the colony. Reverend Marsden, who had been dismissed as magistrate by Macquarie, was delighted to be re-instated.

However, good terms between Marsden and the new governor soon soured, and within months Brisbane dismissed him. Marsden had been outraged that a fellow magistrate, the free surgeon Henry Douglas had a convict, Ann Rumsby, as his mistress. Despite her denial of this relationship, she was arrested. In court she refused to testify and Marsden, and his bench, ordered her to spend the remainder of her sentence in Port Macquarie. Brisbane realised that she had been unfairly and perhaps illegally tried. He dismissed Marsden and overturned the sentence.[7] Once again, a governor who believed in equal justice for all had thwarted Marsden's part-time legal ambitions.

John Macarthur, who had met Thomas Brisbane in England, was another candidate for magistrate and expected to be appointed a week after Macquarie's departure. But there were complaints about his candidature from Judge Barron Field, who was a qualified lawyer, and Macarthur's appointment was withdrawn. Brisbane thought Macarthur had been unfairly maligned and asked Secretary Bathurst in England to support his reappointment.[8] Bathurst declined, fearing it would rekindle friction over Bligh's arrest. He suggested that one of Macarthur's sons, James or William, be appointed instead. However, both men refused the appointment when it was offered in October 1823.[9]

Considering Brisbane's reputed intellect, his next decision was a surprise. In April 1822 he declared that henceforth goods bought by the government would be paid for in *Spanish dollars*. That is, government entities would now buy grain, and other items, in the foreign currency phased out by Macquarie eight years earlier. The Bank of New South Wales appears to have encouraged this decision – it had tons of this coinage left in its vaults and the bank officials probably realised that it would soon be worthless. Each dollar coin had a face value of 5s, but the market value within the colony was only 4s 2d in colonial bank-issued notes. This effectively devalued the cost of goods received by the government by almost a fifth. Landholders and merchants who supplied the government stores were outraged. A petition from 234 settlers and merchants was sent to the governor condemning the use of the old, devalued coinage. John Rope, John Ryan and Thomas Frost had a lot to lose from these payments, and they were among the petition signatories. The petitioners complained that not only was their income reduced by almost 20% but the currency was also 'a foreign Coin of doubtful and fluctuating value'.[10] The pleas to Brisbane were to no avail. Nevertheless, payments in Spanish dollars were strongly resented and resisted, and within three years the British Parliament passed an act proclaiming Stirling as the only official currency of Australia.

In early 1822 the majority of convicts in Newcastle prisons and mines were transferred to Port Macquarie where a dangerous sandbar at the entrance of the harbour had caused several ships to be stranded and wrecked. Port Macquarie was in urgent need of a rugged lifeboat that could be used in these situations. An 18 ft sailing boat suitable for this role was launched from His Majesty's Dockyard in Sydney in July 1822. It was the first such boat built in the colony, constructed to 'neither remain keel upper-most, nor sink when filled; and the men, being rendered buoyant from the quantity of cork used in the construction, are preserved from danger in the most tempestuous seas'. The boat was to be sent to Port Macquarie where it would 'be sensibly experienced in the preservation of many lives, as the navigation of that harbour is known to be very dangerous'. The 8 x 18 ft lifeboat needed to be sailed and rowed by five men over 200 nautical miles in the open seas along the east coast of New South Wales.[11] One of the crew would be Anthony Rope.

It remains unclear how Anthony was selected to be part of the lifeboat crew. As a settler on the South Creek, a long way from the Sydney docks, he would not have known of the lifeboat project without help. Moreover, at 66 years of age, he must have been considered elderly for such an arduous task. A likely explanation is that he was known in the Hawkesbury district as a good swimmer – uncommon in those times – and someone with experience in small boats. Whatever the reasons for his selection, the money offered would have been sufficient attraction for Anthony to snap it up. The venture was to almost cost him his life.

In July 1822 the lifeboat with its five-man crew set out from Port Jackson and reached the Hunter River at Newcastle a week later. On the next leg, they encountered strong gales and high waves off Port Stephens, about 50 km north of Newcastle. Their mast splintered and they had no alternative in the heavy seas but to head for shore and risk beaching the boat in the surf. On the shore run the boat overturned in tremendous surf; four men swam to shore after discarding their heavy clothes, but the fifth crewmember drowned. The men wrestled the boat onto the sand and recovered as much of the boat contents and clothes as they could. It was decided that one man should guard the lifeboat while the other three walked back along the beach to Newcastle. A temporary shelter was erected with a sail over the remaining food and water. Anthony Rope, being the oldest, was probably the person left to look after the boat – a task not without risks, as local aborigines may have objected to the incursion on their beach. The other three crewmembers reached Newcastle the following morning and a large pilot boat was immediately sent to recover the lifeboat and crewman to bring them back to Newcastle to make repairs.

When the news of the beaching reached Sydney, *The Sydney*

Gazette reported, rather naively, 'that no accident could possibly have happened, had the boat been kept off shore'.[12] Manoeuvring a mast-less small boat in heavy seas is a challenge for skilled sailors, but apparently not for the intrepid *Gazette* journalist. The beaching occurred during a major storm, and another boat carrying lime had been lost in the same area a week earlier. The lifeboat received a new mast in Newcastle, and the four men successfully sailed to Port Macquarie. They had lost or ruined most of their clothing on the journey, and in Port Macquarie applied for compensation. At the end of the year Anthony Rope, James Crighton, William Ward and John Hughes received a clothing stipend of £10.[13] It is not known how much the men were paid to deliver the lifeboat, but it would have been substantial.

During Anthony's absence, Elizabeth and the rest of the family were unlikely to have known much of the adventure, and it would have been unsettling time for all of them. John Ryan and Thomas Frost, who were literate, might have read in the newspaper about the beaching of the lifeboat and loss of life. Since no names were given, Elizabeth would have greatly feared that Anthony was the one who had drowned. In late August 1822 Anthony returned from Port Macquarie. His appearance on the farm would have been a time of rejoicing, and he undoubtedly recounted the story of the storm in graphic detail. For the Ropes it was a tale of great excitement and wonder and would have certainly been repeated often around the family hearth.

Watercolour painting of Port Macquarie in 1825 with the notorious sandbar in the centre. Anthony Rope helped sail a lifeboat to Port Macquarie from Sydney in 1822.

Returning to the issue of how Anthony became part of this venture. Unquestionably, payment would have been the main incentive for taking on such a hazardous task. That he had survived the storm and beaching as a 66-year-old, justifies his hiring. During the South Creek and the Hawkesbury River floods, he had probably helped in boating rescues. It is also likely that he worked on the grain ferries in the Nepean and Hawkesbury rivers, and even on Andrew Thompson's boats shipping produce between Sydney and the Hawkesbury districts. This, and previous sailing experience as a younger man, were qualifications enough, though it seems surprising that there were not more experienced seamen in the Sydney area. To offer the job to such a remote settler suggests that either Anthony was well known in the colony as a fine boatman, or he had very good friends in the Sydney ship building circles.

The September 1822 General Muster provides us with details of the settlers' goods and chattels, the last complete survey of farm possessions and stockholdings to be held in the colony. Later musters were less detailed and surveyed only convicts. The 1822 muster lists Anthony Rope as landholder of a 20 acres lease, with Elizabeth, two children and government servant, John Lary, in the house. It shows that the Ropes had 9 acres in wheat crop, 4 acres maize, ¼ acre in potatoes, and a ½ acre garden and orchard. They held in storage for personal consumption 2 bushels of wheat, 10 bushels of maize and owned 12 pigs.[14] A wide variety of fruits and vegetables were cultivated in settlers' gardens and orchards. These were for personal use as well as to sell at markets. Alexander Harris, who worked in the district for years, writes in his memoirs that settlers grew figs, gooseberries, currants, lemons, oranges, melons, peaches 'as large as good sized breakfast cup and of the most exquisite flavour', potatoes, pumpkins 'as big as a large bucket', cabbages, radishes, onions, beans and peas.[15]

In March 1823 the government initiated the new practice of buying supplies, such as grain, by tender. This form of competitive pricing favoured larger farms over the smaller ones. In the first season the government bought only three-month's supply of grain at half of the price paid in the previous year, leaving considerable surplus grain in the hands of grain dealers and growers. Some farmers faced financial ruin. Having no proper storage for their grain, many growers had no option but to use the unsold grain to feed livestock.[16] The government's tampering with the grain market had a 'truly lamentable and demoralising effect in the lower classes of the colonial population'.

Nature was about to add to the misery of the farmers; a severe drought followed. Poor harvests led to a scarcity of grain, and wheat prices increased massively. By then, returning to the old grain marketing practices did not help. The colony was threatened by famine again, and mostly because of the government's mismanagement and greed. The price of wheat per bushel rose from 3s 9d to £1 4s, a six-fold increase. The small farmers, most of whom had reduced their seeding because of a perceived oversupply, did not benefit because they had nothing to sell to the government stores.[17] Brisbane was forced in August 1824 to send a merchant ship to Batavia to secure a cargo of grain.[18]

As a consequence of this marketing fiasco both government and farmers lost heavily. To add insult to injury for farmers, the government had paid for their grain in Spanish dollars, and the farmers' loans had to be repaid in pounds Sterling. These exchange differences exaggerated the losses. Many settlers went bankrupt, and farms were seized and sold at a quarter of their value.[19] It is a sad chapter in Australia's banking and farming history – the government's financial incompetency had ruined many farmers. But as is so often the case in such crises, some benefited from this mismanagement; banks and loan vendors were able to assume ownership by purchasing 'cheap' land in forced sales. There is no record of how the Rope family fared during this difficult period, but almost certainly they struggled to keep afloat financially. And no doubt they would have complained about the need for sensible and benevolent governance, and appreciated, more than ever, the prosperity they enjoyed under Macquarie.

After 35 years of autocratic colonial rule, the British Parliament announced in 1823 a long-overdue shift towards democratisation in the colony: the Legislative Council of New South Wales was to be formed. This permitted the establishment of an independent Supreme Court, Courts of Quarter Sessions, and a limited provision for trial by jury in civil cases. The reconstitution of the courts and the abolition of the Judge Advocate court meant the removal of the last vestiges of military rule. The Legislative Council had little independence from Britain, but it was the first small step on the path to future autonomy. On 17 May 1824, a new Charter of Justice was declared in Sydney when the Supreme Court was formally opened under the new Chief Justice Francis Forbes. Not everyone welcomed these changes. They provoked anger among the exclusives who believed that increased civil rights for the commoners would diminish their influence.

By early 1824 quarrels between Governor Brisbane and Secretary Goulburn were paralysing the administration. Whereas Macquarie wanted to break down the barriers between the exclusives and the emancipists, Goulburn strongly supported the business elite, and was eager to restore them to their former power and influence. Brisbane certainly did not share Macquarie's conviction for social equality, but he did believe in meritocracy from his scientific training and wanted to promote as much cohesion as possible in the community. Goulburn, and his supporters, opposed wherever possible any action Brisbane made to improve the civil opportunities for emancipist inhabitants.

In April 1824, Goulburn well and truly exceeded his official powers. He withheld correspondence from the governor and disobeyed some of his explicit instructions. He even issued official orders of his own. Brisbane wanted an uncomplicated life in which astronomy was the main focus and had tolerated Goulburn's transgressions until he wanted all government orders to be validated by his office. On 1 May 1824 Brisbane informed the Colonial Office of Goulburn's misconduct and requested his dismissal.[20]

On 25 Aug 1824, the first Legislative Council met to advise the government on legislative matters presided over by the governor and five other members appointed by King George IV. The Council was advisory only, possessing no real law-making power; only the governor could introduce a bill.[21] Proposed laws were discussed in the council, but the governor could override any he disagreed with. Moreover, a bill only became law if the chief justice certified that it was consistent with the laws of England and the colony.

Such political matters were of scant concern to most settlers. For the Ropes at Jordan Hill, their life was governed by the seasons, and 1824 was a year of highs and lows. On one hand, they were overjoyed at receiving new land grants, but troubled by family issues. Their daughter Susannah had arranged for her husband, John Bradley, to be assigned to her as a government servant, but he was arrested while working as a constable. The details are unknown, but in June 1824 Bradley was charged with embezzlement and sentenced to one year's labour at the Port Macquarie penal settlement.[22] Having visited this location, Anthony was well aware of the harsh treatment convicts received there. Susannah and her three daughters, the youngest only three weeks old, were now dependent on the support of her parents until she could find work.

The Brisbane administration continued to explore ways of improving the government finances, and in July 1824 it offered crown land for sale, claiming that it was the 'most legitimate sources of Revenue for this Colony'. An acre of land was offered at between 5s and 10s to residents who had a proven ability to improve the land and produce food for the colony.[23] Most small farmers were worried about this offer. Macarthur's suggestions in the past had always favoured wealthy landowners who could afford to pay for land and were anxious that it signalled the end of free land grants from the government.

And probably because of this fear, a month later four Rope

family members, Anthony, William, John, and Sarah petitioned Governor Brisbane for a land grant. Both William and Sarah wrote that they were the children of 'Anthony Roape [*sic*], who arrived by the First Fleet upwards of 35 Years ago'.[24] Anthony, at 68 years, and Elizabeth, at 62, were among the oldest people in the colony. Without any provision for support or pension when they became too old to work, they believed a land grant would be financial security in their retirement. On 31 Aug 1824, Anthony applied for a land grant in the following words:

> That your Excellencys Memorialist came to this Colony in the first fleet, in the year 1789 [*sic*]. That Memorialist is married and has a large family whom he supports from the produce of a rented farm, he occupies in the District of Evan. That since the period of his arrival in the Colony his character has been honest and upright, and his demeanour such, as to merit the approbation of his superiors. That ardently wishing to make some permanent provision for the increasing infirmities of age, which are fast approaching Memorialist and wife, he approaches your Excellency as one of the oldest inhabitants of the Colony praying for a share in your kind & beneficent indulgence.[25]

Traditionally elderly settlers relied on their children's support in their closing years. In 1824 the Ropes were both still active and productive. Indeed they were responsible for supporting family members on their farm. Susannah, her girls and 16-year-old Elizabeth Ann were dependent on them. Mary's son George also remained in their care. With three generations living in the house, the elderly Ropes needed to plan for the future. On 12 Aug 1824 the Ropes had another mouth to feed; Elizabeth Ann gave birth to a boy, James Rope.

In September 1824 John and William Rope were notified by the land grant administration that they would each receive 60 acres. Sarah was not successful, the reply stated that a 'Grant of Land would be contrary to practise' – that is, the government did not yet give land grants to females. Anthony also missed out, most likely because he was too old to be considered. Apparently strong young women and active old men were considered unlikely to become successful farmers.[26]

But Sarah had her mother's spirit and was spurred on by her brothers' success. Sarah and her husband Thomas, along with her sister Mary's husband John, petitioned the governor in November 1824 for a land grant.[27] In February 1825 both men were notified that they had been successful, and each received 50 acres.[28] There would have been quite a celebration in the family that night, and probably a few sore heads the next morning. Brisbane had granted four land grants to the Ropes' children in the space of a several months. The location of the land grants had yet to be specified. The grantee could nominate a preferred site, but it could not be occupied until surveyed, and a land deed issued. The families now had to wait upon the survey office.

The younger Rope family members were typical of the new generation of free colonialists, commonly known as the 'currency lads and lasses'. This was the expression used in the colony to describe those who were Australian born with emancipist or convict parentage. This generation grew up in an adult society in which free immigrants often made slights and barbs about their origins – they were 'the offspring of thieves' and 'good for nothings'. But the spirit and energy of this new breed had its admirers. Surgeon Peter Miller Cunningham was optimistic about the 'currency youth'.

> Our colonial-born brethren are best known here by the name of *Currency*, in contradistinction to *Sterling*, or those born in the mother-country. ... Our Currency lads and lasses are a fine interesting race, and do honour to the country whence they originated. ... The Currency youths are warmly attached to their country, which they deem unsurpassable, and few ever visit England without hailing the day of their return as the most delightful in their lives....[29]

The currency lads and lasses were also referred to as *Corn Stalks* because they were taller than their British counterparts the *Sterlings*, and they had a distinct way of talking. The children of exclusives saw themselves as the pure bloods of the colony and, if they came from large estates, as the *Pure Merinos*. Among the colony's youth, the currency lads stood together and if one was attacked the 'whole hive sally to his aid'. Interestingly, drunkenness was much less common among the currency youth than their parents or the adult population as a whole.[30]

Most had at least one convict or ex-convict parent but, to the surprise of their elite contemporaries, they were generally law-abiding. Work was plentiful in the colony, and many had respectable well-paid jobs. In fact, there were far fewer temptations for youth to commit crime in the colony than in the overcrowded and underemployed British cities. Australia had shown itself to be a land of promise for the parents of the currency youth, and so it would be for them. Toby Ryan, as the son of a convict father, reflected on this in his book *Reminiscences*.

> Many of the early Australians sprang from the well-behaved emancipists and military men, who settled down at once, uncontaminated by drink, disease, or other enervating diseases; the result was fine men and women. Of course, hard work and wholesome food were partly the means of raising so fine a race.... Their red cheeks showed the bloom of health and beauty, and they required no artificial means to make them representable.

They moved with agility, and were straight and well-formed, showing that their ancestors came from a good stock.[31]

For most emancipists and their children Australia was their home, and they had no intention of returning to the Mother Country. They formed a strong political block that sought to ensure lawful access to all levels in Australian society. In 1821 the emancipists sent a petition to King George IV requesting the removal of any impediments to legal representation and rights. Some members of the community, and particularly the exclusives, government officials, and even governors, consistently discriminated against them. Their work opportunities were improving, but they now feared that the rapid increase in new free immigrants arriving would slow their acceptance into Australian society.

Equal opportunity remained a hot issue in the colony. In August 1824 the currency lad, William Wentworth, returned to Sydney after studying law in England. He was the son of Surgeon D'Arcy Wentworth and convict Catherine Crowley, who both arrived on the same ship, the *Neptune*, in 1790. An English friend and barrister, Robert Wardell, came with William to Australia. Wardell had sold *The Statesman* newspaper in London with the aim of starting a new journal in Sydney. Soon after their arrival, Governor Brisbane granted the two men permission to publish the first independent newspaper in Australia, *The Australian*. On 14 Oct 1824 the first edition went to press, and in an editorial Wentworth informed readers that 'A free press is the most legitimate, and at the same time the most powerful weapon that can be employed to annihilate such influence, frustrate the designs of tyranny, and restrain the arm of oppression'.[32]

The next day Governor Brisbane announced that freedom of the press in the colony was essential, and the censorship of *The Sydney Gazette* would end.[33] Soon *The Australian* was supporting the emancipists in their campaign for equal rights. Wentworth used every opportunity to attack exclusive society and became one of the colony's leading political figures of the 1820s and 1830s. His causes were often controversial, and he later became a tenacious enemy of Governor Darling, who was a strong supporter of John Macarthur and the exclusives.

The Ropes' relatively small farm was surrounded by large and wealthy estates that employed between 100 and 150 convict servants, all assigned for the duration of their sentences. Most estate owners were magistrates with their own constables and overseers, and, when necessary, a constable could take an offending servant to court for punishment. Toby Ryan remembered 'the overseers and constables were generally ticket of leave men, the very worst type of tyrants that could be chosen for that infamous service'.[34] Convict servants were still assigned to small settlers but, unlike the large landholders, they were permitted to replace them at short notice if they were unsuitable. Unquestionably, the life of a convict servant assigned to a settler in the Castlereagh district would have been hard, but not nearly as harsh was labouring in road gangs, or on the Emu Plain convict farm. Still, convicts preferred to be assigned to an ex-convict settler, where they were treated more humanely.

In February 1825 Anthony Rope returned the servant Samuel Lawn to the government, and a week later received John McIlvee, who had previously worked for his daughter-in-law's father Edward Field.[35] McIlvee had laboured for three years at the Emu Plains government farm, and in 1823 asked to work for a settler because his wife had just arrived as a convict.[36] Within months of being assigned to the Ropes, he received his ticket of leave. Anthony must have given McIlvee a very good reference.[37] They would have been sympathetic of McIlvee wanting to be with his wife, who was working in the Parramatta female factory. After receiving his ticket of leave he left the Rope farm assignment, and a few months later, in September 1825, Anthony took on a new servant, Frank Timmings.[38]

In 1824 the British Parliament approved the establishment of the *Australian Agricultural Company* (AAC), which was to be responsible for improving merino fine wool, cattle, tobacco, flax production, and other crops for export. The company was intended to attract wealthy settlers to the colony, and to provide employment for a large number of convicts at no cost to the government.[39] This was part of a scheme to export more Australian wool, a project long cherished and promoted by John Macarthur. In 1822 Governor Brisbane had given the green light to the creation of the AAC, with Macarthur as a founding member and shareholder. The son of the earlier Governor King, Phillip Parker King, was another wealthy landowner and shareholder. King and Macarthur were among those appointed to the advisory board of the company.[40]

Many settlers feared that the AAC would give large landholders and new immigrants access to the best farmland. They had good reasons to be concerned. Those previously granted small land holdings could not yet occupy the properties because of long delays in the official surveying. This included the lands granted to the Rope family members, who still had no title deeds permitting them to cultivate the land. Further massive land granted to the AAC exacerbated the surveying delays.

There were also concerns in the farming community that "common land" would be sold to the AAC. Common land was a designated area that could be grazed on by all farmers in the district. In April 1825, Rev. Fulton sent a petition signed by 52 farmers in the Castlereagh district to the governor. Anthony and John Rope, John Ryan and Thomas Frost were among the signatories. The petitioners pleaded that the 5000 acres of common land near Castlereagh granted to Captain King on a temporary grazing permit, be returned to its former purpose. The petition stated that Governor Macquarie had set aside this land in 1813 to be used by all settlers for their cattle, and as a source of timber. Captain King had already erected fences around an area, and farmers saw this as the first step to a permanent enclosure, just as it had been 18th century England. The petition sought assurances that this land would not be granted permanently to King, or to anyone else. It pointed out that King's fencing had already deprived surrounding landholders of valuable pastures for their stock and timber resources.[41]

Until now, Brisbane had shown cautious liberalism on the sale of land and was, in principle, not unsympathetic towards emancipists. But in May 1825 he was instructed by the Colonial Office to grant the land to Captain King, who also had permission to buy 2000 acres of crown land.[42] When this became known there was great concern in the settler community. Fortunately it was not the plot the Castlereagh settlers were worried about, and that land was returned to common use.

Nonetheless, by the end of 1825 the AAC was granted *one million acres* of land and selected their land at Port Stephens, north of Newcastle with harbour rights at Newcastle.[43] News of such an enormous free land grant was not well received. *The Sydney Gazette* claimed that the ACC's intent was nothing less 'than the enrichment of themselves at the expense of the Colonists of New South Wales'. For many it confirmed the belief that the AAC was just a mechanism for Macarthur to profiteer from the government and that it 'must entail inevitable destruction on the industry of every loyal subject in the Colony'.[44] More major acquisitions would soon follow. A year later, the next governor, Ralph Darling, a known friend of John Macarthur, would give the company a 31-year lease to mine coal at Newcastle.[45]

Further orders from the Colonial Office enforced stricter conditions on convict servitude. Brisbane was instructed to re-occupy Norfolk Island as a place for the secondary punishment of reoffending convicts. Moreover, the ship *Phoenix* was converted into a prison hulk moored in Port Jackson at Lavender Bay. This became known as *The Hulk* or the *Phoenix Bay* and remained in use until 1837.[46]

Brisbane's reluctance to apply the Bigge reforms in full made him a target of the colony's conservatives. They sent critical letters to the Earl of Bathurst complaining about this, and that the governor seemed more interested in astronomy than in governing the colony. In May 1825 Brisbane received a reply from Bathurst about his criticism of Secretary Goulburn. The letter concluded with the statement that both he and

Goulburn would soon be replaced. They were asked to stay put until the arrival of the next governor.[47]

A month later, Brisbane was asked by the Colonial Office to carry out a general survey and valuation of the colony. No further land was to be granted until the survey complete. These Colonial Office edicts made it clear that there were now to be two distinct classes of settlers. The first acquired land through purchase, and the second through grants. First-class settlers, the wealthy colonists and immigrants, contributed directly to the prosperity of the colony, and should receive preferential treatment. Second-class settlers, the smaller property owners, were eligible for a free land grant of up to 320 acres, but only if they could show sufficient capital to farm this area.[48]

These requirements reflected the contempt Secretary Bathurst held for the emancipist "upstarts". He firmly believed that this 'class of people' was unsuitable for 'agricultural labour of any description'. In his view, people without capital would certainly fail, and 'agricultural projects, undertaken upon no better basis than this, must rather retard than advance the general prosperity of the Country'.[49] The instructions sent to Brisbane effectively placed land ownership beyond the reach of most ordinary emancipists and poor free settlers.

Since the start of the colony, governors had granted land without any significant planning of boundaries or roads. In the last forty years this had led to a multitude of oddly shaped plots and made surveying and mapping the farming districts administratively difficult. So much so that disputes over farm boundaries were common. It also placed an enormous strain on the survey office, which lacked trained staff. Needless to say, the surveying of official boundaries became the rate-determining step in the issuance of title deeds. Not unexpectedly, the first-class landowners were generally at the front of the queue at the surveyor's office, and even employed their own surveyors. Their land was always measured, and their deeds issued, before the plots of the second-class settlers.

The delays in surveying the land to the Rope family members were long, and they would wait interminably for title deeds. These bottlenecks caused considerable financial loss to settlers, some of whom had not yet received deeds for land granted years before by Governor Macquarie. It was a scandal, but at least the land granted by Macquarie could be occupied before the officially surveyed boundaries were issued.[50] Land granted by Brisbane could not.

Brisbane's return to Britain was imminent. Most in the colony considered him a fair man, but his lack of assistance to the struggling small farmers meant he had few supporters among the emancipists in remote areas. Quixotically, this would change in his last days in office; Sir Thomas was about to become popular with the commoners. Indeed, his closing acts as governor gained him a degree of fame that almost erased his earlier political and financial blunders. During most of his tenure Brisbane had never been comfortable with the emancipists, but on the eve of departure he accepted a dinner invitation from their leaders.[51] During the dinner Brisbane was lauded for promoting a free press. He responded that the newspapers had been his best friends in the colony and stated that he had given the press support in their campaign for improving the rights of emancipists, and the fairer treatment of convicts.[52] These points rather impressed the emancipists, especially as the exclusives opposed a free press. Brisbane had, overnight, significantly increased his support, but he was about to do even better.

The Australian informed readers that the times for the 'Nimrods of the Territory once domineered over Prisoners, Emancipists and Free alike' were drawing to a close. Until now, regardless of official regulations, they had trampled on common rights with 'the cat-o-nine-tail Law'. Governor Brisbane had permitted free press and as a consequence New South Wales was no longer a penal settlement.[53]

Probably in response to this editorial, the governor was invited by leading conservatives to a public farewell dinner. He gladly accepted provided that some of the leading emancipists be invited as well. The exclusives were aghast, and his invitation was withdrawn.[54] The news of this spread like a wildfire through the colony, and by his final farewell decision as governor, Sir Thomas Brisbane had managed to become the toast of a colony he had ruled over for four years. This gesture of equality meant that the settlers finally considered him a "good bloke", even if he had taken a long time to reveal his better side.

Brisbane's contemporary, clergyman John Dunmore Lang, wrote that he was a man 'of the very best intentions', but lacked the energy required to carry them into action. He also wrote that, because Brisbane had mostly delegated his power, 'his good intentions were seldom realised' and 'his promises too frequently forgotten'.[55] Brisbane, a hero on the battlefield and a keen astronomer, had shown little interest in the daily business of the government. He disliked politics, and in a colony where Macarthur was active, there was a lot of this to deal with. Compared to a military post, Sir Thomas had found commanding a civilian colony to be much less pleasant and, its occupants, a lot less responsive to his orders.

As a trained astronomer, Sir Thomas Brisbane had built at his own expense an observatory in Parramatta. Here, with the help of two assistants, Carl Rümker and James Dunlop, he had brought out from England, Brisbane made 40,000 observations over 2½ years and catalogued about 7000 stars. He had also given enthusiastic support to the cause of science in the colony, and in 1821 he was made the first President of the Philosophical Society of Australasia, later renamed as the Royal Society of New South Wales. Brisbane established the first agricultural college in the colony and was the first patron of the Agricultural Society.

When Sir Thomas and his family sailed to England on 1 Dec 1825, the official farewell was decidedly low key. There were none of the colourful parades and flags displayed for Governor Macquarie's departure, but one suspects that this did not concern him unduly.[56] On returning to England his family moved to Scotland, where Sir Thomas pursued his astronomical interests and built another observatory. In the following decades he promoted science and became a member of the Royal Society of Edinburgh and President of the British Association for the Advancement of Science. Sir Thomas Brisbane died in 1860 at the impressive age of 87.

Chapter 23

DESPOTISM & DYSFUNCTION 1825-1831

This is the age of cant – cant political and cant religious. It is contagious – for it has extended even to the antipodes.[1]

The army officer Lt. General Ralph Darling was to be the seventh Governor of New South Wales. In a previous posting he had been the acting Governor of Mauritius, where he oversaw plantations worked by slaves. Darling arrived in Port Jackson on 18 Dec 1825 and the Sydney crowds largely refrained from the customary practice of cheering the new governor when he landed.[2] The knowledge of his service in Mauritius had preceded him, and the residents of a free colony were uncomfortable with the appointment of someone who had administered a slave colony.

The new governor seemed determined to make an immediate imprint on the colony. Two days after taking office, Ralph Darling proclaimed that the NSW Legislative Council membership would be increased to seven – four executive and three other members. One of the non-executives would be John Macarthur.[3] The promise given by Macarthur to the court in England that he would not be involved in the colony's future political activities was about to be broken.

Darling also set about reorganising the colony's administration. He wanted a government administered along military lines, with strict adherence to regulations and the unquestioning loyalty of subordinates. Whereas Brisbane had softened the Bigge reforms in order to lessen the impact on emancipists and convicts, the new governor would adhere to them, to the letter. It was clear from the outset that Darling's tenure in Australia was to be a stormy one. Overall the colony had embraced the principles of fair and equitable governance espoused by Macquarie, and Darling's strict interpretation of the Bigge reforms met strong resistance across the entire community. Free and freed inhabitants expressed a determination to resist the loss of any civil rights, and to promote the improved treatment of those in servitude.

Darling's term came at a time when emancipists were asserting their right to become full British citizens. John Macarthur, and other conservatives, which included the governor, opposed such recognition, and so did the Tory government in London. The latter still wanted Australia to be a penal colony and the last refuge for unwanted felons. They insisted that the support for *full* emancipation must be suppressed. The visions of a future Australia by these two sides could not be more clearly defined, Darling favoured the elite minority and distanced himself from the common people, even though they were the vast majority of the inhabitants he had been sent to govern.

The year 1826 was to prove difficult for the entire colony – it started with a severe drought that would last for almost three years. The unrelenting dryness threatened the survival of most farms and was to be the financial ruin of many families. On top of the drought worries, the Ropes were about to have their little world turned upside down. Anthony was charged with harbouring and releasing an escaped convict. On 10 Jan 1826 he appeared before the Justices of the Peace, Reverend Fulton, John McHenry and Alexander Kinghorne in the Penrith Court House. He had been accused by William Hayes, supervisor of Phillip King's neighbouring farm, of 'rescuing, detaining and suffering to escape Owen Mullaghan a runaway prisoner of the Crown from the service of Captain King'.[4]

At the hearing, Patrick Ellmore, a servant of Phillip King, stated that on the night of January 6th, Hayes had informed him that Mullaghan had escaped to Rope's farm, and he should go to their house and apprehend the runaway. At around 2 am Mullaghan was seen going into the hut of one of Rope's servants, and here Ellmore took him into custody. A servant in the hut called his master, Anthony Rope, who came with his son William and another free man. The three questioned Ellmore's identity, thinking he might be a bushranger. Ellmore protested and asked that Rope detain him and Mullaghan overnight, and check with Hayes the next morning. Ellmore bedded down in the servant's hut, while Mullaghan went with Anthony to the house. In the morning Mullaghan had escaped. After hearing the evidence, the Penrith court committed Anthony to the next Quarter Sessions in Windsor.

Following the hearing, two of Anthony's friends, George Colliss and Thomas Higgins, approached Rev. Henry Fulton about a temporary release, and bail was set at £100 (about $15,000 today). Colliss and Higgins put up £25 each, and Anthony £50. The bail conditions required Anthony to appear before the Windsor court and not leave the country.[5] Although his friends knew that Anthony would not try to escape, it was a lot of money for them to commit and indicates the extent to which settlers would go to support mates when they were in trouble. Mateship and family ties in these small communities had tangible benefits. Anthony and emancipist George Colliss had known each other for more than 25 years, and farmed land bordering John Rope's farm. The Irish ex-convict Thomas Higgins became part of the larger Rope family when he married Sophia Field, the younger sister of John Rope's wife, Maria.

Four months later, on 10 May 1826, Anthony appeared at the Windsor Quarter Sessions. He was accused of releasing the runaway Owen Mullaghan from Captain King's servant Patrick Ellmore, who had captured and beaten him. The court noted that the ill treatment of Mullaghan was an 'evil example of all other in the like care offending and against the peace of our said Lord the King, His Crown and Dignity' but nevertheless declared Anthony *guilty*. The existing court records are fragmentary and pages 378 and 379 detailing the sentence issued on May 11th are missing.[6] As many in the community would have vouched for Anthony's honesty and integrity, the punishment may have been just a fine. Also, considering that Mullaghan had been maltreated as a servant, it is quite possible that Anthony received only a caution. Whatever transpired, he certainly did not go to gaol.

Convicts and the emancipists alike were soon to feel the full impact of Darling's strict compliance to the Colonial Office order that the Bigge reforms be enforced to the hilt. One such reform was to do with land surveys. Crown land, both sold or granted, must now be officially surveyed before occupation, and the registration of land sales had priority over land grants. It meant that, under Darling, the currency youth of the colony had little hope of receiving a land grant. William Wentworth and *The Australian* took up their cause. He declared 'every young man in the Colony ought to be able to look forward with certainty to the prospect of having his own farm, and, of being able to settle upon it, as soon as he arrives at years of maturity'.[7] Darling largely ignored this plea and his battles with Wentworth were about to begin.

The perfidy of Darling's administration soon became evident. He was prepared to soften Colonial Office instructions when it suited him, but the emancipist community felt the full force of the law and the stricter regulations. The new Viceroy shared Earl Bathurst's unfavourable opinion of ex-convicts, and believed they simply were not worthy of his consideration, let alone generous treatment.

The routine punishment of convicts now became draconian. A system of iron-chain gangs was introduced as secondary punishment, and these gangs were used to build roads and bridges for expanding settlements. The gangs worked in leg-irons during the day and were shackled together at night in a stockade. Darling also favoured sending convicts to the penal settlements Port Macquarie, Moreton Bay and

Norfolk Island. Discipline in these prisons was strict and enforcement brutal. In Darling's view prisoners in the penal settlements should work in irons as an example to others contemplating crimes. Rations were meagre and no additional provisions were given those doing for hard labour.[8] Darling's time in Mauritius was clearly guiding his actions.

The ruin to farmlands from drought in 1826-29 was made worse by widespread fires that destroyed pastureland and grain crops across the colony. During these parched years, the wheat yields were so low there was not enough grain to feed the colony. It was said by the oldest settlers that vegetation and pasture had 'never known to be so scanty' and the face of the country had never been in such a 'deplorable plight'.[9]

Sometime in 1826 the Ropes moved to a neighbouring 20-acre plot, which they leased from William Faithful at Jordan Hill. Their daughter, Mary Ryan, and her family rented the farm they had vacated. The reason for the move is unknown, but the drought and resulting debts are likely causes. The Rope's farm property probably exceeded the needs of the older couple, and they offered it to their daughter. Anthony would have built a new hut on the neighbouring plot with the help of William and grandson George who was still living with them. Later, George worked with his uncle William as a wheelwright, building and repairing carts, carriages and wagons. Two years later, George would move in with his mother Mary and stepfather John Ryan. Toby Ryan recalled that he and George became good friends.[10]

The Ryan family remained on the Jordan Hill farm until about 1837. During this time Toby saw a lot of his grandparents and became very attached to them. He writes in his book that he liked shooting, but had no gun, and used a bow and arrows to shoot birds. For that he got into trouble from his parents. But his grandfather Anthony was very kind and 'gave him an old Queen Anne's musket, very long and heavy, the lock minus a hammer, which struck against the pan in the old guns, before the percussion was invented'. The boys had great fun and it sounded like the 'thundering of artillery' when they were shooting ducks on the nearby pond.[11]

Darling's administration made it increasingly hard for convicts to marry. It was a relief when, in July 1826, the Ropes' daughter Elizabeth Ann, 18, was given permission by Rev. Marsden in Parramatta to wed convict John Battley, 27.[12] For unknown reasons the wedding ceremony never took place. Elizabeth Ann was underage and needed her parents' consent to marry, and perhaps they refused it. The Ropes knew that partnering a convict on a 14-year sentence would be a hard life, as Battley had little chance of a ticket of leave or a pardon. Opportunities for release during Darling's administration were few, and convicts were treated badly. Anthony and Elizabeth knew all too well just how miserable it had been for Susannah when her husband was sent to the Port Macquarie penal settlement for a year.

Elizabeth Ann seems not to have been heartbroken by the decision and found another partner. On 30 Oct 1826 Rev. Henry Fulton, with the consent of her parents, married Elizabeth Ann to emancipist Thomas Player, 34, in the Castlereagh Church. The witnesses were Elizabeth Ann's sister Susannah Bradley and John Proctor. In 1814, Thomas Player had been found guilty of stealing goods to the value of 28s 6d, sentenced to 7 years transportation. Thomas Player and John Bradley arrived together on the *Baring*. In 1820, Player became the servant of Sarah Rope's husband, Thomas Frost, and was still working for him in 1825, well past the end of his sentence.[13]

Thomas and Elizabeth Ann moved onto a 5-acre lease at Jordan Hill, close to the Rope's farm where her 2-year-old son James was cared for. To earn extra money Thomas worked as a bricklayer and it is likely that Anthony taught him the trade. Many large estates surrounded their small farms that needed building workers. Five months later Elizabeth Ann left her husband, and Thomas placed a notice into the newspaper.

> WHEREAS MY WIFE, ELIZABETH PLAYER, having left her house and home without any just cause or provocation on my part - I, the undersigned do hereby caution all persons against giving her trust or credit in my name, as I will not be responsible for any debts contracted by her after this date. And I hereby further caution any person or persons whatsoever from harbouring, concealing, maintaining, or employing the said Elizabeth Player, as I am determined to prosecute any persons so offending to the utmost rigour of the law.[14]

Elizabeth Ann later returned to live with Thomas, and they had children in 1827 and 1829. She had another five children after 1831; the father was unrecorded, but they are attributed to Player. A few years later she had a son by Edward Sullivan.

A government notice published in *The Sydney Gazette* on 7 Oct 1826 aroused hope that title deeds to long-outstanding land grants would soon be issued. The notice stated that anyone who had received a free grant and had not been notified of the official boundaries should apply to the Land Board with proof that they possessed the necessary funds to stock and cultivate their land.[15] Settlers across the farming districts immediately sent in proof of their eligibility. For instance, John Rope listed farm stock and plant to a total value of £195 – considerable wealth for a small farmer. At the time John was renting 30 acres from William Bowman on the banks of the Nepean River and was judged by the emancipist landholder Samuel Terry to be 'a very good character'.[16]

However, most applicants were advised that the boundaries of their selections could not be surveyed soon. This was an understatement; the survey office was years behind in providing official boundaries, and, when they did, the land was often not in the location selected by the grantee. On 29 Oct 1826, 24 settlers in the Evan district petitioned Darling to have their selected properties in Kurrajong, on the west side of the Nepean, surveyed, claiming that they were suffering serious losses. The names of John and William Rope, Thomas Frost and John Ryan, as well as Thomas Higgins and George Colliss, were on the petition. All the petitioners were small settlers in the Castlereagh district who had grants of land ranging from 30 to 100 acres.[17] It would not be until late 1831, seven years after receiving the grants that John and William Rope, Thomas Frost and John Ryan, were provided with surveyed boundaries of their properties, but, even then, no deeds were issued.

In 1826, despite additional staff being appointed to the survey office, massive backlogs in the issuing of deeds existed when the Surveyor General John Oxley wrote a report for the government. This claimed that most of the land granted by Governor Macquarie that had not surveyed when he left in 1821, had now been assigned boundaries. But only half of the grants given by Governor Brisbane had been surveyed. Oxley agreed that this was ruinous to settlers who were 'Compelled to remain idle and without an homestead, until certain Parishes have been surveyed and put up for Sale. It must be the object of every Settler to get on his lands, as speedily as possible'.[18] But the delays in surveys and deeds continued and got worse when Oxley quarrelled with Darling over his refusal to appoint more staff to the survey office.

It was not uncommon in the colony for soldiers to intentionally commit a minor crime that led to their discharge from the army. Many soldiers saw a convict's life as being easier than that of a Private, and they were prepared to serve out a short sentence to get out of the military, after which they expected to prosper as a civilian. In November 1826, two privates in the 3rd Regiment, Joseph Sudds and Patrick Thompson deliberately stole for this reason. Governor Darling was made aware of the background to this crime, and he was determined to make an example of the men. Rather than send the theft to a court-martial, it was referred to the Court of Quarter Sessions. The soldiers were found guilty and sentenced to seven years in a penal settlement. Darling commuted this to seven years hard labour on a road chain gang, and ordered the men be heavily chained with spiked iron collars round their necks attached by chains to leg irons.[19] A week later Sudds died in his irons.

Newspaper editors were outraged. And when it was disclosed that Joseph Sudds had been ill before being put in irons, the press claimed his treatment was torture. William Wentworth of *The Australian*, and Edward Smith Hall of the newly established newspaper *The Monitor*, accused Darling of abusing his authority. Chief Justice Francis Forbes agreed with the newspapers, and said the punishment was contrary to law. Wentworth reported the alleged illegality of Darling's act in a letter to Colonial Office Secretary Bathurst and demanded his impeachment. The whole affair rapidly developed into a bitter feud. Darling claimed the press was promoting 'mutiny and insurrection' and had to be restrained. In his view, newspapers and public comments were dangerous, and he was about to make several attempts to restrain the press.[20]

The continuing drought in 1828 was the last straw for many farmers and their farms had to be sold. The grain losses on Hawkesbury farms were intolerable, particularly when land was not near a creek or river. In some places, sufficient rain had fallen to grow a small wheat crop, just enough to feed families and to pay back some debts. Other farmers had been smart enough to plant drought-tolerant maize and they received a better yield.[21] Almost no settlers received government support during the drought, and wheat became so scarce it had to be imported from Van Diemen's Land. Ludicrously, Darling blamed the settlers for the grain shortage. He wrote to the Colonial Secretary Huskisson that the 'improvidence of the lower Class of Settlers, who never make provision for a season of scarcity when they are so fortunate as to have an Abundant Harvest, have exposed this Class in particular to very serious inconvenience on the present occasion'.[22]

But even Darling had to admit that it was the small farmers who grew most of the colony's grain, and farms in the Hawkesbury were the main suppliers of the Sydney market. Darling had no interest in farming and did not appreciate that grain yields often had little to do with the farmers themselves. Moreover, he had never felt the pangs of hunger and the loss of property that followed floods and droughts, nor had he suffered from the financial stress when loan sharks hovered to claim the debtor's money or land. Because of this, Darling blamed settlers for the 'very inconvenience' of having to despatch ships to Tasmania and the Cape for grain. Astoundingly, he seemed more concerned that the cattle of the wealthy graziers perished for want of fresh fodder.[23] The government farm at Emu Plains had sold their cattle but there were few buyers.[24] The Rope, Ryan and Frost families would have been interested if they had the cash and, based on later muster records, John Rope appears to have done just that.

A dry 1829 meant that a serious food crisis faced the colony. It was only then that Darling reluctantly agreed that the small settlers needed assistance to survive, and government stores were ordered to supply them with grain for seed and for bread. The farmers were grateful for the relief, and *The Sydney Gazette* reported that it was moving to witness the eagerness with which poor farmers rushed to where corn was issued, and 'the light hearts with which they returned to their homes, bearing precious seed'. These were extremely hard times for the Rope families with the South Creek now just a chain of stagnant ponds.[25]

Captain Philip Parker King, with his wife Harriett and children had returned to England in 1822. In May 1826 Captain King was commissioned by the Royal Navy to survey the coasts of Peru, Chile and Patagonia aboard HMS *Adventure*. HMS *Beagle* also took part in this extensive survey, which was not completed until 1830. In 1827 Harriett and the children returned to Australia to take up residence at their *Dunheved* farming estate. While the Kings were in England, William Hayes had managed *Dunheved* and it was he who had accused Anthony Rope of aiding the escape of the assigned convict Mullaghan. Shortly after Harriett King returned Hayes was dismissed, and a new manager, John Flanagan, was appointed. The Kings knew their Rope neighbours, and the charges against Anthony may have influenced Hayes' dismissal.

Toby Ryan writes that under John Flanagan's administration the *Dunheved* farm became the 'pattern farm to the whole colony; they had as fine farming men as ever left England'. Toby praised the new management for their treatment of convicts. As the Rope's grandson, he had met Mrs King often as a child, and wrote that 'Lady King soon became well-known in the district; her never-tiring disposition to do good to the poor was obvious to all and appreciated'. Harriett King had a portable medicine chest, and she treated the sick and poor in the district. Toby recalled that she vaccinated him against smallpox as a child, along with his siblings and other children in the district, 'she was highly esteemed by all who knew her'.[26] Being neighbours, the Ropes probably visited Harriett when they were sick, and the close proximity of her care may have contributed to their remarkable longevity.

Free or emancipist settlers were no longer required to attend the annual convict Muster. However, by an Act of the NSW Legislative Council, Australia's first official census was held in November 1828.[27] This records that Anthony Rope lived on a farm at Jordan Hill with 11 acres, all cultivated, and 5 cattle. The census states that the household included Anthony, 65, Elizabeth, 64, William, 24, and grandson James, 4 (the actual ages of Anthony and Elizabeth were 72 and 66). William was still unable to occupy his land grant and was living at home working as a fencer and farmer. The listed cattle belonged to William who was building up livestock for his future farm.[28] Without William's help his parents would not have been able to farm as much land.

The census shows that Mary and John Ryan lived with their six children and one servant on a rented farm next to the Ropes at Jordan Hill, with 40 acres under cultivation, 40 cattle and one horse. John and Maria Rope's household included their four children and two government servants. John had two farms in Evan, 25 acres on a rented property called *Staniard* with 12 cattle, and 60 acres on a farm called *Ropes* with its land still uncleared.[29] With a total of 85 acres, John Rope was one of the larger small farmers in the Evan district.

Sarah and Thomas Frost and their five children were living on a rented farm called *Woodriffs* near the Nepean River. They had 15 acres of cultivated land, three horses and one cow. Thomas Frost also worked as a constable with the Penrith police. Elizabeth Ann and Thomas Player, and their son, farmed at Jordan Hill leasing 5 acres of land. Susannah had separated from John Bradley, and she lived at South Creek working as a washerwoman to support her three daughters.[30] On May 1829 Susannah gave birth to a son, John. The father was recorded as John Proctor, with whom she and her children were now living. Proctor, transported for life for stealing goods worth 40s, arrived in 1814. By 1821 he was the keeper of the new gaol and courthouse in Penrith, and in 1825 became the district constable and gaoler. In 1830, after serving 16 years, he received a conditional pardon for good behaviour.[31]

Between 1822 and 1828, 13,300 convicts had arrived in New South Wales. The population of the colony had risen to 36,598, of which, almost one half were convicts (15,668). Every fifth person was an ex-convict (7530), every fourth was born in the colony (8727) and every tenth was a free immigrant (4673). The male female ratio among convicts was 9 to 1; in the total population, the ratio was about 3 to 1.[32]

Newspaper attacks on Governor Darling and his administration continued unabated. He decided to put an end to these criticisms once and for all. He levied a tax on each newspaper sold, and, between 1827 and 1829, launched a series of libel suits against the editors. Barristers William Wentworth and Robert Wardell defended the libel cases[33] Wardell and Wentworth had sold their shares in *The Australian* in 1828 to concentrate on their law practice. In April 1828 Darling successfully convicted and imprisoned the editors Edward Smith Hall of *The Monitor*, and Attwell Edwin Hayes of *The Australian*, for seditious libel.

For several years Hall's vitriolic pen had assailed many citizens in the colony from the governor down and had appeared in court 12 times.[34] He criticised the despotic measures instigated by the Bigge report, the tyranny of country magistrates and the poor treatment of the convicts. He became a strong advocate for better convict conditions and 'espoused the cause of any convict, should he be ever so vile, who was punished contrary to law'. In Hall's view, the junta of Magistrates were 'much the same as that of the Overseers of the Plantations in the West Indies is to their slaves'.[35] The convicts and emancipists, unaccustomed to such public support, held Edward Smith Hall in some awe.

In March 1829 William Wentworth retaliated against Darling's libel suits with a long open letter to the Colonial Secretary Murray. In this he alleged that the governor's treatment of Joseph Sudds was 'high misdemeanour at the least, if not of murder', and that he was guilty of a 'series of fraud, tyranny and corruption' incidents unprecedented in the history of the colony. He accused Darling of a 'system of misdemeanours, of which murder itself glares as the centre' and called for his impeachment.[36]

On a slightly different tack, E. S. Hall attacked Darling's land distribution policy for favouring wealthy graziers. In July 1829, he wrote that the question most asked in the colony was:

> what is to become of the Settlers of the Colony, some aged, some native born, who comprise our chief landed population, when so much good land is thus being picked and occupied by twenty nine persons only, and a large portion of it by four families closely allied to the Executive?[37]

Hall claimed that the four families, the Macarthurs, the McLeays, the Berrys and the Throsbys, were a political cabal in the colony, and these greedy men were all close friends of members of the Legislative council, and responsible for laws by which 'the poor of this Country are now being every day sacrificed to the rich'.[38] In Hall's view, Darling's prejudices 'have tended to weaken the attachment of all classes here to the Mother Country, particularly the Australian born male adults'.[39] The governor ignored the allegations.

The Macarthur "cabal" had formed strong links with the Tory politicians in Britain. The emancipists and William Wentworth had much more in common with the English Whig landowners. The wife of Judge Forbes, Mary, labelled the 'Exclusives' and 'Emancipists' as local Tories and Liberals, respectively. Governor Darling's political inclinations were decidedly with the former, and in the late 1820s they dominated the NSW Legislative Council, and certainly had no desire to entertain democracy for the majority of the colony.[40]

In Britain there was growing concern about the competency of Ralph Darling as governor. By early 1830 his critics in Australia had the support of the English press, and the MPs John Stewart, Joseph Hume and Daniel O'Connell started impeachment proceedings in the House of Commons. The incumbent Tory government supported Darling, and the Colonial Office Secretary George Murray opposed any impeachment.[41] His support was to be temporary. In November, the Whig party led by Earl Grey defeated the Tories and assumed power in Britain. These political shifts greatly worried Darling and his supporters. He was now in real need of more influential friends both at home and abroad.

Even John Macarthur's son, James, expressed the opinion that Darling was 'so unpopular a man and has so few friends ... that I shall not be surprised if he is very soon removed from the Government'.[42] James' father did not agree and remained one of the governor's most influential backers in the colony. But John Macarthur's political clout was declining. He had serious health issues and for some years had been confined to his Parramatta estate. From there he plotted against his enemies, which were many, but they did not include Darling.

John Macarthur had been elected to the NSW Legislative Council in 1825, but he rarely attended meetings. As early as 1826 Darling had questioned the soundness of Macarthur's mind, suggesting that he acted 'like a wayward Child'.[43] This rift was short lived. The two men had too many interests in common, and Darling needed to hold onto influential residents who could help him politically. The two families remained friendly until 1831 when Darling departed for England. It is interesting to note that Macarthur, who was infamous for his opposition to all previous governors, avoided criticising Darling and gave him unquestioned support for most of his term of office.[44]

William Wentworth and the emancipists did the exact opposite. They criticised and opposed his administration relentlessly. In an attempt to silence his fiercest critics, Darling threatened to enforce a law banishing anyone convicted twice for seditious libel to a penal district.[45] To Darling's chagrin, the recently appointed Whig parliament in Britain repealed this law, and the new Secretary of the Colonial Office Goderich reprimanded him for attempting to suppress free speech. He instructed Darling to placate any criticism of his administration by better governance. The end was nigh for Darling, and in March 1831 he was notified that his six-year contract would not be renewed.[46]

Nevertheless Darling's perfidy persisted. Despite Brisbane's ruling that free land must not be granted, he continued issuing land grants to gain favour with influential families. He gave land to widows as pensions, and to young ladies about to marry into prominent families as dowries. In September 1831, shortly before his departure, Darling received instructions from the Colonial Office to stop granting land as 'marriage portions'. By then he had given away nearly 30,000 acres of land to wealthy members of the colony.[47]

DESPOTISM & DYSFUNCTION 1825-1831

Through this largess many of the wealthy families in the colony were indebted to the governor's patronage, and his name adorns a remarkable number of places across New South Wales. At the same time, the vast majority of residents in the colony, and particularly the emancipists, saw little of this generosity. It is not surprising that Darling was so widely disliked and mistrusted. Many small settlers, including the Rope families, were still waiting for the deed titles of land granted to them many years before. Indeed, the dysfunctional survey office was symptomatic of the Darling administration as a whole. The large landholders promptly received deeds to their land, while the poor small farmers were put at the end of a very long queue.

In late 1831, after a seven-year delay, John Rope, William Rope, John Ryan, and Thomas Frost, were issued the titles and boundaries for land they had been granted in September 1824 and February 1825. Their initial elation was short lived. The boundaries surveyed were not for the fertile properties they had selected, but for poorer land closer to Castlereagh at The Chain of Ponds district of Evan. The allotments for all family members were in the same area, 8 km north of Castlereagh and 6 km south of Richmond. They were only 10 km northwest of Jordan Hill where Anthony and Elizabeth were living. John and William's land bordered the Northern Road in the west.[48]

After the seven-year survey delay, the deeds required to farm their land remained unissued. William Rope and John Ryan would eventually receive their deeds in April 1832. It was much more serious for John Rope. Despite repeated complaints, he still had no deeds for the South Creek land granted in 1814, an incredible 17 years earlier, or the deed for the Chain of Ponds land near Castlereagh surveyed in 1831.[49] It was a ridiculous situation and he decided to sell both properties without deeds, and let the buyers sort it out. The land sale proceeded only after the buyers, Samuel Terry and Robert Aull, had pleaded those deeds be issued prior to settlement. The Chain of Ponds arrived late in 1832, but nothing was heard about the South Creek property until June 1835. It was then that John Rope received an apology from the Deputy Surveyor General Samuel Augustus Perry that the records had incorrectly shown that deeds for the South Creek land had already been issued in 1814.

After 20 years, the survey office admitted the fault was theirs.[50] This error had caused John and his parents endless worries over many years and is just one example of the absurd incompetence or outright corruption experienced by small settlers. If you were influential your land survey was given priority but deed registrations for small settler may take years. The Darling administration was a serious impediment to small farmers' livelihoods.

Not unsurprisingly the emancipists, currency youth and convicts rejoiced at Ralph Darling's recall. He was the seventh governor under whom Anthony and Elizabeth had toiled, and, apart from the temporary administrators Grose, Johnson, Paterson and Foveaux, he was probably the most inept and corrupt. Governance over the past 40 years had come with varying degrees of competency because the ability to govern was not a necessary qualification for the post. Appointments then (and, for many years after) were determined more by *whom* you knew, rather than by *what* you knew, and whether you were willing to travel *to the ends of the earth*. With this in mind, it was fortunate that over half the governors were effective leaders and administrators. From a convict-emancipist perspective, governors were judged not just on competency but for their treatment of the less privileged in the colony. Phillip and Macquarie were admired for their humanity and generosity, and Bligh, Hunter and King for their fairness.

Portrait of Sir Thomas Brisbane, the colony's sixth governor (1821-1825).

Portrait of Ralph Darling, the colony's seventh governor (1825-1831).

Throughout the four decades of roller-coaster governance, the colony had grown fitfully from a tiny desperate penal settlement to a prosperous and predominantly free community, in which emancipist small settlers thrived. They had contributed to and benefited from these advances and would have considered themselves fortunate to be part of the colony's success. Most settlers would have welcomed the rumours that the new governor, Major-General Richard Bourke had Whig leanings and was a humanitarian. His arrival was keenly anticipated.

DESPOTISM & DYSFUNCTION 1825-1831

On 22 Oct 1831 Ralph Darling and his family left Sydney on the ship *Hooghley*, and the departure was celebrated. The headlines of *The Monitor* 'HE'S OFF! THE REIGN OF TERROR ENDED!' reflected the sentiments of its editor E. S. Hall and readers.[51] The front page of *The Australian* declared 'Rejoice, Australia! DARLING'S reign has passed!'[52] William Wentworth organised a party at his Vaucluse mansion on the day that Darling departed. Over 4000 people partook of the free food and wine and enjoyed bonfires and fireworks at night. The early guests were able to heartily cheer the *Hooghley* as she exited Port Jackson past Vaucluse.

The settlers in the Windsor and Castlereagh districts would have been particularly pleased to see the back of Ralph Darling, though few are likely to have attended Wentworth's grand soiree. They needed to work hard to bring in this years' harvest, which, considering the earlier heavy rains and floods, was surprisingly abundant.[53] In the less salubrious parts of town and in the country, survival and paying debts were a more pressing concern than partying with the Vaucluse set.

The colony had drifted towards despotism and totalitarianism during Darling's governorship. The Scottish clergyman, John Dunmore Lang, observed that Darling was 'naturally desirous to stand well with his superior officers' and 'to think or to act for himself' was 'a sort of disobedience'. Lang concluded that Darling had 'allowed himself to be guided by the opinions of men who were unqualified to direct him'.[54] These "men" were the members of both the Colonial Office and the exclusives, and probably the British Tories. Their mantra was that strict discipline be maintained in the 'prison colony', and increased rights and democracy were not to be tolerated. As soon as Darling had catered to the demands of this faction, his ability to govern fairly evaporated. For this reason, his corrupt leadership was the daily fare in the Sydney newspapers for his six years in office. And almost from the outset of his term in office Darling was labelled a 'tyrant, monster and scoundrel'.[55]

Ralph Darling arrived back in England in May 1832. Three years later, in 1835, his conduct as Governor of New South Wales was criticised in the British Parliament and a Select Committee was appointed. The inquiry exonerated Darling. On the day of this finding, in a remarkable display of political bombast, King William IV knighted him. Further promotion and honorary awards followed, but Sir Ralph Darling received no further military or political appointments. He died comfortably in 1858, aged 86.

Chapter 24

END OF THE CONVICT ERA
1832-1843

The early emancipists raised some of the best men and women in the colony, who became the pioneers of Australia, seeking fresh fields and pastures new, formed the nucleus of a population, many of whom were raised to both affluence and influence.[1]

The eighth Governor of New South Wales was the 54-year-old Irish-born army Major-General Richard Bourke, an avowed libertarian. Bourke had been a successful Lt. Governor of the British Cape of Good Hope, and his reputation for fairness preceded him. When he arrived in Port Jackson on the transport *Margaret*, on 2 Dec 1831, hundreds of people had flocked to the harbour where he was welcomed with a 19-gun salute and the flying of military colours. Sydney took on a party atmosphere that night, with houses illuminated and crowds in the streets. The residents, no matter their social standing, 'gave vent to their loyalty and satisfaction by repeated hurrahs, to the success in his Government'.[2] *The Australian* exuberantly declared that the new governor 'was welcomed with hearty congratulations, and a joy chastened by long suffering ... So will he benefit the Colony and help to raise the Colonists from what they are, to what they ought to be!'[3] The infectious optimism of the welcomers gave Bourke a favourable impression of the colony he was to govern for the next six years. Unfortunately he had an early personal tragedy – his wife died six months later, in May 1832.[4]

Bourke quickly gave a new and positive face to the government and not since Macquarie's time had the colony been on such easy terms with the governor. Whereas Darling had kept the common people at arms-length, Bourke, within days of his arrival, walked the streets of Sydney like a local and planned to visit the surrounding districts. *The Australian* applauded his approachability, informing readers 'His Excellency will find it pleasant and profitable to move about the country. Let him keep the McLeay and the Macarthur faction at a very respectful distance and show a confidence in the "people". He will not be sorry for it.'[5] Alexander McLeay had been Goulburn's replacement as Colonial

Secretary in 1826. As a staunch Tory, McLeay supported the harsher convict discipline recommended by the Colonial Office, which rewarded him for it. By imposing these stricter regulations, he had earned the same unpopularity in the colony as Governor Darling.

Within weeks of becoming governor, Bourke totally abolished free land grants, and sold crown land by public auction at a reserve price of 5s per acre.[6] With this change, the power of patronage held by governors was curtailed and Bourke's credibility in the farming community was enhanced. The revenue raised from selling crown land was used exclusively to finance the passage of free immigrants. In an effort to balance the male-female ratio in the colony, he initiated a plan encouraging 800 females from the rural areas of England to migrate.[7]

Like Macquarie, Bourke was determined to improve the overall prosperity and progress in the colony for all inhabitants. In April 1832, he set up the *Savings' Bank*, with the specific aim of protecting the money brought by convicts and free settlers from England. It also took deposits from the emerging working class and small settlers in the districts and provided them with security and interest on deposits.[8] Such initiatives increased the general level of optimism across the colony.

The currency youth, emancipists and liberals were overjoyed to have Bourke's innovative hand on the government reins. By mid 1832 *The Sydney Herald* hailed Bourke as 'the friend of Australia' who had revived patriotic feelings in the colony, and 'the Country at large will have reason to regard him as its best benefactor'.[9] Bourke further championed the rights of the colony by ensuring a free press. The newspapers and emancipists, as well as William Wentworth, praised his initiatives, which were also skilfully supported by Chief Justice Francis Forbes. Forbes became a close friend of Bourke and a valuable ally in his battles with local Tories and the British Colonial Office.

The Tory-dominated Legislative Council resisted Bourke's initiatives. Nevertheless, with Chief Justice Forbes' backing, he was able to replace the military juries in courts with the British system of trial by jury for criminal cases. Military courts had been in place since the First Fleet and had always been populated by the prominent members of the community. The Legislative Council refused to have emancipists as jurors, even though there was no legal reason to exclude them.[10] The governor wrote to the Colonial Office Secretary Howick about the need for trial by jury and for emancipists to sit as jurors.

> The envy and ill will, which have been engendered by the competition offered by these Persons in the pursuit of wealth by the free Settlers, and the success, which has attended the efforts of the former, will not permit the latter to see that wealthy

> Emancipists have as great an Interest as themselves in putting down robbery and violence, and promoting the due administration of criminal justice. ... the smaller Settlers, and nearly all who have been born in the Colony, feel no repugnance to the admission of Emancipists on Juries, and call loudly for the abolition of what is called the Military Commission.[11]

Just as Governor Macquarie had advocated, Bourke strived to eliminate class prejudice and bias in the colony. Fortunately he was much more of a diplomat than Lachlan Macquarie, and he coupled his reforms with efforts to promote harmony and cooperation across the community 'to hope that confidence is in great measure restored, animosity subsided, and a foundation laid for future peace and goodwill'.[12]

In September 1832, John Macarthur's erratic behaviour led Bourke, with support from community leaders, to question his ability to serve on the Legislative Council. It was decided that his state of mind gave 'little hope of his restoration' and he was removed from the Council on the grounds of being 'pronounced a Lunatic'.[13] Later Macarthur was declared insane and placed under restraint at his home in Camden. He died in 1834, aged 67.[14]

From the outset, Bourke had been appalled by the Bigge Report's recommendation of harsher treatment for convicts. Floggings were now frequent in the colony, and the punishments imposed by remote rural courts were even more excessive. Bourke tried to put a stop to this, but he knew that the largest employers of convict labour, the large estate owners, opposed him. They asserted that floggings kept the workforce under control. The prospect of reduced convict punishments had immediately led to complaints from the elites in the settlements.

In October 1832, Bourke diluted convict punishments by simplifying the offences list, and restricting sentences imposed to less than 50 lashes. He also lessened the types of offences for which convicts were sent to remote penal settlements.[15] Many magistrates agreed with these changes, but others supported the large landowners, and they wrote a petition to King William IV complaining of Bourke's interference in the judicial system.[16] The authority of the opposing magistrates and their influential backers held sway, and convict punishments remained harsh and frequent, particularly in road-gangs and at the penal settlements.

The emancipist families would have given total support to the governor's efforts to curb the punishment regime that had done excessive harm and misery to convicts in their district. They could do little themselves to reduce these punishments but remained optimistic that the lives of the most marginal members of the settlement would improve under Bourke. Anthony, at 76 years, was still physically active on his farm but probably not in district politics. In all likelihood he encouraged the younger settlers and members of his family to attend public meetings, participate in district politics and support the worthiest petitions. The next generation was now expected to uphold the rights of small farmers. His youngest son William was still living at home. In May 1832 he was appointed as a Constable with the Penrith police but resigned at the end of the year.[17] He had finally received the deeds to his granted land and decided that farming offered a better living than policing. In early 1833 William was living at Jordan Hill when convict Charles Watson was assigned to him as a house servant. He would have helped his elderly parents, who, at 77 and 71 years of age, were still active but worked mostly in the house and vegetable garden.[18]

The 9-year-old grandson, James, son of Elizabeth Ann, still lived with his grandparents. Twenty years later, James married his cousin Elizabeth Rope, the daughter of John and Maria Rope. When James died in 1895, aged 72, the funeral notice read: 'The deceased came from that hale hardy class of yeomanry that the Hawkesbury district was once notorious for, and had he not met with this accident, must have lived a good many years longer. ... as a farmer of the old school had few equals behind the plough'.[19] James would have almost certainly learned the tough ploughman's trade from his grandfather, just as Anthony had learnt it from his father John in rural Norfolk.

In mid 1832 the British Whig government abolished the death penalty for most minor offences and replaced it with a sentence of transportation for life.[20] Many English newspapers were critical of the changes, and *The Leicester Chronicle* claimed that automatic life sentences for petty crimes would lead to injustices. In 1832 a Chelmsford Court, the same court where Anthony had been convicted in 1785, sentenced two men to transportation for life; one for stealing a lamb, the other for stealing 90 sovereigns in a house burglary. *The Leicester Chronicle* concluded that if trivial and serious offences earned the same sentence 'one may as well be hanged for a sheep as a lamb'.[21]

When news of the abolition of the death penalty and its replacement with transportation-for-life eventually reached the colony, it would have been a hot topic of discussion among the settler community. Many of them had been sentenced to death before being pardoned to transportation. Elizabeth had 48 years previously been sentenced to hang for burglary and would have been overjoyed to hear of the abolition of the death penalty. The discussion on the subject would have certainly resurrected the dread and terror she felt when the judge put on his black cap and sentenced her to death. However, she would have been puzzled by the fact that the new law would have committed her to be *a convict for life*, whereas in 1783 with the King's pardon she had to be released after 7 years. In effect, the new law removed the death sentence – and with it the possibility of remission by Royal Pardon – and replaced it with *transportation for life with hard labour*. The conundrum that this supposedly "improvement" offered would definitely not have been lost on the convicts and emancipists. One step forward, two steps back!

Most residents in the major settlements were, in all likelihood, ambivalent about the British sentence changes. They probably reinforced a growing concern that the continuance of transported convict labour was unlikely to be in Sydney's best interests. Increasingly, free settlers and influential emancipists in the community questioned whether convict labour was essential to their future prosperity. Calls for the total abolition of convict transportation grew stronger, and three years later, in 1835, the British government established a national prison system replacing transportation with local imprisonment.[22]

Reducing or removing convict transportation almost certainly resurrected in many inhabitants' minds vivid memories of their experiences in the British prison system. They would wonder what had happened to fellow inmates in prisons, hulks, ships and encampments they had occupied over the years. Anthony and Elizabeth Rope were now "ancients" among their peers, and most of their convict acquaintances had already died. Susannah Kable, who Elizabeth knew as an inmate in Norwich Castle gaol and the First Fleet ship *Friendship*, died in 1825 aged 63. It is unlikely that Elizabeth would have given any thought to her nemesis on the *Friendship*, Ralph Clark. She may have heard on the convict grapevine about his conduct on Norfolk Island, and his return to England in 1792. Two years later Clark's whole family perished; his wife dying in childbirth, and Ralph and their son succumbing to yellow fever aboard a ship bound for the West Indies.[23]

Of the 729 First Fleet convicts who landed in Sydney Cove 110 are known to have returned to England, but an unrecorded number may have as well. Of those who remained, the death dates of only 398 are known. By the close of 1831, about 84 First Fleet emancipists were alive.

The first organised attempt to promote serious reforms to the NSW Legislative Council was made at a public meeting in Sydney in January 1833. Those at this meeting advocated that the membership of the legislature be made up of elected representatives of the whole community.[24] The liberally minded Bourke supported these changes. At the end of 1833 he wrote to the Colonial Office proposing that a new council be composed of 24 nominated and elected members.[25] The Colonial Office turned down the proposal. They knew that assembling a representative council that would be acceptable to all was an impossible task, considering the diverse political factions present in the colony.

Despite the determination of the previous Tory government in Britain to keep Australia a penal colony, it had developed a free, prosperous and progressive society. Whereas the British Whig government supported in principle more rights for emancipists, it was uncertain about the very ambitious egalitarian movement in the colony. Bourke was now nourishing the seeds of equality that Phillip and Macquarie had sown, and there was overwhelming local support for a comprehensive democracy in Australia. However, even the more liberally minded politicians in Britain were nervous about such a radical shift to a classless society. Indeed, some saw it as a threat to the monarchy itself!

Bourke had expected the number of convicts transported to the colony to decrease before his term of office closed, and perhaps even stop entirely. Instead, the year 1833 saw the highest number of convicts ever to arrive in Australia, 4115 to New South Wales and 2665 to Van Diemen's Land. At the same time 2685 free emigrants arrived in New South Wales.[26]

In January 1834 Bourke renewed his efforts to improve the conditions for assigned convict servants. He protested again to the Colonial Office about the severity of punishments inflicted, and length of time that convicts had to work in irons before being eligible for a ticket of leave. Bourke claimed that this treatment meant 'fifteen years of Slavery' and was 'more likely to impede than promote reformation'.[27]

Protests in both Britain and Australia against convict servitude had increased significantly. Black slavery was now abolished in Britain, while 'white slavery' was allowed to continue in Australia. *The Monitor* headlined that a 'dreadful state of white slavery' existed in the colony and predicted that the rampant crime rate in England 'arising out of increased misery' would make 'transportation worse than death'.[28] *The Sydney Herald* criticised convict servitude for different reasons. It voiced the views of the exclusives and Tories who argued that transportation was no longer appropriate for a free colony, and should, without delay, be brought to an end. Britain 'must reform her criminals within their own bosom, or exclusive penal settlements must be founded to take our place'. Somewhat ironically, it proclaimed that with a large free and virtuous population, the criminals 'banished from a country where they are not worthy to remain as members' were *polluting* Australian society.[29]

Governor Bourke wanted transportation to cease and agreed that, from a convict's perspective, it was a form of slavery. He claimed 'the condition of the Convict is that of a Slave', the only difference being that in the colony only magistrates had the power to inflict physical punishment. He questioned whether lashes needed to be imposed on convicts at all. In a letter to the Colonial Office Secretary, Bourke wrote that punishment would 'induce a state of despair in the mind of the Convict which is found to be utterly at variance with reformation'.[30]

In November 1834 an epidemic of influenza swept through New South Wales 'like the plague or the cholera', and it brought 'sickness into every family'. The epidemic led to many deaths.[31] On 12 Dec 1834, the Rope's youngest son, William, died at age 29. The reason for his death is not known but it was probably influenza. His early death would have been an enormous loss for his parents, who had in recent years relied on, and benefited from, his support and hard work. William was buried in the Castlereagh cemetery. The ceremony was officiated by Rev. Henry Fulton. On 9 Jan 1835, Anthony and Elizabeth's son John sold the deceased 60-acre estate to Rev. Fulton for £20 10s.[32]

Anthony and Elizabeth remained on their farm despite the tragic loss of their youngest son and carer. The elderly Ropes continued to pay rent for their land, and their 10-year-old grandson James helped with the farming. Fortunately, their daughter Mary and her family were living close by, as were other members of the family, and they assisted their parents where they could. The love that Anthony and Elizabeth invested in their children and grandchildren had its rewards in their infirm years.

In January 1835, Governor Bourke was created a Knight Commander of the Most Honourable Order of the Bath and was now to be addressed as Sir Richard Bourke.[33] The knighthood would have pleased him, but he was mostly preoccupied with the opposition to his reforms from the Legislative Council. He received constant acrimony from the local Tories, who included Alexander McLeay and Treasurer Campbell Riddell. Ralph Darling had appointed most of these men and they were not sympathetic to the Whig tendencies of Sir Richard Bourke. Of course Bourke had strong supporters, and William Wentworth was among them. The two men had much in common. Even so, Bourke was unable to persuade Wentworth to accept a nomination to the Legislative Council.

Wentworth despised Alexander McLeay and had savaged him two years earlier in *The Sydney Herald*, calling him a 'useless public officer' and 'a bloated Pensioner'.[34] When, in August 1835, McLeay announced he was going to retire, Bourke nominated his son-in-law Edward Thomson as Colonial Secretary. Thomson had been the Clerk of the Council for the past six years and, nepotism aside, Bourke argued that he depended on the unerring support of this position.[35] London agreed and sent instructions that McLeay be allowed, in consideration of his long service, to set the date of his retirement.[36] Bourke gave him until January

1837, after which he would replace him with his son-in-law.[37]

The government assisted immigrant scheme had become a contentious issue. It was managed from London but paid for by the colony from the sale of crown land. Bourke agreed with many of the complaints that migrants lacked skills, and in 1835 he appointed a select committee to examine all aspects of immigration.[38] In late 1835, he put forward a plan, supported by both political factions in the colony, offering a 'bounty' for skilled immigrants. An agent was sent to England to ensure that migrants met the colony's needs, and to give prospective immigrants realistic information. In the new scheme settlers or agents could also select suitable emigrants and bring them to the colony. The government would then reimburse them for the cost of the passage.[39]

In mid 1835, William Wentworth founded Australia's first political party, the *Australian Patriotic Association*, on a platform of amending the constitution to have a *bona fide representative* government instead of the Legislative Council.[40] This was the start of a fierce contest between the so-called 'Botany Bay Whigs' and 'Botany Bay Tories'.[41]

Another memorable event in Australia's early history was the visit of Charles Darwin. Captain Phillip Parker King had commanded HMS *Beagle* on its first expedition to South America (1826-30) and his midshipman son Philip Gidley King (the same name as his grandfather) had accompanied him. The young King also sailed on HMS *Beagle* for its second voyage (1831-36) after his father had returned to Australia. A 27-year-old naturalist named Charles Darwin was a botanist on the second voyage, on which he conceived many of his conclusions on the *origin of species* and had become acquainted with the young midshipman. When, on 12 Jan 1836, HMS *Beagle* sailed into Port Jackson, Darwin noted the 'beautiful villas and nice cottages are here and there scattered along the beach'. After disembarking, he explored the Sydney settlement:

> [I] returned full of admiration at the whole scene. It is a most magnificent testimony to the power of the British nation. Here, in a less promising country, scores of years have done many more times more than an equal number of centuries have effected in South America.[42]

He noted that Sydney could 'faithfully' be compared to the large suburbs of London or Birmingham and although a number of large houses had just been finished 'every one complained of the high rents and difficulty in procuring a house'.[43] In that respect, little has changed in Sydney two centuries later.

On his last days in Australia, Darwin dined with Phillip King on his father's estate *Dunheved*. Despite its shortcomings, he thought the system of transforming villains into honest people was working.

> On the whole, as a place of punishment, the object is scarcely gained; as a real system of reform it has failed, as perhaps would every other plan; but as a means of making men outwardly honest, – of converting vagabonds, most useless in one hemisphere, into active citizens in another, and thus giving birth to a new and splendid country – a grand centre of civilisation – it has succeeded to a degree perhaps unparalleled in history.[44]

The Ropes would not have been aware that the future-famous Darwin was visiting next door. Even if they had met him on his way to *Dunheved*, he would have been just another toff visiting the neighbouring estate.

By early 1836 Governor Bourke had decided to dismiss his civil court officers because of their persistent hostility in the Legislative Council. He replaced them with new magistrates who had actively supported his reforms; one of them was his friend and ally, William Wentworth.[45] These appointments infuriated the Botany Bay Tories who feared the increased Whig numbers in Bourke's administration would diminish their role in determining the colony's political directions, and, in particular, the future drafting of a Constitution for New South Wales. Both political camps had drawn up petitions stating their reasons for changing the legislative, transportation and immigration regulations. Influential members of the colony tried to delay elective representation until a sufficient number of free emigrants of 'virtuous and industrious habits' had arrived to outnumber the emancipists. They claimed Bourke's laxity in imposing convict discipline had increased the crime rate.[46]

Wentworth defended the Whig proposals, announcing in *The Sydney Herald* 'I am happy that we have at last got a Government that an honest man can support'.[47] At a public meeting he spoke passionately in support of Governor Bourke 'We've now got a Whig Governor – myself being a Whig', and launched a petition from the free inhabitants to King William IV. In this Wentworth maintained that any change to the constitution must be based on the Whig principle that those with a stake in the country must exercise political power. His petition asked for the immediate creation of an *elected* legislative assembly, and commended Bourke and his policies, denying that they had anything to do with any increases in crime rate.[48]

The two opposing petitions were presented to the public, and they were asked to sign the version they preferred. The Whig proposals received 6000 signatures while the Tory petition received less than 400. If public opinion meant anything the preference of the residents was clear. In July 1836 both petitions were sent to England. James Macarthur, John Macarthur's son, now the leader of the exclusives, accompanied the Tory petition to England.[49]

END OF THE CONVICT ERA 1832-1843

The diametrically opposed views in the colony about the petition proposals continued to cause a furore among the currency youth, emancipists and liberals. They were especially angry when *The Sydney Herald* labelled the public meeting held by William Wentworth as a gathering of the 'unwashed' mob.[50] Headlines and passionate articles in the newspapers on the 'Relinquishment of Transportation' raised the hopes of many residents that the convict intake would stop, but disappointed others.[51] Large landholders and merchants, who were in the minority, continued to assert that convicts provided an essential workforce. For most of the population the rise of egalitarianism in a free Australia was unstoppable. They were soon to find out, however, that Britain was not yet ready to consider major political reform.

For many emancipist families the petition proposals, written mainly by lawyers, would have seemed complex, and a little bewildering. The illiterate members of a family relied on others to read the petitions and newspaper articles, and, as with much second-hand communication, what they heard was filtered by the reader and biased by the teller. The Ropes would not have expected transportation to end in their lifetimes or that they could elect their own representatives. Along with most emancipists who trusted Bourke, they welcomed progress but were unsure how these changes would affect their lives and their farms.

Discussions about such matters at meals were vital for the Rope family. Their comprehension of the printed word was limited so the verbal exchange of ideas, information and gossip enabled them to understand the world around them. It was also a time for entertainment, singing and storytelling. On many occasions Anthony and Elizabeth are likely to have recounted Governor Phillip's speech on 7 Feb 1788, when he told them to 'make the Day of their Transportation to this Place, the happiest Day they had ever seen'.[52] For the Ropes, and many other convicts, this had been a turning point in their lives. Yes, it had meant enduring hard labour, floggings and road gangs, but the promise of freedom and independence ahead was always the incentive for them to raise and nurture a family. Transportation had not been a cakewalk, but nor was life and work in rural Britain. At least here, where ambition and a willingness to work was rewarded, they had the opportunity to improve their lot. All such arguments would be discussed over and over again while trying to make sense of the changes to convict transportation and the legislative council elections proposed in the petitions.

Over the years the Ropes had sometimes used convict assigned servants to help with heavy-duty farm work. Assigned servants certainly helped improve productivity but they were a relative luxury, and only large estates could afford them in large numbers. Apart from the cost, as ex-convicts, most settlers felt uneasy exploiting a servitude system they had once been part of. Anthony and Elizabeth had never worked as assigned servants, but their sons-in-law certainly had. Their children were married to convicts or emancipists, and the greater Rope clan would have definitely supported the removal of assigned convict labour.

As a child Richard Bourke had seen sectarian intolerance in Ireland, and he was opposed to all forms of religious discrimination. In 1836 he advocated state assisted education for all church denominations. The government would subsidise, on a per-capita basis, the building of churches and schools, thus breaking the monopoly of the Church of England on schooling.[53] Some districts had no schools while others had only Anglican provincial schools of a poor standard. Governor Bourke proposed a national school system, in which the government was to build schools and appoint trained teachers according to the population. However, Bourke's educational reforms were well before their time, and they were strongly resisted by powerful members of the community. The Colonial Office had approved his plan in late 1835, but the Legislative Council led by McLeay, and the protestant clergy headed by Bishop William Broughton strenuously opposed it. The support of the Catholic Bishop only re-enforced the protestant opposition, and, to Bourke's great disappointment, the scheme had to be abandoned.[54]

By the end of 1836, 48 years since the formation of the New South Wales colony, the population comprised 77,096 people. With the steady arrival of free immigrants, fewer than one-in-three residents were convicts (27,831). Eight years prior, in 1828, every second person was a convict. Now every third free resident was an emancipist.[55]

Alexander McLeay had still not resigned as Colonial Secretary by 3 Jan 1837, so Bourke dismissed him and appointed Edward Thomson as his replacement. Thomson also became a member of the Legislative Council, a position he would hold for nearly 20 years.[56] He was the best choice for the office, both in terms of his experience and ability, but the local Tories were disgusted. *The Sydney Herald* protested that the 'wealth, intelligence and respectability' of the colony was in jeopardy and this 'dirty intrigue' that bound the Whigs 'at the feet of the Bourke family'. Thomson's appointment had given the Whigs another vote in the NSW Legislative Council.[57] Throughout January the Tories continued their vicious attacks on the governor and his political allies. On 30 Jan 1837 Bourke formally resigned, blaming the intransigence of the Tories.[58] In July 1837 the Colonial Office accepted Bourke's resignation but he remained in office until 5 Dec 1837.[59] In the meantime, Sir George Gipps was commissioned as the new Governor of New South Wales.

END OF THE CONVICT ERA 1832-1843

Governor Bourke's final year, 1837, proved a difficult one, as it was for the Rope families. Two years prior, the Rope's 17-year-old grandson, Toby Ryan, had vanished in the Hunter River district following an altercation with the Penrith police at a house-warming party. It had been a riotous affair and police officers had been pelted with rocks. To avoid arrest Toby had "hopped it and gone bush". For the past two years the family had not heard from him and assumed he was dead. But in 1837 Toby returned home to Jordan Hill and found his father had been gaoled for three months for non-payment of debts, and Mary and the whole Ryan family in the process of selling off their few belongings and moving to another rented farm on the Nepean. During the move Toby recalled that 'On the way we had to pass grandfather and grandmother, and bid them farewell for a time'.[60] Despite their joy at seeing Toby alive, the Ropes would have been upset at the forced departure of their daughter Mary. Unlike earlier times, they were unable to help her. With William gone, and Mary's family moving to the Nepean, the elderly Ropes needed to be more self-reliant. Fortunately their other children living in the area would periodically check on them.

A few months later, on 9 Aug 1837, the matriarch of the Rope family, Elizabeth, died at the age of 75. Reverend Fulton officiated at the funeral on August 11th and she was buried in the Castlereagh cemetery next to her son William and granddaughter Eliza Frost. The Ropes had been married for almost 50 years, and Elizabeth's death would have been devastating for Anthony, and extremely sad for the rest of the clan. From the few personal insights we have into Anthony and Elizabeth's life together, she appears to have been the anchor in the family and had lent both her strength and good sense to their farming life. This had always revolved around their children, and Elizabeth had ensured that those family links were never broken. She and Anthony cultivated the protectiveness that neither had experienced as children. As an orphan Elizabeth had received no parental nurturing and she strived to give this to her own children. Their house was always open to the family, and they provided physical and emotional support to all who were in need.

As an orphan at the age of six, Elizabeth's early life had been one of hardship, hunger and poverty. She had been imprisoned several times from the age of 18, and at the age of 25 was transported to Sydney Cove where she met and married Anthony. Despite the rigours of a hard convict life, the birth of eight children, the last at the age of 46, and 50 years as a wife and mother, Elizabeth had outlived most of her peers. Everything we know about her suggests she was a strong affectionate wife and mother. Her frugal approach to life contributed to the Ropes' wellbeing, and likely accounted for their longevity. In the early colony when drunkenness and indebtedness was common, Elizabeth's sensibility had kept these scourges to a minimum in the greater family. There certainly had been problems, hardships and disappointments in their lives but no more than expected in these pioneering times.

In a rural bushland setting on the outer edge of the Penrith suburb of Cranebrook, Elizabeth's grave still lies in the Castlereagh General Cemetery. In 1985, 150 years after her death, the *Fellowship of First Fleeters* restored her gravestone and erected a memorial plaque.[61]

On 4 Dec 1837, a day before Governor Bourke departed for England, a public meeting was held in his honour, at which William Wentworth gave a moving tribute to his achievements. Wentworth declared that Bourke had transformed the poor colony into a prosperous one where the population had doubled, the commercial resources tripled, and the revenue of the colony quadrupled. Wentworth claimed that such uninterrupted progress commercially and agriculturally was unparalleled in Australian's history.[62]

On the day of departure the troops assembled in front of Government House with the band playing. As Bourke boarded the cargo ship *Samuel Winter*, people lined the cove and gave the Governor a continuous cheer along the water's edge. Casting political allegiances aside *The Monitor* declared 'that the Colony had lost a friend and benefactor'. *The Sydney Gazette* was less enthusiastic and claimed it was not the higher and respectable classes who cheered the governor, but 'the cheers of felon mobs ... the shirtless and shoeless' who waved their hats and the 'ruffians followed him by land [and] by water too'. Clearly, it was the convicts' and emancipist's governor who was leaving, and he would be greatly missed.[63]

On returning to England Bourke declined further official duties and settled on his estate in Ireland. In 1851, Sir Richard Bourke was promoted to General. He died on 12 Aug 1855, aged 78.

In early January 1838, *The Colonist* informed its readers about a preliminary report of the British parliament's committee on transportation. Headed by Sir William Molesworth, the committee recommended the abolition of convict assignment to private individuals and the end of transportation to New South Wales. Judge Forbes, Reverend Lang and James Macarthur had gone to England to give evidence to the committee in support of abolishing transportation and convict servitude. It was anticipated that the new Governor Gipps would in future have the existing convicts in the colony, exclusively employed in public works.[64]

On 23 Feb 1838, the ninth governor, the 47-year-old army

Major Sir George Gipps, arrived on the immigrant ship *Upton Castle*. About 2000 people assembled the following day at Government House to hear the governor sworn in. The attendees were surprised that the new governor did not appear on the veranda to greet them.[65] They would soon learn that Sir George was not a person to mingle readily with the *hoi polloi*.

Gipps arrived amid the disagreements surrounding the abolition of transportation and convict assignments, and these issues confronted him from the moment he landed in Sydney. The wealthier colonialists continued their disapproval at the sudden withdrawal of assigned servants and wanted to know who was going to do the labouring in the future. Proposals were made to bring cheap labour from India or China, but Gipps thought this to be 'evil of the highest magnitude'.[66] While the English government now maintained that transportation was an inefficient form of punishment and rehabilitation, and that convict assignments were a form of slavery, the colony's landowners continued to argue that assigned servants provided a cheap efficient workforce. Over 570 landholders and magistrates petitioned Governor Gipps complaining that the social and moral state of the colony had been misrepresented in England and the evidence given to the committee had been biased. Their petition argued that depriving the colonies of convict labour reduced their means of purchasing crown land and consequently reduced the government's funds to pay for assisted immigration. That is, the survival of assisted immigration depended on the continuance of the convict assignment system.

The petition had little effect. The rising cost of convict assignments and transportation had been heavily criticised in England, and the British had made up their mind.[67] In any case, government colonial policy was determined with little regard to the sentiments of the colony's residents. The British were now ready to make changes to the convict system in the colony, but what the locals thought about it really did not matter.

After receiving instructions from the Colonial Office, Governor Gipps announced on 19 Dec 1838 that the assignment of male convicts within the towns, for the purpose of 'luxury, or as domestic servants', would cease from 1 Jan 1839.[68] The decision outraged the owners of large estates but, somewhat unexpectedly, it was not just the exclusives who wanted this decision reversed. The *Australian Patriotic Association* and its leaders William Wentworth and Sir John Jamison also opposed the change.[69] Wentworth had become one of the largest landowners in the colony, and he and some associates had planned to purchase "for a song" nearly a third of New Zealand's South Island from Maori chieftains. Gipps had blocked it, and Wentworth never forgave him.[70]

END OF THE CONVICT ERA 1832-1843

Portrait of Richard Bourke, the colony's eight's governor (1831-1837).

Portrait of Sir George Gipps, the colony's ninth governor (1838-1846).

From then on Wentworth opposed the governor at every opportunity, and he no longer fought for the causes of the wider aspirant community. It was a surprising reversal for a young man who, years before, had taught the currency youth – of which he was one himself – the meaning of the word *liberty*. It seemed that he now had more personal, and more lucrative, matters to fight for. Political allegiances in the colony were shifting rapidly. The increased numbers of free immigrants arriving were opposed to both transportation and assigned servants, and they supported Gipps. The new immigrants resented competition from low-paid assigned convicts and detested the presence of convict "slaves" in the colony.

On 22 May 1840, by an Order-in-Council, the British Parliament enacted the decision to end transportation to New South Wales. It became officially law in August. The *Eden* and the *Pekoe* were intended to be the last convict ships to be sent to Sydney and arrived in late 1840. But the case for convict labour continued to be supported in some quarters.[71] After heavy lobbying by landowners desirous of cheap labour, the NSW Legislative Council agreed in 1842, despite widespread protests, to import 236 high-class convicts. Another 1400 convicts were transported to New South Wales in subsequent years, the last in 1850. Van Diemen's Land received convict ships until 1853. The Swan River colony founded in 1829, initially refused convicts but in 1850 requested them and they worked on major public building projects until 1868 when

END OF THE CONVICT ERA 1832-1843

transportation to Australia totally ceased. In 80 years, about 164,000 convicts were transported to the Australian colonies on board 806 ships.

Census surveys of the colony had been gathered every year since 1828. For many of these early surveys, only the general statistical data has survived intact – most information on individual people has been lost. The surviving records of the March 1841 census show few personal details. These contain only the data on the number of people living in each household, their ages, gender, occupation and religion and the type of accommodation.

The 1841 census records that Anthony Rope, aged 84, was living alone in the Parish of Castlereagh in a timber house, and was employed in agriculture. Anthony attended the census with his son John, who was listed directly below him in the Nepean district registration, though in a different house.[72] The location of Anthony's house is not known but is likely to have been on his son's farm. Anthony must have still been a fit and active person to live alone at this age at a time when men rarely lived beyond 60. Anthony had worked as a convict and farmer for over 50 years. Moreover, he had always sought additional work on farms and boats to supplement the family's income. This was a man with *an extraordinary number of miles on his personal odometer.* He may have looked old and gnarled, but he remained a tough, determined individual.

The census also records the changing demographics following the end of transportation. With large numbers of immigrants arriving in New South Wales, the population had risen to 130,856 inhabitants, and the number of convicts still serving their sentence had dropped to 26,977 (21%). The gender balance had improved to one female for every two males.[73]

In late 1841, Anthony was no longer able to support himself, and he moved to Penrith with his daughter Susannah Bradley and her partner John Proctor, the local Chief Constable. Susannah was recorded as John Proctor's housekeeper.[74] Her three daughters were now married and only Susannah and John's 12-year-old son John was still living at the Proctor house.

On 26 Jan 1842, the 54th anniversary of the founding of the Sydney Cove settlement was celebrated all over the colony. To commemorate the occasion *The Sydney Gazette* claimed that the government was about to pay a pension to the "last three" surviving members of the First Fleet.

> THE FIRST FLEETERS. – The Government have ordered a pension of one shilling per diem to be paid to the survivors of those who came by the first vessel into the Colony. The number of these really "old hands" is now reduced to three, of whom,

two are now in the Benevolent Asylum, and the other is a fine hale old fellow, who can do a day's work with more spirit than many of the young fellows lately arrived in the Colony. We are glad that the Government have commemorated the auspicious day of our anniversary in so handsome a manner.[75]

Anthony's family must have been notified of this announcement and realised that their father had been overlooked. On February 21st they sent a request for a pension to Governor Gipps.

> That memorialist arrived in the Colony Per Ship *Alexander* in the year 1787 – in the First Fleet – and observing a Paragraph in the Sydney Gazette of the 20th of January that your Excellency has been graciously pleased to render the few Survivors that remain one Shilling per Day memorialist most humbly hopes your Excellency will be Pleased in consideration of his present age being Eighty Eigth years – and rendered too feeble to earn a living. Be Benevolently Pleased to consider him a fit object for such Humanity.
>
> And memorialist is in Duty Bound for the short Period he may Remain in this world will forever Pray.
> Anthony Rope, per Ship Alexander
> at Mr John Proctor, Penrith 21st Febry 1842[76]

From the remarks later added to the margins of this request by the governor and his staff, it is evident that they had no knowledge of the pension. Gipps wrote that Anthony 'must be informed that the Govt. has not authorised the publication of any notice such as that mentioned in his petition'.[77] Unquestionably the surviving First Fleet convicts would have rejoiced at the prospect of a pension, but Gipps was not about to change his mind and no pensions were offered. *The Gazette* had also underestimated the number of living First Fleet convicts. In fact, 17 were still alive in New South Wales and 10 in Van Diemen's Land in 1842.[78]

Four months later in June 1842, John Proctor, the partner of Anthony's daughter Susannah, died at the age of 65. It would have been a sad and difficult time for Susannah, aged 41, since she would now have to find work to support her son and her father. Two months later John Rope's wife Maria died in childbirth aged 40, leaving John with a family of six; his eldest daughter Ann had married in 1835 at the age of 16. The death of Maria was tragic but worse was to come; their father John died only three years later at the age of 49.

On 20 Apr 1843, Anthony Rope passed away at the grand age of 86. He was buried in the Castlereagh cemetery on April 22nd; the ceremony officiated by Reverend John Vincent. At some point over the next 150 years Anthony's gravestone was lost in the unmaintained bush cemetery, and his grave location is unknown. In 1995 the *Rope-Pulley Family Heritage Association* had a new headstone erected next to Elizabeth's grave, which was the most likely burial place. The *Fellowship of First Fleeters* added a memorial plaque to the headstone.[79]

Anthony was 30 years of age when he boarded the First Fleet. The convicts who outlived him would have been much younger when they landed in Sydney Cove. In later years Anthony was one of the oldest men in the colony and he had lived unaided and with full mental faculties to be just short of 87 years. The average lifespan for First Fleet convicts was 56 years.[80]

The graves of Elizabeth and Anthony Rope in the Castlereagh General Cemetery on Church Street, Cranebrook. It is a pioneer burial place in an Australian bush setting.

The First Fleet convicts Anthony Rope and Elizabeth Pulley played crucial, but largely unappreciated, roles in the early years of the New South Wales colony. They were just one of the many emancipist families who contributed enormously to the economic and political evolution of Australia in its formative years. Regrettably, few of these families have been properly acknowledged in our history; indeed modern narratives tend to portray the lives of early convicts in mostly negative roles. In this respect, the Rope family has been fortunate. They have been remembered as pioneer settlers with the naming of a Blacktown suburb *Ropes Crossing* which is close to *Ropes Creek*. The streets named *Pulley Drive, Ropes Crossing Boulevard* in this suburb, and *Rope Street* in

Dundas Valley (previously, the Ponds) commemorate their pioneering contributions to the district. Such recognition for emancipist settlers is rare. Many other families who played equivalent or greater roles in establishing the New South Wales colony and making the Australian society and culture what it is today, have received no recognition at all.

The narrative adopted in this history is an attempt to rectify these oversights, and to establish the important role emancipist settlers played in the founding of Australia. Small emancipist farmers were the backbone of food production during periods when the New South Wales colony teetered on the brink of starvation and collapse. Without their efforts Australia would be a much different place today, and it is possible the British may have abandoned the settlement entirely.

Most early Australian histories centre on the efforts and activities of prominent educated members of the colony. This had led the Australian author William Fielding Fearn-Wannan (better known as Bill Wannan) to make the following observation.

> The writing of history in Australia has, until comparatively recent times and with some few exceptions, been influenced by the values and standards of conduct of the land-takers and merchant princes of the nineteenth century.[81]

Wannan backs up this claim recalling that William Wentworth wrote his treatise, *A Statistical, Historical and Political Account of New South Wales (1819)*, when he was 29 and seeking to become John Macarthur's son-in-law. Consequently, Wentworth's account of Bligh's arrest casts the governor in a poor light, and lauds Macarthur. In truth John Macarthur was a ruthless demagogue and racketeer, who menaced anyone that stood in the way of his political or commercial interests. He certainly deserves a place in our history but not as the iconic early pioneer he is so often portrayed to be.[82]

Surely successful emancipists, such as the farmer, brewer, tanner, shipper and magistrate Andrew Thompson – a person who made pivotal contributions to the success of the colony – deserve much more prominence in our history. And so do the many emancipist settlers who led hard and dangerous lives on remote farms that produced most of the colony's food. In particular, the stoic farmers on the Hawkesbury, South Creek and Nepean waterways, who battled incessantly against floods, droughts, debts and discrimination for little reward or gratitude while alive, need to be much more acclaimed in the modern day accounts of this period.

It is an enormous pity that the absence of written material about illiterate pioneering families prevents their story from being told in much greater detail. Had they been able to write journals and letters, their testimonies would have been even more fascinating than those of the most famous chroniclers of the colony, David Collins and Watkin Tench. In this sense, these two diarists would certainly have concurred with the likely sentiments of these largely forgotten early settlers, that:

written words reveal only a glimpse of our past,

and, alas,

history rarely tells herstory.

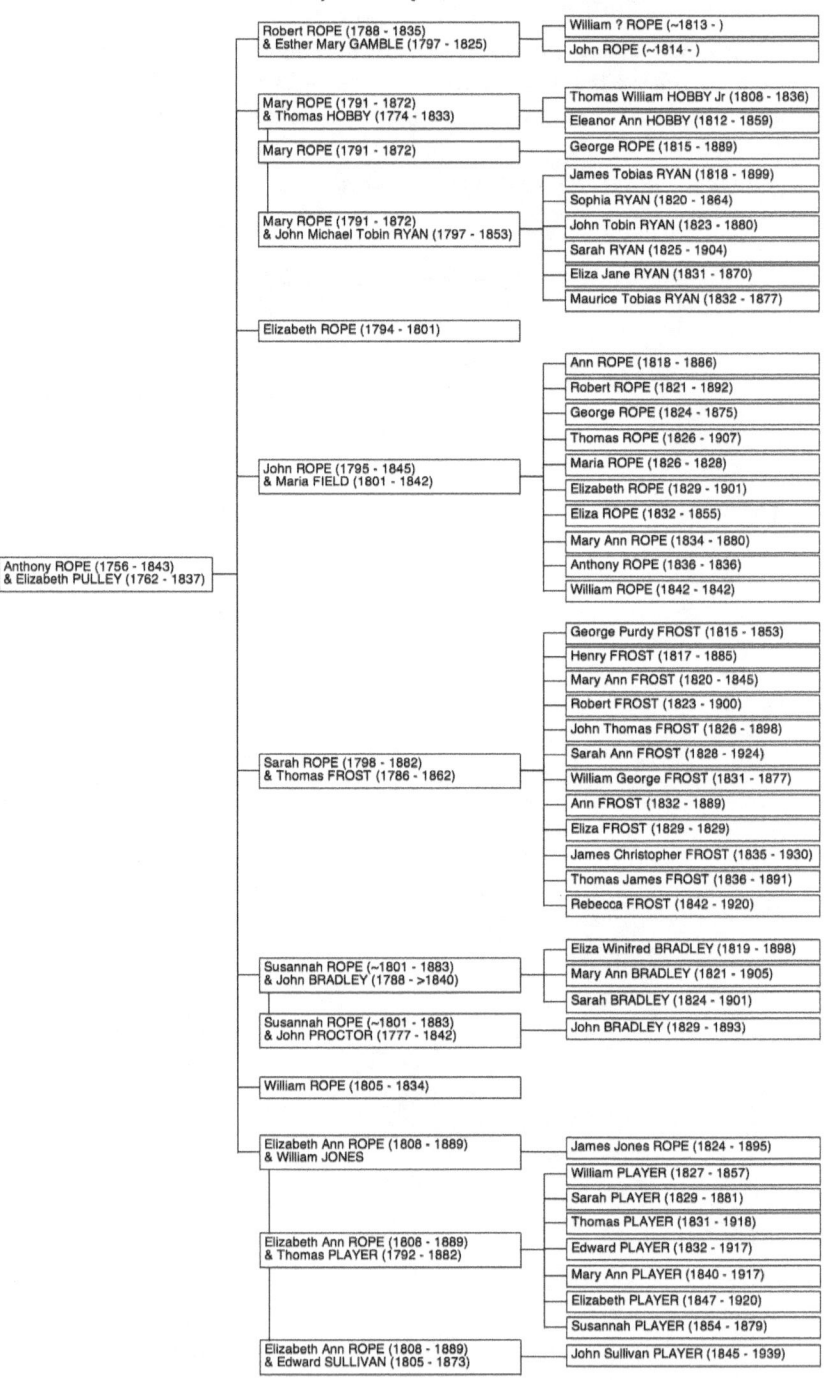

Rope & Pulley Children and Grandchildren

Acknowledgements

In researching this book I was given access to 18th and 19th century historical documents and letters in the libraries and archives of England and Australia. Transcripts and original records were made freely available, and professional staff generously assisted in tracking down the more elusive historical references. Although most First Fleet diaries and journals are now published as books, these were also made available as original manuscripts from the online First Fleet Collection held in the Mitchell and Dixon Libraries. For permission to access these documents and repositories, I am greatly indebted.

I also acknowledge the use of original genealogical and historical material available over the Internet. Without ready access to the digitised global data archives of newspapers, books and documents, researching this history would have been much more time consuming. In this context, the web facility TROVE at the National Library of Australia deserves special mention. Their increasingly extensive archival facilities have been invaluable. Day-to-day details on colonial life were gleaned from a raft of early newspapers, government gazettes and publications stored electronically in the NLA library.

The Mitchell Library and the State Archives and Records of New South Wales provided the bulk of official records, letters, dispatches and convict records of the First Fleet, and the early settlements. The wonderfully detailed and descriptive writings of the colonial diarists – Tench, King, Collins and Phillip, in particular – provided much of the information concerning the voyage of the First Fleet and the establishment of the colony. The court records from the State Archives and Records of New South Wales were especially important to tracing the legal battles of the struggling settlers, and other official documents and letters for the period 1785 to 1845 underpinned much of the detail on land transactions.

This book includes numerous illustrations as sketches, drawings and paintings of early landscapes and portraits. For these I acknowledge access to the digital online images of the State Library of New South Wales, the Mitchell and Dixon Libraries, the National Library of Australia, the University of Melbourne Library and the National Maritime Museum in England, and the Norfolk Museums Service (UK). I thank the Office of the Registrar General for permitting the reproduction of several early parish maps.

I am particularly grateful for the assistance of the staff at the libraries, archives and societies who have provided the documents and books referred to in my citations: the State Library of New South Wales,

ACKNOWLEDGEMENTS

the Mitchell Library, the State Archives and Records of New South Wales, the Penrith Library, the Norfolk Record Office (UK), the Norfolk Family History Society (UK), The National Archives (UK), The University of Western Australia Library, the Nedlands Library, the State Library of Western Australia for use of their British newspaper collections, the Fellowship of First Fleeters and the Rope-Pulley Family Heritage Association.

I am beholden to Jon Fearon, Robert Tonkinson, Barbara Hall and Ruth Guss for their reading of early drafts of the manuscript. I am especially grateful to Jon for his feedback at a time when he was very busy, and cousin Barbara for her determined and expert retrieval of records from the State Archives and Records of New South Wales.

The least straightforward aspect of publishing this book has been its physical production, and I am truly grateful for the advice on this topic from authors Alan Frost, Grace Karskens and Michael Pembroke, and the Director of UWA Publishing, Terri-ann White. I also want to thank Alan Frost for his valuable critique on the first edition.

I particularly wish to thank friends and family whose enthusiasm and encouragement during the compilation and writing of this story helped me complete the task – none more so than to my husband, Sydney, whose support and contributions on many fronts have been indispensable. Finally, special thanks to Robert for the selection and design of the cover, and to Jennifer for her editorial input.

BIBLIOGRAPHY

ARCHIVES AND RECORDS
ADB	Australian Dictionary of Biography
BDA	Biographical Database of Australia
HLRV	Historical Land Records Viewer, New South Wales
HRA	Historical Records Australia
HRNSW	Historical Records of New South Wales
UML	University of Melbourne Library
NLA	National Library of Australia
NMM	National Maritime Museum, England
NRO: PD	Norfolk Record Office, Parish Records, England
NWHCM	Norfolk Museums Service
SLNSW	State Library of New South Wales
SLNSW DX	... Dixon Library
SLNSW ML	... Mitchell Library
SANSW	State Archives & Records of New South Wales
SLVIC	State Library of Victoria
TAHO	Tasmanian Archive and Heritage Office
TNA	The National Archives, England

BIRTH, DEATH AND MARRIAGES
Norton Subcourse, England	NRO: PD 675/2, PD 675/3
Haveringland, Felthorp, England	NRO: PD 35/2, PD 35/3, PD 45/2
Norwich, England	NRO: PD 484/5
St John's Church, Parramatta	SLNSW: SAG 55-56
St Matthew's Church, Windsor	SLNSW: SAG 53
Christ Church, Castlereagh	SLNSW: SAG 89, SANSW: ARK Reel 5002, Vol. 3

PRIMARY SOURCES
Arago, Jacques, *Narrative of a Voyage Round the World*, Treuttel and Wurtz, London, 1823.

Bligh, William, *Account of the Rebellion of the New South Wales Corps*, Ed. J. Curry, The Banks Society, Colony Press, Malvern, 2011.

Bradley, William, *A Voyage to New South Wales - The Journal of Lieutenant William Bradley of HMS Sirius, 1786-1792*, Trustees of the Public Library of New South Wales, Ure Smith, Sydney, 1969.

Clark, Ralph, *The Journal and Letters from Lt. Ralph Clark, 1787-1792*, eds. P. Fidlon and R. Ryan, Australian Documents Library, Sydney, 1981.

Collins, David, *An Account of the English Colony in New South Wales*, Vol I - II, ed. B. Fletcher, Royal Australian Historical Society, Reed, Sydney, 1975.

Colquhoun, Patrick, *A Treatise on the Police of the Metropolis*, J. Mawman, London, 1806.

Cunningham, Peter, *Two Years in New South Wales*, Vol II, Henry Colburn, London, 1827, Facs. Ed., Libraries Board South Australia, 1966.

BIBLIOGRAPHY

Darwin, Charles, *The Voyage of the Beagle*, Harvard Classics, Collier & Sons, New York, 1909.

Easty, John, *Memorandum of the Transactions of a Voyage from England to Botany Bay 1787-1793*, Trustees of the Public Library of New South Wales, Angus and Robertson, Sydney, 1965.

Harte, Walter, *Essays on Husbandry*, London, 1764.

Harris, Alexander, *Settlers and Convicts, or Recollections of Sixteen Year's Labour in the Australian Backwoods*, C. Cox, London, 1847.

House of Commons, *Report from the Select Committee on Transportation*, London, 1812.

Historical Records Australia, Vol I - XIX, ed. Frederick Watson, Library Committee of the Commonwealth, Government Printer, Sydney, 1914 - 1924.

Historical Records of New South Wales, ed. A. Briton and F. M. Bladen, Vol I - VII, Charles Potter, Government Printer, Sydney, 1892-1901.

Hunter, John, *An Historical Journal of Events at Sydney and at Sea 1787-1792*, ed. J. Bach, Royal Australian Historical Society, Angus and Robertson, Sydney, 1968.

Howard, John, *The State of the Prisons in England and Wales*, Warrington, printed by W. Eyres, 1st Ed., 1777.

Howard, John, *The State of the Prisons in England and Wales*, Warrington, printed by J. Johnson, C. Dilly and T. Cadell, London, 4th Ed., 1792.

King, Philip Gidley, *The Journal of Lieutenant King (Afterwards Governor)*, Historical Records of New South Wales, Vol. II, 1793-1795, Government Printer, Sydney, 1893, pp. 513-660.

Lang, John Dunmore, *An Historical and Statistical Account of New South Wales*, London, A. J. Valpy, 1837.

Macquarie, Lachlan, *Lachlan Macquarie, Governor of New South Wales, Journals of his tours in New South Wales and Diemen's Land 1810-1822*, Trustee of the Public Library New South Wales, Sydney, 1956.

Macquarie, Lachlan, *Letter to Viscount Sidmouth on the Transportation Laws*, by the Hon. Henry Grey Bennet, MP, Ridgway, London, 1819.

Macquarie, Lachlan, *A Letter to the Right Honourable Viscount Sidmouth in Refutation of Statements made by the Hon. Henry Grey Bennet, MP*, McMillian, London, 1821.

Nagle, Jacob, *The Nagle Journal*, ed. J. C. Dann, Weidenfeld & Nicolson, New York, 1988.

Nicol, John, *The Life and Adventures of John Nicol, Mariner*, Cadell, London, 1822.

Phillip, Arthur, *The Voyage of Governor Phillip to Botany Bay*, ed. James J. Auchmuty, Royal Australian Historical Society, Angus and Robertson, Sydney, 1970.

Ryan, James T., *Reminiscences of Australia*, George Robertson, Sydney, 1895, Facs. Ed., Nepean Family History Society, South Penrith, 1982.

Scott, James, *Remarks on a Passage to Botany Bay, 1787 –1792*, Trustee of the Public Library of New South Wales, Angus and Robertson, Sydney, 1963.

Smyth, Arthur Bowes, *The Journal of Arthur Bowes Smyth: Surgeon, Lady Penrhyn,*

BIBLIOGRAPHY

1787-1789, eds. P. Fidlon and R. Ryan, Australian Documents Library, Sydney, 1979.
Tench, Watkin, *1788*, ed. T. Flannery, Melbourne, Text Publishing, 2012.
White, John, *Journal of a Voyage to New South Wales*, ed. A. C. Chisholm, Royal Australian Historical Society, Angus and Robertson, Sydney, 1962.
Worgan, George, *Journal of a First Fleet Surgeon*, Library of Australian History, Sydney, 1978.

SECONDARY SOURCES

Atkinson, Alan, *The Europeans in Australia. Vol. 1, The Beginning*, Oxford University Press, Melbourne, 1997.
Barkley-Jack, Jan, *Hawkesbury Settlement Revealed: A New Look at Australia's Third Mainland Settlement 1793-1802*, Rosenberg, Dural, 2009.
Bateson, Charles, *The Convict Ships, 1787 – 1868*, Reed, Sydney, 1974.
Baxter, Carol, *Muster and Lists, New South Wales and Norfolk Island*, Volumes: 1800-1802; 1805-1806; 1814; 1822; 1823, 1824, 1825, ABGR in association with Society of Australian Genealogists, Sydney, 1987-1999.
Becke, Louis and Jeffrey, Walter, *Admiral Phillip: The Founding of New South Wales*, T. Fisher Unwin, London, 1899.
Brooke, Alan and Brandon, David, *Bound for Botany Bay, British Convict Voyages to Australia*, The National Archives Kew, 2005.
Clark, Manning, *A History of Australia, Vol. 1, From the Earliest Times to the Age of Macquarie*, Melbourne University Press, Carlton, 1979.
——— A History of Australia, Vol 2, New South Wales and Van Diemen's Land, 1822-1838, Melbourne University Press, Carlton, 1968.
——— *Manning Clark's History of Australia*, abridged M. Cathcart, Melbourne University Press, Carlton, 1997.
Clune, David & Turner, Ken, *The Governors of New South Wales, 1788 – 2010*, Federation Press, 2009.
Cobley, John, *The Crimes of the First Fleet Convicts*, Angus & Robertson, Sydney, 1985.
——— *Sydney Cove 1788, in the Words of Australia's First Settlers, the True Story of a Nation's Birt*h, Angus & Robertson, Sydney, 1987.
——— *Sydney Cove 1789-1790*, Angus and Robertson, Sydney, 1963.
——— *Sydney Cove 1791-1792*, Angus and Robertson, Sydney, 1965.
——— *Sydney Cove 1793-1795, The Spread of Settlement*, Angus & Robertson, Sydney, 1983.
——— *Sydney Cove 1795-1800, The Second Governor*, Angus & Robertson, Sydney, 1986.
Currey, C. H., *The Brothers Bent*, Sydney University Press, Sydney, 1968.
Currey, John, *David Collins: A Colonial Life*, Melbourne University Press, Carlton, 2000.
Davis, Russell Earls, *Bligh in Australia, A new appraisal of William Bligh and the Rum Rebellion*, Woodslane, Warriewood, 2010.
Dillon, Harry and Butler, Peter, *Macquarie: From colony to country*, William

Heinemann, Sydney, 2010.

Ellis, M.H., *Lachlan Macquarie, His Life, Adventures and Times*, Angus & Robertson, Sydney, 1969.

Ekirch, Roger, *Bound for America: The Transportation of British Convicts to the Colonies, 1718-1775*, Clarendon Press, Oxford, 1987.

Evatt, H. V., *Rum Rebellion: A Study of the Overthrow of Governor Bligh by John Macarthur and the New South Wales Corps*, Angus and Robertson Sydney, 1943.

Fitzgerald, Ross and Hearn, Mark, *Bligh, Macarthur and the Rum Rebellion*, Kangaroo Press, Kenthurst, 1988.

Fletcher, Brian, *Ralph Darling, A Governor Maligned*, Oxford University Press, Melbourne, 1984.

Frost, Alan, *Botany Bay Mirages*, Melbourne University Press, Carlton, 1994.

――― *Botany Bay: The Real Story*, Black Inc., Melbourne, 2012.

――― *The First Fleet: The Real Story*, Black Inc., Melbourne, 2011.

――― *Arthur Phillip, 1738-1814, His Voyaging*, Oxford University Press, Melbourne, 1987.

――― *The Planting of New South Wales: Sir Joseph Banks and the creation of an Antipodean Europe*, in *Sir Joseph Banks: a global perspective*, eds R.E.R. Banks, et al, Royal Botanic Gardens, Kew, London, 1994, pp. 133-147.

――― *Convicts & Empire, A Naval Question*, Oxford University Press, Melbourne, 1980.

Gillen, Mollie, *The Founders of Australia, A Biographical Dictionary of the First Fleet*, Library of Australian History, Sydney, 1989.

Groom, Linda, *A Steady Hand, Governor Hunter & His First Fleet Sketchbook*, National Library of Australia, 2012.

Hewison, Anthony, *The Macquarie Decade, Documents illustrating the History of New South Wales 1810-1820*, Cassell, Melbourne, 1972.

Heyck, Thomas William and Veldham, Meredith, *The People of the British Isles*, Lyceum Books, US, 2014.

Hill, Bridget, *Servants: English Domestics in the Eighteenth Century*, Clarendon Press, Oxford, 1996.

Hill, David, *1788: The Brutal Truth of the First Fleet*, Heinemann, Sydney, 2008.

――― *The Making of Australia*, William Heinemann, Sydney, 2015.

Hughes, Robert, *The Fatal Shore, A History of the Transportation of Convicts to Australia 1787-1868*, The Folio Society, London, 1998.

Karskens, Grace, *The Colony – A History of Early Australia*, Allen & Unwin, Crows Nest, 2010.

Keneally, Tom, *The Commonwealth of Thieves*, Random House, Sydney, 2005.

Australians, Origins to Eureka, Allen & Unwin, Crows Nest, 2009.

King, Jonathan, *The First Fleet, The Convict Voyage that founded Australia 1787-88*, Macmillan, Melbourne, 1982.

――― *Australia's First Fleet, The Voyage and The Re-enactment 1788/1988*, Fairfax, Robertsbridge, Sydney, 1987.

――― *The First Settlement, the Convict Village that Founded Australia 1788-90*, Macmillan, Melbourne, 1984.

Mingay, Gordon E., *Parliamentary Enclosure in England: An Introduction to its Causes*,

BIBLIOGRAPHY

Incidence and Impact 1750-1850, Longman, London, 1997.
Mundle, Rob, *The First Fleet*, ABC Books, HarperCollins, 2014.
———— *Bligh, Master Mariner*, Hachette Australia, 2010.
Murray, Robert and White, Kate, *Dharug & Dungaree - The History of Penrith and St Marys to 1860*, Hargreen, City of Penrith, 1988.
Nagle, J.F., *Collins, the courts & the colony: law & society in colonial New South Wales, 1788-1796*, UNSW Press, Sydney, 1996.
O'Brien, Eris, *The Foundation of Australia*, Angus and Robertson, Sydney, 1950.
Oldham, Wilfrid, *Britain's Convicts to the Colonies*, Library of Australian History, Sydney, 1990.
Pembroke, Michael, *Arthur Phillip - Sailor, Mercenary, Governor, Spy*, Hardie Grant Books, Melbourne, 2013.
Ritchie, John, *Lachlan Macquarie: A Biography*, Melbourne University Press, Carlton, 1986.
Robson, Leslie Lloyd, *The Convict Settlers of Australia*, Melbourne University Press, Carlton, 1994.
Ryan, R. J., *Land Grants 1788-1809*, Australian Documents Library, Sydney, 1981.
Shaw, A. G. L., *The Story of Australia*, Faber & Faber, London, 1955.
———— *Convicts & the Colonies, A Study of Penal Transportation from Great Britain & Ireland to Australia & other parts of the British Empire*, Melbourne University Press, Carlton, 1978.
Slattery, Luke, *The First Dismissal*, Penguin Specials, Melbourne, 2014.
Smith, Babette, *Australian Birthstain*, Allen & Unwin, Sydney, 2008.
Taylor, Sylvia, *Strands of Rope & Pulley*, Toormina, S. Taylor, ed Joan Fisher, 2000.
Withington, Ron, D*ispatched Downunder, Tracing the Resting Places of the First Fleeter*s, Fellowship of First Fleeters, Woolloomooloo, 2013.

ELECTRONIC SOURCES

Ancestry	www.ancestry.com.au
Australian Dictionary of Biography	adb.anu.edu.au
Birth, Death & Marriages NSW	www.bdm.nsw.gov.au
Biographical Database of Australia	www.bda-online.org.au
FamilySearch	www.familysearch.org
Fellowship of First Fleeters	www.fellowshipfirstfleeters.org.au
Findmypast	www.findmypast.com.au
Historical Land Record Viewer	hlrv.nswlrs.com.au
National Archives, UK	www.nationalarchives.gov.uk
National Library of Australia	www.nla.gov.au
Norfolk Family History Society, UK	www.norfolkfhs.org.uk
Norfolk Record Office, UK	www.archives.norfolk.gov.uk
Rope-Pulley Family Heritage Association	www.ropepulley.org
State Library NSW	www.sl.nsw.gov.au
State Archives & Records NSW	www.records.nsw.gov.au
Tasmanian Archive and Heritage Office	www.linc.tas.gov.au
Trove	www.trove.nla.gov.au

NOTES

PROLOGUE   A TRULY EPIC ADVENTURE

1   Arthur Phillip, *Governor Sailor Spy*, DVD, ABC, 2015.
2   Collins, 13 May 1787, I, p. Iv.
3   Arthur Phillip, *Governor Sailor Spy*, DVD, ABC, 2015.

CHAPTER 1   POVERTY & PUNISHMENT

1   Howard, 1st Ed, p. 7.
2   O'Brien, p. 23.
3   Mingay, p. 16.
4   Harte, p. 166.
5   Tomalin, Claire, *Jane Austen*, Vintage Books, New York, 1999, p. 98.
6   Colquhoun, pp. 437-440.
7   Brooke and Brandon, p. 18.
8   Ekirch, p. 1.
9   Ekirch, p. 151.
10 Oldham, p. 32.
11 Howard, 1st Ed, pp. 2-3, 16-17.
12 Howard, 4th Ed, p. 465.
13 Frost, *Botany Bay Mirages*, pp. 16, 25.
14 Oldham, pp. 47-48.
15 Howard, 4th Ed, p. 492.
16 Frost, *Botany Bay Mirages*, p. 20.
17 Howard, 1st Ed, p. 7.
18 Howard, 4th Ed, p. 492.
19 Howard, 4th Ed, p. 1.

CHAPTER 2   POOR RURAL YOUTH

1   Everett, Anthony, *Hadrian and the Triumph of Rome*, Random House, 2009, p. xiii.
2   Ibid.
3   The baptism date is 1 Aug 1756, not 1755, which is cited incorrectly in other histories.
4   A Copy of the Poll for the Knights of the Shire for the County of Norfolk, taken at Norwich, May 22, 1734, Norfolk, p. 117.
5   Heyck and Veldham, pp. 49, 57-58.
6   TNA: PRO (Taylor, p. 5).
7   Howard, 1st Ed, p. 217.
8   Howard, 4th Ed, pp. 259-261.
9   Cobley, *Crimes*, pp. 238-239.
10 TNA: T 1/637.
11 *Chelmsford Chronicle*, 11 Mar 1785.

12 *Chelmsford Chronicle*, 15 Jul 1785.
13 Convicts on *Ceres* hulk, 12 Apr – 12 Jul 1786, TNA: T 1/637.
14 Oldham, p. 62.
15 Oldham, Chap. 3; Frost, *Botany Bay Mirages*, pp. 28-29.
16 Convicts on *Justitia* hulk, 12 Apr – 12 Jul 1786, TNA: T 1/634.
17 Convicts on *Justitia* hulk, 12 Jul – 12 Oct 1786, TNA: T 1/638.
18 Oldham, pp. 199-200.
19 *Public Advertiser*, 29 Sep 1786.
20 Nepean to Shelton, 1 Jan 1787, HRNSW, I, ii, pp. 42-43; TNA: T1/641; Alexander Log, 6 Jan 1787, HRNSW, II, pp. 399; Oldham, p. 135.
21 Warrant for Transportation, 3 Jan 1787, TNA: HO 13/5, pp. 1-6.
22 Ibid.
23 Convicts on *Justitia* hulk, 12 Oct 1786 – 12 Jan 1787, TNA: T 1/641.

CHAPTER 3   FEMALE SERVITUDE

1 Hill, Bridget, p. 47.
2 Phillip, p. 277; TNA: HO 10/7; Cobley, *Crimes*, p. 225; Clark, p. 8.
3 TNA: IR 1/51, f 190.
4 Hill, Bridget, pp. 129-131.
5 NRO: C/S 1/2, MF 653.
6 *Norfolk Chronicle*, 17 July 1779.
7 Rope-Pulley Family Heritage Association, Newsletter, Mar 2012.
8 NRO: PD 184/11, p. 76.
9 Hill, Bridget, p. 53.
10 *Norfolk Chronicle*, 1 Jul 1780.
11 NRO: C/S 1/2, MF 653.
12 *Norfolk Chronicle*, 15 Jul 1780.
13 Howard, 4th Ed, p. 293.
14 Hill, Bridget, pp. 46-51.
15 Howard, 1st Ed, p. 295.
16 Karskens, p. 316.
17 Hill, Bridget, pp. 47-57.
18 Norwich Calendar of Prisoners, NRO: MF/RO 36/1.
19 *Norfolk Chronicle*, 11 Aug 1781.
20 Howard, 4th Ed, p. 295.
21 Howard, 4th Ed, pp. 4-5.
22 TNA: HO 42/9, p. 312.
23 *Norfolk Chronicle*, 11 Jan 1783.
24 Howard, 4th Ed, pp. 293-294.
25 Cobley, *Crimes*, p. 225.
26 *Norfolk Chronicle*, 22 Mar 1783.
27 Howard, 4th Ed, pp. 293-294.
28 Gillen, pp. 62, 176.
29 TNA: HO 13/1, pp. 300-302.

NOTES

30 TNA: HO 42/9.
31 NRO: MF/RO 36/1; *Norfolk Chronicle*, 14 Aug 1784 and 23 Jul 1785.
32 TNA: HO 13/4, p. 273.
33 *Bury and Norwich Post*, 1 Nov 1786.
34 *Norwich Chronicle*, 11 Nov 1786.
35 Ibid.
36 *Derby Mercury*, 30 Nov 1786.
37 Howard, 4th Ed, p. 293.
38 Convicts on *Dunkirk* hulk, 25 Sep – 25 Dec 1786, TNA: T 1/641.
39 Convicts on *Dunkirk* hulk, 26 Dec – 25 Mar 1787, TNA: T 1/644.

CHAPTER 4   BOTANY BAY SCHEME

1   *Morning Post and Daily Advertiser*, 17 Oct 1786.
2   Matra's Proposal, 23 Aug 1783, HRNSW, I, ii, pp. 1-8.
3   Ibid.
4   *London Chronicle*, 21 Nov 1786.
5   Heads of a Plan, 18 Aug 1786, HRNSW, I, ii, p. 17.
6   Sydney to Treasury, 18 Aug 1786, HRNSW, I, ii, p. 14.
7   Heads of a Plan, 18 Aug 1786, HRNSW, I, ii, p. 17.
8   Sydney to Admiralty, 31 Aug 1786, HRNSW, I, ii, pp. 20-22.
9   *Whitehall Evening Post*, 2 Sep 1786.
10 *London Chronicle*, 7 Sep 1786.
11 12 Sep 1786: *London Chronicle*; *Whitehall Evening News*; *British Evening Post*.
12 *London Chronicle*, 19 Sep 1786; *General Evening Post*, 28 Sep 1786.
13 *London Chronicle*, 23 Sep 1786.
14 *Norfolk Chronicle*, 14 Oct 1786.
15 *Morning Chronicle and London Advertiser*, 3 Oct 1786.
16 *Norfolk Chronicle*, 23 Sep 1786.
17 *Northampton Mercury*, 23 Sep 1786.
18 *Morning Post and Daily Advertiser*, 6 Oct 1786.
19 *Lloyd's Evening P*ost, 13 Oct 1786.
20 *Morning Post and Daily Advertiser*, 11 Nov 1786.
21 *Morning Post and Daily Advertiser*, 17 Oct 1786.
22 *Derby Mercury*, 12 Oct 1786; *General Advertiser*, 12 Oct 1786.
23 *General Evening Post*, 14 Oct 1786.
24 *Morning Herald*, 17 Nov 1786.
25 *Morning Herald*, 19 Nov 1786.
26 *Hereford Journal*, 23 Nov 1786.
27 *Morning Chronicle and London Advertiser*, 20 Oct 1786.
28 *General Evening Post*, 9 Nov 1786.
29 Frost, *First Fleet*, p. 25.
30 *Northampton Mercury*, 30 Sep 1786.
31 *Morning Herald*, 11 and 21 Nov 1786.
32 *General Evening Post*, 14 Dec 1786; *Morning Herald*, 19 Dec 1786.

33 *Gazetteer and New Daily Advertiser*, 5 Dec 1786.
34 *General Advertiser*, 8 Dec 1786.
35 *Morning Chronicle and London Advertiser*, 4 Dec 1786.
36 *General Evening Post*, 6 Jan 1787; *Norfolk Chronicle*, 13 Jan 1787.
37 *British Chronicle*, 12 Feb 1787.
38 Howe to Sydney, 3 Sep 1786, HRNSW, I, ii, p. 22.
39 Frost, *Arthur Phillip*; Pembroke, *Arthur Phillip*.
40 Pembroke, p. ix.
41 Frost, *Arthur Phillip*, pp. 3-7; Pembroke, pp. 1-12.
42 Pembroke, pp. 1-12.
43 Frost, *Arthur Phillip*, pp. 49-55.
44 Governor Phillip's First Commission, 12 Oct 1786, HRA, I, pp. 1-2.
45 Smyth, 7 Feb 1788, p. 68.
46 Governor Phillip's Second Commission, 2 Apr 1787, HRA, I, pp. 2-8; Governor Phillip's Instructions, 25 Apr 1787, HRA, I, pp. 9-16.
47 Phillip's Views, 28 Feb 1787, HRNSW, I, ii, p. 53.
48 Ibid
49 Frost, *First Fleet*, pp. 32-33.
50 Bateson, pp. 94-97; Mundle, *First Fleet*, pp. 315-334.
51 King, Philip Gidley, p. 514.
52 Order for Transportation, 6 Dec 1786, HRNSW, I, ii, pp. 30-31.
53 Warrant for Transportation, 3 Jan 1787, HRNSW, I, ii, p. 44.
54 *London Chronicle*, 19 Sep 1786.
55 Rations for marines, HRNSW, I, ii, p. 29.
56 Phillip to Nepean, 18 Mar 1787, HRNSW, I, ii, pp. 58-59.
57 Articles sent by First Fleet to Botany Bay, HRNSW, II, p. 388.
58 Navy Board Meeting, 7 Sep 1786, HRNSW, II, pp. 367-368.
59 Ibid.

CHAPTER 5   ASSEMBLING THE FLEET

1   Hunter, p. 1.
2   Admiralty to Sydney, 12 Oct 1786, HRNSW, I, ii, p. 24.
3   King, p. 513.
4   Second Captain of the Sirius, 15 Dec 1786, HRNSW, I, ii, p. 37.
5   *Alexander* logbook, 6 Jan 1787, HRNSW, II, p. 399; Phillip to Nepean, 11 Jan 1787, HRNSW, I, ii, p. 46.
6   Phillip to Nepean, 18 Mar 1787, HRNSW, I, ii, p. 59.
7   *Lady Penrhyn* Logbook, 6 Jan 1787, HRNSW, II, p. 406.
8   Johnston to Phillip, 11 Jan 1787, TNA: CO 201/2.
9   Phillip to Nepean, 11 Jan 1787, HRNSW, I, ii, p. 46.
10 *Alexander* logbook, 19 Jan 1787, HRNSW, II, p. 399.
11 Bradley, 19 Jan 1787, p. 5.
12 *Alexander* logbook, 19 Jan 1787, HRNSW, II, p. 400.
13 Surgeon White to Phillip, 7 Feb 1787, HRNSW, I, ii, p. 48.

14 Bradley, 5 - 22 Feb 1787, pp. 7-9.
15 White, March 1787, pp. 48-49.
16 Frost, *Botany Bay Mirages*, pp. 117-118; Oldham, pp. 136-137.
17 Phillip to Sydney, 28 Feb 1787, HRNSW, I, ii, p. 50.
18 Phillip to Sydney, 12 Mar 1787, HRNSW, I, ii, p. 57.
19 White, March 1787, p. 50.
20 Gillen, *Founders*; Mundle, *First Fleet*; Withington, *Dispatched Downunder*; Fellowship of First Fleeters.
21 *Northampton Mercury*, 31 Mar 1787.
22 White, March 1787, p. 51, *Alexander* logbook, 13 Mar – 2 Apr 1787, HRNSW, II, p. 400; Bradley, 23 Mar 1787, p. 10.
23 Frost, *First Fleet*, pp. 4, 147-148.
24 Phillip's Views, 28 Feb 1787, HRNSW, I, ii, p. 50; Phillip to Nepean, 1 Mar 1787, HRNSW, I, ii, p. 55.
25 TNA: T 1/644.
26 White, March 1787, p. 47.
27 Phillip to Nepean, 18 Mar 1787, HRNSW, I, ii, p. 59.
28 Clark, 13 Mar 1787, p. 1.; White, p. 47.
29 *British Chronicle*, 4 Jan 1787.
30 Bradley, 2 Mar 1787, p. 9; *Chelmsford Chronicle*, 2 Mar 1787.
31 Frost, *First Fleet*, p. 124.
32 Bradley, 2 Mar 1787, p. 9.
33 Bradley, 16 Mar 1787, p. 10; Tench, p. 17.
34 Hunter, p. 12.
35 Tench, p. 17.
36 Smyth, April 1787, pp. 11, 13.
37 Phillip's Second Commission, 2 Apr 1787, HRA, I, pp. 2-8; Phillip's Instructions, 25 Apr 1787, HRA, I, pp. 9-16.
38 Pembroke, p. 153.
39 Tench, pp. 17-18.
40 Ibid.
41 O'Brien, p. 282: 759 convicts (564 male and 191 females). Return of the Botany Bay detachment and convicts, 15 Apr 1787, HRNSW, I, ii, p. 79; Collins, I, p. Iv (756 convicts); Tench, p. 19 (757 convicts); Bradley, p. 16 (561 male, 192 female, 13 children); King, p. 514 (752 convicts).
42 Cobley, *Crimes*; Gillen, *Founders;* Fellowship of First Fleeters; Mundle, *First Fleet*.
43 King, pp. 513-514.
44 Ibid.
45 Phillip, p. 7; Return of Marines, 15 Apr 1787, HRNSW, I, ii, p. 79; Bradley, p. 15.
46 Cobley, *Crimes*; Gillen, *Founders;* Withington, *Dispatched Downunder*; Fellowship of First Fleeters; Mundle, *First Fleet*.
47 King, p. 514.
48 Gillen, *Founders*; Mundle, *First Fleet*; Fellowship of First Fleeters.

NOTES

49 Ibid.
50 Ibid.
51 Phillip to Nepean, 8 May 1787, HRNSW, I, ii, pp. 101-102.
52 Collins, 10 May 1787, I, pp. liv-lv.
53 White, 12 May 1787, p. 51.
54 Collins, 13 May 1787, I, p. lv; White, 13 May 1787, p. 52.

CHAPTER 6   PORTSMOUTH TO RIO

1   Phillip, p. 8.
2   Tench, p. 19.
3   Clark, 16 May 1787, p. 12.
4   Easty, 18 May 1787, p. 7; Phillip, p. 8; Hunter, 21 May 1787, pp. 3-4; White, 20 May 1787, p. 52.
5   *London Chronicle*, 2-5 Jun 1787.
6   Hunter, 15 May 1787, p. 4.
7   Tench, p. 20.
8   Clark, 20 May 1787, p. 13.
9   Clark, Details of Convicts, pp. 8-9.
10 Tench, p. 19.
11 Clark, pp. 2-9.
12 Sloan, Bernarr, *Convicts, Currency Folk and Chance*, 1993.
13 Clark, 18 and 22 Jul 1787, pp. 27, 29.
14 Nagle, p. 86.
15 Collins, 3 Jun 1787, I, p. lviii.
16 Phillip, p. 9.
17 Hunter, p. 6; King, Jun 1787, p. 519.
18 Phillip to Sydney, 5 Jun 1787, HRNSW, I, ii, pp. 106-107; Phillip to Nepean, 5 Jun 1787, HRNSW, I, ii, p. 108.
19 Clark, 4 Jun 1787, p. 16.
20 King, Jun 1787, pp. 520-521.
21 White, 23 Jun 1787, pp. 62-63.
22 Clark, 19 Jun 1787, p. 19.
23 White, 23 Jun 1787, p. 63.
24 White, 22 Jul 1787, p. 68.
25 White, 25 Jun 1787, p. 63.
26 Tench, p. 25.
27 Clark, 3 Jul 1787, p. 22.
28 Ibid.
29 Bradley, 5 Jul 1787, p. 29; White, 6 Jul 1787, p. 65.
30 White, 18 Jul 1787, p. 67.
31 White, 18 Jul 1787, p. 68.
32 Clark, 22 Jul 1787, p. 29.
33 Clark, 24 Jul 1787, p. 30.
34 Clark, 26 Jul 1787, p. 30.

NOTES

35 Clark, 1 Aug 1787, p. 32.
36 Clark, 2 Aug 1787, p. 32.
37 Clark, 3 Jul 1787, pp. 32-33.
38 Bradley, 2-6 Aug 1787, pp. 31-35.
39 Phillip, p. 15.
40 Nagle, p. 90.
41 Phillip to Nepean, 2 Sep 1787, HRNSW, I, ii, pp. 111-113; Phillip to Stephens, 2 Sep 1787, HRNSW, I, ii, pp. 114-115; Collins, Sep 1787, I, p. lxxv.
42 King, August 1787; p. 523; Phillip to Nepean, 2 Sep 1787, HRNSW, I, ii, p. 112.
43 Collins, Sep 1787, I, p. lxxv.
44 Phillip to Sydney, 2 Sep 1787, HRNSW, I, ii, pp. 110-112; Phillip to Nepean, 2 Sep 1787, HRNSW, I, ii, p. 113.
45 Hunter, Aug 1787, p. 12.
46 Easty, 12 Aug 1787, p. 30.
47 Collins, Aug 1787, I, p. lxxiv; Hunter, Aug 1787, p. 13.
48 Phillip to Nepean, 2 Sep 1787, HRNSW, I, ii, pp. 111-112.
49 Smyth, 10 Dec 1787, p. 48.
50 Phillip, p. 16.
51 Collins, Sep 1787, I, p. lxxv.
52 The pianoforte is preserved in good order at Edith Cowen University Musical School, Perth, WA.
53 Smyth, 7 and 20 Aug 1787, pp. 29, 35.
54 Smyth, 14 Aug 1787, p. 33.
55 Clark, 9 Aug 1787, p. 35.
56 White, 11 Aug 1787, p. 73.
57 Easty, 13 Aug 1787, p. 30.
58 Collins, Aug 1787, I, p. lxxiv.
59 Clark, 13 Aug 1787, p. 37.
60 *Alexander* logbook, 2 Sep 1787, HRNSW, II, p. 400.
61 Smyth, 9 Oct 1787, p. 39.

CHAPTER 7   FEMALE CONVICT BEHAVIOUR

1 Fidlon & Ryan, Introduction, *The Journal and Letters from Lt. Ralph Clark*, p. xvi.
2 Tench, p. 30.
3 Phillip, 4 Sep 1787, p. 17.
4 Hunter, 4 Sep 1787, p. 14.
5 Clark, 9 Sep 1787, p. 44.
6 Clark, 25 Sep 1787, p. 48.
7 Clark, 3 Oct 1787, p. 51.
8 4 Oct 1787: Collins, I, p. lxxvii; *Alexander* logbook, HRNSW, II, ii, p. 400.
9 Bradley, 6 Oct 1787, p. 41; Collins, Oct 1787, I, p. lxxvii.

NOTES

10 Smyth, 9 Oct 1787, p. 39.
11 Collins, Oct 1787, I, pp. 1xxvii-1xxviii.
12 King, 14 Oct 1787, HRNSW, II, p. 528; Collins, Oct 1787, I, p. 1xxviii.
13 Phillip to Stephens, 10 Nov 1787, HRNSW, I, ii, pp. 118-119; Collins, Oct 1787, I, p. 1xxviii; King, Oct 1787, HRNSW, II, p. 528.
14 Phillip to Stephens, 10 Nov 1787, HRNSW, I, ii, p. 119; Smyth, 14 Oct 1787, p. 40.
15 Collins, 9 Nov 1787, I, p. 1xxix.
16 Clark, *Letter to Kempster*, 8 Nov 1787, p. 259.
17 Collins, Nov 1787, I, 1xxix.
18 Smyth, 13 Oct 1787, p. 40.
19 Collins, Nov 1787, I, p. 1xxxi.
20 Collins, Oct 1787, I, pp. 1xxviii-1xxix.
21 Worgan, p. 1.
22 Bradley, 28 Oct 1787, p. 43; White, October 1787, p. 91.
23 Clark, 28 Oct 1787, pp. 61-62.
24 Clark, Letter to Kempster, 8 Nov 1787, p. 259.
25 *Prince of Wales* logbook, 28 Oct 1787, HRNSW, II, p. 404.
26 White, 11 Nov 1787, p. 101.
27 Fidlon & Ryan, Introduction, *The Journal and Letters from Lt. Ralph Clark*, pp. xvi-xvii.
28 Clark, 19 Jun 1787, p. 19.
29 Clark, 3 Jul 1787, p. 22.
30 Clark, 16 May 1787, p. 12.
31 Flannery, Tim, *The Birth of Sydney*, Text Publishing, Melbourne, 1999, p. 51.
32 Clark, *Letters*, pp. 241-245.
33 Fidlon & Ryan, front cover flap, The Journal and Letters from Lt. Ralph Clark.
34 Fidlon & Ryan, Introduction, *The Journal and Letters from Lt. Ralph Clark*, pp. xvi-xvii.
35 Keneally, pp. 293-297.
36 Ibid.
37 MacLaren, Mary, *The Four Elizabeths*, 2011, Xlibris, Bloomington, USA and *Elizabeth's New Life*, 2011, Xlibris, Bloomington, USA.
38 King, Jonathan, p. 17.
39 *Banished*, BBC TV Series, 2015.
40 Cobley, *Crimes*.

CHAPTER 8   LONG HAUL TO BOTANY BAY

1 Collins, 12 Nov 1787, I, pp. 1xxxv-1xxxvi.
2 Collins, 11-12 Nov 1787, I, p. 1xxxv.
3 Scott, 12 Nov 1787, p. 24.
4 Tench, p. 33.
5 Collins, Nov 1787, I, pp. 1xxxvi-1xxxvii.

NOTES

6   Ibid.
7   Phillip's Views, 1 Mar 1787, HRNSW, I, ii, pp. 50-51.
8   King, 19 Nov 1787, p. 531, Tench, p. 35; Collins, 16 Nov 1787, I, p. lxxxvii; Smyth, 19 Nov 1787, p. 43.
9   Smyth, 25 Nov 1787, pp. 44-45.
10 Ibid.
11 Tench, p. 35.
12 Hunter, 27 Nov 1787, p. 22.
13 Smyth, 29 Dec 1787 - 1 Jan 1788, p. 52.
14 Smyth, 1 Dec 1787, pp. 45-46.
15 Ibid.
16 Hunter, 1 Jan 1788, p. 24; Smyth, 9 Jan 1788, p. 54.
17 White, 20 Dec 1787, pp. 103-104.
18 *Alexander* logbook, 28 Dec 1787, HRNSW, II, p. 401.
19 King, 3 Jan 1788, p. 536; Phillip, 3 Jan 1788, p. 21.
20 *Alexander* logbook, 28 Dec 1787, HRNSW, II, p. 401.
21 Tench, 7 Jan 1788, pp. 35-36.
22 Smyth, 10 Jan 1788, p. 55.
23 Phillip, 18 Jan 1788, p. 21.
24 King, 18 Jan 1788, p. 539.
25 Ibid.
26 King, 19 Jan 1788, p. 540; Smyth, 19 Jan 1788, p. 56.
27 Tench, 19 Jan 1788, p. 37.
28 Phillip to Sydney, 15 May 1788, HRNSW, I, ii, p. 121.
29 Collins, Jan 1788, I, p. 1.
30 Ibid.
31 Collins, 31 Dec 1788, I, p. 41; Phillip, 30 Jun 1788, p. 67; White, p. 204.
32 Gillen, *Founders*; Fellowship of First Fleeters; Withington, *Dispatched Downunder*.
33 Hunter, 20 Jan 1788, p. 28.
34 Phillip, 20 Jan 1788, p. 23; *Alexander* logbook, 22 Jan 1788, HRNSW, II, p. 401.
35 Phillip, 22 Jan 1788, p. 23.
36 Hunter, 21 Jan 1788, p. 29.
37 Ibid.
38 Pembroke, pp. 117-118.
39 24 Jan 1788: Phillip, p. 27; Tench, pp. 38-39; King, p. 543.
40 Frost, *Arthur Phillip*, p. 166.
41 25 Jan 1788: Phillip, p. 27; King, p. 543; White, p. 111.

CHAPTER 9   A COLONY AT SYDNEY COVE

1   Tench, p. 77.
2   King, 26 Jan 1788, p. 543; Worgan, p. 7.
3   26 Jan 1788: Clark, p. 93; Smyth, p. 64.

NOTES

4   26 Jan 1788: Hunter, p. 29; Collins, I, p. 4.
5   Collins, Jan 1788, I, p. 5.
6   Ibid.
7   Smyth, 5 Feb 1788, p. 66.
8   Smyth, 6 Feb 1788, p. 67.
9   Ibid.
10 Ibid.
11 Clark, 7 Feb 1788, p. 96.
12 Karskens, Grace, *The myth of Sydney's foundational orgy* 2011, dictionaryofsydney.org/entry/the_myth_of_sydneys_foundational_orgy.
13 Ibid.
14 Karskens, pp. 313-315.
15 Tench, p. 45.
16 Phillip's Instructions, 25 Apr 1787, HRNSW, I, ii, p. 85.
17 7 Feb 1788: Smyth, pp. 67-69; Tench, pp. 47-50.
18 Phillip, 7 Feb 1788, p. 35.
19 Worgan, pp. 35-36; Smyth, 7 Feb 1788, p. 68.
20 Phillip, 7 Feb 1788, p.35; Worgan, p. 36.
21 Cobley, *1788*, p. 67.
22 Clark, 11 Feb 1788, p. 97.
23 Clark, 9, 11 and 20 Feb 1788, pp. 96-97, 100.
24 Tench, p. 49.
25 Hunter, pp. 49-50.
26 Phillip to Sydney, 15 May 1788, HRNSW, I, ii, p. 134.
27 Collins, February 1788, I, p. 7; Smyth, 8 Mar 1788, p. 77.
28 Phillip to Nepean, 16 May 1788, HRNSW, I, ii, pp. 138-139.
29 Collins, Feb 1788, I, p. 5; Smyth, 29 Feb 1788, p. 76.
30 Collins, Feb 1788, I, p. 11.
31 Phillip to Sydney, 16 May 1788, HRNSW, I, ii, p. 139.
32 Collins, Feb 1788, I, p. 8.
33 Ibid.
34 Smyth, 11 Feb 1788, p. 70.
35 King, Feb 1788, HRNSW, II, pp. 547-548.
36 Phillip, Mar 1788, p. 47.
37 Phillip, May 1788, p. 60.
38 Campbell, James, *Letters to Lord Ducie*, 12 Jul 1788, SLNSW: MLMSS 5366.
39 Ross to Nepean, 10 Jul 1788, HRNSW, I, ii, p. 176.
40 Cobley, *1788*, pp. 104-108.
41 Articles sent to Botany Bay, 10 May 1787, HRNSW, II, p. 388.
42 Phillip, p. 70.
43 Worgan, p. 10.
44 White, Mar 1788, p. 119; Phillip, p. 70.
45 Tench, p. 77.
46 Collins, Apr 1788, I, p. 20.
47 Tench, p. 77.

48   Collins, Jun 1788, I, p. 26.
49   Letter from Female Convict, 14 Nov 1788, HRNSW, II, pp. 746-747.
50   White, Jun 1788, p. 145.
51   Collins, I, pp. 16, 28, 71.
52   Bradley, 5-8 May 1788, p. 105; Phillip, 6 May 1788, p. 165.
53   Logbooks, 13-14 Jul 1788, HRNSW, II, pp. 399-401.
54   Hunter to Stephen, 20 Jan 1789, HRNSW, I, ii, pp. 225-226.
55   White, 15 Mar 1788, p. 119.
56   Tench, p. 64.
57   Phillip, p. 69.

CHAPTER 10   A HEARTY WEDDING SUPPER

1   Worgan, 2 Jun 1788, p. 52.
2   Gillen, p. 383.
3   Smyth, 10 Dec 1787, p. 48.
4   St. Philip's Church marriage register; SLNSW: SAG 90.
5   Cobley, *1788*, p. 153.
6   SANSW: NRS 2700, [5/1147A, pp. 37-43], Reel 2391.
7   Ibid.
8   4 June 1788: Collins, I, p. 25; Phillip, pp. 64-65; White, pp. 140-141; Worgan, pp. 52-54.
9   White, 4 Jun 1788, p. 140; Fowell, Newton, *Letters to his family*, 12 Jul 1788, SLNSW: SAFE/MLMSS 4895/1/18.
10   4 Jun 1788: Phillip, p. 64; Worgan, pp. 53-54.
11   Blackburn, David, *Letter to Richard Knight*, 12 Jul 1788, p. 10, SLNSW: Safe 1/120.
12   Collins, Jun 1788, I, p. 25.
13   Cobley, *1788*, pp. 172, 176.
14   Neal, David, *The Rule of Law in a Penal Colony: Law and Politics in Early New South Wales*, Cambridge University Press, 1991, p. 6.
15   Tench, p. 92.
16   Collins, Aug 1788, I, p. 30.
17   Collins, Oct 1788, I, p. 34.
18   Bradley, p. 136; White, p. 175.
19   Phillip to Stephens, 10 Jul 1788, HRNSW, I, ii, pp. 168-169.
20   Phillip to Nepean, 28 Sep 1788, HRNSW, I, ii, pp. 183-184.
21   Cobley, *1788*, p. 245; SLNSW: D 362.
22   Ryan, *Reminiscences*, p. 1.
23   Phillip to Nepean, HRNSW, I, ii, 9 Jul 1788, p. 154.
24   Phillip to Sydney, 15 May 1788, HRNSW, I, ii, pp. 126-127.
25   Phillip to Sydney, 9 Jul 1788, HRNSW, I, ii, p. 146.
26   Phillip to Nepean, 9 Jul 1788, HRNSW, I, ii, p. 155.
27   Phillip to Sydney, 28 Sep 1788, HRNSW, I, ii, pp. 185-193; Cobley, *1788*, 24 Sep 1788, p. 227.

28 State of the Stores in Sydney, HRA, I, p. 80.
29 Phillip to Nepean, 28 Sep 1788, HRNSW, I, ii, pp. 182-183; Phillip, 2 Oct 1788, p.79.
30 Collins, 2 Nov 1788, I, p. 37; Tench, 3 Nov 1788, p. 92.
31 Logbook *Fishburn*, 19 Nov 1788, HRNSW, II, p. 410.
32 Tench, p. 93.
33 Collins, 31 Dec 1788, I, p. 41.

CHAPTER 11   A STRUGGLING COLONY

1   Tench, p. 92.
2   Collins, Jan 1789, I, p. 42.
3   Hunter, King's Journal, Mar 1789, p. 241.
4   Tench, 6 Dec 1791, p. 219.
5   Cobley, *1789-1790*, 11 Feb 1789, p. 12.
6   Collins, Oct 1788, I, p. 35
7   Mar 1789: Tench, pp.101-102; Collins, I, pp. 47-48.
8   Collins, I, pp. 47-48.
9   Cobley, *1789-1790*, 7 Mar 1789, p. 19.
10 Cobley, *1789-1790*, 9 Mar 1789, p. 20.
11 Mar 1789: Collins, I, pp. 48-49; Tench, p. 102.
12 Collins, May 1789, I, pp. 54-56; Tench, May 1789, p. 106.
13 4 Jun 1789: Collins, I, pp. 57-58; Tench, p. 109.
14 SLNSW: SAG 90.
15 Gillen, p. 315.
16 Collins, Nov 1789, I, pp. 68-69.
17 Collins, Dec 1789, I, pp. 72-73.
18 Phillip to Sydney, 12 Feb 1790, HRNSW, I, ii, p. 298.
19 Grenville to Phillip, 10 Jun 1789, HRNSW, I, ii, pp. 252-253.
20 Riou to Stephens, 25 Feb 1790, HRNSW, I, ii, p. 311.
21 Ross to Nepean, 10 Jul 1788, HRNSW, I, ii, p. 176.
22 Phillip to Nepean, 20 Feb 1789, HRNSW, I, ii, pp. 228-229.
23 Phillip to Sydney, 5 June 1789, HRNSW, I, ii, pp. 236-239; Cobley, *1789-1790*, pp. 27-34.
24 Collins, Aug 1789, I, p. 63; Tench, Sep 1789, pp. 113-115.
25 Phillip to Sydney, 1 Feb 1790, HRNSW, I, ii, p. 288.
26 Ibid.

CHAPTER 12   SECOND FLEET ARRIVAL

1   Tench, pp. 119-120.
2   Hunter, Jan 1790, p. 117.
3   Hunter, Feb 1790, p. 118.
4   6 Mar 1790: Collins, I, pp. 80-81; Tench, p. 121; Phillip to Sydney, 11 Apr 1790, HRNSW, I, ii, p. 325.

NOTES

5   Hunter, Mar 1790, p. 123.
6   13-19 Mar 1790: Hunter, pp. 119-120; Bradley, pp. 191-195.
7   Phillip to Sydney, 11 Apr 1790, HRNSW, I, ii, p. 325.
8   Collins, Mar 1790, I, p. 81.
9   Letter by female convict, 24 Jul 1790, HRNSW, II, pp. 767-768.
10   Collins, Jul 1790, I, p. 61; Cobley, *1789-1790*, 31 Jul 1789, pp. 74-75.
11   Collins, 27 Mar 1790, I, pp. 81-82; Tench, p. 121.
12   Apr 1790: Collins, I, p.85; Tench, pp. 122-123.
13   Collins, Apr 1790, I, p. 87.
14   White to Skill, 17 Apr 1790, HRNSW, I, ii, pp. 332-333.
15   Collins, Apr 1790, I, p. 87.
16   Gillen, pp. 207-208.
17   Tench, Apr 1790, p. 123.
18   Collins, Apr 1790, I, p. 88.
19   Tench, Apr 1790, p. 124.
20   Collins, May 1790, I, p. 90; Cobley, *1789-1790*, May 1790, pp. 196-197.
21   Tench, 3 Jun 1790, pp. 126-127.
22   Collins, Jun 1790, I, pp. 93-97; Tench, 3 Jun 1790, pp. 127-128.
23   Phillip to Grenville, 20 Jun 1790, HRNSW, I, ii, p. 352.
24   Collins, 6 Jun 1790, I, p. 96.
25   Ibid.
26   Tench, 9 Jun 1790, p. 129.
27   20 June 1790: Collins, I, pp. 97-98; Tench, p. 130.
28   Phillip to Grenville, 13 Jul 1790, HRNSW, I, ii, p. 355; Tench, Jun 1790, p. 131; Collins, Jun 1790, I, p. 100.
29   Collins, Jun 1790, I, p. 99; Tench, p. 132.
30   Letter by female convict, 24 Jul 1790, HRNSW, II, pp. 767-768.
31   Collins, Jun 1790, I, p. 100.
32   Tench, p. 132.
33   O'Brien, pp. 171-172.
34   Phillip to Grenville, 17 Jul 1790, HRNSW, I, ii, pp. 361-362.
35   Phillip to Nepean, 10 Jul 1790, HRNSW, I, ii, p. 354.
36   Cobley, *1789-1790*, p. 228.
37   Phillip to Nepean, 24 Jul 1790, HRNSW, I, ii, p. 365.
38   Hunter, Phillip's Journal, p. 302; Collins, 28 Aug 1790, I, p. 108.
39   Collins, Aug 1790, I, p. 108.
40   Collins, I, pp. 113-114, 119; Tench, pp. 150-151, 178; Hunter, Phillip's Journal, pp. 335-336.
41   Hunter, *Phillip's Journal*, pp. 314, 337; Tench, Nov 1790, p. 151.
42   Tench, p. 132.
43   Collins, Jul 1790, I, p. 103.
44   Collins, Aug 1790, I, p. 108.
45   Hunter, 23 Jul 1790, p. 304; Tench, 6 Dec 1791, p. 219.
46   Phillip to Grenville, 20 Jun 1790, HRNSW, I, ii, p. 352.
47   Tench, 16 Nov 1790, pp. 155-156.

NOTES

48 Ibid.
49 Tench, 16 Nov 1790, p. 159.
50 Collins, Nov 1789, I, p. 71.
51 Tench, p. 126.
52 7 Sep 1790: Collins, I, pp. 110-111; Cobley, *1789-1790*, pp. 281-284; Tench, pp. 138-139; Nagle, p. 104; Hunter, pp. 308-309.
53 Collins, Sep 1790, I, p. 112.

CHAPTER 13   FIRST SETTLERS

1 Frost, *Arthur Phillip*, p. 208.
2 Collins, Jan and Mar 1791, I, pp. 121, 130.
3 Collins, Jan 1791, I, p. 121.
4 Tench, 16 Nov 1790, p. 159.
5 Phillip to Sydney, 12 Feb 1790, HRNSW, I, ii, p. 298.
6 State of the Settlement, 18 Nov 1791, HRNSW, I, ii, pp. 560-561; Tench, 3 Dec 1791, p. 225.
7 Frost, *Botany Bay Mirages*, pp. 213-214.
8 Tench, Dec 1791, p. 235.
9 Letter by Surgeon's Mate, 13 Jan 1790, HRNSW, II, p. 771.
10 Nicol, p. 131.
11 Collins, Feb 1789, I, p. 44.
12 Cobley, *1791-1792*, p. 54.
13 Phillip's Instruction, 25 Apr 1787, HRNSW, I, ii, p. 90; Collins, April 1791, I, pp. 130-131.
14 Collins, Apr 1791, I, p. 132.
15 Phillip to Nepean, 17 Jun 1790, HRNSW, I, ii, p. 349; Hunter, p. 301.
16 Collins, Apr 1791, I, pp. 130, 132; Tench, 1 May 1791, pp. 184-185.
17 Collins, Apr 1791, I, pp. 130-131.
18 Tench, 2 Apr 1791, p. 182.
19 Collins, 4 Jun 1791, I, p. 137; Cobley, *1791-1792*, p. 78.
20 Tench, 4 Jun 1791, p. 203.
21 Collins, 9 Jul 1791, I, p. 140.
22 Grenville to Phillip, 19 Feb 1791, HRA, I, p. 217.
23 Collins, I, pp. 131, 141; Tench, Jul 1791, p. 206.
24 Collins, Aug 1791, I, p. 144.
25 SANSW: NRS 898, [9/2731, p. 8], Fiche 3267.
26 Tench, 5 Dec 1791, pp. 216-217.
27 Hunter, p. 356.
28 Tench, 5 Dec 1791, p. 217.
29 Return of Lands, 5 Nov 1791, HRNSW, I, ii, pp. 540-541.
30 Hunter, p. 351.
31 Tench, 6 Dec 1791, p. 219.
32 Parish Map of Field of Mars, HLRV: AO MAP 25765.
33 Cobley, *1791-1792*, 29 Oct 1791, p. 137.

NOTES

34   Hunter, p. 361.
35   Hunter, p. 367.
36   Tench, 6 Dec 1791, p. 220.
37   Phillip to Grenville, 5 Nov 1791, HRNSW, I, ii, p. 538; Collins, Oct 1791, I, p. 151.
38   Collins, Sep 1791, I, p. 148.
39   Collins, Aug 1791, I, p. 145.
40   Cobley, *1791-1792*, 15 Nov 1791, p. 157; Collins, Dec 1791, I, p. 156.
41   Phillip to Grenville, 5 Nov 1791, HRNSW, I, ii, p. 533.
42   Currey, C.H., *Mary Bryant*, ADB.
43   Tench, pp. 211-212; Collins, Nov 1791, I, pp. 154-155.
44   Phillip to Grenville, 5 Nov 1791, HRNSW, I, ii, p. 537.
45   Hunter, pp. 371-372.
46   Ibid.
47   Tench, 3 – 8 Dec 1791, pp. 212-224.
48   Tench, 6 Dec 1791, pp. 219-220.
49   Gillen, pp. 121-122.
50   Tench, 6 Dec 1791, p. 220; Gillen, p. 203.
51   Tench, 6 Dec 1791, p. 219.
52   Tench, Dec 1791, p. 210.
53   Cobley, *1791-1792*, 17 Oct 1791, pp. 128-129.
54   Cobley, *1791-1792*, 12, 13 Dec 1791, pp. 190-191; Collins, Dec 1791, I, p. 159.
55   Cobley, *1791-1792*, 16 Dec 1791, p. 195.

CHAPTER 14   **PHILLIP'S DEPARTURE**

1   Cobley, *1791-1792*, 18 Dec 1791, pp. 197-198. Mary Ann Parker was accompanying her husband John Parker, Captain of the HMS *Gorgon* and stayed with Phillip during their time in Sydney.
2   Phillip to Sydney, 15 Apr 1790, HRNSW, I, ii, p. 329.
3   Phillip to Nepean, 15 Apr 1790, HRNSW, I, ii, p. 330.
4   Phillip to Grenville, 25 Mar 1791, HRA, I, p. 262.
5   Cobley, *1791-1792*, 11 Nov 1791, p. 154.
6   Cobley, *1791-1792*, 17 Nov 1791, p. 158.
7   Frost, *Arthur Phillip*, p. 218; Pembroke, p. 214.
8   Tench, 6 Dec 1791, p. 219.
9   Cobley, *1791-1792*, 10 Jan 1792, p. 209.
10   SANSW: NRS 898, [9/2731, p. 8], Fiche 3267; NRS 13836, [7/445], Reel 2560.
11   SANSW: NRS 1215, [SZ75], Reel 2910.
12   Phillip to Dundas, 19 Mar 1792, HRNSW, I, ii, p. 597.
13   Collins, Jan 1792, I, pp. 163-164.
14   Collins, 14 Feb 1792, I, pp. 167-168.
15   Grose to Nepean, 2 Apr 1792, HRNSW, I, ii, p. 613.

NOTES

16 Phillip to Nepean, 29 Mar 1792, HRNSW, I, ii, pp. 610-613.
17 Collins, Apr and May 1792, I, pp. 170, 172, 175.
18 Cobley, *1791-1792*, 20 Apr 1792, p. 251.
19 Phillip to Dundas, 19 Mar 1792, HRNSW, I, ii, p. 597.
20 Collins, Apr 1792, I, p. 172.
21 Collins, May 1792, I, p. 177.
22 Collins, May 1792, I, pp. 176-178.
23 Cobley, *1791-1792*, 21 May 1792, pp. 261-262.
24 Collins, May 1792, I, p. 177.
25 Collins, I, pp. 179-183, 188, 199, 206.
26 Phillip to Dundas, 2 Oct 1792, HRNSW, I, ii, p. 646.
27 Collins, Aug 1792, I, pp. 192-193.
28 Cobley, *1791-1792*, Sep 1792, p. 303.
29 Collins, Oct 1792, I, p. 200.
30 Collins, Oct 1792, I, p. 203; Phillip to Nepean, 16 Oct 1792, HRNSW, I, ii, pp. 669-670.
31 State of the Settlements, 8 Dec 1792, HRNSW, I, ii, pp. 676-677.
32 Collins, Dec 1792, I, pp. 209-210.
33 A Return of Land in Cultivation, 16 Oct 1792, HRA, I, p. 402.
34 Collins, Dec 1792, I, p. 210; SANSW: NRS 898, [9/2731], Fiche 3267.
35 Collins, Dec 1792, I, p. 210.
36 Collins, Dec 1792, I, p. 211.
37 Easty, 11 Dec 1792, pp. 142-143.
38 Phillip to Dundas, 23 Jul 1793, HRNSW, II, p. 59.
39 Phillip to unknown, 26 Oct 1793, HRNSW, II, p. 75; Governor Phillip and his Successor, 30 Dec 1793, HRNSW, II, p. 813.

CHAPTER 15   THE RUM CORPS

1 Cobley, *1793-1795*, Sep 1793, p. 68.
2 Collins, Oct 1794, I, p. 330.
3 Hunter to Portland, 10 Aug 1796, HRNSW, III, p. 65.
4 Dundas to Phillip, 14 Jul 1792, HRNSW, I, ii, p. 632; Phillip to Dundas, 2 Oct 1792, HRNSW, I, ii, p. 647.
5 Phillip to Dundas, 4 Oct 1792, HRNSW, I, ii, p. 651.
6 Clune & Turner, p. 57; Steven, M., *John Macarthur*, ADB.
7 Collins, 12 Dec 1792, I, 213; Cobley, *1791-1792*, 12 Dec 1792, p. 352.
8 Cobley, *1791-1792*, 12 Dec 1792, p. 353.
9 Collins, Dec 1792, I, p. 214.
10 Collins, Dec 1792, I, p. 213.
11 Cobley, *1791-1792*, 12 Dec 1792, p. 352; Collins, I, Dec 1792, p. 214; Grose to Dundas, 9 Jan 1793, HRA, I, p. 414.
12 Karskens, p. 125.
13 Collins, Jan 1793, I, pp. 219-220.
14 Collins, Feb 1793, I, p. 227.

NOTES

15 Cobley, *1793-1795*, 25 Feb 1793, p. 15.
16 Grose to Dundas, 16 Feb 1793, HRNSW, II, p. 15.
17 Collins, Dec 1793, I, p. 275.
18 Collins, Jul 1793, I, p. 251.
19 Cobley, *1793-1795*, Sep 1793, pp. 68-69.
20 Cobley, *1793-1795*, pp. 69, 178.
21 Cobley, *1793-1795*, Jun 1793, p. 47.
22 Collins, Aug 1793, I, p. 259.
23 Collins, Oct 1793, I, p. 269; Ryan, *Land Grants*, pp. 5, 19.
24 Dundas to Grose, 30 Jun 1793, HRNSW, II, pp. 50-51.
25 Grose to Dundas, 3 Sep 1793, HRNSW, II, pp. 62-64; Collins, Sep 1793, I, p. 260.
26 Collins, Dec 1793, I, p. 272.
27 Johnson, 3 Sep 1793, HRNSW, II, p. 65.
28 Collins, Jan 1794, I, p. 284.
29 Collins, Jan 1794, I, p. 285.
30 Collins, Mar 1794, I, pp. 299-300.
31 Collins, Aug 1794, I, p. 322.
32 Collins, Dec 1794, I, p. 337.
33 Collins, I, pp. 161, 337.
34 Collins, Mar 1795, I, p. 344.
35 Grose to Dundas, 31 Aug 1794, HRNSW, II, p. 254.
36 State of the Settlements, 4 Mar 1795, HRNSW, II, p. 289.
37 Hunter to Portland, 12 Nov 1796, HRA, I, p. 667.
38 Ibid.
39 Barkley-Jack, pp. 29-30, 53.
40 Cobley, *1793-1795*, p. 281.
41 Currey, *Collins*, pp. 80-81.
42 Return of Land Grants, 25 Sep 1800, HRA, II, p. 566.
43 Cobley, *1795-1800*, Oct 1795, pp. 8-9; Hunter to Portland, 21 Dec 1795, HRA, I, p. 550.
44 Hunter to Portland, 10 Jan 1798, HRA, II, p. 117.
45 Collins, Oct1795, I, p. 361.
46 Cobley, *1795-1800*, pp. 39-40; Collins, Feb 1796, I, pp. 379-380.
47 Government and General Order, 5 Feb 1796, HRNSW, III, pp. 15-16; Hunter to Paterson, 7 Feb 1796, HRNSW, III, p. 17.
48 Memorandum, 7 Mar 1796, HRNSW, III, pp. 20-22.
49 Portland to Hunter, 31 Aug 1797, HRA, II, p. 106.
50 Government and General Order, 8 Feb 1796, HRNSW, III, pp. 17-18.
51 Macarthur to Hunter, 24 Feb 1796, HRA, II, p. 95.
52 Collins, Jan 1796, I, p. 376.
53 Collins, Jun 1796, I, pp. 399-401.
54 General State of Districts of Settlement, 20 Aug 1796, HRA, I, p. 596; Collins, Jun 1796, I, p. 401.
55 General State of Districts of Settlement, 20 Aug 1796, HRA, I, p. 596.

NOTES

56 Barkley-Jack, pp. 10-13.
57 Collins, Jun 1796, I, pp. 401-402; Cobley, *1795-1800*, Jun 1796, p. 68.
58 Government and General Order, 29 Feb and 11 Jul 1796, HRNSW, III, pp. 29, 58.
59 Cobley, *1795-1800*, Jul 1796, pp. 75-77.
60 HRNSW, III, pp. 119-135.
61 Ryan, *Land Grants*, p. 56; SANSW: NRS 898, [9/2731], Fiche 3267.
62 Currey, John, *David Collins: A Colonial Life*; Nagle, John Flood, *Collins, the courts and the colony: law & society in colonial New South Wales 1788-1796*.

CHAPTER 16   FLOODS & DEBTS

1 Ryan, *Reminiscences*, p. 3.
2 Collins, Feb 1797, II, p. 16; Barkley-Jack, p. 229.
3 Cobley, *1795-1800*, 3-5 Jul 1797, p. 155.
4 Cobley, *1795-1800*, p. 457.
5 Ryan, *Reminiscences*, p. 1.
6 Ryan, *Reminiscences*, pp. 3, 114.
7 Counter, Chris, *Tumbledown Barn*, 1997, Riverstone Historical Society.
8 Barkley-Jack, pp. 110-111, Lot 209.
9 Ryan, *Land Grants*, p. 130; Barkley-Jack, pp. 110-113.
10 Counter, Chris, *Tumbledown Barn*, 1997, Riverstone Historical Society.
11 Collins, Jan 1795, I, p. 339; Barkley-Jack, p. 289; Ryan, *Land Grants*, pp. 32, 132.
12 O'Brien, p. 220.
13 Government and General Order, 14 Jan 1797, HRNSW, III, pp. 189-190.
14 Collins, Mar 1797, II, pp. 18-19; Government and General Order, 14 Apr 1797, HRNSW, III, p. 204.
15 Hunter to Portland, 20 Jun 1797, HRA, II, p. 22.
16 Hunter to Portland, 10 Jan 1798, HRA, II, p. 117.
17 Ibid.
18 Hunter to Portland, 2 Mar 1798, HRA, II, p. 135.
19 Settlers' Statement to Hunter, 19 Feb 1798, HRA, II, pp. 136-140.
20 Report Marsden and Arndell, HRA, II, 2 Mar 1798, pp. 144-146.
21 Settlers' Statement to Hunter, 19 Feb 1798, HRA, II, pp. 136-140.
22 Report Marsden and Arndell, HRA, II, 2 Mar 1798, pp. 144-146.
23 Cobley, *1795-1800*, May 1798, p. 218.
24 Portland to Hunter, 31 Aug 1797, HRNSW, III, p. 297; Portland to Hunter, 5 Nov 1799, HRNSW, III, p. 735.
25 Collins, Apr 1798, II, pp. 77, 84.
26 Portland to Hunter, 22 Feb 1797, HRA, II, p. 7.
27 Macarthur to Portland, 15 Sep 1796, HRA, II, pp. 90-93.
28 Collins, Sep 1796, I, p. 410.
29 Howe, George, *New South Wales Pocket Almanack and Colonial Remembrancer*, 1806.

NOTES

30 Hunter to Portland, 1 May 1799, HRA, II, p. 354-355; Collins, Mar 1799, II, p. 143.
31 Collins, I, pp. 339, 357-358.
32 Collins, Nov 1799, II, p. 195.
33 Government and General Order, 21 Dec 1796, HRNSW, III, p. 186; Hunter to Portland, 7 Jan 1800, HRA, II, pp. 433-434.
34 Expenses of Farming at Hawkesbury, 14 Jan 1800, HRA, II, pp. 435-436.
35 State of the Settlement, 31 Dec 1799, 15 Feb 1800, HRA, II, p. 468-469.
36 Petition of Settlers to Hunter, 1 Feb 1800, HRA, II, pp. 445-446.
37 Hunter's Reply to Hawkesbury Petition, 8 Feb 1800, HRA, II, p. 450.
38 Hunter to Portland, 20 Mar 1800, HRA, II, p. 474; Collins, Mar 1800, II, p. 206.
39 Portland to Hunter, 26 Feb 1799, HRA, II, pp. 338-340.
40 King to King, 3 May 1800, HRA, II, p. 505.
41 Settlers' Muster Book, SLNSW: SAFE/MLMSS 1225 (Safe 1/104).
42 Barkley-Jack, p. 256.
43 Government and General Order, 10 Jul 1800, HRNSW, IV, p.115.
44 King to Paterson, 18 Sep 1800, HRA, II, p. 543; Paterson to King, 18 Sep 1800, HRA, II, p. 544.
45 King to Hunter, 6 Jul 1800, HRA, II, p. 656.
46 O'Brien, p. 251.
47 Hunter, John, *Governor Hunter's Remarks on the Causes of the Colonial Expense of the Establishment of New South Wales*, Printed S. Gosnell, London, 1802.
48 General Orders, 1 Oct 1800, HRA, II, p. 622.
49 Government and General Order, 12 Jan 1801, HRNSW, IV, pp. 288-289.
50 SANSW: NRS 898, [2/8130, pp. 363-365], Reel 6020.
51 Ibid.
52 King to Portland, 10 Mar 1801, HRA, III, p. 10.
53 Ryan, *Reminiscences*, p. 114.
54 Barkley-Jack, pp. 414-415.
55 King to Portland, 10 Mar 1801, HRA, III, p. 10.
56 Petition of Hawkesbury Settlers, Jun 1801, HRA, III, pp. 134-135. (no names are registered)
57 King's General Order, 23 Jun 1801, HRA, III, pp. 135-136.
58 Government and General Order, 20 Jun and 14 Jul 1801, HRNSW, IV, pp. 409-410, 442.
59 Settlers' Muster Book, SLNSW: SAFE/MLMSS 1225 (Safe 1/104).
60 Barkley-Jack, p. 165.
61 Ryan, *Land Grants*, pp. 18, 46.
62 Cobley, *1795-1800*, p. 80, 308; Gillen, p. 62.
63 Baxter, *1800 -1802*.
64 Government and General Orders, 25 May 1802, HRNSW, IV, p. 771.
65 King to Portland, 8 Jul 1801, HRA, III, pp. 111-112.
66 King to Portland, 21 Aug 1801, HRA, III, pp. 187-222, 246.
67 King to Portland, 5 Nov 1801, HRA, III, pp. 276-286.

NOTES

68   King to King, 8 Nov 1801, HRA, III, p. 325.
69   King to Portland, 14 Nov 1801, HRA, III, p. 331.
70   King to King, 14 Nov 1801, HRA, III, p. 345.
71   Tucker, Michelle Scott, *Elizabeth Macarthur*, Text, 2018.

CHAPTER 17   GOVERNORS KING & BLIGH

1   Sydney Settler's to Bligh, 22 Sep 1806, HRNSW, VI, p. 189.
2   King to Johnston, 18 Feb 1803, HRA, IV, p. 216.
3   Introduction, HRA, IV, pp. xi-xii.
4   King to Portland, 10 Feb 1801, HRA, III, p. 48.
5   King to Hobart, 21 Feb 1803, HRA, IV, p. 333.
6   Addresses from Settlers, 29 Mar 1803, HRA, IV, pp. 502-503.
7   King to Hobart, 9 May 1803, HRA, IV, p. 85.
8   King to Portland, 21 Mar 1802, HRA, III, p. 490.
9   Frost, *Banks*, pp. 142-144.
10 Ibid.
11 King to Hobart, 23 Nov 1802, HRA, III, p. 737.
12 King to Bowen, 9 May 1803, HRA, IV, p. 152.
13 King to Hobart, 1 Mar 1804, HRA, IV, pp. 454-455.
14 Johnston to Paterson, 9 Mar 1804, HRA, IV, pp. 569-570; King to Hobart, 12 Mar 1804, HRA, IV, pp. 563-564, 566.
15 King to Hobart, 12 Mar 1804, HRA, IV, pp. 563-564, 577.
16 Ryan, *Reminiscences*, pp. 1-3.
17 Ryan, *Land Grant*, p. 122; Barkley-Jack, pp. 110-111, 113, 439; HLRV: AO MAP 282.
18 *Sydney Gazette*, Sunday 31 Mar 1805.
19 Ibid.
20 Ibid.
21 King to Camden, 20 Jul and 1 Nov 1805, HRA, V, pp. 510, 576.
22 Evatt, pp. 58-59.
23 King to Cooke, 6 Jan 1806, HRA, V, p. 632.
24 Ryan, *Land Grants*, pp. 157, 166.
25 TNA: HO 10/37.
26 Ryan, *Land Grants*, p. 175; Murray and White, pp. 43-44.
27 Frost, *Banks*, p. 142.
28 Ibid.
29 King to Cook, 1 Nov 1805, HRA, V, pp. 613-615.
30 *Sydney Gazette*, 30 Mar 1806; Marsden to King, 26 Mar 1806, HRNSW, VI, p. 827.
31 Inundation of Hawkesbury, SLNSW: FL3505620; Marsden to King, 26 and 28 Mar 1806, HRNSW, VI, pp. 54, 826-827.
32 King to Camden, 7 Apr 1806, HRA, V, p. 698.
33 Ryan, *Land Grants*, p. 157; Byrnes, J. V., *Andrew Thompson*, ADB.
34 Government and General Orders, 11 May 1806, HRNSW, VI, p. 72.

35 *Sydney Gazette*, 11 May 1806.
36 King family correspondence, SLNSW: CY 906, p. 49.
37 TNA: HO 10/37.
38 Castlereagh to King, 13 Jul 1805, HRA, V, p. 489.
39 King to Hobart, 14 Aug 1804, HRA, V, p. 116.
40 Evatt, pp. 69-70.
41 Introduction, HRA, VI, p. xi.
42 Ryan, *Land Grants*, pp. 184, 190-191.
43 Address to Governor Bligh, 14 Aug 1806, HRNSW, VI, pp. 165-166.
44 *Sydney Gazette*, 17 Aug 1806; Hawkesbury Settlers Address, Sep 1806, SLNSW: SAFE/Banks Papers/Series 40.109.
45 Settlers Address, 22 Sep 1806, HRNSW, VI, pp. 188-192.
46 Bligh to Banks, 7 Feb 1807, SLNSW: SAFE/Banks Papers/Series 40.71.
47 Regulations of Vessels, 4 Oct 1806, HRNSW, VI, pp. 193-195.
48 Bligh to Windham, 5 Nov 1806, HRA, VI, pp. 26-27.
49 Bligh to Windham, 7 Feb 1807, HRA, VI, p. 123.
50 Commentary, HRA, VI, p. 731.
51 Ryan, *Reminiscences*, p. 3.
52 Ryan, *Land Grant*, p. 182; HLRV: AO Map 237; Baxter, *Muster 1828*, p. 574.
53 *Sydney Gazette*, 28 May 1814; SANSW: NRS 897, [4/1730, pp. 393-395a], Reel 6044.

CHAPTER 18   THE RUM REBELLION

1   Gore to Castlereagh, 27 Mar 1808, HRNSW, VI, p. 552.
2   Hawkesbury Settlers to Bligh, 29 Jan 1807, HRA, VI, pp. 577-578.
3   Bligh to Windham, 7 Feb 1807, HRA, VI, p. 122.
4   Castlereagh to Bligh, 31 Dec 1807, HRA, VI, p. 201.
5   Government and General Order, 14 Feb 1807, HRNSW, p. 253.
6   Hawkesbury Settlers to Bligh, 25 Feb 1807, SLNSW: SAFE/Banks Papers/Series 40.116.
7   Mrs. King's farm stock books, SLNSW: MLMSS 710, CY 1192.
8   Casey & Lowe Pty Ltd, Archaeological Assessment Central Precinct, St Marys Development, July 2008, pp. 26-27.
9   *Sydney Gazette*, 29 Dec 1821.
10 Proclamation, 3 Jan1807, HRNSW, VI, p. 236.
11 Trial of Macarthur, 5 Jul 1807, HRNSW, VI, pp. 485-488.
12 Evatt, p. 109.
13 Bligh to Windham, 31 Oct 1807, HRA, VI, pp. 188-190.
14 Government and General Order, 23 Jul 1807, HRNSW, VI, p. 276.
15 D'Arcy Wentworth, 17 Oct 1807, HRNSW, VI, pp. 327-328.
16 *Sydney Gazette*, 16 Aug 1807.
17 Bligh to Castlereagh, 31 Oct 1807, HRA, VI, pp. 602-603.
18 Gore to Castlereagh, 31 Oct 1807, HRNSW, VI, p. 371.
19 Bligh to Windham, 31 Oct 1807, HRA, VI, pp. 155-156, 714-715.

NOTES

20 Grimes to Macarthur, 13 Jan 1808, HRNSW, VI, pp. 413-414; Macarthur to Grimes, HRNSW, 14 Jan 1808, VI, p. 417; Introduction, HRA, VI, p. xxii.
21 Bligh to Banks, 10 Oct 1807, SLNSW: SAFE/Banks Papers/Series 40.72.
22 Ibid.
23 Ibid.
24 Bligh to Windham, 31 Oct 1807, HRA, VI, pp. 150, 152.
25 Introduction, HRA, VI, p. xx.
26 Trial of Macarthur, 2 Feb 1808, HRNSW, VI, pp. 466, 471-472; Bligh to Castlereagh, 30 Apr 1808, HRNSW, VI, pp. 609-610.
27 Trial of Macarthur, 2 Feb 1808, HRNSW, VI, p. 471.
28 Johnston to Castlereagh, 11 Apr 1808, HRA, VI, pp. 298, 313.
29 Macarthur to Bligh, 29 Dec 1807, HRNSW, VI, pp. 395-396.
30 Examination of Andrew Thompson, 27 Jan1808, HRNSW, VI, p. 451.
31 Settlers' Address to Bligh, 1 Jan 1808, SLNSW: SAFE/Banks Papers/Series 40.92.
32 Ibid.
33 Evatt, pp. 150-151.
34 Atkins to Bligh, 11 Apr 1808, HRA, VI, p. 238; Trial of Macarthur, 25 Jan 1808, HRNSW, VI, p. 422.
35 Bligh to Johnston, 26 Jan 1808, HRNSW, VI, p. 433.
36 Johnston to Castlereagh, 11 Apr 1808, HRA, VI, pp. 211-212.
37 Johnston to Gaol Keeper, 26 Jan 1808, HRNSW, VI, p. 433; Macarthur to Johnston, 26 Jan 1808, HRA, VI, pp. 240, 723-724.
38 Bligh to Castlereagh, 30 Apr 1808, HRA, VI, p. 432.
39 Bligh to Castlereagh, 30 Apr 1808, HRA, VI, pp. 421, 430-432.
40 Gore to Castlereagh, 27 Mar 1808, HRNSW, VI, p. 558.
41 Evatt, pp. 176-177.
42 Gore to Castlereagh, 27 Mar 1808, HRNSW, VI, p. 560.
43 Finding of Court, 2 Feb 1808, HRNSW, VI, p. 510.
44 Johnston to Castlereagh, 11 Aug 1808, HRA, VI, p. 216-219.
45 Government and General Order, 6 Feb 1808, HRNSW, VI, p. 511.
46 Bligh to Castlereagh, 30 Jun 1808, HRA, VI, pp. 530-531, 550.
47 Steven, M., *John Palmer*, ADB; Bligh to Castlereagh, 30 Apr 1808, HRA, VI, pp. 439-440.
48 Deposition of Captain Kemp, 11 Apr 1808, HRA, VI, p. 397.
49 Settlers to Johnson, 11 Apr 1808, HRNSW, VI, pp. 572-573.
50 Ryan, *Land Grants*, pp. 131; TNA: HO 10/37.
51 Hardy, Bobbie, *Early Hawkesbury Settlers*, Kangaroo Press, 1985, p. 143.
52 Bligh to Castlereagh, 31 Aug 1808, HRA, VI, pp. 588-589.
53 Hall, Annegret, *Doctor Redfern*, pp. 51-52.
54 Proclamation, 31 Jul 1808, HRNSW, VI, p. 701.
55 Foveaux to Paterson, 16 Aug 1808, HRA, VI, p. 633.
56 Bligh to Castlereagh, 30 April, 31 Aug 1808, HRA, VI, pp. 440, 605.
57 *Sydney Gazette*, 28 Aug and 2 Oct 1808; SANSW: NRS 5607, [2/8286, pp. 29-36], Reel 2232.

NOTES

58 Mason to Bligh, 20 Aug 1808, HRNSW, VI, pp. 702-703.
59 Settlers' Petition to Castlereagh, 4 Nov 1808, HRNSW, VI, pp. 802-804.
60 Parsons, V., *George Suttor*, ADB.

CHAPTER 19 BLIGH DEFIES THE REBELS

1 Evatt, p. 275.
2 Foveaux to Castlereagh, 20 Feb 1809, HRA, VII, p. 3.
3 Correspondence, Jan 1809, HRA, VII, pp. 33-35.
4 Fulton to Castlereagh, 23 Mar 1809, HRNSW, VII, p. 88.
5 Settlers to Castlereagh, 17 Feb 1808, HRNSW, VII, p. 34.
6 Correspondences, Jan 1809, HRA, VII, pp. 36-39; Paterson to Bligh, 30 Jan 1809, HRNSW, VII, pp. 12-13; Fulton to Castlereagh, 23 Mar 1809, HRNSW, VII, pp. 86-87.
7 Paterson to Bligh, 2 Feb 1809, HRNSW, VII, p. 16; Agreement Bligh and Paterson, 4 Feb 1809, HRNSW, VII, pp. 17-18; Bligh to Castlereagh, 10 June 1809, HRA, pp. 120-123.
8 Bligh to Castlereagh, 10 Jun 1809, HRA, VII, pp. 123-124.
9 Bligh to Paterson, 22 Feb 1809, HRNSW, VII, p. 45.
10 Hawkesbury Settlers to Bligh, 17 Mar 1809, HRNSW, VII, pp. 78-79.
11 Fulton to Castlereagh, 23 Mar 1809, HRNSW, VII, pp. 86-87; Proclamation by Bligh, 12 Mar 1809, HRNSW, VII, p. 66.
12 Bligh to Castlereagh, 10 June 1809, HRA, p. 124.
13 Paterson to Castlereagh, 12 Mar 1809, HRA, VII, p. 23.
14 Bligh to Castlereagh, 10 June 1809, HRA, VII, pp. 125-128.
15 Settlers to Bligh, 10 Jun 1809, HRA, VII, pp. 159-160; Collins General Order, 8 Jul 1809, HRA, VII, p. 165; Bligh to Castlereagh, 8 Jul 1809, HRA, VII, p.161.
16 Collins, 6 Aug 1809, HRA, VII, pp. 175-176.
17 Settlers to Castlereagh, 4 Nov 1808, HRNSW, VI, pp. 802-804.
18 *Sydney Gazette*, 4 Jun 1809 and 6 Aug 1809.
19 Flood at Hawkesbury, 3 Jun 1809, HRNSW, VII, p. 165; *Sydney Gazette*, 6 Aug 1809.
20 *Sydney Gazette*, 6 Aug 1809; Government and General Order, 8 Aug 1809, HRNSW, VII, p. 204.
21 Introduction, HRA, VII, p. xix.
22 King to Windham, 12 Aug 1806, HRA, V, p. 773; Return of Land Grants, 25 Sep 1800, HRA, II, p. 566; Ryan, *Land Grants*, p. 191.
23 Macquarie to Liverpool, 13 Nov 1812, HRA, VII, p. 549.
24 Ryan, *Land Grants*, pp. 202, 210, 262, 297, 300.
25 Introduction, HRNSW, VI, p. xxx; Admiralty to Cook, 29 Apr 1809, HRNSW, VII, p. 110.
26 Castlereagh to Bligh, 15 May 1809, HRA, VII p. 87; Proclamation, 1 Jan 1810, HRNSW, VII, pp. 252-253; Macquarie to Castlereagh, 8 Mar 1810, HRA, VII, p. 218.

NOTES

27 Castlereagh to Macquarie, 14 May 1809, HRA, VII, pp. 81-82.
28 *Sydney Gazette*, 7 Jan 1810.
29 Proclamation by Macquarie, 11 Jan 1810, HRA, VII, p. 231.
30 Lachlan Macquarie papers, SLNSW: MLMSS 2920X, CY 301; *Sydney Gazette*, 21 Jan 1810.
31 Macquarie to Castlereagh, 30 Apr 1810, HRA, VII, p. 277; Lachlan Macquarie papers, SLNSW: MLMSS 2920X, CY 301, frames 25-26.
32 Lachlan Macquarie papers, SLNSW: MLMSS 2920X, CY 301.
33 Ibid.
34 *Proceedings of a General Court-Martial for the Trial of Lieut. Col. Geo. Johnston*, Sherwood, Neely and Jones, London, 1811.
35 Macquarie to Castlereagh, 30 Apr 1810, HRA, VII, pp. 257-258; Bligh to Banks, 11 Aug 1810, HRNSW, VII, p. 404.
36 Macquarie to Castlereagh, 10 May 1810, HRA, VII, p. 331.
37 SLNSW: Safe 4/5, IE3203670.
38 *Proceedings of a General Court-Martial for the Trial of Lieut. Col. Geo. Johnston*, Sherwood, Neely and Jones London, 1811, pp. 408-409.
39 Michael Duffy, *Man of Honour: John Macarthur*.
40 *Windsor and Richmond Gazette*, 9 Jul 1892; William Bligh, Wikipedia.
41 Ryan, *Reminiscences*, pp. 323-324.
42 Bligh to Castlereagh, 10 June 1809, HRNSW, VII, p. 172.
43 Evatt, *Rum Rebellion*.

CHAPTER 20   MACQUARIE & EQUALITY

1 Macquarie to Bathurst, 28 Jun 1813, HRA, VII, pp. 775-776.
2 Macquarie to Castlereagh, 30 Apr 1810, HRA, VII, p. 276.
3 Government and General Order, 7 Apr 1810, HRNSW, VII, p. 328.
4 Macquarie to Liverpool, 27 Oct 1810, HRA, VII, p. 347; Lachlan Macquarie papers, SLNSW: MLMSS 2920X, CY 301.
5 Macquarie to Castlereagh, 30 Apr 1810, HRA, VII, pp. 249-252; Government Public Notice, 9 Jun 1810, HRNSW, VII, p. 387.
6 Government and General Order, 15 Dec 1810, HRNSW, VII, p. 469.
7 *Sydney Gazette*, 18 Aug 1810.
8 Hassall family - Day sales books, SLNSW: A 862-3, CY 1213, pp. 190-191, 194, 204.
9 Ibid.
10 Ryan, *Reminiscences*, pp. 20-21.
11 Hassall family - Day sales books, SLNSW: A 862-3, CY 1213, pp. 267, 269, 288.
12 Macquarie, *Journals of his tours*, p. 19.
13 Macquarie to Castlereagh, 30 Apr 1810, HRA, VII, p. 249.
14 Macquarie, *Journals of his tours*, p. 32.
15 Macquarie, *Journals of his tours*, p. 39.
16 *Sydney Gazette*, 6 Apr 1811.

NOTES

17 SANSW: NRS 2658, [5/1105], case 163.
18 Old Bailey Proceedings, 18 Jul 1810, t18100718-8; TNA: HO 77/18, HO 10/4.
19 TAHO: 602894, CUS33/1/3 p. 41.
20 Ryan, *Reminiscences*, pp. 13-14.
21 *Sydney Gazette*, 2 Mar 1811.
22 SANSW: NRS 845, [4/8481, p. 63], Reel 2754; *The Monitor*, 7 Jun 1828.
23 *Australian*, 17 Jan 1834; SANSW: NRS 2514, Reel 852 and 855.
24 TAHO: CON31/1/21 p. 279.
25 House of Commons, Report, *1812*, pp. 34, 36, 46.
26 House of Commons, Report, *1812*, pp. 13-15.
27 SANSW: NRS 2659, [5/1108], case 404.
28 Macquarie to Bathurst, 28 Jun 1813, HRA, VII, pp. 775-776.
29 Ibid.
30 Macquarie to Bathurst, 28 Jun 1813, HRA, VII, p. 722.
31 Government and General Order, 5 Feb 1814, HRA, VIII, pp. 257-258.
32 Macquarie to Bathurst, 24 May 1814, HRA, VIII, pp. 255-256.
33 Macquarie to Bathurst, 28 Apr 1814, HRA, VIII, p. 144.
34 SANSW: NRS 898, [9/2652, p. 16], Fiche 3266.
35 Parish of Londonderry, HLRV: AO MAP 237.
36 SANSW: NRS 1273, Reel 2552; Commentary, HRA, X, p. 835.
37 Ryan, *Reminiscences*, p. 51.
38 *Sydney Gazette*, 15 Oct 1814.
39 SANSW: NRS 1260, [4/1225], Reel 1252.
40 Inhabitants, 24 Jun 1815, HRA, VIII, p. 600.
41 Cultivation, 24 Jun 1815, HRA, VIII, p. 601; Macquarie to Liverpool, 17 Nov 1812, HRA, VII, p. 559.
42 BDA, http://www.bda-online.org.au/files/MC1814_Muster.pdf.
43 Macquarie to Bathurst, 28 Apr 1814, HRA, VIII, p. 154.
44 *Sydney Gazette*, 25 Jun 1814.
45 *Sydney Gazette*, 10 Sep 1814; Macquarie to Bathurst, 4 Dec 1817, HRA, IX, p. 509.
46 Ellis, p. 324.
47 Murray and White, pp. 111-115, 336-338; William Cox Journal, SLNSW: SAFE/C 708/2.
48 TNA: HO 27/3 p. 8; HO 9/4; HO 11/2.
49 Macquarie to Bathurst, 24 Mar 1815, HRA, VIII, p. 464.
50 SANSW: NRS 1165, [4/4430, p. 90], Reel 774.
51 Government and General Orders, 31 Dec 1814, HRA, VIII, p. 472.
52 Macquarie to Bathurst, 24 Mar 1815, HRA, VIII, p. 466.
53 General Minutes of the Supreme Court, 11 May 1815, HRA, VIII, p. 515.
54 Macquarie to Bathurst, 22 Jun 1815, HRA, VIII, pp. 483-484.
55 Macquarie to Bathurst, 1 Jul 1815, HRA, VIII, p. 621.
56 Bathurst to Macquarie, 18 Apr 1816, HRA, IX, p. 107.

NOTES

CHAPTER 21 PROSPERITY FOR EMANCIPISTS

1. Macquarie to Bathurst, 31 Mar 1817, HRA, IX, p. 237.
2. SANSW: NRS 4563, [4/7860], case 90.
3. Macquarie to Bathurst, 1 Dec 1817, HRA, IX, pp. 500-501.
4. Old Bailey Proceedings, July 1814, (t18140706-106); TNA: HO 9/7, HO 10/10.
5. Ryan, *Reminiscences*, p. 3.
6. Ryan, *Reminiscences*.
7. Macquarie to Bathurst, 31 Mar 1817, HRA, IX, p. 237.
8. Macquarie to Bathurst, 1 Dec 1817, HRA, IX, p. 499.
9. Macquarie to York, 25 Jul 1817, HRA, IX, p. 444; Macquarie to Torrens, 20 Sep 1817, HRA, IX, p. 487.
10. Number of Convicts, 1810-1816, HRA, X, p. 808.
11. Shaw, Convicts & Colonies, p. 365.
12. King to Hobart, 14 Aug 1804, HRA, V pp. 74-75.
13. *Sydney Gazette*, 10 Sep 1814 and 14 Dec 1816.
14. Ryan, *Reminiscences*, pp. 9-10.
15. Harris, p. 126.
16. SANSW: NRS 897, [4/1773, p. 6], Reel 6059.
17. SANSW: NRS 1273, Reel 2552.
18. *Sydney Gazette*, 22 Jun 1816.
19. Macquarie to Castlereagh, 30 Apr 1810, HRA, VII, p. 265.
20. Macquarie to Bathurst, 29 Mar 1817, HRA, IX, p. 223; Charter of the Bank of New South Wales, 29 Mar 1817, HRA, IX, pp. 223-227, 231.
21. Macquarie to Bathurst, 1 Dec 1817, HRA, IX, pp. 495-501.
22. Macquarie to Goulburn, 24 Sep 1817, HRA, IX, p. 488.
23. *Sydney Gazette*, 20 Jan 1816.
24. Macquarie to Goulburn, 21 Dec 1817, HRA, IX, p. 747.
25. *Sydney Gazette*, 24 and 31 Jan 1818.
26. Macquarie to Marsden 8 Jan 1818, SLNSW: A 797 (Safe 1/385).
27. *Sydney Gazette*, 28 Mar 1818; Ellis, p. 451.
28. SANSW: NRS 12992, Reel 1572.
29. TNA: HO 9/9; HO 10/8, HO 10/1/1.
30. SANSW: NRS 900, [4/1857, pp. 31-31a], Fiche 3192.
31. SANSW: NRS 897, [4/1744, pp. 311-315], Reel 6049.
32. SANSW: NRS 900, [4/1862, p. 27], Fiche 3206.
33. Government Orders, 9 Jul 1813, HRA, VII, pp. 783-784.
34. SANSW: NRS 1264, Reel 1256.
35. Macquarie to Bathurst, 24 Mar 1819, HRA, X, pp. 88-93.
36. SANSW: NRS 1264, Reel 1256.
37. Commission to Bigge, 30 Jan 1819, HRA, X, p. 3.
38. Bathurst to Bigge, 6 Jan 1819, HRA, X, pp. 4-8.
39. Ibid.
40. Macquarie to Bathurst, 22 Feb1 1820, HRA, X, p. 224.

NOTES

41 Macquarie, *Letter to Viscount Sidmouth*, 1819, pp. 91-92.
42 Macquarie, *Letter to Viscount Sidmouth*, 1821, pp. 72, 77.
43 Macquarie to Bathurst, 29 Feb 1820, HRA, X, p. 291.
44 Arago, pp. 160-163.
45 Macquarie to Bathurst, 10 Oct 1823, SLNSW: D Q82/30.
46 Macarthur Onslow, Sibella, *Some early records of the Macarthurs of Camden*, Angus & Robertson, Sydney, 1914, pp. 349-355.
47 Ibid.
48 Bathurst to Macquarie, 15 Jul 1820, HRA, X, p. 314.
49 Macquarie to Bathurst, 1 Sep 1820, HRA, X, p. 352.
50 Macquarie to Bathurst, 1 Sep 1820, HRA, X, pp. 351-364; Wylde to Macquarie, 1 Sep 1820, HRA, X, pp. 363-364.
51 Macquarie to Bathurst, 22 Oct 1821, HRA, X, p. 557.
52 Emancipists to King, 22 Oct 1821, HRA, X, pp. 549-554.
53 SANSW: NRS 899, [4/1837A No. 360 pp. 399-400], Fiche 3088.
54 SANSW: NRS 900, [4/1863, pp. 57-58a], Fiche 3210; NRS 898, [9/2652, pp. 66,71], Fiche 3266.
55 Address to Macquarie, 12, 15 Dec 1821, HRA, X, pp. 702-705.
56 Macquarie to Bathurst, 30 Nov 1821, HRA, X, p. 573.
57 Bathurst to Macquarie, 18 May 1820, HRA, X, p. 306.
58 Macquarie to Bathurst, 21 Mar 1821, HRA, X, p. 481.
59 *Sydney Gazette*, 1 Dec 1821.
60 Population, 30 Nov 1821, HRA, X, p. 575.
61 Lachlan Macquarie papers, SLNSW: MLMSS 2920X, CY 302; *Sydney Gazette*, 15 Feb 1822.
62 Bigge, John Thomas, *Report of the Commissioner of Inquiry into the state of the colony of New South Wales*, London, 1822.
63 *Monitor*, 27 Jan 1827.
64 *Colonist*, 5 Feb 1835.

CHAPTER 22   CURRENCY LADS & LASSES

1 Cunningham, p. 53.
2 Commission of Goulburn, June 1820, HRA, X, p. 664.
3 *Sydney Gazette*, 8 and 22 Dec 1821.
4 Brisbane to Bathurst, 10 Apr 1822, HRA, X, pp. 630-631.
5 *Sydney Gazette*, 25 Jan and 12 Jul 1822.
6 Bathurst to Brisbane, 9 Sep 1822, HRA, X, p. 790.
7 Brisbane to Bathurst, 6 Sep 1822, HRA, X, pp. 761, 849.
8 Brisbane to Bathurst, 27 Feb 1822, HRA, X, p. 625.
9 Bathurst to Brisbane, 26 Mar 1823, HRA, XI, pp. 61-62; James Macarthur to Goulburn, 17 Oct 1823, HRA, XI, pp. 185-186.
10 Memorial from Colonists, August 1822, HRA, X, pp. 738-744.
11 *Sydney Gazette*, 19 July 1822.
12 *Sydney Gazette*, 26 July 1822.

NOTES

13 Wentworth family papers, 1783-1827, SLNSW: CY 774, 1822, p. 1.
14 SANSW: NRS 1260, Reel 1252; Baxter, *1822*, p. 285.
15 Harris, pp. 121-122.
16 Bathurst to Brisbane, 31 Mar 1823, HRA, XI, p. 73.
17 Lang, pp. 204-205.
18 Bathurst to Brisbane, 4 Mar 1825, HRA, XI, p. 529.
19 Lang, p. 206.
20 Brisbane to Bathurst, 1 May 1824, HRA, XI, pp. 254-258.
21 Warrant Appointing a Council, 19 Jan 1824, HRA, XI, pp. 195-196; *Sydney Gazette*, 12 Aug 1824.
22 SANSW: NRS 898, [4/6671, p. 70], Reel 6023; NRS 2514, Roll 850.
23 Brisbane to Bathurst, 24 Jul 1824, HRA, XI, pp. 331-334.
24 SANSW: NRS 899, [4/1839A, No 843, pp. 397, 493], Fiche 3108; NRS 899, [4/1837A, No. 360, pp. 399-400], Fiche 3088.
25 SANSW: NRS 896, [4/1839A, No 842, pp. 489-492], Fiche 3108.
26 SANSW: NRS 937, [4/3512, pp. 356, 375], Reel 6013.
27 SANSW: NRS 899, [4/1837A, No. 361, p. 401], Fiche 3088.
28 SANSW: NRS 937, [4/3513, pp. 457-458], Reel 6014.
29 Cunningham, pp. 53, 56-57.
30 Cunningham, pp. 54, 63, 116.
31 Ryan, *Reminiscences*, p. 301.
32 *Australian*, 14 Oct 1824.
33 Brisbane to Bathurst, 12 Jan 1825, HRA, XI, pp. 470-471.
34 Ryan, *Reminiscences*, pp. 17-18.
35 SANSW: NRS 897, [4/1785 p. 183a], Reel 6063.
36 SANSW: NRS 897, [4/1786, p. 167], Reel 6057.
37 SANSW: NRS 12200, [4/4060], Reel 890.
38 TNA: HO 10/20.
39 Australian Agricultural Company, 17 Apr 1825, HRA, XI, p. 563.
40 *Sydney Gazette*, 4 Nov 1824.
41 SANSW: NRS 937, [4/3513, p. 548], Reel 6014; NRS 938, [4/5782, pp. 299-301], Reel 6017.
42 SANSW: NRS 898, [2/1925, p.11], Fiche 3260.
43 Bathurst to Brisbane, 18 May 1825, HRA, XI, p. 591; *Sydney Gazette*, 15 Dec 1825.
44 *Sydney Gazette*, 22 Dec 1825.
45 Bathurst to Darling 26 Jul 1826, HRA, XII, p. 447.
46 Brisbane to Horton, 24 Mar 1825, HRA, XI, pp. 552-553.
47 Bathurst to Brisbane, 29 Dec 1824, HRA, XI, pp. 429-430; Brisbane to Bathurst, 15 May 1825, HRA, XI, p. 589.
48 Bathurst to Brisbane, 1 Jan 1825, HRA, XI, pp. 436-437, 455-456.
49 Ibid.
50 Oxley to Darling, 22 Jul 1826, HRA, XII, pp. 380-386.
51 Lang, p. 209.
52 *Australian*, 27 Oct 1825.

53 *Australian*, 20 Oct 1825.
54 Lang, p. 214.
55 Lang, pp. 192-193.
56 *Sydney Gazette*, 1 Dec 1825.

CHAPTER 23   DESPOTISM & DYSFUNCTION

1   *Sydney Monitor*, 6 Dec 1828.
2   Introduction, HRA, XII, p. xii; *Sydney Gazette*, 19 Dec 1825.
3   Proclamation, 21 Dec 1825, HRA, XII, p. 128.
4   SANSW: NRS 845, [4/8475, No 39, pp. 371-376], Reel 2753.
5   Ibid.
6   SANSW: NRS 845, [4/8475, No 39, pp. 377, 380], Reel 2753.
7   *Australian*, 19 Jan 1826.
8   Darling to Hay, 10 Feb 1827, HRA, XIII, p. 106.
9   *Australian*, 9 Dec 1826.
10 Ryan, *Reminiscences*, pp. 14, 35.
11 Ryan, *Reminiscences*, pp. 26-27.
12 SANSW: NRS 12212, [4/4511].
13 TNA: HO 9/8; SANSW: NRS 1264, Reel 1253; TNA: HO 10/20.
14 *Australian*, 14 Feb 1827.
15 *Sydney Gazette*, 7 Oct 1826.
16 SANSW: NRS 907, [27/1165].
17 *Timespan*, No 38, 1990.
18 Oxley to Darling, 22 Jul 1826, HRA, XII, p. 386.
19 Darling to Bathurst, 4 Dec 1826, HRA, XII, pp. 715-720.
20 Darling to Horton, 15 Dec 1826, HRA, XII, pp. 761-763.
21 *Sydney Monitor*, 27 Sep 1828.
22 Darling to Huskisson, 20 Jun 1828, HRA, XIV, pp. 231-232.
23 Darling to Huskisson, 10 Apr 1828, HRA, XIV, p. 139.
24 Darling to Huskisson, 23 Sep 1828, HRA, XIV, p. 401.
25 *Sydney Gazette*, 29 Oct 1829.
26 Ryan, *Reminiscences*, pp. 16-17.
27 Darling to Huskisson, 29 Jul 1828, HRA, XIV, p. 258.
28 SANSW: NRS 1273, Reel 2552; NRS 907, [27/1167]; TNA: HO 10/26.
29 SANSW: NRS 1273, Reel 2552.
30 Ibid.
31 TNA: HO 77/21, f. 8; SANSW: NRS 898, [4/424, p. 7], Reel 6039; NRS 1174, [6/884], Reel 798.
32 Shaw, *Convicts & Colonists*, p. 366; SANSW: NRS 1286, Reel 176.
33 Darling to Goderich, 10 Oct 1827, HRA, XIII, p. 547.
34 Lack, Clem, Journal of the Royal Historical Society of Queensland, Vol 9, Issue 2, pp. 28-40.
35 *Monitor*, 17 May 1828.
36 Wentworth to Murray, 1 Mar 1829, HRA, XIV, pp. 800-859.

37 Hall to Murray, 2 May 1829, HRA, XV, pp. 61-67.
38 Ibid.
39 Hall to Murray, 17 Nov 1828, HRA, XIV, p. 581.
40 Fletcher, p. 229.
41 *Sydney Gazette*, 23 Dec 1830.
42 Fletcher, p. 287.
43 Darling to Hay, 2 Sep 1826, HRA, XII, p. 523.
44 Fletcher, p. 291.
45 Darling to Murray, 4 Feb 1830, HRA, XV, pp. 355-356.
46 Goderich to Darling, 6 Jan and 15 Mar 1831, HRA, XVI, pp. 11-12, 111.
47 Darling to Goderich, 14 Sep 1831, HRA, XVI, pp. 353-354.
48 Parish map of Londonderry, HLRV: AO MAP 237.
49 SANSW: NRS 13836, [7/449], Reel 2561; *Sydney Monitor*, 26 Sep and 1 Oct Sep 1831; *Sydney Herald*, 10 Oct 1831; *Government Gazette*, 11 Apr and 31 Oct 1832.
50 SANSW: NRS 907 [34/4801], [34/6138], [34/8280], [35/4633], [34/7704].
51 *Sydney Monitor*, 22 Oct 1831.
52 *Australian*, 21 Oct 1831.
53 *Australian*, 2 Dec 1831.
54 Lang, pp. 235-237.
55 *Sydney Gazette*, 21 Sep 1827.

CHAPTER 24   END OF THE CONVICT ERA

1 Ryan, *Reminiscences*, p. 13.
2 *Sydney Monitor*, 3 and 7 Dec 1831.
3 *Australian*, 9 Dec 1831.
4 King, Hazel, *Sir Richard Bourke*, ADB.
5 *Australian*, 16 Dec 1831.
6 Goderich to Bourke, 10 Jul 1831, HRA, XVI, p. 297; *Sydney Monitor*, 21 Jan 1832.
7 Bourke to Goderich, 27 Feb 1832, HRA, XVI, p. 532.
8 *Government Gazette*, 4 Apr 1832.
9 *Sydney Herald*, 28 May 1832.
10 Bourke to Goderich, 6 and 22 Feb 1832, HRA, XVI, pp. 515, 527.
11 Bourke to Howick, 28 Feb 1832, HRA, XVI, pp. 543-545.
12 Ibid.
13 Bourke to Goderich, 24 Sep 1832, HRA, XVI, p. 760.
14 Clark, Manning, Vol 2, p. 210.
15 Bourke to Goderich, 30 Oct and 3 Nov 1832, HRA, XVI, pp. 780-781, 788-789; Bourke to Stanley, 15 Jan 1834, HRA, XVII, pp. 324-325.
16 Petition, 19 Sep 1834, HRA, XVII, pp. 540-541.
17 *Sydney Gazette*, 31 May 1832; *Sydney Herald*, 7 Jan 1833.
18 *Government Gazette*, 5 Jun 1833.
19 *Windsor and Richmond Gazette*, 18 May 1895.

NOTES

20 *Sydney Gazette*, 8 Dec 1832.
21 *Leicester Chronicle*, 28 Jul 1832.
22 Shaw, *Convicts & Colonies*, p. 148.
23 Hine, Jane D., *Ralph Clark*, ADB.
24 *Sydney Gazette*, 29 Jan 1833.
25 Bourke to Stanley, 25 Dec 1833, HRA, XVII, p. 306.
26 Goderich to Bourke, 6 Nov 1831, p. 443; Shaw, *Convicts & Colonies*, p. 366; Martin, Robert Montgomery, *Statistics of the Colonies of the British Empire*, London, 1839, p. 418.
27 Bourke to Stanley, 15 Jan 1834, HRA, XVII, p. 314.
28 *Sydney Monitor*, 14 Sep 1833.
29 *Sydney Herald*, 13 Feb 1834.
30 Bourke to Stanley, 15 Jan 1834, HRA, XVII, pp. 322-330.
31 *Sydney Monitor*, 5 Nov 1834.
32 SANSW: NRS 12992, Reel 1578.
33 Commentary, HRA, XVII, p. 785.
34 *Sydney Herald*, 6 Jun 1833.
35 Bourke to Aberdeen, 1 Aug 1835, HRA, XVIII, p. 57.
36 Glenelg to Bourke, 26 Feb 1836, HRA, XVIII, p. 297.
37 Bourke to Glenelg, 16 Sep 1836, HRA, XVIII, p. 543.
38 *Sydney Monitor*, 26 Sep 1835.
39 Bourke to Glenelg, 14 Oct 1835, HRA, XVIII, pp. 161-163; *Government Gazette*, 4 Nov 1835.
40 Bourke to Aberdeen, 25 Jul 1835, HRA, XVIII, p. 48.
41 *Sydney Monitor*, 9 Oct 1833; *Sydney Herald*, 16 Nov 1835.
42 Darwin, pp. 455-456.
43 Ibid.
44 Darwin, p. 468-470.
45 *Sydney Monitor*, 6 Jan 1836; Bourke to Glenelg, 1 Mar 1836, HRA, XVIII, p. 333-341.
46 Petition, 13 Apr 1836, HRA, XVIII, pp. 392-395.
47 *Sydney Herald*, 8 Feb 1836.
48 *Australian*, 15 Apr 1836; Petition, 13 Apr 1836, HRA, XVIII, pp. 399-403.
49 Bourke to Glenelg, 25 Jul 1836, HRA, XVIII, p. 456.
50 *Sydney Herald*, 14 Apr 1836.
51 *Sydney Monitor*, 23 Apr 1836.
52 Worgan, p. 36.
53 Bourke to Glenelg, 14 Sep 1836, HRA, XVIII, p. 537.
54 Bourke to Glenelg, 8 Aug and 16 Sep 1836, HRA, XVIII, pp. 466-470, 543; Glenelg to Bourke, 27 Feb 1837, HRA, XVIII, pp. 695-696.
55 *Government Gazette*, 1 Feb 1837.
56 Bourke to Glenelg, 3 Jan 1837, HRA, XVIII, p. 637.
57 *Sydney Herald*, 5 Jan 1837.
58 Bourke to Glenelg, 30 Jan 1837, HRA, XVIII, p. 660.
59 Glenelg to Bourke, 3 Jul 1837, HRA, XIX, p. 4.

NOTES

60 Ryan, *Reminiscences*, pp. 39-40, 73-76.
61 Withington, p. 182.
62 *Australian*, 5 Dec 1837.
63 *Sydney Monitor*, 6 Dec 1837; *Sydney Gazette*, 7 Dec 1837.
64 *Colonist*, 20 Jan 1838.
65 *Commercial Journal*, 28 Feb 1838.
66 Gipps to Glenelg, 1 May 1838, HRA, XIX, p. 401.
67 Gipps to Glenelg, 18 Jul 1838, HRA, XIX, p. 504; *Sydney Gazette*, 28 Jun 1838.
68 Gipps to Glenelg, 8 Oct 1838, HRA, XIX, pp. 603-604; *Government Gazette*, 19 Dec 1838.
69 *Sydney Herald*, 11 Feb 1839.
70 Persse, Michael, *William Wentworth*, ADB.
71 Russell to Gipps, 6 Jul 1840, HRA, XX, pp. 700-703; *Sydney Herald*, 23 Oct 1840.
72 SANSW: NRS 1282, Reel 2222.
73 *Government Gazette*, 31 Aug 1841.
74 *Commercial Journal*, 11 May 1839.
75 *Sydney Gazette*, 29 Jan 1842.
76 SANSW: NRS 905, [42/1584].
77 Ibid.
78 Gillen, *Founders*; Withington, *Dispatched Downunder*; Fellowship of First Fleeters.
79 Withington, p. 182.
80 Gillen, *Founders*; Withington, *Dispatched Downunder*; Fellowship of First Fleeters.
81 Wannan, Bill, *Very Strange Tales*, p. 11.
82 Duffy, Michael, *Man of Honour: John Macarthur*.

INDEX

18th Century Britain, 3-8, 10, 12, 14, 21-26, 52, 81, 116, 132, 141, 267, 284
Abbott, Edward, 198
Aborigines, 44, 100, 101, 103, 122, 133, 138, 139, 146, 149, 158, 173, 183
Admiral Gambier, ship, 231, 233
Admiral Gifford, ship, 248
Age of Enlightenment, 5, 26
Agnes Banks, 196, 205, 206, 208, 212
Agricultural Society, 287
Albion, 114
Alexander, ship, 1, 19, 45, 50-53, 57, 63, 65, 67, 68, 70, 72, 74, 75, 85, 86, 87, 88, 90, 105-107, 109, 115, 123, 124, 303, 318
Alt, Augustus, 49, 107, 119
Altree, John, 49
American Colonies, 2, 4, 8, 9, 31, 40
Anderson, John, 151
Anna Josepha, ship, 199
Antislavery laws, 8
Arkwright, Richard, 4
Arndell, Thomas, 49, 64, 68, 176, 185, 186
Asia, ship, 23
Atkins, Richard, 157-160, 165, 173, 177, 178, 180, 211, 218, 220-222, 224, 236
Atlantic ocean, 56, 60, 62, 65, 73
Atlantic, ship, 149, 159, 160, 161
Austen, Jane, 6
Australian, The, 282, 286, 290, 294, 296, 301, 302
Australian Agricultural Company, 283
Australian Patriotic Association, 309, 315
Aylsham bridewell, 28, 29
Badgery, James, 205-208
Badgery's Farm, 206, 208
Baker, William, 247

Ball, Henry, 102, 111, 131
Balmain, William, 49, 52, 175
Bank of New South Wales, 261, 274
Banks, Joseph, 35-37, 89, 153, 178, 209, 210, 220
Barber, Elizabeth, 63, 64, 68, 71, 72
Bare Island, 101, 114
Baring, ship, 263, 292
Bass Strait, 188, 202, 232
Bass, George, 173, 174, 188, 202
Bathurst, Earl, 259, 264, 270, 284
Battley, John, 291
Baudin, Nicolas, 202
Baughan, John, 175
Bayliss, Joseph, 206, 208
Bayly, Nicholas, 249
Beazley, John, 142
Bennelong, 138, 139, 162, 173
Bennet, Henry, 259, 265, 266
Bent, Ellis, 256
Bent, Jeffrey, 256, 259
Bigge, John Thomas, 259, 264-268, 271-273, 284, 288, 290, 296, 304
Bigge Report, 272, 296, 300, 304
Biggers, Thomas, 207, 234
Birds Eye Corner, 205
Bishop, Joseph, 146, 151
Bishop, Mary, 116
Blackburn, David, 114
Blacktown, 319
Blaxcell, Garnham, 225, 228
Blaxland, Gregory, 255
Bligh, Elizabeth, 210
Bligh, Mary, 209, 210, 216, 231, 236, 237
Bligh, William, 198, 201, 209-250, 256, 262, 268, 274, 300, 320
Bloodworth, James, 103, 107
Blue Mountains, 188, 246, 248, 255
Borrowdale, ship, 45, 50, 57, 85, 106
Botany Bay, 18, 19, 20, 32, 33, 35-42, 44, 46, 47, 53, 56, 57, 61, 74-76, 79, 83, 85, 87-89, 90-92, 100, 101, 115, 122

362

INDEX

Botany Bay Scheme, 1, 3, 38, 40, 41, 42, 50, 52
Boulton, Matthew, 4
Bourke, Richard, 300, 302-314, 316
Bowen, John, 202
Bowman, John, 263
Bowman, William, 258, 293
Brabyn, John, 223
Bradley, John, 263, 264, 279, 292, 296
Bradley, Robert, 15, 16
Bradley, William, 51
Brand, Curtis, 151
Brazil, John, 228
Brickfield, 103, 107, 111, 115, 122
Bridewell, 10, 11, 25, 26, 28, 29
Brighton, Alice, 22
Brisbane, Thomas, 252, 270-274, 278-280, 282-288, 293, 298, 300
Britannia, ship, 159, 167, 178
British Chronicle, 54
British Evening Post, 39
Brooks, Richards, 252
Broughton, William, 312
Bryant, Mary, 149
Bryant, William, 149
Burdett, Joseph, 183
Bury and Norwich Post, 32
Bury, Fleetwood, 29
Camden, Lord, 205
Campbell, Duncan, 9, 10, 17, 19, 41
Campbell, James, 102, 104, 125
Cape of Good Hope, 46, 75, 302
Cape Town, 47, 53, 72, 73-77, 83, 107, 109, 119, 123, 125, 130, 164
Cape Verde Islands, 65
Castle Hill, 203
Castlereagh, 195, 196, 205, 206, 213, 228, 246, 247, 252, 253, 255, 258, 283, 284, 293, 299, 301, 308, 317
Castlereagh cemetery, 247, 308, 313, 314, 318, 319
Castlereagh church, 201, 253, 255, 261, 263, 292
Castlereagh school, 254, 258
Castlereagh, Viscount, 214, 219, 228, 229, 236, 237, 246

Catchpole, Margaret, 195, 196
Censor, hulk, 10, 17, 19, 50
Census, 213, 295, 296, 317
Ceres, hulk, 10, 16, 17, 19, 50
Charlotte, ship, 45, 50, 53-57, 60, 62, 63, 66, 72, 74, 76-78, 82, 85, 92, 94, 106
Chelmsford, 15-20, 305
Chelmsford, Assizes Court, 15
Chelmsford Chronicle, 16, 20
China, 40, 42, 46, 106, 129, 149, 150, 315
Clark, Elizabeth Ann, 177, 178, 180, 247
Clark, Ralph, 21, 54, 60-64, 66-69, 72-74, 76-82, 95, 98, 99, 128, 129, 306
Clark, Thomas, 177, 178
Clark's farm, 177, 180, 247, 263
Collins, David, 49, 70, 76, 83, 84, 88, 89, 93, 97, 100, 101, 103, 105, 110, 111, 113, 115, 120-123, 125, 126, 129, 131, 134, 138, 141, 149, 152, 154-157, 160, 162-166, 168, 173, 174, 176-178, 202, 203, 233, 321
Colliss, George, 213, 289, 290, 293
Colonial Office, 203, 205, 209, 210, 211, 214, 219-221, 226, 228, 231, 232, 235, 245, 246, 250, 251, 256, 259, 261, 262, 264, 268, 271-273, 279, 284, 285, 290, 294, 298, 301, 303, 306-308, 312, 315
Considen, Dennis, 49
Convict clothing, 70, 116, 133
Cook, James, 35, 37, 39, 41, 43, 45, 55, 56, 69, 86-90, 209
Cowpastures, 205, 214
Cox, William, 248, 255
Craig, James, 208
Cranebrook, 247, 314, 319
Crighton, James, 276
Crime, 6-9, 12, 15, 17, 28, 42, 44, 58, 59, 63, 97, 101, 103, 104, 141, 143, 150, 153, 181, 239, 260, 264, 265, 266, 270, 281, 291, 293, 305, 307, 310

363

INDEX

Christmas, 29, 87, 119, 120
Crossley, George, 224, 256
Crumby, Robert, 208
Cumberland County, 114
Cunningham, Peter, 281
Cunningham, Philip, 203
Currency lads, 272, 281, 282, 290, 300, 303, 311, 316
Currency, Holey dollar and Dump, 250, 251
Currency, Spanish dollar, 274, 278
Curtis, Robert, 13, 116
Curtis, Susanna, 13
Darling, Ralph, 103, 252, 271, 282, 284, 288-291, 293-303, 308
Darwin, Charles, 309, 310
Das Voltas, 37
Dawes, William, 70
Day, Samuel, 110, 111, 113, 116, 122, 133
Denison, Charlotte, 43
Deptford docks, 48-51
Derby Mercury, 33, 40
Dickens, Charles, 242
Dixon, James, 201
Dodd, Henry, 99, 119, 136
Douglas, Henry, 274
Drayton, 22, 24, 25
Ducey, Patrick, 205
Dudgeon, Elizabeth, 63, 64, 66-68
Duke of Wellington, ship, 248, 270
Dundas Valley, 320
Dundas, Henry, 166
Dunheved, 244, 295, 309, 310
Dunkirk, hulk, 10, 17, 31, 32-37, 54, 63, 64, 115
Dunlop, James, 286
Dunn, John, 197, 204
Eagar, Edward, 256, 269
East India Company, 42, 46, 106, 163
Eastern Creek, 180-183, 189
Eden, ship, 316
Eivers, Mark, 228
Elliot, Edward, 151, 176
Ellmore, Patrick, 289, 290
Emu Ford, 255, 257

Emu Plains, 258, 283, 294
Enclosure Act, 5, 6, 267
Evans, George, 255
Evatt, H.V., 205, 218, 222, 240
Everingham, Mathew, 151
Everitt, Michael, 43
Eyre, James, 29, 30, 31
Faddy, William, 61
Faithful, William, 213, 252, 291
Farrel, Matthew, 197
Farrell, Peter, 182, 183
Fellowship of First Fleeters, 314, 319, 324
Felthorpe, 21, 22, 24
Female fertility, 141, 142
Female servitude, 21, 27, 144
Fidlon, P.G., 80
Field of Mars, 147, 176, 181, 186
Field, Barron, 269, 274
Field, Edward, 234, 261, 283
Field, Maria, 261, 290
Field, Sophia, 290
Field, William, 146, 151
Finucane, James, 228
First Fleet, 1, 2, 10, 12, 19-21, 26, 31, 40, 42, 45, 46, 48, 49-51, 53, 56-60, 62-64, 73, 78, 80-82, 89-91, 98, 104, 106, 107, 117, 119, 135, 141, 144, 145, 149, 155, 156, 162, 172, 178, 191, 211, 233, 260, 280, 303, 306, 317, 318, 319
Fishburn, ship, 45, 50, 57, 85, 119
FitzSimons, Peter, 95
Flanagan, John, 295
Flannery, Tim, 95
Flinders, Matthew, 173, 188, 202, 249, 262
Flogging, 25, 26, 64, 67, 72, 80, 98, 101, 102, 122, 123, 132, 143, 158, 204, 215, 254, 261, 263, 304, 308
Flood, 184, 189-191, 194-197, 205, 207, 208, 211, 212, 214, 225, 233, 234, 264
Forbes, Francis, 278, 294, 303
Forbes, Mary, 297
Fortune, ship, 43
Fortunée, hulk, 10, 17, 37

INDEX

Foundational orgy, 94-96
Foveaux, Joseph, 164, 165, 226-230, 234-236, 238, 239, 300
Franklin, Benjamin, 5
Freeman, James, 101
French Revolution, 7
Freycinet, Louis de, 266
Friends, ship, 247
Friendship, ship, 1, 32-34, 45, 50, 53, 54, 57, 59-64, 66, 68, 69, 71-74, 76-82, 85, 87, 88, 92, 106, 107, 109, 123, 306
Frost, Alan, 91
Frost, Eliza, 313
Frost, George, 254
Frost, Henry, 254
Frost, Thomas, 201, 255, 257, 260, 263, 269, 274, 276, 280, 284, 292, 293, 294, 296, 299
Fulton, Henry, 200, 201, 223-225, 227, 230, 237, 240, 253, 254, 258, 261, 263, 283, 289, 292, 308, 313
Gamble, Ester Mary, 247
Gandell, John, 249
Gaol, 7, 9-11, 15-18, 24, 25, 30, 32, 37, 41, 46, 49, 50, 53, 101, 135, 142, 194, 196, 219, 223
Garden Island, 99, 104
Gazetteer, 9, 42
General Advertiser, 42
General Evening Post, 39, 40, 41
Geographe, ship, 202
Georges River, 245
Gipps, George, 312, 314-316, 318
Goderich, Viscount, 298
Golden Grove, ship, 45, 50, 57, 85, 119
Gordon, George, 42
Gore, William, 223, 224, 237
Gosling, Robert, 15, 16
Goulburn, Frederick, 272, 278, 279, 303
Gould, Henry, 15
Government House, 107, 120, 132, 196, 218, 223-225, 231, 232, 236, 242, 263, 270, 314, 315

Green Hills, 188, 196, 208, 227, 233, 246
Grenville, Lord, 133, 152
Griffin, Edmund, 227
Grimes, Charles, 224
Grose, Francis, 141, 156, 161, 163-178, 180, 197, 205, 207, 221, 235, 300
Guardian, 125, 131, 133, 137
Hall, Edward Smith, 294, 296, 297, 301
Hall, Margaret, 64, 66, 68
Hargreaves, James, 4
Harris, Alexander, 277
Harris, John, 223
Harrison, John, 56
Hassall, Rowland, 216, 243-245, 262
Hatton, Joseph, 111, 112
Haveringland, 22
Hawkesbury River, 149, 152, 169, 172, 179, 180, 184, 189, 195, 206, 208, 212, 233, 246, 254, 277
Hawkesbury settlers, 176, 190, 196, 201, 210, 211, 215, 221, 226, 228, 229, 232, 239, 269
Hayes, Attwell Edwin, 296
Hayes, William, 289, 295
Heads of a Plan, 38
Heigham, 25
Hethersett, 24, 27-30
Higgins, Thomas, 289, 290, 293
Hill, Bridget, 22, 23, 27
Hill, William, 152
HMS *Adventure*, ship, 295
HMS *Beagle*, ship, 295, 309
HMS *Bounty*, ship, 209
HMS *Buffalo*, ship, 191, 192, 210
HMS *Dromedary*, ship, 237
HMS *Endeavour*, ship, 35
HMS *Gorgon*, ship, 135, 144, 148-152
HMS *Guardian*, ship, 125, 131, 137
HMS *Hindostan*, ship, 235, 237
HMS *Hyaena*, ship, 59-62
HMS *Porpoise*, ship, 209, 230-233, 235-237
HMS *Reliance*, ship, 172, 173, 178

365

INDEX

HMS *Resolution*, ship, 209
HMS *Sirius*, ship, 2, 45, 49, 51, 52, 57, 59-61, 69-71, 74, 76, 83, 85-87, 107, 114, 119, 123, 124, 128-130, 136, 142
HMS *Supply*, 45, 49, 51, 52, 57, 59, 61, 69, 70, 75, 85, 87, 88, 91, 92, 102, 114, 119, 124, 128, 129, 131, 136, 172
Hobart town, 203, 233, 235
Hobart, Lord, 203, 209
Hobby, Ann, 227, 248
Hobby, Thomas, 227, 234, 240, 248, 255
Holmes, Susannah, 31-34, 54, 77, 98, 115, 306
Home Office, 19, 32, 36-39, 45-47, 51, 53, 55, 71, 84, 85, 87, 92, 102, 104, 116, 117, 119, 125, 131, 133-135, 137, 143, 144, 150, 152, 153, 157, 159, 160, 164, 166, 168, 170, 173, 175, 177, 178, 185-187, 190-193, 196, 198, 199, 205
Hooghley, ship, 301
Horsford, 21, 22
House of Commons, 35, 36, 265, 298
Houston, John, 213, 252
Howard, John, 10, 11, 15, 26, 28, 30, 34
Howard, Thomas, 154
Howard's farm, 154, 180, 247, 263
Howes, Thomas, 24, 25
Howick, Viscount, 303
Hubbard, William, 151
Huffnell, Susannah, 124
Hughes, John, 276
Hughes, Robert, 95
Hugo, Victor, 5
Hulk, 9, 10, 17-19, 35, 37, 39, 41, 50, 53, 54, 306
Hulks Act, 9, 10
Hume, Joseph, 297
Hunter, ship, 199
Hunter, John, 49, 70, 72, 73, 84-86, 88-92, 107, 111, 118, 119, 128, 129, 136, 162, 164, 170, 172-178, 181, 183-188, 190-193, 200, 211, 212, 220, 234, 235, 240, 249, 300
Huts, 105, 109, 120, 126, 167, 189
Indefatigable, ship, 258
Indian ocean, 39, 56, 75
Indian, ship, 255
Inett, Ann, 131, 149, 178
Investigator, ship, 202
Ipswich Journal, 16
Jamison, John, 257, 315
Johnson, George, 300
Johnson, Richard, 49, 71, 76, 101, 110, 116, 117, 120, 136, 169, 180, 249
Johnston, George, 111, 155, 162, 203, 211, 222, 223, 231-233, 239, 253
Jordan Hill, 117, 195, 212, 213, 216, 245, 252, 279, 291, 292, 295, 296, 299, 305, 313
Justinian, ship, 134
Justitia, hulk, 9, 10, 17, 19, 50, 109
Kable, Henry, 31, 32, 54, 77, 98, 100, 115, 197, 198, 207, 219, 223, 226, 228, 234
Karskens, Grace, 26, 95, 165
Kay, John, 4
Kelly, Thomas, 146, 151
Kemp, Anthony, 223
Keneally, Thomas, 80
Kennedy, Marcella, 248
Kenny, John, 204, 205
Kent, William, 180
King estate, 216, 244, 245
King George, ship, 207
King George III, 5, 92, 93, 114, 124, 133
King George IV, 269, 279, 282
King William IV, 301
King, Anna Josepha, 149, 210, 212, 216
King, Harriett, 295
King, Maria, 216
King, Norfolk, 131, 149
King, Philip Gidley, 46, 49, 57, 75, 88, 102, 131, 148, 162, 170, 178, 191-194, 196, 198-205, 207-212,

219, 220, 227, 235, 251, 260, 262, 300, 309
King, Phillip Parker, 216, 283, 284, 289
King, Sydney, 131
Kinghorne, Alexander, 289
La Boussole, ship, 91
Lady Juliana, ship, 125, 133, 134, 135
Lady Penrhyn, ship, 45, 50, 51, 52, 55, 57, 59, 60, 71, 77, 78, 85, 86, 92, 94, 106, 173
Land grants, 44, 143, 145, 146, 151, 154, 161, 164, 166, 169, 171, 172, 174, 177, 179, 181, 197, 205, 206, 210, 212-215, 226, 231, 234-236, 243, 244, 249, 252, 255, 267-269, 273, 279-281, 283-285, 290, 292, 293, 295, 298, 299, 303
Lang, John Dunmore, 286, 301
Lapérouse, de, Jean-François, 91
Larkam, John, 180
Lary, John, 277
L'Astrolabe, ship, 91
Lavender, Martha, 23
Lawn, Samuel, 283
Lawson, William, 223, 255
Laycock, Thomas, 223
Legislative Council, 278, 279, 288, 295, 297, 298, 303, 304, 306, 308, 309, 310, 312, 316
Leicester Chronicle, 305
Lemain Island, 36
Liverpool, 245
London Chronicle, 39, 46, 61
Londonderry, 213, 252
Lord, Simeon, 207, 219, 223, 226, 242
Love, John, 168
L'Uranie, ship, 266
Macarthur, Elizabeth, 135, 199
Macarthur, James, 274, 298, 310
Macarthur, John, 135, 164-166, 171, 174, 175, 177, 187, 191, 192, 198-200, 205, 209, 211, 214, 215, 217-226, 228, 230, 231, 233-236, 239, 240, 262, 267, 268, 273, 274, 279,

282-284, 286, 288, 289, 297, 298, 302, 304, 314, 320, 328
Macarthur, William, 274
MacLaren, Mary, 80
Macquarie, Elizabeth, 235, 245
Macquarie, Lachlan, vii, ix, 227, 234-238, 240-247, 249-274, 278, 279, 284, 285, 287, 288, 293, 300, 302-304, 307
Marrott, John, 142
Marsden, Samuel, 174, 176, 181, 182, 185, 186, 188, 204, 242, 251, 254, 256, 259, 262, 263, 265, 267, 268, 273, 274, 291
Marshall, James, 198
Marshall, Joseph, 151
Mary Ann, ship, 144
Mason, Elizabeth, 109-112
Mason, Martin, 229
Matra, James, 35, 36
McCarthy, Dennis, 204, 205
McCormick, Sarah, 67, 68, 69, 74
McHenry, John, 289
McIlvee, John, 283
McLeay, Alexander, 297, 302, 303, 308, 312
Mercury, ship, 59, 63, 64, 81
Meredith, James, 61, 62, 63, 64, 66, 72, 111
Minchin, William, 206, 223
Minns, Mrs Elizabeth, 29
Mitchell, Elizabeth, 261
Molesworth, William, 314
Molle, George, 259
Monitor, 294, 296, 301, 307, 314
Moore, William, 223
Moreton Bay, 290
Morning Chronicle, 39, 41, 42
Morning Chronicle and London Advertiser, 39
Morning Herald, 40, 41, 42
Morning Post, 40
Mulgrave Place, 172, 176, 180
Mullaghan, Owen, 289, 290, 295
Murray, George, 298
Murry, Robert, 167

INDEX

Muster, 138, 161, 173, 180, 192, 193, 196, 197, 208, 252, 253, 264, 277, 295
Mutiny, 42, 59, 61-64, 72, 74, 209, 230, 235, 236, 238, 239, 294
Naturaliste, ship, 202
Nepean River, 152, 167, 174, 182, 205, 206, 208, 214, 227, 255, 258, 293
Nepean, Evan, 19, 36, 37, 50, 53, 54, 65, 71, 84, 102, 116, 117, 125, 135
Neptune, ship, 134, 135, 282
New Holland, 1, 3, 18, 35-7, 39, 45, 49, 87, 188, 202, 262
Newcastle, 256, 275, 284
Newgate Prison, 41, 42, 50, 56
Newton, Isaac, 5
Nicol, John, 142
Nightingall, Miles, 235
Norfolk, 1, 6, 12, 13, 21-23, 25, 30, 31, 42, 102, 128, 129, 145, 305
Norfolk Assizes, 23, 27, 29
Norfolk Chronicle, 23-25, 27, 29, 30, 32, 33, 39
Norfolk Court Calender, 27
Norfolk Island, 80, 102, 110, 121, 124, 128, 129, 131, 135, 148, 149, 152, 161, 170, 178, 191, 198, 211, 226, 228, 231, 233, 284, 291, 306
Norfolk Quarter Sessions, 25, 29
Northampton Mercury, 39, 41, 52
Norton Subcourse, 13-15, 20, 56
Norwich, 13, 21-25, 32, 33
Norwich Assizes, 27
Norwich Castle gaol, 23-25, 27, 29-33
Norwich Workhouse, 24
NSW Corps, 135, 146, 148, 152, 156, 163-168, 170, 171-177, 181-183, 185-187, 189, 193, 197-200, 203, 209-212, 215, 216, 218, 220-224, 226-232, 234-237, 240, 241, 247, 261
O'Connell, Daniel, 297
O'Connell, Maurice, 236, 237
Ocraft, John, 142

Old Bailey, 58, 247, 257
Old Hawkesbury Road, 180
Oxley, John, 270, 293
Paine, Thomas, 5, 7
Palmer, Charles, 206
Palmer, John, 155, 166, 226, 227, 232, 237, 249
Pardon, 44, 200, 236, 249, 268, 273
Pardon, absolute, 200, 208, 268
Pardon, conditional, 200, 201, 208, 255, 263, 264, 268, 269, 296
Pardon, Royal, 8, 31, 306
Parramatta, 137, 144-148, 150, 159, 221, 227, 243, 245, 254
Parramatta River, 119
Paterson, William, 170-175, 178, 181, 198, 203, 226-228, 230-232, 234-237, 300
Pekoe, ship, 316
Pembroke, Michael, 2, 43
Penrith, 247, 254, 255, 258, 289, 296, 305, 313, 314, 317, 318, 323, 326, 329
Perry, Samuel Augustus, 299
Perryn, Richard, 16
Petherick, John, 146
Phillip, Arthur, 1, 2, 32, 39, 41-45, 49, 50-56, 59-75, 77, 79, 82-107, 114-119, 121-139, 141, 143-150, 152-171, 173, 174, 176, 178, 186, 187, 190, 200, 202, 203, 219, 233, 234, 243, 246, 262, 300, 307, 309, 311
Phoenix, ship and hulk, 284
Pightling, Samuel, 27, 28
Pious perjury, 7, 16
Pitt, ship, 156, 157
Pitt government, 18, 37, 38
Pitt Town, 169, 180, 212, 227, 246
Pitt, William, 35, 36, 42, 246
Player, Thomas, 292, 296
Plymouth, 10, 17, 32, 33, 37, 39, 50, 53, 54, 63
Pooley, *see Pulley*
Population, 4, 5, 35, 70, 129, 135, 138, 141, 159, 161, 172, 190, 207,

INDEX

253, 255, 266, 270, 277, 296, 297, 307, 312, 314, 317
Port Dalrymple, 203
Port Jackson, 56, 89-93, 100, 104, 106, 119, 123, 125, 128, 131, 133, 136, 138, 139, 144, 162, 167, 170, 172, 178, 188, 191, 202, 224, 232, 235, 237, 258, 263, 266, 270, 275, 284, 288, 302, 309
Port Macquarie, 270, 274-276, 279, 290, 292
Port Stephens, 275, 284
Porteous, John, 231
Portland, Duke, 137, 164, 175, 177, 185, 187, 191, 193, 199
Portsmouth, 1, 2, 10, 17, 19, 37, 39-41, 44, 47, 50-56, 58, 61, 64, 89, 125, 133, 162
Poulden, John, 111
Powley, *see Pulley*
Price, James, 105, 110-113
Prince of Wales, ship, 45, 52, 55, 57, 59, 61, 77, 83, 85, 87, 92, 94, 106, 109, 142
Proctor, John, 292, 296, 317, 318
Prospect Hill, 145, 150, 176
Provisions, 39, 47, 60, 79, 136
Public Advertiser, 18
Pulley, Elizabeth, 1, 2, 3, 6, 8, 12, 21-34, 54, 56, 63, 64, 66-69, 72, 74, 77, 78, 80, 82, 89, 94, 96, 98, 100, 103, 105, 109, 110, 143, 173, 319
Pulley, Tobias, 21, 22, 23
Pulley, William, 22, 23
Putland, John, 209, 210
Queen, ship, 148, 150, 157
Ramsay, John, 146, 151
Rations, 17, 18, 28, 47, 53, 60, 64, 67, 68, 70, 74, 76, 87, 95, 100, 104, 110, 113, 115, 118, 119, 121-124, 128, 130, 132-134, 136, 140-144, 148-150, 156-161, 164, 168-171, 173, 177, 179, 192, 193, 194, 197, 198, 205, 208, 245, 253, 291
Redfern, William, 265, 269
Reid, William, 143

Retribution, hulk, 258
Richards, John, 151, 168
Richards, William, 19, 45, 47
Richardson, William, 124
Richie, Robert, 228
Richmond, 180, 246, 248, 252, 254, 299
Riddell, Campbell, 308
Rio de Janeiro, 47, 53, 60, 64, 65, 69-76, 85, 106
Riverstone, 181
Roberts, William, 111
Robertson, Tony, 95
Robinson, Richard, 149
Rochford, 15, 16
Rope children, 14, 184, 189, 244
Rope family, 20, 130, 137, 146, 158, 161, 169, 172, 180, 181, 183, 188, 192, 195, 197, 201, 205, 206, 208, 212, 213, 243, 246, 251, 262, 269, 278, 280, 281, 283, 285, 290, 319
Rope, Ann, 13
Rope, Anthony, 1-3, 6, 7, 10, 12-21, 32, 50, 56, 63, 65, 72, 86, 89, 96, 98, 100, 103, 105, 109, 110-116, 119, 121-124, 129, 130, 132, 133, 137, 138, 140, 142-148, 151, 154, 155, 158, 161, 168, 177, 179-183, 188, 190, 192, 194, 196, 204-206, 208, 211, 216, 217, 221, 227, 229, 234, 235, 243-247, 249, 251-253, 257, 260, 263, 264, 275-277, 279, 280, 283, 284, 289, 290-292, 295, 305, 308, 313, 317-319
Rope, Anthony and Elizabeth, 14, 106, 109, 110, 112, 113, 116, 120, 129, 130, 135, 137, 138, 140, 143, 145, 147, 151, 154, 155, 157, 158, 161, 165, 167-174, 177, 179-182, 184, 188-191, 194-198, 201, 204-208, 210, 212, 213, 216, 217, 225, 227, 228, 234, 243-248, 250-255, 257, 258, 264, 276, 277, 279, 280, 282, 283, 289, 291, 292, 295, 296, 299, 300, 306, 308, 310-313
Rope, Eleanor Ann, 248, 253, 255, 258

INDEX

Rope, Elizabeth, 10, 111, 113-117, 119, 122-124, 129, 130, 132, 141, 142, 144-148, 158, 161, 168, 169, 174, 183, 188, 189, 192, 196, 197, 204, 205, 217, 227, 244, 252, 253, 264, 276, 277, 280, 295, 305, 313, 314, 319

Rope, Elizabeth Ann, 227, 264, 280, 291, 292, 296

Rope, George, 255, 258, 264, 291

Rope, James, 292, 295, 308

Rope, John, 13, 20, 174, 204, 213, 216, 234, 245, 251, 252, 261, 269, 274, 280, 284, 290, 292-294, 296, 299, 308, 318

Rope, Mary, 13, 14, 146, 158, 168, 169, 181, 183, 192, 227, 234, 240, 248, 251, 255, 257, 258, 269, 280, 291, 296, 308, 313

Rope, Robert, 116, 117, 119, 130, 132, 135, 140, 142, 158, 161, 168, 169, 173, 181, 183, 192, 204, 227-229, 234, 247, 248, 253

Rope, Sarah, 14, 188, 244, 255, 263, 269, 280, 292, 296

Rope, Susannah, 13, 14, 196, 244, 263, 279, 280, 292, 296, 317, 318

Rope, William, 204, 264, 280, 291, 293, 295, 299, 305, 308, 313

Rope's Farm, 146, 147, 151, 154, 177, 180, 183, 189, 204, 216, 244, 245, 248, 289, 291, 292

Rope's Paddock, 245

Rope-Pulley Family Heritage Association, 319, 324

Ropes Creek, 210, 212, 216, 217, 319

Ropes Crossing, 319

Rose Hill, 119, 121, 123, 124, 128, 136-138, 140-145, 151, 155

Ross, Robert, 49, 56, 57, 71, 72, 77, 80, 84, 85, 90, 95, 100-102, 104, 113, 125-130, 148, 151, 152, 156

Rosson, Isabella, 124

Rum Rebellion, 198, 214-229, 240

Rümker, Carl, 286

Rumsby, Ann, 274

Ruse, James, 143, 145, 154, 169

Ryan, James Toby, 116, 117, 181, 195, 204, 213, 240, 245, 248, 252, 254, 258, 281, 282, 291, 295, 313

Ryan, John, 201, 240, 257, 258, 274, 276, 284, 291, 293, 296, 299

Ryan, R.J., 80

Ryan, Robert, 109, 110, 112, 129

Samuel Winter, ship, 314

Santa Cruz, 47, 53, 59, 64, 65, 73

Scarborough, ship, 45, 46, 50, 52, 55, 57, 61, 62, 74, 85, 87, 88, 90, 106, 134, 135

Schaffer, Philip, 143

Scott, James, 78, 83

Scurvy, 53, 67, 70, 74, 76, 84, 87, 99, 100, 102, 106, 116, 119, 120, 123, 124

Sea pie, 110, 112

Second Fleet, 128, 133, 134-136, 142, 144, 148, 218

Shea, John, 125

Sherwin, William, 181, 182

Shortland, John, 45, 52, 85, 94, 106

Simpson, John, 32, 33, 34

Sinclair, ship, 209

Sinclair, Duncan, 19, 50, 87, 115

Skyner, Baron, 27

Slave trade, 4, 7, 8, 134, 246, 307

Slaves, 8, 44, 71, 288, 297, 316

Smith, John, 208

Smyth, Arthur Bowes, 44, 49, 71, 74-76, 78, 85-88, 94-96, 100, 106

South Creek, 167, 172, 179, 180, 182-184, 188, 189, 192-194, 196, 197, 204, 205, 207, 208, 210, 212, 213, 216, 227, 228, 233, 234, 243-245, 249, 254, 264, 275, 277, 295, 296, 299

Speedy, ship, 191

Spithead, 1, 2, 19, 52, 54-56, 59

St Margaret's church, 21, 22

St Mary's church, 13, 14

St Matthew parish, 182

St Matthew's church, 227, 247

St Philip's church, 124, 219, 225

Stewart, John, 297

INDEX

Sudds, Joseph, 293, 294, 297
Summers, John, 109, 110, 122, 146, 151, 168, 188
Supplies, 19, 41, 45, 47, 48, 50, 51, 55, 59, 64, 69, 70, 73, 74, 83, 84, 89, 102, 117, 119, 121, 123, 128-130, 133, 134, 136, 149, 153, 156, 159, 160, 164, 168, 171
Surprize, ship, 134, 135
Surry, ship, 270
Suttor, George, 229
Swilly Farm, 206
Sydney Cove, 90, 92, 93, 95, 99, 102-104, 107-110, 114, 115, 117, 118, 120, 121, 123, 125, 126, 128, 136, 144, 148, 152, 153, 165, 167, 197, 219, 225, 266, 306, 313, 317, 319
Sydney Gazette, 202, 211, 216, 254, 261-263, 271, 276, 282, 284, 292, 295, 314, 317, 318
Sydney Herald, 303, 307, 308, 310, 311, 312
Sydney, Lord, 32, 33, 36-38, 42, 52, 65, 84, 88, 92, 100, 126, 153
Table Bay, 75, 77
Tasman, Abel, 56, 86
Tea, 6, 42, 46, 105, 106, 116, 122, 142, 165, 185, 243, 244
Tench, Watkin, 53, 55, 56, 60, 62, 66, 78, 82-84, 88, 96, 99, 102, 103, 104, 107, 111, 119-121, 123, 131-134, 137, 142, 144, 150-152, 154, 178, 321
Terra Australis, 202
Thackery, Elizabeth, 67, 68
Thames River, 9, 10, 15-19, 35, 37, 39, 48-54
The Downs, 51, 52
The Hulk, hulk, 284
The Lump, ferry, 137
The Ponds, 121, 145, 146, 148, 150, 154, 155, 157, 158, 167, 169, 172, 176, 179-182, 184, 186, 188, 247, 263, 320
The Recruiting Officer, play, 124
Thetford, 29

Thetford Assizes, 30
Third Fleet, 144, 148, 149, 156, 157, 171
Thompson, Andrew, 207, 208, 212, 215, 218, 221, 224, 227, 228, 234, 242, 277, 320
Thompson, Patrick, 293
Thomson, Edward, 308, 312
Ticket of Leave, 201, 249, 250, 255, 258, 263, 273, 283, 291, 307
Timmings, Frank, 283
Toongabbie, 158, 165, 181
Transportation, 1, 2, 4, 7-12, 16, 17, 20, 23, 25, 31, 32, 35-40, 42, 46, 49, 58, 63, 81, 131, 259, 260, 264, 267, 271, 305-307, 311, 314-317
Transportation, Committee on, 18, 35, 36, 124, 239, 249, 250, 255, 314, 315
Trial by jury, 222, 250, 278, 303
Tumble-down Barn, 179, 181, 182, 195, 212, 247
Turnbull, Malcolm Bligh, 240
Turnbull, William Bligh, 240
Turner, Ann (Hannah), 32, 34
Underwood, James, 207, 219, 226
Upton Castle, ship, 315
Van Diemen's Land, 87, 178, 188, 202, 203, 226-228, 230-233, 236, 248, 269, 294, 307, 316, 318
Varndell, Edward, 146, 151
Vincent, John, 318
Vinegar Hill, 203
Voltaire, 5
Waaksamheyd, ship, 136
Walton, Francis, 62
Wannan, Bill, 320
Warburton, Ann, 111
Ward, William, 276
Wardell, Robert, 282, 296
Ware, Charlotte, 64, 66
Warren, Timothy, 249
Waterhouse, Henry, 138, 139, 162, 174
Watson, Charles, 305
Watt, James, 4
Webb, Robert, 143

371

INDEX

Wentworth, D'Arcy, 218, 219, 223, 282
Wentworth, William, 255, 282, 290, 294, 296-298, 301, 303, 308-311, 314, 315, 316, 320
Weston, Charles, 24, 25
White Hall Evening Post, 39
White, John, 39, 49, 51, 52-54, 66-68, 76, 77, 87, 100, 111, 131, 133, 155
Wilberforce, William, 5, 246
Williams, Frances, 109-112, 129
Windham, William, 214, 220
Windsor town, 172, 179, 181, 188, 194, 195, 213, 227, 240, 245-248, 252, 254, 258, 263, 264, 289, 290, 301, 325
Woolwich, 10, 17, 18, 19, 54, 258
Worgan, George, 49, 71, 77, 98, 103
Wymondham Abbey, 24
Wymondham Bridewell, 25, 26
Yeats, Ann, 173, 178
Yellow Mondays Lagoon, 206
Yemmerrawanne, 162, 173

www.ingramcontent.com/pod-product-compliance
Lightning Source LLC
Chambersburg PA
CBHW030431300426
44112CB00009B/946